The Synergy of Sustainable Entrepreneurship

Russ Neu
United Nations Development Programme, Philippines

Xiaojun Qian
Tsinghua University, China

Poshan Yu
Soochow University, China & European Business Institute, Luxembourg & Australian Studies Centre, Shanghai University, China

IGI Global
Scientific Publishing
Publishing Tomorrow's Research Today

Vice President of Editorial — Melissa Wagner
Managing Editor of Acquisitions — Mikaela Felty
Managing Editor of Book Development — Jocelynn Hessler
Production Manager — Mike Brehm
Cover Design — Phillip Shickler

Published in the United States of America by
IGI Global Scientific Publishing
701 East Chocolate Avenue
Hershey, PA, 17033, USA
Tel: 717-533-8845
Fax: 717-533-8661
Website: https://www.igi-global.com E-mail: cust@igi-global.com

Library of Congress Cataloging-in-Publication Data

Names: Neu, Wee Teck, editor. | Qian, Xiaojun, 1956- editor. | Yu, Poshan, editor.
Title: The synergy of sustainable entrepreneurship / edited by Russ Neu, Xiaojun Qian, Poshan Yu.
Description: Hershey, PA : IGI Global Scientific Publishing, [2025] | Includes bibliographical references and index. | Summary: "This book addresses key themes and topics related to sustainable entrepreneurship, providing a multidisciplinary perspective that encompasses various industries, regions, and contexts"-- Provided by publisher.
Identifiers: LCCN 2024053591 (print) | LCCN 2024053592 (ebook) | ISBN 9798369343388 (hardcover) | ISBN 9798369352144 (paperback) | ISBN 9798369343395 (ebook)
Subjects: LCSH: Sustainable development. | Entrepreneurship.
Classification: LCC HC79.E5 S963 2025 (print) | LCC HC79.E5 (ebook) | DDC 338/.04--dc23/eng/20250201
LC record available at https://lccn.loc.gov/2024053591
LC ebook record available at https://lccn.loc.gov/2024053592

British Cataloguing in Publication Data
A Cataloguing in Publication record for this book is available from the British Library.

Editorial Advisory Board

Table of Contents

Detailed Table of Contents

With increasing global awareness of environmental sustainability, GSCM (Green Supply Chain Management) has become a critical strategy for reducing environmental impacts while optimizing resource utilization.The research focuses on the innovation and collaboration mechanisms within GSCM, utilizing CiteSpace to perform a comprehensive literature visualization analysis.Through keyword co-occurrence networks, institution-author co-occurrence analysis, and research hotspot analysis, the paper uncovers key knowledge clusters, research trends, and future directions in the GSCM field.

This case is based on real life setup of a Bengaluru based leading Electric Vehicles (EV) charging network company (pseudonym:E-mobility Solutions) and its strategic initiatives, analysis of financial feasibility of setting up the electric vehicles charging station, and the return on investment in Indian scenario.Electric vehicle charging stations are the backbone of EV ecosystem and depending on the situation and need, electric vehicles (EV) can be charged in a number of methods. Accordingly, charging infrastructure for EVs is of different forms and tailored for varied uses.The case study represents a major step towards the electric vehicle charging infrastructure and will broaden understanding of the presence and lack thereof a connection between the non-financial factor and their impact on profitability. The limitation, however, is that the study was confined to charging station in Bangalore district only. Future studies can also focus on setting up an EV Public Charging Station in a rural area and the return on investment from it.

The circular economy is an alternative to the linear economy, which is based on the take-make-waste model of production and consumption. The circular economy aims to reduce environmental impacts and resource depletion by designing products and services that minimize waste, extend the lifespan of materials, and regenerate natural systems. Entrepreneurs play a key role in the transition to the circular economy, as they can create innovative solutions that address the needs and preferences of customers, while also generating positive environmental and social outcomes. This chapter provides a comprehensive overview of the circular economy concept and its principles, as well as a framework for developing and implementing circular economy business models. It also showcases a variety of examples of successful circular economy ventures from different sectors and regions, highlighting the benefits and challenges of adopting this approach. The chapter concludes with some recommendations for entrepreneurs, policymakers, and educators who want to support and promote circular entrepreneurship.

This study has the aim to analyze the environmental and institutional frameworks implications in entrepreneurship ecosystems. It is assumed that research on entrepreneurship ecosystem micro foundations are sensitive environmental and institutional factors including the agency of actors in their own local communities. The method used is the meta-analytical-reflective and descriptive based on conceptual, theoretical, and empirical literature reviews. It is concluded that the

Foreword

The world faces urgent challenges: climate change, resource depletion, and growing social inequalities. In this context, sustainable entrepreneurship has emerged as a powerful force for change, blending innovation with a commitment to environmental and social responsibility. This book, The Synergy of Sustainable Entrepreneurship, explores how entrepreneurship can be a driving force for a sustainable future.

Sustainable entrepreneurship is more than creating businesses—it is about re-thinking the role of business in society. It challenges the traditional focus on profit alone, shifting towards long-term value creation that benefits people, the planet, and economies.

This book highlights the unique power of entrepreneurship to drive sustainable innovation. Entrepreneurs thrive on solving problems and seizing opportunities. When applied to sustainability, this drive fosters transformative solutions that can reshape industries and communities. From renewable energy to circular economies, the possibilities for change are immense.

The concept of synergy—combining entrepreneurship with sustainability—amplifies their individual impacts. Together, they form a dynamic force capable of driving systemic change, whether in energy, manufacturing, or social innovation. Collaboration is another key theme. Partnerships across governments, businesses, and communities are essential to aligning efforts and leveraging collective expertise. Entrepreneurs, as connectors and innovators, are uniquely positioned to foster these collaborations and achieve shared goals.

This book also recognises the global nature of sustainability. While sustainability principles are universal, their application must account for diverse local contexts. Cultural, economic, and geographic factors shape how solutions are developed and implemented.

Ultimately I believe that sustainable entrepreneurship is not just a strategy; it is a responsibility. By committing to sustainable principles, entrepreneurs can create meaningful change that benefits both current and future generations. They will also play a crucial role in shaping a more resilient, equitable, and prosperous world.

It is my hope that the ideas in this book will inspire new innovations, foster collaboration, and empower individuals to drive the change our world needs.

Xiaojun Qian
Tsinghua University, China

Preface

In the contemporary global landscape, the pursuit of sustainable development has become an overarching and urgent goal. Sustainable entrepreneurship has emerged as a crucial and dynamic concept that holds the promise of revolutionizing economies and societies alike. It is within this context that we, as editors of this volume titled "The Synergy of Sustainable Entrepreneurship," in collaboration with Prof. Russ Wee Teck Neu from UNDP and Prof. Xiaojun Qian from Tsinghua University, are proud to present this comprehensive and in-depth exploration of the subject.

The genesis of this book lies in the recognition of the fragmented nature of research and practice in sustainable entrepreneurship. It was essential to assemble a cohesive body of knowledge that could bridge the gaps and offer a holistic understanding. Chapter 1 initiates this journey by providing a profound examination of innovation and collaboration in Green Supply Chain Management (GSCM) from an entrepreneurial vantage point. Through the utilization of CiteSpace-Based Literature Visualization, it maps out the intellectual terrain, laying a solid foundation for comprehending the significance of sustainable supply chain strategies in the entrepreneurial realm.

Chapter 2 propels us forward into a vision of a greener future, spotlighting the role of EV Charging Networks. It elucidates how such networks are not only a technological marvel but also a vital enabler of sustainable transportation and urban development, presenting fertile ground for entrepreneurial initiatives.

The Circular Economy Models, expounded upon in Chapter 3, offer a revolutionary blueprint for sustainable entrepreneurship. These models shatter the traditional linear economic mold, presenting innovative pathways for businesses to optimize resource utilization, minimize waste, and generate value in a circular and regenerative manner.

Chapter 4 delves into the environmental and institutional frameworks that underpin entrepreneurship ecosystems. Understanding these frameworks is of utmost importance as they define the regulatory, social, and economic context within which sustainable entrepreneurs must navigate, influencing every aspect from market access to compliance and resource allocation.

The role of artificial intelligence in sustainable social entrepreneurship development is the focus of Chapter 5. It dissects how AI can act as a catalyst for social transformation, empowering entrepreneurs to address complex social and environmental challenges with greater efficacy and scalability.

Chapter 6 challenges the traditional paradigms of the fashion industry in the context of Industry 5.0, presenting a new perspective on fashion sustainability. It offers insights into how the industry can embrace sustainable practices throughout the value chain, from design innovation to production and consumption patterns.

Chapter 7 offers a comprehensive review of the opportunities and challenges of sustainable entrepreneurship in a specific regional context, namely Sri Lanka. By examining the unique interplay of cultural, economic, and social factors, it enriches our understanding of how sustainable entrepreneurship unfolds in diverse settings.

The role of social entrepreneurship in sustainable development, as perceived by business experts, is the subject of Chapter 8. Their insights provide valuable guidance on how social entrepreneurs can collaborate with the business community to drive positive change and achieve broader sustainable development objectives.

Chapter 9 draws lessons from emerging economies regarding sustainable entrepreneurship. These economies present a unique blend of challenges and opportunities, and their experiences offer a wealth of knowledge for entrepreneurs and policymakers seeking to foster sustainable growth.

Chapter 10 focuses on sustainable entrepreneurship within the BRICS economies. It uncovers the latent opportunities within these large and influential emerging economies, despite the formidable challenges they face, and proposes strategies for entrepreneurs to thrive and contribute to sustainable development.

Chapter 11 explores sustainable innovation and product development, with a particular emphasis on creating products that are both environmentally friendly and socially responsible. It offers practical frameworks and strategies for entrepreneurs to embed sustainability into the very core of their product design and development processes.

The applications of venture philanthropy in impact entrepreneurship, systems change, and private-public collaboration are dissected in Chapter 12. It highlights the power of collaborative models in amplifying the impact of sustainable entrepreneurship and driving systemic social change.

Finally, Chapter 13 presents a practical application of the Triz Methodology in the design of a water-saving system for a household toilet. This exemplifies how engineering and design principles can be harnessed to address specific environmental challenges, embodying the essence of sustainable entrepreneurship in action.

This book is a synthesis of ideas, research, and best practices that converge to offer a panoramic view of sustainable entrepreneurship. It is our sincere hope that it will serve as an indispensable resource for students, scholars, entrepreneurs, and policymakers, inspiring them to embrace sustainable entrepreneurship and actively contribute to the creation of a more sustainable and prosperous future for all.

We are deeply indebted to all the contributors for their unwavering dedication and profound expertise in enriching this volume. Their insights and research have been the cornerstone of its success. We also extend our gratitude to the numerous individuals and institutions that have lent their support to this project, making it possible to bring this significant body of knowledge to the forefront.

In conclusion, this collaborative effort of the editorial team, which includes myself, Poshan Yu, along with Prof. Russ Wee Teck Neu from UNDP and Prof. Xiaojun Qian from Tsinghua University, has been a journey of discovery and synthesis. We have strived to curate a collection of chapters that not only reflects the current state of sustainable entrepreneurship but also paves the way for future research and practice.

We are confident that this volume will spark meaningful discussions and inspire actionable change in the field. It is our collective hope that it will be a guiding light for those who seek to understand and implement sustainable entrepreneurship principles in diverse contexts.

As we look ahead, we anticipate that the ideas presented herein will continue to germinate and give rise to new and innovative approaches to sustainable economic and social development. We remain committed to the advancement of this important area of study and practice and look forward to the contributions that this book will inspire in the global community.

Russ Neu
United Nations Development Programme, Philippines

Xiaojun Qian
Tsinghua University, China

Poshan Yu
Soochow University in China, the European Business Institute in Luxembourg, and the Australian Studies Centre at Shanghai University in China

Chapter 1
From an Entrepreneurial Perspective:
Innovation and Collaboration in Green Supply Chain Management (GSCM)

Poshan Yu
https://orcid.org/0000-0003-1069-3675
Soochow University, China

Zi Chen
https://orcid.org/0009-0002-6273-7158
Independent Researcher, China

Russ Neu
Quest Ventures, Singapore

Jingtan Pan
Independent Researcher, China

Shengyuan Lu
https://orcid.org/0000-0002-9847-4604
Johns Hopkins University, USA

Kelin Guo
https://orcid.org/0009-0007-7305-0032
emlyon business school, China

ABSTRACT

With increasing global awareness of environmental sustainability, GSCM (Green Supply Chain Management) has become a critical strategy for reducing environmental impacts while optimizing resource utilization.The research focuses on the innovation and collaboration mechanisms within GSCM, utilizing CiteSpace to perform a comprehensive literature visualization analysis.Through keyword co-occurrence networks, institution-author co-occurrence analysis, and research hotspot analysis, the paper uncovers key knowledge clusters, research trends, and future directions in the GSCM field.

DOI: 10.4018/979-8-3693-4338-8.ch001

1. INTRODUCTION

1.1 Research background and objectives

Green Supply Chain Management (GSCM) has emerged as a pivotal approach in the modern business environment, crucial for addressing the dual imperatives of ecological sustainability and economic viability. The advent of GSCM is rooted in the growing recognition of environmental impacts associated with the global supply chain operations, which encompass the entire lifecycle of a product from raw materials through to disposal. As the global marketplace evolves, the implementation of environmentally sustainable practices within supply chains becomes not just a regulatory necessity but a strategic asset that enhances competitiveness and resilience.

The objective of this research is to delineate the innovation and collaboration mechanisms that characterize effective GSCM, particularly within the Asian context. Asia, with its dynamic economies and rapid industrial growth, presents unique challenges and opportunities for the implementation of GSCM practices. The region's diverse economic landscapes, varying levels of technological advancement, and differing regulatory environments make it a critical area for studying GSCM dynamics. This study aims to utilize CiteSpace, a powerful tool for literature visualization and analysis, to map the existing knowledge landscape, identify gaps, and reveal emerging trends within GSCM research. Through keyword co-occurrence networks, institution-author co-occurrence analysis, and research hotspot visualization, this research seeks to uncover key patterns of innovation in GSCM, explore collaborative mechanisms that enhance GSCM effectiveness, analyze current research hotspots with a particular focus on trends specific to Asia, and understand the drivers of collaboration and the specific challenges and opportunities faced in implementing GSCM in the Asian setting.

1.2 Significance of the research

The significance of this research extends across several dimensions. Academically, it contributes to the burgeoning field of sustainable supply chain management by providing a structured and comprehensive analysis of the literature, thus setting a foundation for future scholarly work. The use of CiteSpace enhances the rigor of this analysis by allowing for the visualization of complex datasets, thereby offering clearer insights into the evolution of research themes and the interconnections between different research domains.

From a practical perspective, this study offers critical insights for businesses operating in or entering Asian markets. Understanding the innovation and collaboration mechanisms in GSCM can help companies better integrate sustainable practices into their core operations, thus not only complying with increasing regulatory demands but also gaining strategic advantages in terms of operational efficiency and brand reputation. Additionally, this research highlights the specific challenges faced in diverse Asian contexts, offering tailored strategies that consider local environmental, technological, and regulatory conditions.

Furthermore, the research addresses a critical gap in the current literature by focusing specifically on Asia, a region that has been both a major contributor to and victim of environmental degradation due to industrial activities. By focusing on Asia, the research not only contextualizes GSCM in one of the most economically and environmentally significant regions of the world but also enhances the applicability of its findings, providing relevant and actionable insights for policymakers and business leaders aiming to foster sustainable development in their supply chains.

In sum, the research aims to craft a nuanced understanding of how innovation and collaboration in GSCM can be effectively harnessed to meet the sustainability challenges of today, particularly within the Asian context. This is crucial not only for the academic advancement of GSCM as a field of study but also for the practical implementation of sustainable business practices that are essential for long-term environmental and economic sustainability.

2. LITERATURE REVIEW

2.1 Current Research Progress in GSCM

The imperative for integrating environmental sustainability into supply chain management has catalyzed extensive scholarly focus on Green Supply Chain Management (GSCM), particularly regarding innovation, technological integration, and challenges within the Asian context. Recent literature underscores the importance of innovative practices and green innovation in enhancing the sustainability of supply chains. Linlin Liu highlight that logistics performance significantly reduces carbon emissions in the article"Carbon neutrality through supply chain performance: does green innovation matter in Asia?", suggesting that green innovation is a crucial driver of environmental sustainability in Asian economies.

Technological advancements, specifically the adoption of Industry 4.0 technologies, play a transformative role in GSCM (Tseng, Chiu, Tan, & Siriban-Manalang, 2013). The integration of AI, IoT, and big data analytics is extensively examined as tools that improve efficiency and transparency in green supply chains (Yu & Xiao, 2024). Ming-Lang Tseng discussed how advanced technologies facilitate the implementation of green design and sustainable practices, thereby promoting sustainable consumption and production in Asia.Research on green supply chains is integrating more deeply into corporate sustainability strategies. For instance, enhanced data analytics capabilities not only improve resource utilization efficiency but also enable companies to predict the environmental impacts of products during the design phase. This allows for measures to reduce waste and emissions early in the product lifecycle. Furthermore, as supply chains increasingly transform digitally, their potential impacts on social and environmental justice cannot be overlooked. The benefits of technological advancements are now reaching all participants in the supply chain.

Despite the progress, several barriers impede the full adoption of GSCM practices. Economic constraints, technological infrastructure deficiencies, and regulatory inconsistencies are commonly cited challenges. These barriers often stem from the high costs associated with implementing GSCM and the complexities of technological integration, which are yet to be adequately addressed across varying Asian contexts.

Furthermore, the role of policy and regulatory frameworks in shaping GSCM practices is a critical area of investigation. Research indicates that supportive governmental policies and international regulations can significantly influence the adoption of green practices (Chen et al., 2023) . For instance, Ziqin Yu elaborates on how environmental regulations in Asian countries impact GSCM, pointing out that regulatory support is crucial for enhancing green practice adoption. Looking ahead, the literature signals a growing emphasis on the circular economy within GSCM, promoting not just recycling and reuse but also the redesign of supply chain processes to minimize environmental impacts (Agyabeng-Mensah, Baah, Afum, & Kumi, 2023). This shift towards a more integrated approach that encompasses economic, environmental, and social sustainability dimensions is poised to define the future trajectory of GSCM research.

The current body of literature on GSCM demonstrates a robust engagement with the themes of innovation, technology, and policy, driven by the urgent need to address environmental sustainability within the supply chain. The dynamic nature of this field reflects ongoing efforts to adapt to emerging technologies and evolving regulatory landscapes, particularly in the economically and environmentally diverse settings of Asia.

2.2 Research Gap

The current body of Green Supply Chain Management (GSCM) research, while extensive, reveals several areas requiring deeper inquiry, particularly within the complex regulatory and cultural landscapes of Asian economies. A significant gap exists in understanding how GSCM innovations are adapted and disseminated across diverse regulatory environments. This lack of detailed study into the interplay between technological adoption and local regulations may hinder the effective integration of sustainable practices tailored to specific regional needs.

Moreover, the granularity required to effectively manage supply chains across Asia's economically diverse landscape is often overlooked. There is a pressing need for studies that dissect the impact of economic heterogeneity on GSCM effectiveness, considering the unique challenges and opportunities presented by both emerging and developed markets within the region. This gap underscores the necessity for a nuanced approach that evaluates how socio-economic disparities influence the implementation and outcomes of GSCM.

Additionally, the empirical research focusing on the direct impact of GSCM on business performance metrics such as cost savings, revenue growth, and market share is notably scarce. The predominance of theoretical and qualitative studies over hard data leaves a gap in the literature that, if filled, could strengthen the case for GSCM by highlighting its tangible benefits to business performance.

2.3 Contribution of the research

The research seeks to enrich the GSCM discourse by delving into these identified gaps, offering a nuanced analysis of how green innovations and collaborative efforts are specifically shaped by and for the Asian context. By exploring the dynamic interaction between GSCM practices and local regulatory frameworks, this study will shed light on the ways policies can be designed to better facilitate the adoption of sustainable practices within supply chains. Such insights are crucial for policymakers aiming to craft regulations that are both supportive of technological advancements and aligned with sustainability objectives.

The use of advanced analytical frameworks such as keyword co-occurrence and institution-author co-occurrence deepens the understanding of interrelationships within the GSCM literature, pinpointing pivotal institutions and authors. This reveals the collaborative networks that shape the field's evolution and highlights where future interventions could be most effective. Such insights are crucial for identifying leverage points that facilitate the adoption of innovative GSCM practices.

By examining the specific challenges and opportunities that GSCM faces, particularly in the diverse markets of Asia, the study provides actionable insights for stakeholders. These insights assist in tailoring strategies to overcome barriers and optimize GSCM practices effectively. As a result, the research not only enriches the academic field but also serves as a practical guide for companies, policymakers, and other stakeholders engaged in designing and implementing sustainable supply chain strategies across Asia.

Lastly, the proactive discussion of limitations and future research directions sets the stage for subsequent studies, ensuring they build on a solid foundation. This approach fosters a continual evolution of research within GSCM, particularly in harnessing the potential of digital technologies for environmental sustainability. The integration of theoretical depth with practical insights ensures that the contributions of this study are actionable and relevant to real-world applications, enhancing sustainability practices throughout the region.

Through these contributions, the research will facilitate a deeper understanding of GSCM in Asia, offering actionable insights and robust, evidence-based strategies to enhance the effectiveness and adoption of green practices in supply chains throughout the region. The fusion of academic insight with practical applications serves to not only advance the field of GSCM but also to champion the broader implementation of environmentally sustainable practices in a key global region.

3. METHODOLOGY

3.1 Data Collection and Screening

3.1.1 Literature searching and identification

The research utilizes the scientometric analysis tool CiteSpace to visualize and quantify the relationships between key terms, identify research trends, and conduct a comprehensive assessment. During the systematic review process, as of June 2024, we have collected relevant literature data from the Web of Science Core Collection database. The search utilized the following keywords: Green Supply Chain Management (GSCM), Asia, collaboration and innovation. Reflecting the characteristics of the research subject, we retrieved literature from the years 2000 to 2024, initially filtering based on titles, abstracts, and keywords. Ultimately, we collected 1039 articles (with 234 records automatically removed), providing a solid data foundation for subsequent analysis. This analysis also gathered bibliometric information such as publication year, author identities, citation counts, and co-citation networks, to track the evolution of research themes and identify influential research clusters. Statistical analysis was conducted by the authors to explore trends in publications, collaboration patterns, and more.

3.1.2 Screening and assessing for eligibility

Building on the initial screening, we further reviewed the abstracts of the initially retrieved papers. Given that our research is conducted from an Asian perspective, we excluded content on the application of GSCM innovations and collaborative frameworks in other regions, focusing exclusively on studies related to Asia. Additionally, we selected only those articles published in peer-reviewed journals, written in English, and with full texts available, to ensure the comprehensiveness and representativeness of the data. After a series of screenings, the authors ultimately obtained 659 relevant articles.

3.2 Data Analysis

3.2.1 Keyword Co-occurrence Networks

The visual representation provided by the CiteSpace analysis (Fig 3.2.1) offers a compelling overview of the intricate relationships and thematic clusters within the realm of Green Supply Chain Management (GSCM), particularly from an Asian perspective. This keyword co-occurrence network not only illuminates the most prominent themes in the current literature but also highlights the dynamic interplay between various elements that contribute to the field's complexity and richness.

Central to the network is the concept of 'green supply chain management' itself, strategically positioned as a nexus linking diverse themes such as 'environmental performance', 'sustainability', 'collaboration', and 'innovation'. This configuration suggests that the core focus of GSCM research revolves around enhancing environmental metrics within supply chain processes while simultaneously driving innovation to foster sustainable practices. The prominence of 'environmental performance' and its close association with 'sustainability' underscores a significant research trend towards quantifying and improving the ecological impacts of supply chain operations. Additionally, the integration of 'collaboration' into this cluster highlights the critical role of cooperative strategies among various stakeholders in achieving these sustainability goals, indicating that effective GSCM is not only about technological or process innovation but also about fostering collaborative networks that enhance collective environmental performance.

Adjacent to these central themes, 'collaboration' emerges as a pivotal node, connected with 'performance', indicating that collaborative efforts within supply chains are crucial for achieving superior environmental and firm performance. This relationship is critical as it encapsulates the essence of GSCM's success, which hinges not only on individual corporate initiatives but on the synergistic efforts of all stakeholders involved.

Furthermore, the network reveals a strong link between 'management' and 'innovation', highlighting that effective management practices are essential for the introduction and integration of innovative technologies and processes in GSCM. The presence of terms like 'AI', 'IoT', and 'big data analytics' near these nodes points to the increasing reliance on advanced technologies to drive GSCM forward, reflecting the integration of Industry 4.0 technologies as discussed in earlier sections of the paper.

The inclusion of geographic-specific nodes such as 'Asia' and 'China' emphasizes the regional focus of much of the GSCM research, which is particularly pertinent given the unique environmental challenges and rapid industrial growth experienced in these areas. The linkage of these geographical terms with 'policy', 'regulatory frameworks', and 'economic growth' illustrates the critical interdependencies between regional market conditions, regulatory environments, and GSCM practices.

Moreover, the keyword 'circular economy' appears connected to the central themes, signifying an evolving focus in GSCM literature towards models that emphasize not just recycling and reuse but also the redesign of business processes to minimize resource wastage and environmental impact. This shift towards a circular economy approach within GSCM is indicative of a broader trend in sustainable business practices, seeking to create closed-loop systems that contribute to long-term sustainability goals

Through the analysis of this keyword co-occurrence network, it becomes evident that GSCM research is increasingly interdisciplinary, drawing upon fields such as environmental science, technology, management, and economics to address the complex challenges of sustainability. Each node and link in the network not only represents a specific area of focus but also contributes to a broader understanding of how integrated efforts can enhance the efficacy and impact of GSCM initiatives.

The comprehensive analysis not only deepens the understanding of the thematic landscape of GSCM research but also provides a strategic roadmap for future studies and implementations. By identifying key areas of current research emphasis and potential gaps where further exploration is needed, this network analysis lays a solid foundation for advancing GSCM practices, particularly in the context of Asian economic and environmental conditions. As such, the insights garnered from this visual mapping are instrumental for both academics looking to further explore these themes and practitioners aiming to implement effective GSCM strategies within their operations.

Figure 1. Keyword Co-occurrence Network

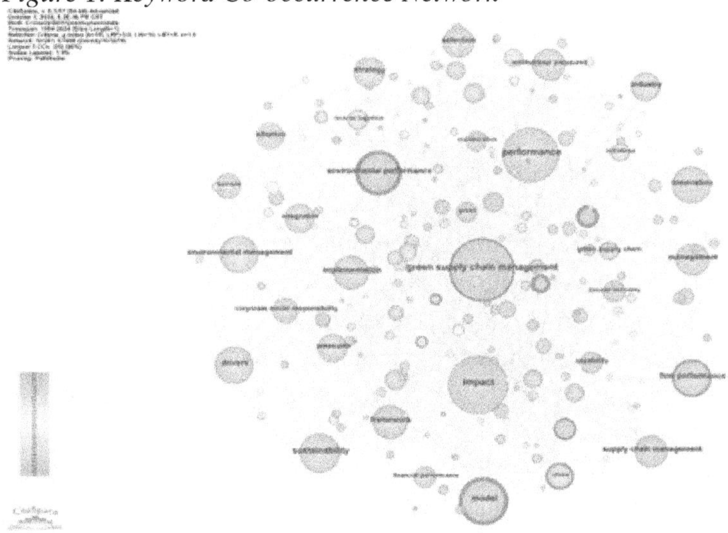

3.2.2 Institution-Author Co-occurrence Analysis

The Institution-Author Co-occurrence Analysis (Fig 3.2.2) provides a vivid representation of the collaborative networks and influential figures within the realm of Green Supply Chain Management (GSCM), particularly highlighting the significance of certain scholars and their affiliations. The analysis not only sheds light on who is leading the charge in GSCM research but also underscores the importance of collaborative networks that span across various geographic and institutional boundaries.

At the heart of this Institution-Author co-occurrence network, Ming-Lang Tseng, i.e. merges as a particularly significant node, indicative of his extensive contributions to the field and his central role in connecting various research streams within GSCM. His connections to other notable scholars and institutions illustrate the collaborative nature of GSCM research, where cross-institutional partnerships foster a deeper understanding and wider application of sustainable practices within supply chains. The prominent position of Tseng, alongside other key figures such as Joseph Sarkis, and Qinghua Zhu points to a concentrated cluster of expertise that has been pivotal in advancing GSCM theory and practice.

The network also reveals the diverse yet interconnected roles played by researchers from different regions, reflecting the global scale of GSCM challenges and the collaborative efforts required to address them. For instance, the links between Asian scholars with their counterparts in Europe and North America suggest a rich exchange of ideas and methodologies that enhance the global knowledge base in

GSCM. This is crucial, as the successful implementation of GSCM practices often requires adaptation to local contexts, which can be greatly informed by international collaboration.Furthermore, the presence of clusters around certain institutions indicates centers of excellence in GSCM research. These hubs act as beacons of innovation, drawing researchers and projects that contribute to the evolving landscape of GSCM. For example, the cluster around authors like Kee-hung Lai and Kannan Govindan, who are frequently cited with Ming-Lang Tseng, highlights the collaborative efforts within certain research institutions that are leading the way in integrating sustainability into supply chain management.

The analysis not only helps in identifying where significant research is being conducted but also in understanding how these research collaborations impact the field of GSCM. By examining the ties between these authors and their respective institutions, one can discern patterns of influence and innovation spread. Such patterns are indicative of how new ideas in GSCM are generated, validated, and disseminated across the academic and practical realms. Also, the analysis serves as a map for emerging researchers and practitioners in the field, indicating which institutions and authors they might look to for groundbreaking work and potential collaboration. It also helps funding bodies and policy makers see which clusters of researchers are most influential, possibly guiding decisions on where to allocate resources to maximize the impact of research funding in enhancing GSCM practices globally.

Figure 2. Institution-Author Co-occurrence Network

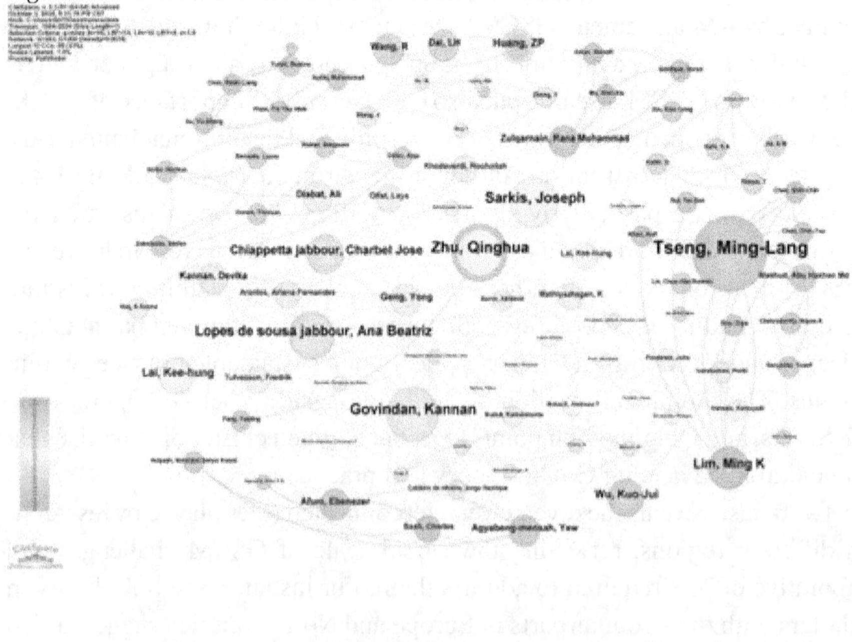

3.2.3 Research Hotspot Analysis

The research hotspot analysis (Fig 3.2.3) highlights key themes and their evolution in Green Supply Chain Management (GSCM) over time. The central node of Green Supply Chain Management anchors the analysis, with surrounding themes like innovation, collaboration, performance, and sustainability reflecting the core research interests in this field.

Innovation emerges as a major hotspot, emphasizing the critical role of technological advancements such as Industry 4.0 technologies (AI, IoT, big data) in driving green supply chain efficiency and environmental sustainability. Research has focused on how innovations in product design and process optimization reduce environmental impact, positioning green innovation as a strategic tool for competitive advantage. Collaboration also plays a significant role, underscoring the need for cooperation among suppliers, manufacturers, and logistics partners to ensure green practices across the entire supply chain. The analysis highlights how collaborative efforts, especially in reverse logistics and closed-loop supply chains, enhance sustainability outcomes. These partnerships are vital for achieving long-term green objectives.

Performance metrics, especially firm performance and environmental performance, remain critical areas of study. Scholars examine the impact of GSCM on financial results, with a focus on how green practices contribute to competitive advantage, cost reduction, and improved corporate reputation while fulfilling environmental targets. The node for sustainability further reflects growing emphasis on circular economy, resource efficiency, and the transition from linear to circular supply chain models. This shift is driven by increasing regulatory and consumer pressures, pushing businesses to adopt sustainable practices.

In recent years, the analysis shows a rising focus on GSCM within Asia, particularly in economies like China and India. Research here explores how local regulatory environments, economic conditions, and technological capabilities influence the adoption and effectiveness of GSCM practices. Government policies and regulatory enforcement are seen as key drivers, while barriers like costs and technological limitations continue to pose challenges. Besides, newer trends such as big data analytics, blockchain, and digitalization are emerging, with companies leveraging these technologies to enhance transparency and efficiency in sustainable supply chain management. These innovations point to a future where digital tools play a critical role in GSCM success.

Figure 3. Research Hotspot Time Zone Map

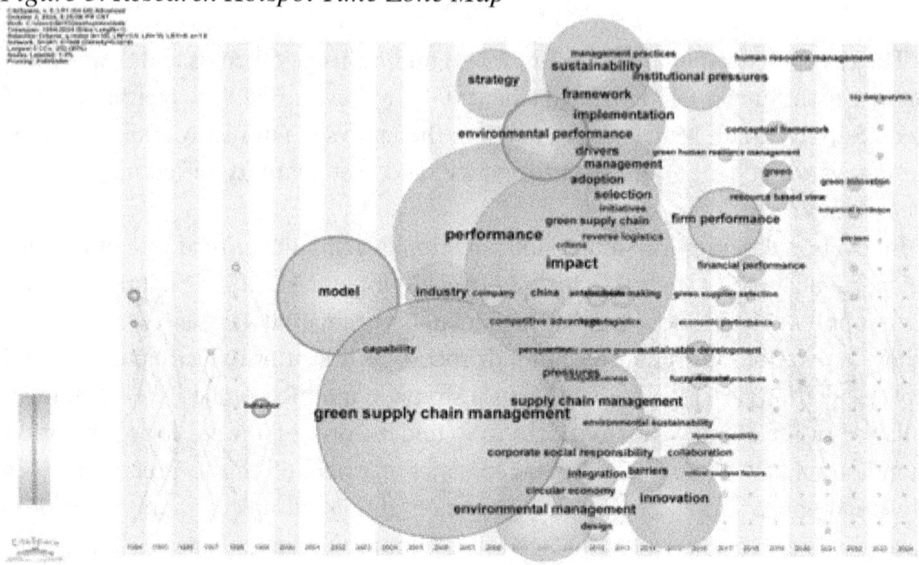

3.2.4 Future research trends

The rapid evolution of Green Supply Chain Management (GSCM) in Asia, as evidenced by recent citation bursts, underscores the dynamic interplay between green innovation, economic growth, and strategic human resource management. This trend analysis delves into the data derived from the top 21 keywords with the strongest citation bursts, revealing how pivotal themes are shaping the future of sustainable practices in regional economies. "Green innovation" remains a central pillar, reflecting its critical role in enhancing environmental performance and operational efficiency within supply chains. The sustained focus on this area highlights its potential to drive significant reductions in environmental impact while boosting economic viability. Concurrently, the keyword "economic growth" correlates strongly with the integration of sustainable practices, suggesting that environmental sustainability is becoming synonymous with economic necessity in Asia. This relationship is further supported by the rise of "human resource management" as a key theme, indicating a growing recognition of the role that effective management of human capital plays in implementing and sustaining green practices. The strong citations for "empirical evidence" highlight the increasing demand for data-driven insights into the efficacy of GSCM initiatives, emphasizing the need for robust, quantifiable outcomes that can validate the impact of these practices on both the environment and corporate profitability.

Within this context, future research will likely explore deeper into how innovative green technologies and strategies can be integrated into corporate governance structures to enhance economic outcomes while preserving ecological balance. The intersection of "green innovation" with "economic growth" offers fertile ground for examining how sustainability initiatives can be optimized to support expansive economic objectives without compromising environmental integrity. Moreover, studies focusing on "human resource management" are expected to shed light on the strategies that most effectively engage employees in sustainability goals, fostering a culture that prioritizes green practices in every facet of business operations. Lastly, the emphasis on "empirical evidence" calls for a methodological refinement in future studies, advocating for sophisticated analytical techniques that can dissect and demonstrate the tangible benefits of GSCM more convincingly to stakeholders across various sectors.

This holistic approach not only enriches the scholarly discourse around GSCM but also provides a practical blueprint for corporations, policymakers, and other stakeholders committed to advancing sustainable development within Asia's vibrant economic landscape.

Figure 4. Top 21 keywords with the strongest citation bursts

Top 21 Keywords with the Strongest Citation Bursts

Keywords	Year	Strength	Begin	End	1994 - 2024
china	2010	5.38	**2010**	2017	
environmental management	2010	5.31	**2012**	2016	
analytic network process	2012	4.27	**2012**	2018	
fuzzy set theory	2013	5.07	**2013**	2014	
company	2008	5	**2013**	2017	
initiatives	2013	4.79	**2013**	2016	
selection	2013	4.62	**2013**	2016	
implementation	2013	3.51	**2013**	2016	
model	2002	4.15	**2014**	2016	
reverse logistics	2013	5.61	**2015**	2019	
fuzzy dematel	2016	4.35	**2016**	2019	
institutional pressures	2016	5.18	**2017**	2018	
operational practices	2017	4.25	**2017**	2020	
green	2019	4.14	**2019**	2021	
economic performance	2017	3.97	**2020**	2022	
economic growth	2021	3.94	**2021**	2022	
green innovation	2022	5.11	**2022**	2024	
human resource management	2020	3.95	**2022**	2024	
empirical evidence	2022	3.62	**2022**	2024	
pls sem	2022	3.53	**2022**	2024	
behavior	1999	3.52	**2022**	2024	

4. DISCUSSION

4.1 Key Innovation Patterns in GSCM

In the realm of Green Supply Chain Management (GSCM), innovation patterns manifest as a dynamic interplay between technological advancements and strategic shifts toward sustainability, redefining traditional industry norms and operational paradigms. The integration of cutting-edge technologies like the Internet of Things (IoT), artificial intelligence (AI), and blockchain is pivotal, enhancing transparency and efficiency across supply chains. These technologies facilitate real-time tracking, predictive analytics, and secure, transparent transactions, which are essential for creating interconnected, optimized supply chain ecosystems that minimize waste and maximize resource efficiency. For example, IoT devices can monitor conditions throughout the supply chain, ensuring that the most efficient routes and methods are employed to reduce carbon footprints and enhance operational efficacy.

Simultaneously, process innovations emphasize the adoption of circular economy models, which challenge the traditional linear consumption and disposal patterns by prioritizing resource efficiency and waste reduction. This shift towards regenerative approaches, where end-of-life products are reintegrated into the production cycle through practices like reverse logistics and remanufacturing, transforms regulatory compliance into value-creating opportunities. Such strategic innovations not only align companies with global sustainability goals but also enhance their market image and competitive edge.

The effectiveness of these technological and process innovations is further amplified through enhanced stakeholder engagement and collaboration. Engaging suppliers, customers, and regulatory bodies in the innovation process enables companies to develop more cohesive and adaptive supply chain strategies, particularly crucial in regions like Asia with diverse regulatory environments and market conditions. Tools like supplier sustainability indices and platforms for sharing best practices exemplify structured approaches to fostering stakeholder collaboration, driving collective progress towards sustainability.

At the foundation of these innovation patterns lies the critical role of empirical insights and data-driven decision-making. As GSCM grows in complexity, leveraging advanced data analytics to monitor, optimize, and predict supply chain activities becomes indispensable. This emphasis on data not only enhances the monitoring and optimization of supply chain activities but also enables companies to anticipate market shifts and adapt their strategies accordingly. Comprehensive empirical research supports these initiatives, offering nuanced understandings of the impacts and guiding more effective future innovation efforts.

The most profound innovations in GSCM are those intricately woven into the fabric of corporate strategies, reflecting an organization's deep-rooted commitment to sustainability across all operations. This strategic integration ensures that GSCM practices are central to a company's core objectives, receiving robust support from top management and permeating the corporate culture. Such alignment underscores the notion that sustainability is not an ancillary consideration but a fundamental aspect of business planning and execution, pivotal for the enduring success of GSCM initiatives.

4.2 Collaboration Mechanisms among stakeholders enhance the effectiveness of GSCM

Collaboration in Green Supply Chain Management (GSCM) serves as a pivotal element in overcoming the inherent complexities and achieving sustainability goals across global supply chains. This multifaceted collaboration spans various layers of the supply chain from suppliers, manufacturers, distributors, to consumers and regulatory bodies. The sheer scale of modern supply chains, which often extend across multiple international borders and regulatory environments, particularly in economically and environmentally diverse regions like Asia, requires an integrated approach that harnesses collective efforts and resources.

The diversity in environmental standards and economic conditions across countries emphasizes the need for a synthesized effort where stakeholders are not merely participants but active contributors to sustainability. By pooling resources, knowledge, and innovations, stakeholders can forge a more cohesive and effective approach to managing environmental impacts. This cooperative network is crucial in meeting the ambitious environmental goals that are increasingly demanded by both consumers and regulatory authorities.

At the core of successful GSCM collaboration lies the establishment and adoption of shared standards and practices. This alignment is crucial, as it ensures that all parties are working towards common goals under a unified framework. However, achieving this alignment is inherently challenging due to the varying objectives, capabilities, and levels of commitment among stakeholders. It necessitates rigorous communication and often complex negotiations. Digital technologies, particularly advanced data platforms, play a crucial role in facilitating this aspect of GSCM by enabling real-time data exchange and enhancing supply chain transparency. Blockchain technology, for example, can create a verifiable and tamper-proof record of compliance with sustainability standards by different parties, thereby fostering accountability and trust among stakeholders.The use of such technologies not only supports the operational aspects of collaboration but also helps in tracking the sustainability of supply chain components. It ensures that all stakeholders can verify each other's compliance with agreed-upon environmental standards, thus maintaining the integrity of the green supply chain. Moreover, technologies like IoT and AI can be leveraged to optimize resource use and improve the overall efficiency of supply chains, further contributing to sustainability goals.

In addition to technological integration, financial collaboration is also vital. Joint investments in sustainable technologies and shared resources for recycling and waste management can help distribute the costs and risks associated with these initiatives. This financial collaboration makes it feasible for smaller entities to adopt and implement GSCM practices, democratizing the ability to contribute to sustainability efforts. By reducing financial barriers, collaborative investments not only enhance the environmental footprint of supply chains but also improve economic outcomes by minimizing redundancies and enhancing operational efficiency.

Collaborative problem-solving sessions that bring together multiple stakeholders can spark innovation and lead to the development of tailored solutions that address specific sustainability challenges unique to different regions or sectors. These sessions provide a platform for exchanging ideas and testing new approaches in a collaborative environment, which can accelerate the innovation process and lead to more effective solutions.Furthermore, the role of governmental and non-governmental organizations is critical in catalyzing and supporting these collaborative efforts. Governments can influence GSCM practices by providing incentives such as subsidies or tax breaks for adopting sustainable practices, or conversely, by imposing penalties for non-compliance. NGOs play a complementary role by facilitating knowledge sharing and capacity building among stakeholders. They often act as neutral parties that can bring together competitors to collaborate on common sustainability challenges without the risk of compromising competitive advantage.

These collaborative efforts require a foundational change in how businesses perceive their role in the larger environmental context. Instead of viewing GSCM practices as a compliance or marketing strategy, they should be seen as integral components of a business's operational and strategic frameworks. This shift is critical for the long-term success and sustainability of GSCM initiatives.

The future of GSCM hinges on the ability to create and sustain these collaborative networks. By bridging diverse capabilities and perspectives, and by integrating technological, financial, and strategic resources, stakeholders can collectively tackle the complex environmental challenges that no single entity could address alone. The path forward for GSCM is therefore defined not only by the technologies and processes that underpin it but significantly by the strength, depth, and effectiveness of the collaborative networks that support it. As these networks grow and deepen, they will continually enhance the capacity of supply chains to meet the dual challenges of environmental sustainability and economic viability, paving the way for a greener future.

4.3 Challenges and Opportunities GSCM is facing

The landscape of Green Supply Chain Management (GSCM) is shaped by an intricate web of challenges and opportunities that reflect its complexity and crucial role in promoting environmental responsibility across global industries. Implementing GSCM requires navigating a myriad of international, national, and local environmental regulations. The regulatory landscape varies significantly across different regions, particularly in Asia, where economic development levels greatly influence environmental policies. Companies face the daunting task of ensuring compliance with these diverse and sometimes conflicting regulations, which often involve substantial costs and organizational adjustments.

Adding to the complexity, technological integration poses its own set of challenges. The adoption of advanced technologies such as artificial intelligence (AI), the Internet of Things (IoT), and blockchain is essential for effective GSCM, but integrating these technologies into existing supply chain infrastructures can be costly and disruptive. Businesses must invest not only in the technologies themselves but also in training their workforce to utilize these new tools effectively. The rapid pace of technological advancement necessitates continuous investment to maintain state-of-the-art systems, which can strain financial resources.

Supply chains today are vast and complex networks that span multiple countries and involve countless stakeholders. Achieving transparency across such expansive networks is extremely challenging but crucial for monitoring GSCM practices effectively and ensuring that every link in the chain adheres to sustainability standards. This lack of visibility can complicate efforts to measure the environmental impacts accurately and manage the sustainability practices of suppliers, especially those in regions with less stringent environmental standards.

Internally, organizations often encounter cultural and structural resistance to integrating GSCM practices. Changing the entrenched behaviors and perceptions that prioritize short-term productivity and cost-saving over long-term sustainability requires a fundamental shift in corporate culture. This resistance can stem from a lack of understanding of the tangible benefits that sustainable practices can offer, such as cost savings through increased efficiency and enhanced company reputation.

Despite these challenges, GSCM presents substantial opportunities for innovation and creating competitive advantage. Companies that pioneer in integrating sustainable practices can distinguish themselves in a marketplace where consumers increasingly favor environmentally responsible products. This shift can lead to improved market share and the ability to command premium prices. Moreover, GSCM can significantly enhance operational efficiencies by minimizing waste and optimizing resource use, which not only reduces costs but also mitigates risks associated with resource scarcity and price volatility.

Furthermore, a strong commitment to sustainable practices can substantially boost a company's brand value and reputation, attracting loyal customers and skilled employees who share the company's environmental values. Engaging suppliers in sustainable practices extends these benefits across the supply chain, fostering resilience and strategic advantages in procurement and innovation.

Leveraging the latest technological advancements also unlocks new possibilities for enhancing GSCM. Technologies like AI and big data analytics can optimize supply chain operations and predict future trends, while blockchain can provide unprecedented transparency and traceability. These technological tools enable more effective monitoring and compliance with environmental regulations, making GSCM both feasible and efficient.

The journey of integrating GSCM involves navigating through a terrain filled with significant obstacles, but it also opens up pathways to substantial business value and societal benefits. The evolving dynamics of GSCM will likely continue to be driven by both the challenges it seeks to overcome and the opportunities it endeavors to capitalize on, guided by innovation and a commitment to sustainability. As industries globally recognize these benefits, the adoption and refinement of GSCM practices are expected to accelerate, marking a crucial step towards sustainable development in the corporate world.

5. CONCLUSION

The research has comprehensively explored the multifaceted aspects of Green Supply Chain Management (GSCM), illuminating its critical role in promoting sustainable business practices across global industries, with a particular focus on the Asian context. Through a detailed analysis facilitated by CiteSpace, this study has not only mapped the existing landscape of GSCM but also identified emergent trends, pivotal challenges, and substantial opportunities that define this field. The insights garnered have profound implications for both practitioners and theorists in the domain of supply chain management, especially in contexts where environmental considerations are becoming increasingly integral to corporate strategy and consumer preferences.

The discourse on GSCM began with an in-depth examination of the key innovative patterns that are shaping its landscape. It is evident from the research that technological advancements play a pivotal role in enhancing the sustainability and efficiency of supply chains.The integration of sophisticated technologies such as Artificial Intelligence (AI), the Internet of Things (IoT), and blockchain is pivotal, fundamentally transforming supply chains toward heightened sustainability and efficiency. AI leverages predictive analytics to anticipate disruptions and optimize resource allocation, significantly minimizing waste and enhancing responsiveness to both market demands and environmental regulations. IoT technology augments this by enabling unprecedented real-time monitoring and control, embedding devices that continuously relay data to ensure compliance with environmental standards and operational efficiency. Blockchain complements these advancements by providing transparent, immutable records of transactions, thereby bolstering trust among stakeholders and certifying the sustainability of supply chain practices. Concurrently, the shift towards circular economy models promotes recycling, remanufacturing, and the reuse of materials, which not only mitigates environmental impact but also integrates resources back into the production cycle. This strategic fusion of cutting-edge technologies and sustainable processes is revolutionizing traditional supply chain management, steering it towards more sustainable, efficient, and resilient frameworks. These innovations are not just enhancing operational capabilities but are also instigating a comprehensive shift towards systems that synergize economic viability with environmental responsibility, signaling a transformative era in supply chain management where sustainability becomes a cornerstone of operational excellence and corporate strategy.

Collaboration among various stakeholders has been identified as another critical factor in the effective implementation of GSCM. The complexities of modern supply chains, which often span diverse geographical and regulatory landscapes, necessitate a collaborative approach to manage environmental responsibilities effectively. This study has highlighted the synthesis of efforts across different sectors and regions, demonstrating that collaborative networks significantly enhance the capability to achieve collective environmental goals. Such networks leverage shared knowledge, distribute risks, and optimize resource utilization, making sustainable practices more effective and economically viable.

Collaboration among various stakeholders has emerged as a cornerstone in the successful implementation of Green Supply Chain Management (GSCM), essential for managing the multifaceted demands of modern, global supply chains. These supply chains span a vast array of geographical and regulatory landscapes, each with its unique challenges and requirements. Effective collaboration is crucial not only for aligning diverse environmental standards but also for harmonizing business practices across borders. This study underscores the importance of building robust collaborative networks that transcend sectoral and regional boundaries, enhancing the capacity to achieve comprehensive environmental goals. By pooling resources, knowledge, and technologies, these networks can tackle complex sustainability challenges more effectively than any single entity. For instance, multinational corporations working with local suppliers can foster sustainability practices that adapt and respect local environmental conditions while maintaining global quality standards. Additionally, collaborative efforts often lead to the development of shared technological platforms that facilitate real-time data exchange and enhance transparency across the supply chain. Such platforms can track the carbon footprint of products, monitor resource use, and ensure that all stakeholders adhere to agreed sustainability practices, thus fostering a culture of accountability and continuous improvement.

Moreover, these collaborative networks play a pivotal role in risk distribution, especially in projects involving significant investments in green technologies or processes that might be financially burdensome for individual players. By sharing the financial and operational risks, companies can undertake more ambitious sustainability projects, driving innovation while mitigating individual exposure to financial setbacks. This risk-sharing is particularly important in regions where environmental regulations are stringent or rapidly evolving, requiring agile responses and adaptive measures. Furthermore, collaboration enables the optimization of resource utilization across the supply chain. Shared logistics, joint recycling initiatives, and collaborative product development efforts are examples of how resources can be used more efficiently, reducing waste and lowering costs. These cooperative strategies not only improve the environmental footprint of the entire supply chain but also enhance economic outcomes by minimizing redundancies and maximizing the value extracted from each resource. The synthesis of collaborative efforts across different sectors and regions not only boosts the capability to meet environmental objectives but also creates a more resilient supply chain capable of withstanding disruptions and adapting to new environmental policies. As such, the future of GSCM relies heavily on strengthening stakeholder relationships and fostering a culture of cooperation and shared responsibility, ensuring that sustainability becomes a fundamental aspect of supply chain operations worldwide.

However, integrating GSCM is fraught with challenges. Regulatory diversity across different regions, especially in Asia, imposes a substantial burden on companies striving to comply with environmental standards. The varying and sometimes conflicting nature of these regulations complicates compliance efforts and can lead to significant costs. Additionally, the technological integration necessary for effective GSCM presents financial and operational challenges. These include the high costs associated with adopting new technologies, potential disruptions during integration, and the ongoing need for training personnel to effectively use these technologies. Furthermore, achieving transparency in extensive, multi-layered supply chains is exceptionally challenging but crucial for verifying compliance with sustainability standards.

Despite the significant challenges associated with Green Supply Chain Management (GSCM), the opportunities it presents are transformative and extensive, offering substantial competitive and operational advantages in a marketplace increasingly influenced by environmental sustainability. Companies that effectively integrate GSCM practices not only align themselves with stringent regulatory frameworks but also enhance their positioning in a consumer market that is progressively prioritizing eco-friendly products, driving demand for transparent and sustainable business practices. Implementing effective GSCM practices leads to considerable operational efficiencies and cost reductions across multiple facets of the supply chain by minimizing waste and optimizing resource utilization, which can significantly decrease environmental footprints while improving profitability. These efficiencies stem from enhanced logistics that streamline supply chain operations, reduce resource consumption, lower energy costs, and facilitate the recycling and more effective use of materials, thereby reducing reliance on volatile raw materials. Beyond operational efficiencies, a strong commitment to sustainable practices enhances a company's brand reputation, making it more attractive to a growing segment of environmentally conscious consumers and a workforce that values corporate responsibility, which is crucial for building a motivated and engaged team pivotal in driving long-term business success. Moreover, companies excelling in GSCM are likely to attract more investors as the financial community increasingly factors sustainability into risk assessments and investment decisions, providing not just capital but also further legitimacy and support for their sustainability initiatives. Furthermore, GSCM encourages innovation by pushing companies to rethink and redesign their processes and products from a sustainability perspective, leading to the development of new, more efficient, and cleaner technologies that not only reduce environmental impact but also provide companies with unique products and services to offer the market, such as the use of biodegradable materials or the adoption of renewable energy sources, which can open up new markets and customer segments, driving growth and diversification. In conclusion, the integration of GSCM practices offers a multitude of benefits that extend across the operational, strategic, and corporate levels of a business, helping companies navigate the complexities of modern environmental regulations and consumer expectations while enhancing market competitiveness and aligning business success with sustainable development goals, thus providing compelling reasons for its widespread adoption and continued refinement in the corporate world despite initial challenges.

The research conducted offers profound strategic implications for a diverse range of stakeholders, illuminating the critical need for a cohesive regulatory framework that not only supports but actively promotes the adoption of Green Supply Chain Management (GSCM) practices. For policymakers, the findings underscore the importance of developing regulations that are not merely punitive but also incentivizing, providing clear pathways and substantial support for businesses transitioning towards sustainable practices. Such frameworks should aim to reduce the bureaucratic and financial burdens that currently hinder the adoption of GSCM, making it accessible not just for large corporations but also for small and medium enterprises which often struggle with the resources necessary for such transformations. In parallel, there is a significant need for international cooperation to standardize regulations that address the global nature of modern supply chains, ensuring that sustainability standards are consistent across borders to prevent disparities that can lead to competitive disadvantages. For business leaders, this study highlights the imperative of investing in cutting-edge technologies such as artificial intelligence, blockchain, and the Internet of Things that can drive significant improvements in supply chain transparency, efficiency, and sustainability. The integration of these technologies can help in better forecasting, resource management, and even in reducing the carbon footprint through optimized logistics and product lifecycle management. However, technology alone is not sufficient; there is a concurrent need to foster collaborative networks that can facilitate shared learning and resource utilization, spreading best practices across industries and geographies. This approach not only enhances individual company performance but strengthens the entire sector by raising the standard of environmental responsibility and sustainability.

Moreover, cultivating a corporate culture that prioritizes sustainability is essential for the long-term integration of GSCM. This involves training and motivating employees at all levels to engage with sustainability goals actively, and creating reward systems that recognize and incentivize eco-friendly innovations and operations. Such a culture encourages sustainability to be viewed as a core aspect of business strategy and critical to corporate identity, which can enhance employee satisfaction and attract top talent, particularly from the younger, environmentally conscious workforce. The path forward for GSCM is laden with challenges, including the need to overcome significant initial costs and organizational inertia. However, the opportunities—ranging from cost savings and improved operational efficiency to enhanced corporate reputation and access to new markets—are substantial. Capitalizing on these opportunities requires a proactive approach to innovation and a willingness to redefine traditional business models and processes. The future of supply chain management, particularly within the context of increasing global emphasis on environmental sustainability, will be shaped by the ongoing evolution of GSCM practices. As more businesses adopt these practices, there will likely be a cascading effect, with GSCM becoming a norm rather than an exception, driven by consumer demand, regulatory pressures, and the inherent economic and environmental benefits it offers. In sum, the continuous evolution of GSCM practices is expected to play a pivotal role in the future of supply chain management, shaping how companies interact with the environment, their consumers, and each other. The transition to more sustainable practices is not merely a regulatory or ethical issue but a foundational business strategy that will define market leaders in the decades to come. As this evolution unfolds, it will undoubtedly bring to the fore new technologies, strategies, and challenges, but also a wealth of opportunities for those prepared to lead the charge towards a sustainable future.

In conclusion, the journey toward integrating GSCM across global industries is complex and challenging but also rich with opportunities for significant environmental and economic benefits. As companies and policymakers continue to recognize and act upon these benefits, the adoption and refinement of GSCM practices are expected to accelerate, marking a crucial step towards sustainable development in the corporate sector. This evolution will continue to be driven by innovation, collaboration, and a commitment to sustainability, reshaping the landscape of global supply chain management in profound ways.

6. LIMITATION AND FUTURE RESEARCH

6.1 Limitations of the research

The research on Green Supply Chain Management (GSCM) within the Asian context, while providing valuable insights, has its limitations primarily due to its geographical focus. Concentrating specifically on Asia means the findings are deeply informed by the unique economic and regulatory environments of this region. These environments differ significantly from those in Western Europe, North America, and other parts of the world where economic conditions are more homogeneous and environmental regulations may be more stringent or uniformly enforced. This geographic specificity restricts the broader applicability of the conclusions drawn, potentially limiting their relevance to only similar developing market contexts where economic growth often precedes environmental regulation.

Another notable limitation of this study arises from its methodological reliance on secondary data sources and literature reviews. This reliance inherently restricts the research to the perspectives and data available in published materials, which can introduce a selection bias towards more successful or positive outcomes. Such a bias might skew the overall synthesis of GSCM effectiveness, as studies with negative results or those highlighting the challenges of implementing GSCM might be underreported or entirely absent. This could lead to an overly optimistic portrayal of the readiness and impact of GSCM practices across industries and fail to fully capture the barriers that could impede their adoption.

In addition, the study's dependence on CiteSpace for the analysis of literature trends could also be seen as a limitation. While CiteSpace is effective for mapping out the landscape of existing research and identifying key themes and trends, it may not adequately capture the complexity of individual GSCM practices or the detailed contextual factors that influence their success or failure. This tool's algorithmic approach focuses more on quantifiable data and might overlook nuanced qualitative insights that are critical for understanding the depth of GSCM challenges and the intricacies involved in implementing sustainable supply chain practices. Such a methodological focus could limit the depth of analysis necessary to grasp the multifaceted nature of GSCM initiatives.

To address these limitations and advance the field of GSCM, future research should expand geographically to include diverse economic and regulatory contexts, enhancing the generalizability of findings. Adopting a mixed-methods approach that integrates qualitative and quantitative data could provide a more comprehensive understanding of GSCM complexities. Also, focusing on longitudinal studies could offer insights into the long-term impacts and sustainability of GSCM practices, which are crucial for developing adaptive and resilient supply chain models in the face of global environmental and economic changes.

6.2 Prospective of future research direction

The future research direction for Green Supply Chain Management (GSCM) presents an expansive field, rich with opportunities for deep exploration and significant advancements. As industries and economies continue to evolve in response to global sustainability pressures and technological advancements, the scope for furthering research in GSCM is both necessary and urgent. Such research could provide profound insights into the integration of cutting-edge technologies, the optimization of regulatory frameworks, and the enhancement of collaborative networks, all of which are crucial for the successful implementation of sustainable practices across global supply chains.

One critical area of future research lies in the exploration of GSCM within varying geographic and economic contexts beyond the primarily Asian focus of current studies. Investigating how GSCM practices are implemented in different global regions, such as Africa, Latin America, and varying parts of Europe and North America, can provide a richer, more comprehensive understanding of global GSCM dynamics. This expansion is crucial not only for enhancing the generalizability of existing models but also for adapting and refining GSCM practices to fit diverse environmental, economic, and cultural contexts. For instance, research could focus on the specific challenges and opportunities in implementing GSCM in less developed economies, where regulatory frameworks may be less robust and technological advancements more sporadic.

Also, the rapid development and adoption of new technologies such as AI, IoT, and blockchain suggest a promising direction for future research. Studies could explore in greater depth how these technologies can be specifically tailored and integrated into GSCM to enhance transparency, efficiency, and sustainability. Future research could delve into the development of bespoke technological solutions that address unique supply chain challenges, such as the tracing of raw materials in industries where sourcing practices are under scrutiny for environmental or ethical reasons. Moreover, the potential of emerging technologies like quantum computing and next-generation AI algorithms offers a new frontier for optimizing supply chain logistics and sustainability assessments at an unprecedented scale and speed. Additionally, the evolving regulatory landscape presents another fertile area for research. Future studies could focus on how different global standards and regulations impact the implementation of GSCM practices across industries. This research could critically assess the effectiveness of various regulatory approaches in promoting sustainable supply chains and explore the potential for a more harmonized global regulatory framework. Such studies would be crucial for policymakers and businesses alike, providing them with actionable insights on navigating complex regulatory environments while striving for sustainability.

Obviously, there is a significant need to investigate the socio-economic impacts of GSCM implementation more deeply. Research could extend to understanding how GSCM practices affect labor markets, local communities, and broader economic systems, particularly in regions heavily dependent on industries undergoing significant shifts due to GSCM practices. This includes studying the impact of automation and technology on employment within traditional manufacturing sectors and exploring how GSCM can contribute to economic resilience and sustainability in the face of global economic pressures. The role of consumer behavior and market demand in driving GSCM adoption offers a compelling research avenue. Future studies could examine how consumer preferences influence corporate strategies around sustainability and how these preferences are shaped by socio-cultural factors, media influence, and economic conditions. Understanding the dynamic relationship between consumer behavior and GSCM could aid companies in designing products and supply chains that not only meet sustainability criteria but also resonate with evolving market demands.

In sum, the prospective directions for future research in GSCM are vast and varied, encompassing technological innovations, regulatory adaptations, economic impacts, and cultural influences on sustainability practices. Each of these areas offers the potential to significantly advance the field of GSCM, contributing to a deeper understanding and more effective implementation of practices that could shape the future of global supply chains in an environmentally sustainable direction. This multidisciplinary approach will be vital for developing robust, adaptable, and forward-looking GSCM strategies that can meet the challenges of the 21st century.

ADDITIONAL READING

Popescu, C. R., & Yu, P. (Eds.). (2024). *Intersecting Environmental Social Governance and AI for Business Sustainability*. IGI Global., DOI: 10.4018/979-8-3693-1151-6

Popescu, C. R., Yu, P., & Wei, Y. (Eds.). (2023). *Achieving the Sustainable Development Goals Through Infrastructure Development*. IGI Global., DOI: 10.4018/979-8-3693-0794-6

Yu, P., Chen, D., & Ahuja, A. (2022). Smart and Sustainable Economy: How COVID-19 Has Acted as a Catalyst for China's Digital Transformation. In Kautish, S., & Kaur, G. (Eds.), *AI-Enabled Agile Internet of Things for Sustainable FinTech Ecosystems* (pp. 106–146). IGI Global., DOI: 10.4018/978-1-6684-4176-3.ch006

Yu, P., Chen, J., Sampat, M., & Misuko, N. (2022). The Digital Transformation of Rural Agricultural Business Management: A Case Study of China. In Bilgaiyan, S., Singh, J., & Das, H. (Eds.), *Empirical Research for Futuristic E-Commerce Systems: Foundations and Applications* (pp. 23–52). IGI Global., DOI: 10.4018/978-1-6684-4969-1.ch002

Yu, P., Ge, Y., Mandizvidza, K., & Mulli, J. (2023). How Can Small and Medium Enterprises in the Chinese Market Achieve Sustainable Development Goals Through Blockchain? In Taleb, D., Abdelli, M., Khalil, A., & Sghaier, A. (Eds.), *Examining the Vital Financial Role of SMEs in Achieving the Sustainable Development Goals* (pp. 52–85). IGI Global., DOI: 10.4018/978-1-6684-4834-2.ch004

Yu, P., Gong, R., & Sampat, M. (2022). Blockchain Technology in China's Digital Economy: Balancing Regulation and Innovation. In Tehrani, P. (Ed.), *Regulatory Aspects of Artificial Intelligence on Blockchain* (pp. 132–157). IGI Global., DOI: 10.4018/978-1-7998-7927-5.ch007

Yu, P., Gu, H., Zhao, Y., & Ahuja, A. (2022). Digital Transformation Driven by Internet Data Center: Case Studies on China. In Piaggesi, D., Landazuri, H., & Jia, B. (Eds.), *Cases on Applying Knowledge Economy Principles for Economic Growth in Developing Nations* (pp. 203–230). IGI Global., DOI: 10.4018/978-1-7998-8417-0.ch011

Yu, P., Hu, X., Prakash, A., Misuko, N. W., & Haiyue, G. (Eds.). (2023). *Opportunities and Challenges of Industrial IoT in 5G and 6G Networks*. IGI Global., DOI: 10.4018/978-1-7998-9266-3

Yu, P., Jiao, A., & Sampat, M. (2022). The Effect of Chinese Green Transformation on Competitiveness and the Environment. In Ordóñez de Pablos, P., Zhang, X., & Almunawar, M. (Eds.), *Handbook of Research on Green, Circular, and Digital Economies as Tools for Recovery and Sustainability* (pp. 257–279). IGI Global., DOI: 10.4018/978-1-7998-9664-7.ch014

Yu, P., Lang, H., Galang, J. I., & Xu, Y. (2023). The Role of Digital Twin in Accelerating the Digital

Transformation of Smart Cities. Case Studies in China. In Yu, P., Hu, X., Prakash, A., Misuko, N., & Haiyue, G. (Eds.), *Opportunities and Challenges of Industrial IoT in 5G and 6G Networks* (pp. 155–177). IGI Global., DOI: 10.4018/978-1-7998-9266-3.ch008

Yu, P., Liu, X., Mahendran, R., & Lu, S. (2022). Analysis and Comparison of Business Models of Leading Enterprises in the Chinese Hydrogen Energy Industry. In Felseghi, R., Cobîrzan, N., & Raboaca, M. (Eds.), *Clean Technologies and Sustainable Development in Civil Engineering* (pp. 179–216). IGI Global., DOI: 10.4018/978-1-7998-9810-8.ch008

Yu, P., Liu, Z., & Hanes, E. (2022). Supply Chain Resiliency, Efficiency, and Visibility in the Post-Pandemic Era in China: Case Studies of MeiTuan Waimai, and Ele. me. In Ramakrishna, Y. (Ed.), *Handbook of Research on Supply Chain Resiliency, Efficiency, and Visibility in the Post-Pandemic Era* (pp. 195–225). IGI Global., DOI: 10.4018/978-1-7998-9506-0.ch011

Yu, P., Liu, Z., Hanes, E., & Mumtaz, J. (2022). Integration of IoT and Blockchain for Smart and Secured Supply Chain Management: Case Studies of China. In Goyal, S., Pradeep, N., Shukla, P., Ghonge, M., & Ravi, R. (Eds.), *Utilizing Blockchain Technologies in Manufacturing and Logistics Management* (pp. 179–207). IGI Global., DOI: 10.4018/978-1-7998-8697-6.ch010

Yu, P., Liu, Z., & Sampat, M. (2023). Enhancing the Resilience of Food Cold Chain Logistics Through Digital Transformation: A Case Study of China. In Masudin, I., Almunawar, M., Restuputri, D., & Sud-On, P. (Eds.), *Handbook of Research on Promoting Logistics and Supply Chain Resilience Through Digital Transformation* (pp. 200–224). IGI Global., DOI: 10.4018/978-1-6684-5882-2.ch014

Yu, P., Lu, S., Hanes, E., & Chen, Y. (2022). The Role of Blockchain Technology in Harnessing the Sustainability of Chinese Digital Finance. In Swarnalatha, P., & Prabu, S. (Eds.), *Blockchain Technologies for Sustainable Development in Smart Cities* (pp. 155–186). IGI Global., DOI: 10.4018/978-1-7998-9274-8.ch009

Yu, P., Song, J., Sampat, M., & Hanes, E. (2023). Digital Twins: Accelerating the Digital Transformation in the Chinese Transportation Sector. In Fields, Z. (Ed.), *Multidisciplinary Approaches in AI, Creativity, Innovation, and Green Collaboration* (pp. 121–154). IGI Global., DOI: 10.4018/978-1-6684-6366-6.ch007

Yu, P., Xue, W., & Mahendran, R. (2022). The Development and Impact of China's Digital Transformation in the Medical Industry. In Rodrigues, M., & Proença, J. (Eds.), *Impact of Digital Transformation on the Development of New Business Models and Consumer Experience* (pp. 97–128). IGI Global., DOI: 10.4018/978-1-7998-9179-6.ch006

Yu, P., Zhang, Y., Sampat, M., & Chen, Y. (2023). Research on Cross-Industry Digital Transformation Under the New Normal: A Case Study of China. In Marco-Lajara, B., Martínez-Falcó, J., & Millán-Tudela, L. (Eds.), *Corporate Sustainability as a Tool for Improving Economic, Social, and Environmental Performance* (pp. 246–277). IGI Global., DOI: 10.4018/978-1-6684-7422-8.ch013

REFERENCES

Agyabeng-Mensah, Y., Baah, C., & Afum, E. (2024). Do the roles of green supply chain learning, green employee creativity, and green organizational citizenship behavior really matter in circular supply chain performance? *Journal of Environmental Planning and Management*, 67(3), 609–631. DOI: 10.1080/09640568.2022.2130036

Ali, Z. (2023). Predicting SMEs performance through green supply chain practices: A mediation model link of business process performance. *Asia Pacific Journal of Marketing and Logistics*, 35(2), 432–450. DOI: 10.1108/APJML-05-2021-0296

Baah, C., Agyabeng-Mensah, Y., Afum, E., Acquah, I. S. K., & Essel, D. (2023). Government influence on logistics and supply chain innovations: assessing implications for firm performance and societal impact in an emerging economy. INTERNATIONAL JOURNAL OF EMERGING MARKETS. DOI: 10.1108/IJOEM-09-2021-1348

Chen, S., Zhou, F. L., Su, J. F., Li, L. X., Yang, B. Y., & He, Y. D. (2021). Pricing policies of a dynamic green supply chain with strategies of retail service. *Asia Pacific Journal of Marketing and Logistics*, 33(1), 296–329. DOI: 10.1108/APJML-07-2019-0423

Dhaigude, A. S., Gupta, N., Sardana, D., Kumar, V., & Terziovski, M. (2023). The catalytic role of "responsible investments" in innovation and firm performance link: In the context of manufacturing in Asia-Pacific. *Asia Pacific Journal of Management*. Advance online publication. DOI: 10.1007/s10490-023-09882-9

Farooque, M., Zhang, A., & Liu, Y. P. (2019). Barriers to circular food supply chains in China. *Supply Chain Management*, 24(5), 677–696. DOI: 10.1108/SCM-10-2018-0345

Jalil, F., Yang, J. H., Al-Okaily, M., & Rehman, S. U. (2024). E-commerce for a sustainable future: Integrating trust, green supply chain management and online shopping satisfaction. *Asia Pacific Journal of Marketing and Logistics*, 36(10), 2354–2370. Advance online publication. DOI: 10.1108/APJML-12-2023-1188

Liu, J., Yuan, C. H., Hafeez, M., & Yuan, Q. Y. (2018). The relationship between environment and logistics performance: Evidence from Asian countries. *Journal of Cleaner Production*, 204, 282–291. DOI: 10.1016/j.jclepro.2018.08.310

Liu, L. L., Wu, H., Hafeez, M., Albaity, M. S. A., & Ullah, S. (2022). Carbon neutrality through supply chain performance: does green innovation matter in Asia? ECONOMIC RESEARCH-EKONOMSKA ISTRAZIVANJA. DOI: 10.1080/1331677X.2022.2149588

Majumdar, A., & Sinha, S. K. (2019). Analyzing the barriers of green textile supply chain management in Southeast Asia using interpretive structural modeling. *Sustainable Production and Consumption*, 17, 176–187. DOI: 10.1016/j.spc.2018.10.005

Peng, Q. Y., Wang, C. X., & Goh, M. (2023). Green innovation decision and coordination of supply chain under corporate social responsibility and risk preferences. *Computers & Industrial Engineering*, 185, 109703. Advance online publication. DOI: 10.1016/j.cie.2023.109703

Sheu, J. B., Kundu, T., & Choi, T. M. (2024). International Sustainable Supply Chain Management Under Bilateral Governments' Policy Intervention and Power Asymmetry. *IEEE Transactions on Engineering Management*, 71, 138–150. DOI: 10.1109/TEM.2021.3108975

Somsuk, N., & Laosirihongthong, T. (2017). Prioritization of applicable drivers for green supply chain management implementation toward sustainability in Thailand. *International Journal of Sustainable Development and World Ecology*, 24(2), 175–191. DOI: 10.1080/13504509.2016.1187210

Sundarakani, B., de Souza, R., Goh, M., Wagner, S. M., & Manikandan, S. (2010). Modeling carbon footprints across the supply chain. *International Journal of Production Economics*, 128(1), 43–50. DOI: 10.1016/j.ijpe.2010.01.018

Tamayo-Torres, I., Gutierrez-Gutierrez, L., & Ruiz-Moreno, A. (2019). Boosting sustainability and financial performance: The role of supply chain controversies. *International Journal of Production Research*, 57(11), 3719–3734. DOI: 10.1080/00207543.2018.1562248

Tseng, M. L., Islam, M. S., Karia, N., Fauzi, F. A., & Afrin, S. (2019). A literature review on green supply chain management: Trends and future challenges. *Resources, Conservation and Recycling*, 141, 145–162. DOI: 10.1016/j.resconrec.2018.10.009

Tseng, M. L., Wu, K. J., Hu, J. Y., & Wang, C. H. (2018). Decision-making model for sustainable supply chain finance under uncertainties. *International Journal of Production Economics*, 205, 30–36. DOI: 10.1016/j.ijpe.2018.08.024

Xie, J. P., Li, J., Liang, L., Fang, X., Yang, G., & Wei, L. H. (2020). Contracting Emissions Reduction Supply Chain Based on Market Low-Carbon Preference and Carbon Intensity Constraint. *Asia-Pacific Journal of Operational Research*, 37(2), 2050003. Advance online publication. DOI: 10.1142/S0217595920500037

Yu, Y., Zhu, W. W., & Tian, Y. (2021). Green Supply Chain Management, Environmental Degradation, and Energy: Evidence from Asian Countries. *Discrete Dynamics in Nature and Society*, 2021, 1–14. Advance online publication. DOI: 10.1155/2021/5179964

Yu, Z. Q., & Xiao, X. (2024). Green supply chain management and innovation persistence-Based on environmental turbulence perspective. *European Journal of Innovation Management*, 27(4), 1299–1337. DOI: 10.1108/EJIM-05-2022-0230

Zhang, Q. S., Yang, L., Cheng, J. Z., & Feng, T. W. (2024). How green human resource management and institutional pressure drive performance via green image: The equifinal paths and their performance outcomes. *Asia Pacific Journal of Human Resources*, 62(1), e12389. Advance online publication. DOI: 10.1111/1744-7941.12389

Chapter 2
Beginning of March Towards Greener Future Through EV Charging Network

Vedashree Mali
Dr. Vishwanath Karad MIT World Peace University, India

Roshan Joseph Punnen
Dr. Vishwanath Karad MIT World Peace University, India

ABSTRACT

This case is based on real life setup of a Bengaluru based leading Electric Vehicles (EV) charging network company (pseudonym:E-mobility Solutions) and its strategic initiatives, analysis of financial feasibility of setting up the electric vehicles charging station, and the return on investment in Indian scenario.Electric vehicle charging stations are the backbone of EV ecosystem and depending on the situation and need, electric vehicles (EV) can be charged in a number of methods. Accordingly, charging infrastructure for EVs is of different forms and tailored for varied uses.The case study represents a major step towards the electric vehicle charging infrastructure and will broaden understanding of the presence and lack thereof a connection between the non-financial factor and their impact on profitability. The limitation, however, is that the study was confined to charging station in Bangalore district only. Future studies can also focus on setting up an EV Public Charging Station in a rural area and the return on investment from it.

DOI: 10.4018/979-8-3693-4338-8.ch002

ELECTRIC VEHICLE INDUSTRY

The promotion of Electric Vehicles (EVs) has been a crucial step towards addressing the environmental challenges posed by climate change. In recent years, there has been a significant increase in awareness about EVs as well as a shift in preferences towards replacing traditional petrol/diesel vehicles with EVs. As a result, the sales of EVs have experienced exponential growth. Owning an EV eliminates the need for reliance on petrol because, unlike conventional fuel vehicles that utilize internal ignition engines, EVs are powered by electric motors. These motors are powered by a large automobile battery, which can be charged through a power outlet or an electric vehicle supply equipment (EVSE). Since EVs run on electricity, there are no emissions from engines, and there is no need for components like fuel pumps, fuel lines, or fuel tanks.

Electric cars have minimal operating costs since they have fewer mechanical components that require maintenance. Additionally, they are highly environmentally beneficial as they consume minimal fossil fuels (petrol or diesel). While some EVs previously used lead acid or nickel metal hydride batteries, lithium-ion batteries have become the standard for modern battery electric cars due to their longer lifespan and superior energy storage capabilities, with a self-discharge rate of just 5% per month.

In recent years, electric vehicles have gained significant attention due to the growing concerns over carbon footprints and the environmental impact of traditional fuel-powered vehicles. The concept of electric vehicles has been around for a while, but it is in the past decade that it has truly captured the spotlight. One of the key advancements in electric vehicle technology is regenerative braking, which allows these vehicles to capture and store energy that would otherwise be wasted during braking. By utilizing the electric motor as a generator, the energy is stored in the vehicle's battery for later use. This development, coupled with the increasing focus on renewable energy sources and the desire to mitigate transportation's contribution to climate change and air pollution, has led to a significant surge in electric vehicle sales. A pivotal moment in the fight against climate change was the signing of the Paris Agreement in 2015. This global agreement saw all 196 member countries commit to finding solutions to combat global warming and limit temperature rise to below 2 degrees Celsius. Under the accord, the Paris Declaration on Electro-Mobility and Climate Change was issued, highlighting the need for a greater emphasis on electric mobility.

India is among the nations that have shown interest in adopting electric cars, and this interest remains strong. In fact, India has set an ambitious goal of achieving 100 percent electric mobility by 2030. According to a UN assessment, the number of passenger vehicles is projected to increase more than fourfold to 1.2 billion by 2050, resulting in a significant rise in carbon emissions. The transportation industry, heavily reliant on fossil fuels, currently contributes to 23% of global CO_2 emissions, and this percentage is expected to reach 40% by 2040 if no measures are taken to promote electric mobility. The global Electric Vehicle (EV) industry is forecasted to grow at a Compound Annual Growth Rate (CAGR) of 21.7% by 2030. This growth can be attributed to the increasing popularity of zero-emission vehicles, government policies, and tax incentives, which have created a high demand for EVs and subsequently fuelled the expansion of the EV market. Since 2020, the investment in EVs and connected car technology has exceeded $100 billion, indicating the significant interest and potential in this sector. Recognizing the growing demand, major vehicle manufacturers worldwide have introduced electric vehicles to cater to this market.

The electric vehicle charging station industry experienced significant growth in 2021, reaching a value of 17.59 billion USD. It is projected to further expand to 111.90 billion USD by 2030, with a compound annual growth rate of 30.25%. This remarkable growth can be attributed to the high demand and increasing popularity of electric vehicles in the market. Governments worldwide have implemented various schemes and subsidies to promote the development of charging stations, contributing to the industry's rapid expansion. These stations serve as a vital source of energy for electric vehicles, utilizing advanced technologies such as metered connections and network connectivity to enhance their functionality. Although the EV industry faced some challenges in 2020 due to the pandemic and disruptions in the supply chain, it continues to thrive as efforts towards a greener earth persist.

EV INDUSTRY IN INDIA

The electric vehicle sector in India ranks as the fifth largest globally and is projected to climb to the third spot by 2030. In 2021, India witnessed a remarkable 168% growth rate in EVs compared to the previous year, with a total of 122,607 units. According to IQ Air (2019), India was listed as the 25th out of 50 cities with the worst air quality worldwide, leading to 74,000 deaths in 2015 due to vehicle emissions. The government has significantly ramped up its efforts to promote electric mobility over the past decade. The National Electric Mobility Mission Plan 2020 was launched in 2013 with the goal of deploying 6-7 million electric vehicles by the end of 2020. Subsequent initiatives like the Faster Adoption and Manufacturing of Hybrid and Electric Vehicles (FAME) program were introduced to support the objectives of NEMMP, although the country fell short of meeting those targets. The Council on Energy, Environment, and Water (CEEW) stated that if India fulfills its Clean Energy Ministerial (CEM) EV30@30 commitment, the EV industry could be worth $206 billion USD by 2030. The CEM, a global platform, has been collaborating with nations worldwide to ensure that 30% of new vehicle sales by

2030 are electric. With the current pace of infrastructure development, achieving this target appears feasible.

The EV sector in India was dominated by two wheelers and three wheelers. With increasing crude price, increasing environmental awareness and emission norms have increased the demand for electric vehicle. It was expected that the price of the electric vehicles was also expected to decline in the coming years which will add further attention to the electric vehicles. The EV sales in India were led by 2-wheeler and 3-wheeler as shown in the below figure:

Figure 1. Sales of 2W and 3W from 2018 to 2021

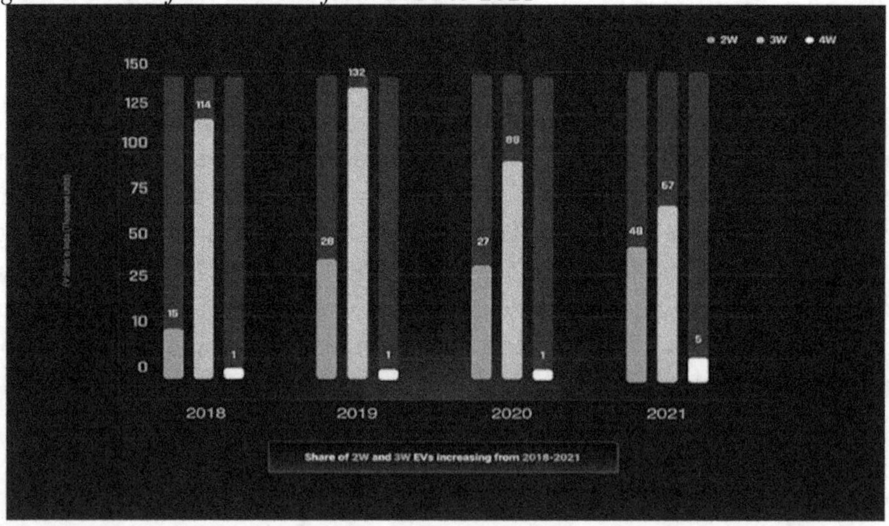

Source: company records

The EV charging infrastructure in India has experienced significant growth in the past five months, expanding by over 2.5 times. With a focus on vehicles with a range of less than 500km, charging stations play a vital role in establishing a robust EV ecosystem in the country. As of March 15, 2021, the Department of Heavy Industry (DHI) has approved 3397 charging stations for the FAME project. Key charge points operators in India include Charge Grid, Kazam, GoME, EVRE, Charge Zone, BOLT, and Electric Pe. Over the next 4-5 years, approximately 48,000 chargers are planned to be added to the network, with a total investment of Rs 14000 crore.

A recent consumer research study in India revealed that 55% of consumers have either switched or are willing to switch to electric vehicles. The lack of infrastructure is identified as the biggest deterrent to adoption. It is important to consider the specific requirements of each city when determining whether to increase the number of home chargers or public chargers. Metropolitan cities with apartment complexes tend to prefer home charging, while cities with dispersed populations prioritize quick public charging. However, due to overurbanization and high population densities in many Indian cities, the availability of fast public charging is crucial for EV users. According to the Council on Energy, Environment, and Water (CEEW) and the Centre for Energy Finance, it is estimated that India will witness the sale of approximately 102 million electric vehicles between 2021 and 2030.

Figure 2. Expected Sales of EVs from 2021 to 2030

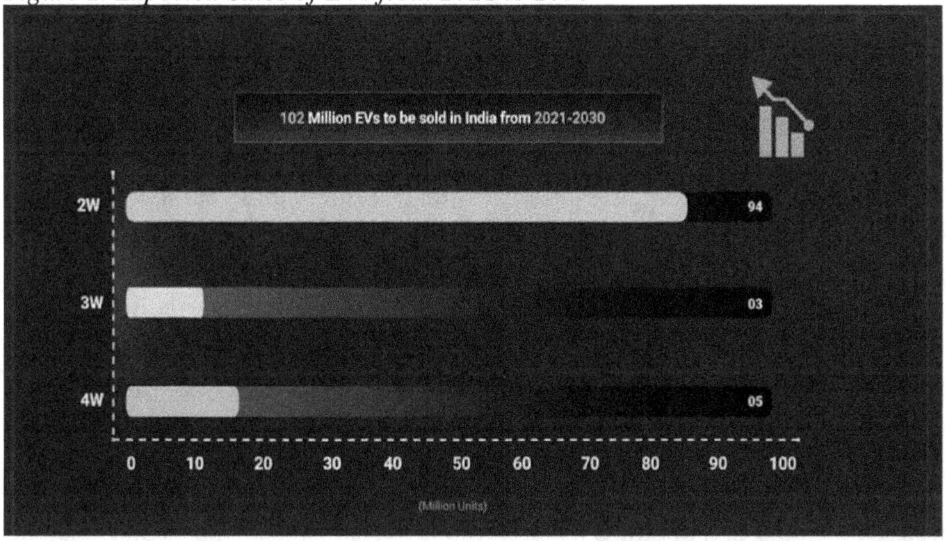

Source: company records

LITERATURE REVIEW

The Paris Agreement brought together all 196 member states in a joint effort to address global warming and cap the temperature increase at 2 degrees Celsius(Ahmad, 2020). India has set a target of achieving 100% electric mobility by 2030; however, it encounters obstacles such as the insufficient charging infrastructure. An analysis utilizing the system of innovation framework pinpointed hurdles including land scarcity and governmental inefficacies. (Chokkalingam et al., 2017) The significant increase in electric vehicle (EV) adoption has paved the way for advancements in charging infrastructure. Seamless connectivity between charging stations is crucial for widespread EV usage to address concerns about driving range. Current charging stations lack efficient power allocation and scheduling management. Enhancing the existing infrastructure could involve providing users with real-time data on charging station availability and reserves to help them locate the nearest charging point for their EV. This research paper discusses the development of an interactive user application using SQL and PHP to allocate charging slots based on battery parameters, utilizing data communication with charging stations to check slot availability. The proposed real-time forecasting charging infrastructure, operated by a server, minimizes waiting times and effectively manages scheduling to prevent EVs from running out of battery power on the road. The model is implemented using a cost-effective microcontroller and has undergone system testing. The exhaustive nature of fossil fuels and environmental concerns linked to greenhouse gases are the primary factors driving the shift from conventional vehicles to electric vehicles (EVs). (As a result, scientists and researchers have focused their efforts on exploring charging stations due to the electrification of the transportation sector and the growing popularity of EVs. However, the lack of developed charging infrastructure, determining the optimal placement of charging stations, and managing charge scheduling pose significant challenges for the widespread adoption of EVs. These challenges also impact other aspects of EVs, such as vehicle price and driving range, which can be partially addressed with a well-established charging infrastructure. The existing outdated infrastructure poses limitations in achieving the ideal placement of charging stations, as it was not designed with EVs in mind when it was initially developed. Over the past few years, researchers have dedicated their studies to determining the best placement and sizing of EV charging stations. They have employed various approaches, objective functions, and optimization algorithms to tackle this complex and dynamic problem. This review study aims to provide the research community with the latest advancements and findings in the field of charging infrastructure planning for EVs. The authors of this study (Aditya and Kartik, 2015) propose a method to expand the number of charging stations by tapping into the electricity provided by electric poles to charge electric vehicles. This process involves regulating the charging rate through a controller that receives input from an electronic data capture machine. This strategy aims to accelerate the adoption of Electric Vehicles by leveraging the current electric infrastructure. It also promotes the ownership of Electric Vehicles, which in turn encourages Original Equipment Manufacturers (OEMs) to introduce new products. India is striving to enhance its EV charging infrastructure by utilizing the existing network of electric poles. By repurposing these poles as potential charging stations, the country can facilitate the growth of Electric Vehicles and reduce emissions. Increasing the number of charging stations in India will not only encourage more people to own Electric Vehicles but also support the country's goal of developing a robust electric vehicle charging infrastructure. By offering incentives for off-peak charging, the peak load on the electric grid can be minimized. (Surbhi et al., 2020) The paper delves into the fundamental terminologies related to charging stations, encompassing types, levels, and diverse technologies. It also provides a concise overview of lithium-ion battery charging strategies and battery management systems. The Indian government incentivizes the adoption of electric vehicles by offering tax reductions and subsidies for EV charging. Guidelines established by the Ministry of Power and Housing facilitate the setup process. Challenges faced by Electric Vehicle Charging Stations (EVCS) include grid overloading, load forecasting, charging time, and traffic management. The Indian government's support for EV deployment is evident through tax reductions and subsidies. The focus is on addressing EVCS challenges and exploring opportunities for electric vehicles, including discussions on technologies, grid overloading, and government initiatives aimed at promoting EV deployment.

The rise (Gupta et al., 2021) in the use of traditional fuel in the transportation industry has led to a rapid depletion of resources. Consequently, the focus of research in the transportation sector has shifted towards electrification over the past decade. Electric Vehicles (EVs) have been increasingly replacing internal combustion engines in recent years. The growing number of EVs on the road has had a significant negative impact on the current electric grid, resulting in reliability issues. To address these challenges, measures need to be implemented to mitigate the adverse effects of the increased demand for charging stations. This paper provides a detailed analysis of the current EV landscape, charging infrastructure, EV effects, and the optimal allocation of Electric Vehicles. Specifically, it examines the optimal placement of fast charging stations based on economic advantages and grid considerations. The paper also addresses the obstacles to adoption and explores future trends in the industry, including sourcing energy from renewable sources and leveraging vehicle-to-grid technology. (Sajan,2022). The economic viability of setting up an electric vehicle charging station (EVCS) in accordance with government regulations is analysed using the net present value (NPV) method. Electric vehicles (EVs) have the potential to reduce greenhouse gas emissions and decrease reliance on traditional fuels in India. The presence of affordable and dependable charging infrastructure is essential for the widespread acceptance of EVs. This study specifically examines the economic feasibility of EV charging stations in India, highlighting the factors that influence the selection of charging infrastructure locations and the existing standards for EV charging. The NPV method is employed to evaluate the economic viability of establishing EVCS. It is found that setting up EVCS at existing parking facilities can be a profitable venture, presenting a lucrative business opportunity. The availability of charging infrastructure plays a critical role in facilitating the widespread adoption of electric vehicles. (Arigela et al.,2022) The establishment of an electric vehicle (EV) charging infrastructure is of utmost importance for the widespread adoption of EVs on a large scale. This is particularly true in the Indian context, where there are unique challenges to overcome. The increasing popularity of EVs has led to a growing demand for charging stations, which in turn makes the setup financially viable. To ensure the cost-effectiveness of charging stations, it is crucial to rely on research findings and developments in the field. This paper focuses on data analysis that specifically addresses the demand for EV charging station infrastructure in India. The findings highlight the necessity for strategic planning and development to support the large-scale deployment of EVs in urban areas. One of the key challenges explored in this study is the establishment of an effective charging infrastructure. It emphasizes the significance of ideal positioning and charge scheduling to ensure efficient operations and widespread adoption of EVs in the Indian market. By addressing these challenges, the aim is to facilitate the smooth integration of EVs into the existing transportation system. Furthermore, this study provides valuable insights into the latest developments and research findings related to charging infrastructure for EVs in India. The intention is to support the research community and policymakers in addressing the infrastructure needs for EVs in the country. By leveraging these insights, stakeholders can make informed decisions and implement effective strategies to meet the growing demand for EV charging infrastructure in India. (D. A. Hussien, 2023) The optimization of charging and discharging schedules in electric vehicle charging stations is crucial for maximizing revenue and ensuring financial feasibility. By implementing coordinated charging strategies, revenue can be significantly increased compared to uncoordinated approaches. This study formulates the scheduling issue as a linear optimization problem and utilizes the Particle Swarm Optimization (PSO) technique to find the optimal solution. Not only does coordinated charging scheduling maximize revenue for charging stations, but it also minimizes negative impacts on the electric network. (Avinash et.al,2020) The research underscores the necessity of establishing EV charging station infrastructure in India, underscoring the importance of strategic planning and development to facilitate the extensive uptake of EVs in the nation. Optimal placement, efficient charging schedules, and comprehensive infrastructure enhancement are pivotal elements recognized for the effective assimilation and acceptance of EVs in the Indian market. Examination of market-driven and regulatory issues for financial viability. The selection of strategic sites to promote EV adoption and mitigate risks constitutes the primary focus of the study. The paper delves into the potential requirement for electric vehicles (EVs), charging station (CS) infrastructure, and the associated challenges within the Indian context. However, the authors do not delve into the potential implications of EVs on the Indian electricity market. The location of EV charging stations is critical for EV adoption and risk management. The necessity for EV charging station infrastructure in India, along with the challenges and risks linked to EV adoption, is highlighted. The study also outlines challenges, governmental policies, and EV specifications.

EVs are recognized as a promising technology for reducing urban emissions by transferring them to centralized power plants in rural regions, underscoring the significance of electrifying the transportation sector. The challenges and potential solutions related to the adoption of electric vehicle charging infrastructure in India are discussed (Arsalan Syed et al.,2022). An economic analysis is conducted to evaluate the feasibility of deploying wireless charging infrastructure in the country. The lack of commercially viable charging infrastructure in India is highlighted. The research paper includes a detailed economic assessment of implementing wireless charging infrastructure in India to determine its viability in the current context. Mathematical models and simulation results are presented to analyze the inductive (wireless) charging system for electric vehicles in the Indian setting. The study considers international standards for wireless charging in the development of hardware to address safety, environmental, and regulatory issues. Economic factors such as installation costs, power supply requirements, and infrastructure design are examined to comprehend the financial implications of establishing wireless charging stations in India. (Walid et al., 2023) The article presents a linear optimization approach to address the issue of coordinated charging and discharging scheduling for electric vehicles at charging stations. By formulating the problem as a linear optimization problem and employing the Particle Swarm Optimization (PSO) technique, the proposed method effectively solves the problem. The coordinated charging and discharging scheduling strategy not only enhances the revenue of charging stations but also outperforms uncoordinated charging methods. (Colin Sheppard et al., 2016) The study utilized an agent-based simulation modeling platform to investigate the cost-effective placement of electric vehicle charging stations (EVCS) in the National Capital Territory (NCT) of Delhi, India. The research focuses on identifying optimal locations for EVCS in densely populated and frequented areas. With a 1% penetration rate, it was found that 2764 chargers could be strategically deployed at a cost of $4.4 million. The study underscores the importance of public PEV charging infrastructure in reducing emissions and decreasing reliance on imported oil. Furthermore, it highlights the necessity for additional infrastructure to support electric vehicles, especially in areas where home chargers are not readily available, and where range anxiety may impact charging capacity. A novel profit maximization model (Se, Hoon et al., 2018) for electric vehicle (EV) charging stations in Korea has been proposed in this study. The authors aim to encourage participation in the EV charging business by formulating a method to determine the optimal number of EV chargers and the capacity of auxiliary equipment. The objective is to maximize the profit of the charging station operator (CSO) while considering regulatory, economic, and physical constraints. By improving the profitability of EV charging infrastructure, individual CSOs can benefit economically. Furthermore, this approach promotes the participation of CSOs in the EV charging business, which in turn contributes to environmental benefits. It is important to note that the profitability of the EV charging business is influenced by the initial capital investment. The proposed method offers a means to maximize profit for charging station operators. Additionally, the study highlights the significance of EVs in reducing greenhouse gas emissions and emphasizes the support of global policies in this regard. However, Korea faces challenges in the introduction of EVs due to the lack of infrastructure.

DRIVING FORCES BEHIND THE DEMAND FOR ELECTRIC VEHICLES

After examining the historical data on electric vehicle (EV) sales in India, it is evident that there has been a significant surge in the demand for EVs both globally and within the country. Among all types of EVs, the two-wheeler sector has experienced the highest growth rate. Several factors have contributed to this sudden increase in demand for EVs in India, including:

1. Pollution Control Laws: Governments and organizations worldwide have been setting and achieving various sustainability targets, many of which focus on reducing CO2 emissions, pollution, and noise levels while enhancing productivity. As a result, several governmental organizations have offered tax credits and other incentives to individuals purchasing electric vehicles, making EVs more accessible to the general public.
2. Urbanization: In metropolitan areas, where average daily driving distances are shorter and smaller, fuel-efficient vehicles are more prevalent. With the projected increase in the global urban population by 2030, it is expected that the demand for electric cars will continue to rise.
3. Battery Range Extensions: As battery technology continues to advance, the range of electric cars has significantly improved. This expansion in range has made EVs more practical for individuals who need to travel longer distances. Additionally, advancements in charger performance and battery technology have made high-speed charging more efficient, minimizing downtime during travel.
4. Growing Number of Charging Stations: To meet the increasing demand for charging stations, many communities have been expanding the number of accessible ports each year. The availability of charging stations in supermarkets, airports, and other public places has made EVs a more viable option for consumers.

5. Increased Variety of Options: Initially, there were limited types and models of electric cars available, and many of them were prohibitively expensive. However, as EVs have gained popularity, a wider range of car types and models have become accessible, catering to a larger number of consumers with different preferences and demands.
6. Changing Market Trends: Market statistics indicate that while sales of conventional vehicles have remained steady or declined, the demand for EVs has been steadily increasing. This shift in market trends has further contributed to the rise in EV sales.

In conclusion, the sudden surge in demand for electric vehicles in India can be attributed to various factors such as pollution control laws, urbanization, battery range extensions, the growing number of charging stations, increased variety of options, and changing market trends. These factors have collectively propelled the growth of EVs and made them a more attractive choice for consumers.

KEY COMPONENTS OF AN ELECTRIC VEHICLE:

- Battery Pack: An energy storage unit in a vehicle that holds power for the electric motor.
- Electric motor: The motor that receives power from the vehicle's battery to drive the wheels, with some cars using motor generators for both propulsion and energy regeneration.
- Electronic power controller: Equipment that manages the energy flow from the traction battery, controlling the speed and torque output of the electric motor.
- Onboard charger: Converts AC current from the charge port into DC current to charge the motor battery, while also analyzing battery properties like voltage, current, temperature, and charge status.
- Charging port: The connection point that links the vehicle to an external power source for recharging the electric battery pack.
- Transmission (electric): Responsible for transferring mechanical power from the electric motor to the wheels.
- Cooling system: Maintains safe operating temperatures for the engine, electric motor, power electronics, and other vehicle components.
- DC/DC converter: Converts high-voltage DC power from the vehicle battery into lower-voltage DC power needed to operate vehicle systems and recharge the auxiliary battery.

- Battery: The auxiliary battery in an electric vehicle supplies power for operating vehicle accessories.

THE COMPANY

E-mobility Solutions had established one of the largest charging networks worldwide. Their network spanned across India, with Electric Vehicle (EV) charging stations suitable for all types of EVs, including two wheelers, three wheelers, and four wheelers. The company had already installed over 10,000 EV charging points globally and had ambitious plan to install an additional 100,000 charging points by 2025. Furthermore, they aimed to install 250,000 charging points within the country, including rural areas, by 2024.

One of the key features of their chargers was the universal charging point, manufactured in India, which was compatible with any EV charger and could work with the current AC supply. To enhance user convenience, the company had also introduced a mobile app that allowed users to easily locate and book the nearest charging station. These unique initiatives made E-mobility Solutions' charging station network highly reliable throughout India. The company provided a comprehensive software experience and aimed to establish a robust network of Electric Vehicle charging points across the country. Their ultimate goal was to expand and create the best EV charging network globally.

In addition, E-mobility Solutions offered a potential earning opportunity for users, allowing them to set the rate for a single charge. This enabled common people to participate in the EV revolution without owning an Electric vehicle. The installation process for E-mobility Solutions' chargers was simple and could be carried out by any electrician.

Charging Network-

The installation process of the company's charging unit was both quick and hassle-free. It only took 30 minutes to complete the installation, making it convenient for individuals or electricians. The process involved three simple steps:

1. Mounting the device and poster to the wall: Begin by fixing the device and poster to the wall using the screws provided in the box. Once the poster is mounted, place the QR code on it.
2. Connecting to electricity: After mounting the device, the next step is to connect the charger to the electricity source.

3. Activating the device: To activate the device, simply scan the QR code using the company's dedicated app. Once scanned, the device is ready to be used.

The Business Model

Business Model of the company comprised of the following components-

Operating System

The company had created an operating system that provided a customized platform for users to tailor to their preferences, enabling them to stay connected in an intelligent and efficient network. This operating system facilitated the establishment of a sophisticated ecosystem where all charging stations were linked, enhancing the accessibility of the electric vehicle experience. Furthermore, this operating system could be smoothly integrated into current Original Equipment Manufacturers' systems.

The company offered unique OS features that were not found on other platforms, including:

- An app with a virtual speedometer
- The ability to playback trips
- Real-time monitoring of vehicles
- Advanced diagnostic and control capabilities for vehicles
- Analytics specifically designed for vehicles
- A rental module for easy vehicle rental management
- A speed lock feature for children's safety
- Geofencing functionality for location-based restrictions
- Seamless connectivity between vehicles and the cloud through Vehicle to Cloud (V2C) and Cloud to Vehicle (C2V) connections.

Unique selling points of the organization's operating system:

- Smart mobile application: This operating system enables users to connect to their smartphones, providing access to various features including navigation, smart alerts, and vehicle diagnostics.
- Live updates: The operating system enabled users to receive real-time notifications regarding the vehicle for the rider, distributor, and service center, ensuring that the vehicle remains connected and up to date.
- Data to the cloud: The utilization of AI and machine learning in this Operating System enables users to gather comprehensive data on every aspect of the vehicle, facilitating the analysis of its performance.

- Easy integration: The operating system proved to be highly compatible with various vehicles, thanks to its seamless packaging. This allowed both OEMs and users to effortlessly prepare their electric vehicles for the future.
- Making vehicle connected: With the utilization of this operating system, comprehensive monitoring of the entire vehicle becomes possible, enabling control over various components such as the battery, motor, lights indicators, and more. This functionality is achieved through the transmission of data to the cloud.
- Experiencing the IoT world: The company's IoT enabled chargers facilitated network visibility for both the user and other ecosystem participants, thanks to the capabilities of this operating system.

Income generation through the installation of an EV charging system

The installation of the company's chargers provided an opportunity for owners to generate income by sharing their charging points. As per the company's statement, individuals who share their chargers for 5 hours daily could potentially earn Rs 3,000 per month. This allowed owners to generate passive income through the installation of the EV charging system Upon completion of the installation and sharing of the charging points, the charger will become accessible through the company's application. Consequently, other drivers will have the ability to locate the charger or charging station. Additionally, the chargers will receive the most recent version updates through OTA updates. Users will have the convenience of monitoring power usage, the quantity of bookings made, and other relevant information through the application.

Infrastructural Requirements of an EV Charging Station

- The installation of a transformer, substation, and implementation of safety measures was deemed essential.
- Provision of a 33/11KV cable and the necessary equipment for metering/termination was required.
- Sufficient civil works had to be completed to ensure smooth operations.
- Ample space was necessary to accommodate the charging of electric cars and provide convenient entrance/exit points.
- Any local certifications that may be required had to be considered, as state laws may vary in this regard.

Algorithm for Choosing Charging Stations

The Charging Station Selection Server (CSS) performs the task of determining the current location of a vehicle and evaluating the distance it needs to cover. Its primary recommendation is to utilize all available charging stations in order to reach the desired charging level. To provide an estimate of the time and energy required to reach a specific charging station, CSS establishes connections with other vehicles and considers the prevailing traffic conditions. In situations where traffic congestion is severe, CSS also suggests alternative routes to the nearest charging station.

To minimize waiting time, the driver selects the preferred charging method and reserves a spot at the charging station with the shortest queue. The CSS facilitates communication between the vehicle and the Charging Stations (CS) through a mobile network. Furthermore, it compares the pricing of one charging station with others and presents the existing metering system available at that particular station. An alternative approach is the implementation of a demand-based metering system, where electric vehicles are charged based on peak load and specific time periods.

Figure 3. Algorithm in Choosing Charging Stations

Source: prepared by author

Electric vehicles face distinct challenges when it comes to the electrical grid. The main problem lies in the vehicle's power consumption during charging, as electricity is supplied from the grid to the batteries. However, the distribution grid is solely responsible for transmitting electric energy, which limits the amount of energy that can be transported through the transmission lines of the transportation network.

Financial aspect of Setting Electric Charging Station in India

The company had shared following details about the cost structure it observed while setting up the charging stations-

- Installation expenses: The expenses associated with setting up an electric vehicle (EV) charging station in India typically vary between Rs. 100,000 and Rs. 4,000,000. The actual cost depends on the type of chargers utilized and the total amount of funds needed. Considering a broader scenario and a supply of 250KVA EV Stations, the company has derived the following approximate estimation. The 60KW charger type had an estimated cost of Rs.9,00,000, while the 7/22KW AC charger cost Rs.100,000. Setting up the standard DC 48V charger amounted to approximately Rs.240,000, whereas the normal 10KW AC charger had a setup cost of Rs.60,000. Ultimately, the cost of setting up the charger varied depending on the specific type utilized

- New Electricity Installation: Acquiring a new electricity connection with a capacity of 250 KVA amounted to approximately Rs.750,000.
- Civil Works: The civil works involved in establishing the charging station amounted to approximately Rs.250,000 to Rs.300,000.
- EVSE management, software, and integration: The installation and software integration of the Electric Vehicle Supply Equipment (EVSE) incurred a cost ranging from Rs.40,000 to Rs.60,000. The EVSE obtains electricity from the power grid and employs a control system and wired connection to ensure the safe charging of the vehicle. In addition to the aforementioned setup cost, there was also an operational expense associated with it which encompass various elements, such as engineers and labor. The annual expenditure for technicians and manpower involved in maintenance and repair amounted to approximately Rs.4,00,000 to Rs.6,00,000. Another aspect to consider is the cost of advertising and promotion, which varied between Rs.30,000 and Rs.50,000. Additionally, the rental cost for land is contingent upon the specific area and locality. The expense for leasing land ranged around Rs.600,000 per year.

So, the annual maintenance cost for the EV charging station in the second year amounted to approximately Rs.10,00,000, which includes the rent for the land t.

Taking into account the aforementioned information, the subsequent breakdown of expenses is provided, using one of the categories as an illustration -

Table 1. Financial Information

PARTICULARS	APPROX COST (in Rs.)
DC Level 3 (30 kW) per unit cost = 6,50,000 * 2 unit	13,00,000
New Electricity Connection (Cabling 50m, Panels, breakers, Fire Extinguishers, etc.)	2,26,500
Civil Works (Flooring, Panels, Charger foundation, Shed/Cover etc.)	2,84,000
Software Management and Charger integration	50,000
Technicians (1person at 15k per month for full year)	1,80,000

continued on following page

Table 1. Continued

PARTICULARS	APPROX COST (in Rs.)
Network Service Provider Fee	10,000
Land Lease Rental @ 10k per month for a parking slot * 3 parking slot *12 months	3,60,000
Advertising @ 2500 per month	30,000

Revenue Model of a Public Charging Station

The company has presented a revenue projection for a Public Charging Station, considering the following expectations:

- The Public Charging station experienced capacity utilization rates of 15% in the first year, 25% in the second year, 40% in the third year, 65% in the fourth year, and 85% in the fifth year.
- On average, it takes one hour for a vehicle to charge.
- The assumed maximum power consumption per day was 480 kWh per charger * 2 DC, resulting in a power consumption of 20 kWh per DC per hour.
- A margin of Rs 5 per kWh used was factored into the electricity tariff.

Given the increasing demand for electric vehicles (EVs), it has become imperative to establish charging stations at various locations to facilitate their usage. Consequently, numerous business centres have commenced providing EV charging facilities to cater to their customers' needs.

Advantages of incorporating electric vehicle charging stations at various commercial establishments

The installation of the company's EV charging stations at various business centres yielded several advantages.

In restaurants, visitors tended to stay longer as they utilized the charging station, resulting in increased opportunities for them to order additional items such as desserts, beverages, or coffee, thereby benefiting the restaurant. Moreover, the presence of an EV charging station was perceived as environmentally friendly, enhancing the business's reputation among customers who were highly concerned about the environmental impact of their choices.

In hotels, the charging stations generated revenue through fee-based charges or by providing a complimentary service. They also attracted premium ecotourism and electric vehicle drivers, thereby increasing earnings for each available room. Additionally, the business centres received improved ratings and reviews on well-known travel websites.

In shopping malls, the EV charging stations encouraged EV drivers to visit, which in turn boosted consumer spending. Furthermore, the stations facilitated store mapping and fostered a relationship with customers. Additionally, special discounts were offered to EV drivers, further enhancing their shopping experience.

CONCLUSION

The global market for electric vehicles (EVs) is steadily expanding at a compound annualized growth rate of 21.7%. By 2030, it is projected to grow from 8.1 million units to 39.21 million units. EVs are undoubtedly the future of transportation and driving. In order to establish a comprehensive EV ecosystem, it is crucial to have a robust charging infrastructure. A well-developed network of EV charging stations must be established to address potential buyers' concerns about range. It is imperative for various companies and individuals to comprehend the commercial viability of an EV charging station. Based on the findings of this study, the authors propose the following recommendations and initiatives:

1. Participate in the EV ecosystem and invest in a cleaner and economically sustainable future, while also contributing to the global effort of limiting global warming to 2 degrees Celsius by the second half of this century.
2. Companies should focus on building a stronger grid that can support the substantial demand generated by EV charging.
3. Companies in the sector can seek government support to minimize the costs associated with setting up charging stations. These costs include rent, charging equipment, and permits.
4. The relevant authorities should streamline the process of obtaining permits and approvals required for setting up charging stations.
5. Companies aiming to strengthen the EV charging ecosystem should expand the charging infrastructure by adding more charging stations along highways and in cities.

REFERENCES

Ahmad, M. N. (2020). Electric vehicle charging stations in India (the challenges and barriers being faced by charge point operators and a look at possible solutions)

Arigela, S. (2022, December). Veerendra., Manam, Ravindra., Adireddy, Ramesh., K., Manoz, Kumar, Reddy., Chandra, Sekhar. (2022). Electric vehicles charging in India: Infrastructure planning and policy aspects. *Energy Storage*, 4(6), e335. Advance online publication. DOI: 10.1002/est2.335

Baik, S. H., Jin, Y. G., & Yoon, Y. T. (2018). Determining equipment capacity of electric vehicle charging station operator for profit maximization. *Energies*, 11(9), 2301.

Chokkalingam, B., Padmanaban, S., Siano, P., Krishnamoorthy, R., & Selvaraj, R. (2017). Real-time forecasting of EV charging station scheduling for smart energy systems. *Energies*, 10(3), 377. DOI: 10.3390/en10030377

Deb, S., Tammi, K., Kalita, K., & Mahanta, P. (2018). Review of recent trends in charging infrastructure planning for electric vehicles. *Wiley Interdisciplinary Reviews. Energy and Environment*, 7(6), e306. DOI: 10.1002/wene.306

Deb, S., Tammi, K., Kalita, K., & Mahanta, P. (2019). Charging station placement for electric vehicles: A case study of Guwahati city, India. *IEEE Access : Practical Innovations, Open Solutions*, 7, 100270–100282. DOI: 10.1109/ACCESS.2019.2931055

Deshpande, A. M., & Deshpande, K. U. (2015, August). Creating a platform to foster the growth of electric vehicles in Indian market by increasing the electric vehicle public charging stations. In *2015 IEEE International Transportation Electrification Conference (ITEC)* (pp. 1-4). IEEE.

EV infrastructure, (2022, June) Part 1: Assessment of India's Current Electric Vehicle (EV) Charging Infrastructure.

EV infrastructure, (2022, June) Part 2: Developing Electric Vehicle Charging Infrastructure in India–Business Opportunities and Risks.

EV infrastructure, (2022, June) Part 3: EV Charging Infrastructure in India – Strategic Recommendations

Gupta, R. S., Tyagi, A., & Anand, S. (2021). Optimal allocation of electric vehicles charging infrastructure, policies and future trends. *Journal of Energy Storage*, 43, 103291. DOI: 10.1016/j.est.2021.103291

Hemavathi, S., & Shinisha, A. (2022). A study on trends and developments in electric vehicle charging technologies. *Journal of Energy Storage*, 52, 105013. DOI: 10.1016/j.est.2022.105013

Hussien, D. A., Omran, W. A., & Sharkawy, R. M. (2023, March). Smart charging of electric vehicles in charging stations. In 2023 5th International Youth Conference on Radio Electronics, Electrical and Power Engineering (REEPE) (Vol. 5, pp. 1-5). IEEE.

Kalakanti, A. K., & Rao, S. (2022). Charging Station Planning for Electric Vehicles. *Systems*, 10(1), 6. DOI: 10.3390/systems10010006

Kavianipour, M., Fakhrmoosavi, F., Singh, H., Ghamami, M., Zockaie, A., Ouyang, Y., & Jackson, R. (2021). Electric vehicle fast charging infrastructure planning in urban networks considering daily travel and charging behaviour. *Transportation Research Part D, Transport and Environment*, 93, 102769. DOI: 10.1016/j.trd.2021.102769

Khan, W., Ahmad, F., Ahmad, A., Alam, M. S., & Ahuja, A. (2018). Electric vehicle charging infrastructure in India: viability analysis. In *ISGW 2017: Compendium of Technical Cases* (pp. 193–206). Springer. DOI: 10.1007/978-981-10-8249-8_17

Kizhakkan, A. R., Rathore, A. K., & Awasthi, A. (2019, December). Review of electric vehicle charging station location planning. In 2019 IEEE Transportation Electrification Conference (ITEC-India) (pp. 1-5). IEEE. DOI: 10.1109/ITEC-India48457.2019.ITECINDIA2019-226

Kore, H. H., & Koul, S. (2022). Electric vehicle charging infrastructure: Positioning in India. *Management of Environmental Quality*, 33(3), 776–799. DOI: 10.1108/MEQ-10-2021-0234

Kumar, K, J., Kumar, S., & VS, N. (. (2022). Standards for electric vehicle charging stations in India: A review. *Energy Storage*, 4(1), e261. DOI: 10.1002/est2.261

Kumar, P., & Dash, K. (2013). Potential need for electric vehicles, charging station infrastructure and its challenges for the Indian market. *Advance in Electronic and Electric Engineering*, 3(4), 471–476.

Lam, A. Y., Leung, Y. W., & Chu, X. (2013, October). Electric vehicle charging station placement. In *2013 IEEE International Conference on Smart Grid Communications (SmartGridComm)* (pp. 510-515). IEEE. DOI: 10.1109/SmartGridComm.2013.6688009

Lam, A. Y., Leung, Y. W., & Chu, X. (2014). Electric vehicle charging station placement: Formulation, complexity, and solutions. *IEEE Transactions on Smart Grid*, 5(6), 2846–2856. DOI: 10.1109/TSG.2014.2344684

Mishra, S., Verma, S., Chowdhury, S., Gaur, A., Mohapatra, S., Dwivedi, G., & Verma, P. (2021). A comprehensive review on developments in electric vehicle charging station infrastructure and present scenario of India. *Sustainability (Basel)*, 13(4), 2396. DOI: 10.3390/su13042396

Nair, S., Rao, N., Mishra, S., & Patil, A. (2017, December). India's charging infrastructure— biggest single point impediment in EV adaptation in India. In 2017 IEEE transportation electrification conference (ITEC-India) IEEE.

Nelder, C., & Rogers, E. (2019). *Reducing EV charging infrastructure costs*. Rocky Mountain Institute.

Pareek, S., Sujil, A., Ratra, S., & Kumar, R. (2020, February). Electric vehicle charging station Challenges and opportunities: a future perspective. In 2020 International Conference on Emerging Trends in Communication, Control and Computing (ICONC3) IEEE. DOI: 10.1109/ICONC345789.2020.9117473

Pareek, S., Sujil, A., Ratra, S., & Kumar, R. (2020, February). Electric vehicle charging station challenges and opportunities: A future perspective. In 2020 International Conference on Emerging Trends in Communication, Control and Computing (ICONC3) (pp. 1-6). IEEE.

Pareek, S., Sujil, A., Ratra, S., & Kumar, R. (2020, February). Electric vehicle charging station challenges and opportunities: A future perspective. In 2020 International Conference on Emerging Trends in Communication, Control and Computing (ICONC3) (pp. 1-6). IEEE.

Rabiee, A., Ghiasian, A., & Chermahini, M. A. (2018). Long term profit maximization strategy for charging scheduling of electric vehicle charging station. *IET Generation, Transmission & Distribution*, 12(18), 4134–4141. DOI: 10.1049/iet-gtd.2018.5592

Sajan, Jerome. (2022). An Economic Feasibility Study of Electric Vehicle Charging Stations in India. DOI: 10.1007/978-981-19-2091-2_17

Save, B., Sheikh, A., & Goswami, P. (2019, December). Recent developments, challenges, and possible action plans for electric vehicle charging infrastructure in India. In 2019 9th International Conference on Power and Energy Systems (ICPES) DOI: 10.1109/ICPES47639.2019.9105530

Sheppard, C. J., Gopal, A. R., Harris, A., & Jacobson, A. (2016). Cost-effective electric vehicle charging infrastructure siting for Delhi. *Environmental Research Letters*, 11(6), 064010.

Sheppard, C. J., Gopal, A. R., Harris, A., & Jacobson, A. (2016). Cost-effective electric vehicle charging infrastructure siting for Delhi. *Environmental Research Letters*, 11(6), 064010. DOI: 10.1088/1748-9326/11/6/064010

Shrivastav, A. V., Khan, S. S., Gupta, R. K., Ekshinge, P. R., & Parmeshwar, N. (2020). Electric Vehicle Charging Station (Case study on infrastructure of EV charging station). *Journal of Emerging Technologies and Innovative Research*, 7, 2017–2033.

Syed Mohammed, A., Anuj, Lodhi, A. S., & Murtaza, Q. (2022). Techno-economic feasibility of hydrogen based electric vehicle charging station: A case study. *International Journal of Energy Research*, 46(10), 14145–14160.

Tarei, P. K., Chand, P., & Gupta, H. (2021). Barriers to the adoption of electric vehicles: Evidence from India. *Journal of Cleaner Production*, 291, 125847. DOI: 10.1016/j.jclepro.2021.125847

Trivedi, N., Gujar, N. S., Sarkar, S., & Pundir, S. P. S. (2018, March). Different fast charging methods and topologies for EV charging. In 2018 IEEMA Engineer Infinite Conference (eTechNxT) (pp. 1-5). IEEE. DOI: 10.1109/ETECHNXT.2018.8385313

Tyagi, B., Sasidharan, C., & Das, S. (2019). A case study on potential impact of electric vehicle charging for an electricity distribution utility in India. In *Second large scale integration of renewable energy conference*, Delhi.

Walid, A. (2023). *Omran., R.M., Sharkawy*. Smart Charging of Electric Vehicles in Charging Stations., DOI: 10.1109/REEPE57272.2023.10086885

Chapter 3
Circular Economy Models: A Blueprint for Sustainable Entrepreneurship

Priyanshi Jindal
https://orcid.org/0009-0001-8116-8192
ABES Business School, Ghaziabad, India

Harshit Gouri
https://orcid.org/0009-0006-4507-8989
St. Stephen's College, Delhi, India

ABSTRACT

The circular economy is an alternative to the linear economy, which is based on the take-make-waste model of production and consumption. The circular economy aims to reduce environmental impacts and resource depletion by designing products and services that minimize waste, extend the lifespan of materials, and regenerate natural systems. Entrepreneurs play a key role in the transition to the circular economy, as they can create innovative solutions that address the needs and preferences of customers, while also generating positive environmental and social outcomes. This chapter provides a comprehensive overview of the circular economy concept and its principles, as well as a framework for developing and implementing circular economy business models. It also showcases a variety of examples of successful circular economy ventures from different sectors and regions, highlighting the benefits and challenges of adopting this approach. The chapter concludes with some recommendations for entrepreneurs, policymakers, and educators who want to support and promote circular entrepreneurship.

DOI: 10.4018/979-8-3693-4338-8.ch003

I. INTRODUCTION

Over the past few years, the circular economy has emerged as a compelling and sustainable solution to tackle the urgent environmental and social issues facing our world. The circular economy is a paradigm shift away from the traditional linear "take, make, dispose" model of production and consumption. Instead, it promotes a regenerative approach where resources are continually reused, remanufactured, and recycled, creating a closed-loop system that minimizes waste and environmental impact. (Mura et al., 2024)The ultimate goals of the circular economy include reducing resource depletion, minimizing pollution, and fostering social and economic inclusivity.

The circular economy represents a paradigm shift from traditional linear economic models, focusing on a regenerative approach where resources are reused, repaired, and recycled to minimize waste. Experts like Paul Ekins define it as a system that aims to redefine growth, focusing on positive society-wide benefits. (Grzymala, 2023)It decouples economic activity from the consumption of finite resources and designs waste out of the system. (Popa, 2023)This model not only addresses environmental sustainability but also offers an avenue for economic resilience and innovation, as it encourages the development of new business models and industrial processes that contribute to the natural development of products. (Maldonado Castro et al., 2022) As the European Parliament notes, it involves sharing, leasing, reusing, repairing, refurbishing, and recycling existing materials and products as long as possible, extending their life cycle and reducing waste. In essence, the circular economy is about transforming our take-make-waste system into one that is restorative by design and beneficial for both the environment and the economy.

According to ***Ellen MacArthur****, a prominent advocate for the circular economy, it is "an industrial system that is restorative or regenerative by intention and design. It replaces the end-of-life concept with restoration, shifts towards the use of renewable energy, eliminates the use of toxic chemicals, and aims for the elimination of waste through the superior design of materials, products, systems, and business models."(Grzymala, 2023)*

Building upon this, ***Walter R. Stahel****, often considered a pioneer in the field, emphasizes the cyclical nature of resource use, stating that the circular economy is "a loop concept, of cradle-to-cradle, designed for durability, disassembly, and remanufacturing."(Molchanova, 2023)*

In contrast, some authors highlight the importance of the circular economy not only as a sustainable economic model but also as a fundamental shift in mindset. ***Peter Lacy and Jakob Rutqvist****propose a definition that emphasizes the transformational nature of circularity: "A circular economy is a holistic, regenerative approach to the design, production, and consumption of goods and* *services that seeks to optimize value and minimize waste throughout the product lifecycle."(Zăpucioiu et al., 2023)*

II. GOALS OF THE CIRCULAR ECONOMY

Circular economy principles aim to minimize waste and maximize resource efficiency by creating closed-loop systems where products, materials, and resources are reused, repaired, refurbished, and recycled. The goals of the circular economy converge on several key principles:

1. **Minimizing Resource Use and Waste:**

The circular economy is a transformative approach to production and consumption, which contrasts sharply with the traditional linear economy's "take-make-dispose" model. In a circular system, the lifecycle of materials is maximized, so that items are reused and repurposed rather than discarded. (Lisitsa et al., 2022)This not only conserves resources but also reduces environmental pollution and greenhouse gas emissions associated with manufacturing and waste disposal. Companies and consumers alike play a role in this process: companies by designing products for durability and recyclability, and consumers by choosing sustainable options and participating in recycling programs. The ultimate goal is to create a closed-loop system where every product is part of a continual cycle of use and reuse, promoting sustainability and reducing our ecological footprint.

2. **Reducing Carbon Emissions:**

Circular practices indeed play a crucial role in reducing carbon emissions and mitigating climate change. By reusing, recycling, and repurposing materials, we not only conserve resources but also reduce the energy required for the production of new materials. This energy reduction is significant because it often involves burning fossil fuels, which are the primary source of CO_2 emissions(Stoyanova-Koval et al., 2023) .The circular economy model promotes a sustainable approach by keeping products and materials in use for as long as possible, thus decreasing the demand for new raw materials and the associated emissions from their extraction and processing. Furthermore, this model encourages innovation in design for longevity, reparability, and recyclability, leading to a more resilient and adaptable economic system. Adopting circular practices is a step towards a more sustainable future, where economic growth is decoupled from environmental degradation.

3. **Creating Sustainable Business Sectors and Jobs:**

The circular economy is not just an environmental or resource management approach; it's a transformative economic model that offers a pathway to sustainable development. By redefining products and services to design waste out of the system, it creates a closed-loop system that is restorative by nature. This approach encourages innovation in product design, materials science, and business models, leading to the emergence of new sectors such as recycling technologies, renewable energy, and sustainable product manufacturing. These sectors not only contribute to reducing the ecological footprint but also create job opportunities that support economic growth. In essence, the circular economy intertwines economic prosperity with environmental stewardship, presenting a holistic path forward for sustainable business practices.

4. **Systemic Change and Collaboration:**

The concept of a circular economy is indeed a transformative approach to addressing environmental challenges and fostering sustainable growth. It emphasizes the importance of a systemic shift in the way we view and manage resources, moving away from the traditional linear model of 'take-make-dispose' to a more regenerative and restorative cycle. This shift necessitates a collaborative effort across all sectors of society. (Koval et al., 2022; Stoyanova-Koval et al., 2023)Consumers are encouraged to adopt sustainable practices, businesses are urged to innovate in design and production for longevity and recyclability, and policymakers are tasked with creating an enabling environment through supportive legislation and incentives. The potential economic benefits are significant, with the possibility of unlocking $4.5 trillion in value by 2030, as you mentioned. This economic incentive, coupled with the urgent need to preserve our planet's resources, makes the pursuit of a circular economy an imperative for the present and future generations. (weforum.org)

III. PRINCIPLES OF THE CIRCULAR ECONOMY

The contrast between linear and circular economic systems is highlighted in the comparison table, revealing significant differences in their approaches. The linear model is characterized by high resource use, resulting in substantial waste, minimal recycling, and designs for single-use products. In contrast, the circular model advocates for lower resource use, waste reduction, and robust recycling processes. It encourages the creation of products meant for repeated use, enhancing their lifespan and utility over several cycles.(Özpolat & Nakıpoğlu Özsoy, 2022) The linear model's focus is on immediate financial gain, whereas the circular model is designed for enduring environmental and economic health. The environmental toll is considerable in the linear model due to the exhaustion of resources and accumulation of waste, while the circular model seeks to protect natural ecosystems through efficient use of resources and decreasing waste. (Lisitsa et al., 2022)Innovation in a linear context is often limited and centered around the product, but in a circular context, it is broad, considering the full product lifecycle and material usage. Policy in a linear economy typically addresses waste management post-consumption, but circular policies aim for a thorough management of the product's entire lifecycle. This stark contrast emphasizes the shift towards a sustainable and resource-conscious circular economy.

Table 1. Comparison between Linear Economy and Circular Economy Models

Aspect	Linear Economy	Circular Economy
Resource Consumption	High	Reduced
Waste Generation	High	Minimized
Recycling	Limited	Extensive
Product Design	Linear (One-time use)	Circular (Designed for reuse)
Economic Impact	Short-term profit focus	Long-term sustainability
Environmental Impact	Degradation	Preservation
Innovation	Linear, incremental	Systemic, holistic
Policy Focus	End-of-life management	Full lifecycle management

Exploration of design strategies to minimize waste, extend material lifespan, and regenerate natural systems

The concept of a circular economy emphasizes the importance of reducing waste, maximizing the lifespan of materials, and promoting regeneration of natural systems. In this document, we present strategies that entrepreneurs can adopt to align with the principles of a circular economy.

1. Minimizing Waste

1.1 Design for Disassembly

Design for Disassembly (DfD) is a sustainable design strategy that focuses on creating products that can be easily taken apart. This approach allows components to be separated at the end of the product's life, facilitating repair, refurbishment, or recycling.(Formentini & Ramanujan, 2023) DfD enhances the product lifecycle and minimizes waste by enabling the recovery of valuable materials and parts. When designing for disassembly, engineers and designers consider factors such as the type of fasteners used, the ease of access to components, and the use of materials that can be efficiently separated and processed. (Yadav & Garg, 2023)This not only contributes to the circular economy but also aligns with environmental regulations and consumer demand for sustainable products. By implementing DfD principles, companies can reduce their environmental footprint and create a more sustainable future.

1.2 Reduce Packaging Waste

Reducing packaging waste is a crucial step towards environmental sustainability. By minimizing the use of packaging materials, especially those that are non-recyclable or non-biodegradable, we can significantly decrease the volume of waste that ends up in landfills. Opting for reusable packaging not only reduces waste but also conserves resources by diminishing the demand for new materials. (Shaikh & Hyder, 2023)Biodegradable alternatives, on the other hand, offer a solution that complements the natural decomposition process, thereby reducing the long-term impact on the environment. Businesses and consumers alike can contribute to this effort by choosing products with minimal packaging, supporting companies that prioritize sustainable packaging, and advocating for policies that encourage the reduction of packaging waste. (Brouwer & Thoden van Velzen, 2023)Through collective action and conscious choices, we can make a meaningful difference in preserving our planet for future generations.

1.3 Implement Reverse Logistics

Implementing reverse logistics involves creating a system that allows for the efficient return of products at the end of their lifecycle. This process is essential for sustainable business practices, as it enables the refurbishment, recycling, or remanufacturing of products. To establish such a system, a company must first assess the feasibility of collecting and processing returned items.(Formentini & Ramanujan, 2023) This includes evaluating the cost-effectiveness of transportation and the potential for recovering materials or components. Additionally, the company should develop partnerships with recycling and remanufacturing facilities, which can process the returned items. (Molchanova, 2023)It's also important to create clear guidelines for the end-users on how to return products, and to ensure that the return process is as convenient as possible to encourage participation. Finally, integrating reverse logistics into the company's broader sustainability goals can help in promoting a circular economy, where products and materials are reused and recycled, reducing waste and environmental impact.

2. Extending Material Lifespan

2.1 Use Durable Materials

Incorporating durable materials into product design is a fundamental principle for enhancing longevity and sustainability. Materials such as stainless steel, high-density polyethylene, and anodized aluminum are renowned for their robustness and resistance to wear and tear.(Brouwer & Thoden van Velzen, 2023) By choosing such materials, manufacturers can ensure that products withstand the test of time, reducing the need for frequent replacements and thereby minimizing waste. Additionally, durable materials often require less maintenance, which can lead to cost savings for consumers over the product's lifecycle. Ultimately, the use of durable materials is not only a commitment to quality but also an investment in environmental responsibility and resource efficiency.

2.2 Encourage Repairability

Promoting repairability in product design is a sustainable approach that benefits consumers and the environment. By designing products with repair in mind, manufacturers can extend the lifespan of their products, reduce waste, and decrease the environmental impact of manufacturing new products. Providing access to spare parts ensures that when a product does break down, it can be fixed rather than replaced. (Özpolat & Nakıpoğlu Özsoy, 2022)Additionally, offering repair guides empowers consumers to understand their products better and perform repairs themselves, fostering a culture of sustainability and self-reliance. This approach not only conserves resources but also supports a circular economy, where products are used for as long as possible.

2.3 Promote Sharing Economy

The sharing economy is a sustainable business model that maximizes the utility of products by enabling their shared use, access, or ownership. This approach can significantly reduce waste and resource consumption by facilitating product sharing or rental services. It encourages the efficient use of materials and products, often through platforms that connect users who want to rent out their items with those who need them temporarily. (Maldonado Castro et al., 2022)By promoting the sharing economy, we can contribute to a more resource-efficient world, where the life cycle of products is extended, and the need for production of new items is reduced, leading to a decrease in the overall environmental footprint. This not only supports sustainability but also fosters community engagement and can provide affordable access to goods that might otherwise be inaccessible.

3. Regenerating Natural Systems

3.1 Adopt Biomimicry Principles

Biomimicry is an innovative approach to design that seeks to emulate nature's time-tested patterns and strategies. The goal is to create products, processes, and policies—new ways of living—that are well-adapted to life on earth over the long haul. This approach allows us to learn from the natural world's 3.8 billion years of research and development.(Martino, 2023) By adopting biomimicry principles, designers and engineers can create solutions that are sustainable and efficient, reducing waste, energy consumption, and toxic emissions. For instance, the design of the Eastgate Centre in Harare, Zimbabwe, which uses natural ventilation inspired by termite mounds, or the development of adhesives modeled after the sticky properties of gecko feet, are prime examples of biomimicry in action. (Taieb & Amor, 2023) These innovations not only minimize environmental impact but also often result in cost savings and increased efficiency. Embracing biomimicry not only fosters sustainability but also propels us towards a more harmonious relationship with our environment.

3.2 Support Biodiversity Conservation

Biodiversity conservation is crucial for maintaining the balance of ecosystems and ensuring the survival of various species. Implementing practices that support this can include establishing protected areas to safeguard habitats, promoting sustainable land use to prevent habitat destruction, and engaging in reforestation efforts to restore degraded areas. Additionally, supporting local and indigenous communities in their efforts to protect biodiversity can be highly effective, as they often possess traditional knowledge and a vested interest in the health of their environment. (Saranya K G et al., 2023)Education and awareness campaigns can also play a significant role in biodiversity conservation by informing the public about the importance of biodiversity and how they can contribute to its preservation. Collectively, these actions can help mitigate the loss of species and maintain ecological balance.

3.3 Invest in Renewable Energy

Investing in renewable energy is a strategic move towards a sustainable future. It involves shifting from traditional energy sources that are finite and often harmful to the environment, such as fossil fuels, to more sustainable options like solar, wind, hydro, and geothermal power.(Shaikh & Hyder, 2023) This transition not only helps in conserving our planet's limited resources but also plays a crucial role in combating climate change by reducing greenhouse gas emissions. Moreover, the renewable energy sector has the potential to create numerous jobs, drive technological innovation, and provide energy security for generations to come. It's a forward-thinking approach that benefits both the economy and the environment.

Incorporating sustainable design strategies is essential for businesses aiming to support circular economy models. These strategies can help reduce waste, optimize resource use, and create products that are easier to repair, reuse, or recycle. By doing so, businesses not only contribute to environmental sustainability but also build resilience against resource scarcity and market volatility, ensuring long-term success and a healthier planet.

IV. ENTREPRENEURIAL ROLE IN CIRCULAR ECONOMY TRANSITION

As environmental issues become more pressing and society becomes more aware, the circular economy stands out as a promising path for sustainable growth. This approach is built on reducing waste and enhancing the efficiency of resources, offering a significant shift from the conventional linear economy that follows a "take-make-dispose" pattern. Entrepreneurs play a crucial role in this shift, leveraging innovative solutions to strike a careful equilibrium between meeting consumer demands and promoting beneficial environmental and societal outcomes.

Emphasizing Innovation's Role in Sustainable Business Practices:

Entrepreneurship has long been hailed as a catalyst for change, and within the realm of circular economy, its potential is magnified. (U & R, 2023)The essence of circular entrepreneurship lies in reimagining products, processes, and business models to align with sustainability objectives. Here, innovation serves as the cornerstone, driving the creation of novel solutions that challenge the status quo.

Innovation in circular entrepreneurship encompasses a spectrum of strategies, from eco-design and remanufacturing to resource recovery and sharing platforms. These innovations not only minimize waste and resource depletion but also present lucrative opportunities for entrepreneurs. (Roleders, 2023)By leveraging technologies such as IoT, blockchain, and AI, entrepreneurs can optimize resource utilization, streamline supply chains, and enhance product life cycles.

Moreover, innovation in circular entrepreneurship extends beyond tangible products to encompass service-based offerings and collaborative networks. (Sehnem et al., 2023)Subscription models, product-as-a-service concepts, and sharing platforms exemplify how entrepreneurs can monetize sustainable consumption patterns while fostering community engagement.

Fundamentally, the transformative power of innovation in circular entrepreneurship lies not only in its ability to drive profitability but also in its capacity to catalyze systemic change(Koval et al., 2022). By challenging conventional wisdom and embracing disruptive technologies, entrepreneurs are paving the way for a more regenerative and equitable economy.

Investigating the Methods Entrepreneurs Use to Harmonize Client Demands with Beneficial Environmental and Social Outcomes:

Entrepreneurs embarking on the circular economy journey face a dual challenge: meeting evolving customer expectations while upholding environmental and social responsibility. This necessitates a delicate balancing act wherein profitability is not pursued at the expense of planetary and societal well-being.

One approach to achieving this balance is through consumer education and engagement. By transparently communicating the environmental and social benefits of circular products and services, entrepreneurs can cultivate a sense of purpose-driven consumption among their customer base.(Santos -Corrada et al., 2024) This, in turn, fosters brand loyalty and strengthens the market for sustainable goods and services.

Furthermore, entrepreneurs can harness the power of co-creation and collaboration to ensure that their offerings resonate with diverse stakeholder needs. Engaging with local communities, NGOs, and governmental bodies can provide valuable insights into the specific environmental and social challenges that need to be addressed. (Roleders, 2023; Timofei, 2023)Through inclusive decision-making processes, entrepreneurs can co-design solutions that prioritize both profit and purpose.

Additionally, integrating circularity into the core values and operational practices of the business can help ensure alignment between customer needs and sustainability objectives. From sustainable sourcing and production to end-of-life management, entrepreneurs must embed circular principles throughout the value chain.(Sehnem et al., 2023) This not only enhances the credibility of their brand but also mitigates risks associated with resource scarcity and regulatory compliance.

The successful transition to a circular economy hinge upon the entrepreneurial spirit that embraces innovation and responsibility in equal measure. By harnessing the transformative power of innovation while balancing customer needs with positive environmental and social impacts, entrepreneurs can catalyze a paradigm shift towards a more sustainable and resilient future.

V. FRAMEWORK FOR CIRCULAR ECONOMY BUSINESS MODELS

The Circular PRISM Model is a comprehensive framework for entrepreneurs to develop and implement sustainable, circular business models. (Soroka et al., 2023) This model offers a unique and holistic approach to creating value while minimizing environmental impact.

The Circular PRISM Model

The Circular PRISM Model is an innovative approach that encourages entrepreneurs to create sustainable businesses by rethinking how products are designed, used, and reused. (Bombonatti Filho, n.d.)It consists of five interconnected steps:

1. **Product Circularity:** This step focuses on designing products that can be easily recycled or repurposed at the end of their life cycle. It encourages the use of materials that can be recovered and reused, thus closing the loop and reducing waste.
2. **Reverse Logistics:** This involves setting up systems to take back used products from consumers. By establishing efficient supply chains for the return of products, companies can recover valuable materials and components for reuse, refurbishment, or recycling.
3. **Innovative Business Models:** Entrepreneurs are encouraged to think outside the traditional 'take-make-dispose' model and develop new business strategies that prioritize sustainability. This could include models like product-as-a-service, where customers pay for the use of a product rather than owning it outright, encouraging longer product lifespans and reducing waste.
4. **Stakeholder Synergy:** This step emphasizes the importance of working together with all stakeholders, including customers, suppliers, and local communities. Collaboration can lead to innovative solutions that benefit all parties and support the broader goals of the circular economy.
5. **Multidimensional Enablers:** The transition to a circular economy requires support from various enablers, such as technology, policy, and finance. This step involves leveraging these conditions to create an environment where circular practices are not only possible but also profitable and scalable.

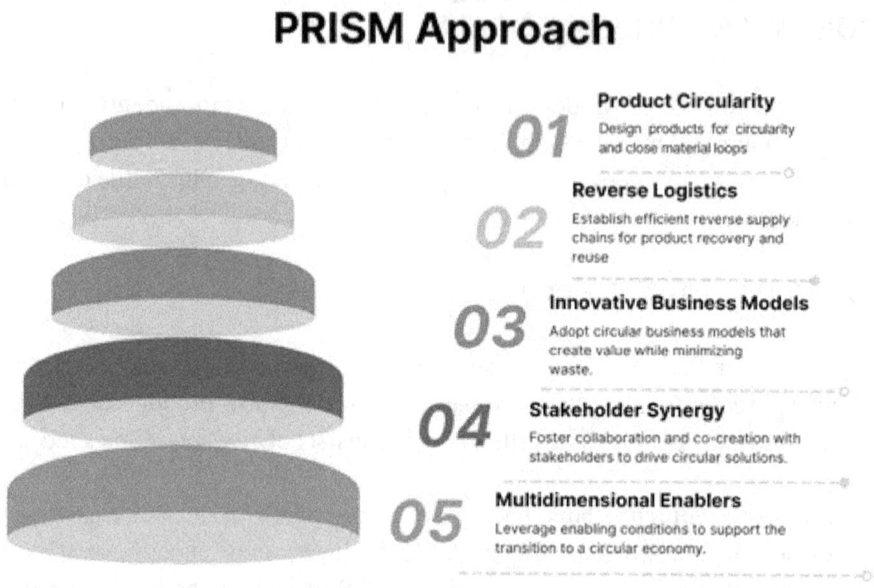

The Circular PRISM Model represents a transformative approach in sustainable business, focusing on the circular economy's principles. EcoCycle, a hypothetical bicycle manufacturer, exemplifies this model through its practices. The company's commitment to product circularity is evident in its design of durable, modular bicycles made from recycled materials, which can be easily disassembled for reuse or recycling. (Ncube et al., 2023)EcoCycle's reverse logistics system encourages customers to return old bicycles, facilitating refurbishment or parts reuse, thereby minimizing waste and reducing material costs. Their innovative leasing business model ensures resource ownership remains with the company, allowing for efficient recovery and recycling post-lease. Collaborative efforts with stakeholders, including local governments, suppliers, and customers, foster a synergistic environment benefiting all parties within the circular economy. Lastly, EcoCycle's use of technology for lifecycle tracking, data analytics for optimizing logistics, and continuous R&D efforts, supported by government incentives for sustainability, are pivotal multidimensional enablers that drive the success of their circular business model.

VI. IMPLEMENTING CIRCULAR BUSINESS MODELS INDEED COMES WITH A VARIETY OF CHALLENGES:

1. **Regulatory Obstacles** - Existing regulations often favor linear economies, making it difficult for circular initiatives to gain traction.
   - **Legacy Regulations**: Many regulations were established during an era when linear economic models were the norm, focusing on production, consumption, and disposal. These regulations often lack provisions for recycling, reuse, or resource recovery.
   - **Compliance Challenges**: Circular businesses may face complex and costly compliance requirements as they attempt to navigate regulations not designed with circularity in mind.
   - **Limited Incentives**: Current regulatory frameworks might not offer enough incentives for businesses to invest in circular practices, reducing the appeal for companies to make the shift.
2. **Technological Constraints** - Outdated or insufficient technology can impede the adoption of circular practices.
   - **Technological Gaps**: Many industries rely on outdated technology that is not compatible with the principles of a circular economy, such as efficient recycling processes or durable product design.
   - **Innovation Barriers**: The development and deployment of new technologies that support circular practices, such as advanced material recovery systems, can be slow and expensive.
   - **Integration Issues**: Incorporating new technologies into existing systems can be challenging, often requiring substantial modifications and investments.
3. **Consumer Behavior** – Changing consumer habits is tough, especially if circular products are seen as less convenient or lower quality.
   - **Perception of Quality**: Consumers may perceive circular products, such as those made from recycled materials, as inferior to new products.
   - **Convenience**: Linear models often offer more convenience, with straightforward purchasing and disposal processes, whereas circular models might require consumers to engage in recycling, returning products, or repairing items.
   - **Behavioral Inertia**: Established consumer habits and preferences are hard to change, and it can take significant effort to educate and encourage consumers to adopt more sustainable practices.
4. **Technological Barriers** – Advanced recycling processes and efficient reverse logistics systems are often required, posing additional technological challenges.

- **Recycling Efficiency**: Advanced recycling technologies that can effectively recover and reuse materials without degradation are still underdeveloped or costly.
- **Reverse Logistics**: Efficient systems for collecting, sorting, and transporting used products back into the production cycle are complex and expensive to implement.
- **Infrastructure Needs**: Developing the necessary infrastructure for a circular economy, such as recycling facilities and logistics networks, requires significant investment.

5. **Consumer Education –** There's a significant lack of awareness about the benefits of circular economy practices among consumers.
    - **Knowledge Gap**: Many consumers are unaware of the environmental and economic benefits of circular economy practices, limiting their participation and support.
    - **Communication Challenges**: Effectively communicating the advantages of circular products and practices can be difficult, especially when competing against the marketing power of linear models.
    - **Educational Initiatives**: There is a need for widespread educational initiatives to inform consumers about how they can contribute to and benefit from a circular economy.
6. **Resistance to Change –** Organizational inertia and resistance from stakeholders accustomed to linear models can be significant hurdles.
    - **Cultural Resistance**: Within organizations, there can be a strong resistance to changing established practices and mindsets that favor linear models.
    - **Stakeholder Pushback**: Stakeholders, including investors, employees, and partners, may be skeptical of the value and feasibility of transitioning to a circular model.
    - **Change Management**: Managing the transition to a circular economy requires significant effort in change management, including training, communication, and re-aligning business objectives.

VII. CASE STUDIES: SUCCESSFUL CIRCULAR ECONOMY VENTURES

I. Unilever - Closing the Loop in Packaging

Background:

Unilever, a multinational consumer goods company founded in 1930, operates in various sectors, including food and beverages, cleaning agents, beauty, and personal care. (Seier et al., 2023)With an extensive product portfolio, Unilever recognizes the environmental impact associated with packaging waste, prompting the company to take bold steps towards a circular economy model.

Initiatives:

1. **Sustainable Living Plan:** Unilever's Sustainable Living Plan, launched in 2010, represents a significant shift in the corporate approach to sustainability. The ambitious goal to ensure all plastic packaging is recyclable, reusable, or compostable by 2025 (Kaestner et al., 2023)highlights a commitment to reducing environmental impact while still pursuing business growth. This initiative not only addresses waste management concerns but also encourages innovation in packaging design and materials. By setting such targets, Unilever is contributing to a broader movement towards sustainability in the consumer goods industry, promoting a circular economy where materials are kept in use for as long as possible. The success of this plan could serve as a model for other corporations looking to balance economic objectives with environmental responsibility.
2. **Loop Program:** The "Loop" program is a pioneering initiative in the movement towards sustainability and zero-waste consumerism. (Yang, 2023)By collaborating with TerraCycle, Unilever is taking a significant step in addressing the environmental impact of packaging. This innovative platform not only offers a practical solution to the problem of single-use packaging but also promotes a shift in consumer behavior towards more sustainable practices. The process of returning, cleaning, refilling, and reusing packaging materials helps close the loop in the product lifecycle, potentially reducing the carbon footprint and conserving resources. Such programs are essential as they contribute to the development of a circular economy, where products and materials are kept in use for as long as possible, extracting the maximum value from them while in use and recovering and regenerating products and materials at the end of their service life.

3. **Eco-Friendly Innovations:** Unilever's commitment to sustainability is evident in its investment in research and development for eco-friendly packaging solutions. The company's initiatives are multifaceted, focusing on reducing the environmental impact of packaging by incorporating post-consumer recycled materials, which helps in diverting waste from landfills and reducing the need for virgin materials. (Seier et al., 2023)Additionally, Unilever is at the forefront of developing plant-based packaging options, which are derived from renewable resources and offer a reduced carbon footprint compared to conventional materials. The exploration of alternative materials also signifies a proactive approach to replacing traditional plastics, which are known for their long-term persistence in the environment and potential harm to wildlife.

Benefits and Challenges:

Benefits:

1. **Reduced Environmental Impact:** Unilever's commitment to making all packaging recyclable, compostable, or biodegradable by 2025 is part of a broader strategy to reduce the environmental impact of its products. This aligns with growing consumer expectations for sustainable and eco-friendly practices.(Koval et al., 2022)
2. **Cost Savings:** The adoption of circular packaging solutions not only aligns with sustainability goals but also provides cost advantages. Reusing and recycling materials can lead to economic benefits in the long run, contributing to Unilever's overall business sustainability.

Challenges:

1. **Consumer Education:** The Sustainable Living Plan requires active participation from consumers in proper disposal and recycling practices.(Stoyanova-Koval et al., 2023) Unilever recognizes the need for comprehensive consumer education programs to ensure that sustainability goals are met and that the impact extends beyond corporate policies to individual actions.
2. **Technological Limitations:** Unilever acknowledges the technological challenges in developing fully recyclable or biodegradable packaging materials. However, the company views these challenges as opportunities for innovation and continuous improvement.

Success Story:

Unilever's commitment to sustainable packaging, exemplified through initiatives like the "Loop" program, showcases a practical and innovative approach to closing the loop on packaging waste. The success of these initiatives not only demonstrates progress in reducing packaging waste but also positions(Yang, 2023) Unilever as an industry leader in integrating circular economy principles into its core business strategy. By addressing both environmental concerns and consumer expectations, Unilever sets a precedent for sustainable practices in the fast-moving consumer goods sector.

II. Patagonia - Closing the Loop in Clothing

Background:

Patagonia, founded in 1973 by Yvon Chouinard, is an American outdoor clothing company known for its commitment to environmental sustainability. As a leader in the outdoor apparel industry, Patagonia has long recognized the environmental impact of textile production and consumption, prompting the company to adopt innovative circular economy practices.

'Initiatives:

1. **Worn Wear Program:** Launched in 2013, the Worn Wear program embodies Patagonia's commitment to extending the life of its products. This initiative encourages customers to repair, reuse, and recycle their Patagonia garments. The company provides free repairs for its products, operates a mobile repair service, and sells used Patagonia clothing, reducing waste and promoting a culture of reuse.
2. **Recycled Materials:** Patagonia has made significant strides in incorporating recycled materials into its product line. The company uses recycled polyester made from post-consumer plastic bottles, recycled nylon from fishing nets, and recycled wool from factory scraps. This approach not only reduces waste but also decreases the demand for virgin materials, lowering the overall environmental impact of production.
3. **Design for Durability:** Patagonia's product design philosophy centers on creating long-lasting, high-quality garments that can withstand years of use. This approach naturally aligns with circular economy principles by reducing the frequency of replacement and, consequently, waste generation. The company

also provides detailed care instructions to help customers extend the life of their products.

Benefits and Challenges:

Benefits:

1. **Reduced EnvironmentalImpact:** By promoting repair, reuse, and recycling, Patagonia significantly reduces the environmental footprint associated with clothing production and disposal.
2. **Brand Loyalty:** The company's commitment to sustainability has fostered strong customer loyalty, attracting environmentally conscious consumers who align with Patagonia's values.

Challenges:

1. **Cost Implications:** Implementing circular practices, such as using recycled materials and offering repair services, can increase production costs, potentially affecting profit margins.
2. **Changing Consumer Behavior:** Encouraging customers to repair and reuse clothing rather than buying new items requires a shift in consumer mindset, which can be challenging to achieve on a large scale.

Success Story:

Patagonia's circular economy initiatives have been remarkably successful. The Worn Wear program has repaired over 130,000 items of clothing since its inception, significantly extending the lifespan of these products. In 2019, 68% of Patagonia's fabrics were made with recycled materials, demonstrating substantial progress in closing the loop on textile production. The company's commitment to circular principles has not hindered its financial success; instead, it has contributed to Patagonia's growth and strong brand reputation. In 2018, CEO Rose Marcario stated that the company's repair and reuse model was contributing to record-breaking sales and profits, proving that circular economy practices can be both environmentally and economically beneficial. Patagonia's success in implementing circular economy principles serves as an inspirational model for the fashion industry, demonstrating that sustainability and profitability can go hand in hand. By prioritizing durability, repairability, and recyclability, Patagonia has not only reduced its environmental impact but also created a loyal customer base that values and supports these practices.Top of Form

VIII. RECOMMENDATIONS FOR STAKEHOLDERS

This section provides tailored recommendations for key stakeholders. Entrepreneurs receive guidance on navigating circular entrepreneurship, policymakers learn about creating supportive ecosystems, and educators are encouraged to foster awareness and understanding of the circular economy.

A. Recommendations for Entrepreneurs:

Entrepreneurs venturing into circular economy practices can enhance their success by embracing innovation. Actively seeking and adopting solutions aligned with circular principles, such as redesigning products or exploring new technologies, can minimize waste and resource consumption. Additionally, collaboration and networking within the industry are crucial for the exchange of ideas and resources, fostering support and accelerating the adoption of circular practices. Prioritizing sustainable design principles in product development, focusing on repairability and reusability, contributes significantly to a circular business model. Entrepreneurs should proactively educate stakeholders about the benefits of circular entrepreneurship, building transparency and trust.(U & R, 2023) Furthermore, exploring alternative business models like leasing or take-back schemes can promote circularity by extending product lifespans and creating additional revenue streams. For instance, a cosmetics company could set up a take-back scheme, where customers can return empty product packaging, which the company then collects, cleans, and reuses or recycles the materials, closing the loop.

B. Recommendations for Policymakers:

Policymakers play a pivotal role in fostering a supportive ecosystem for the circular economy. To incentivize circular practices, they should establish regulatory frameworks, offering incentives such as tax breaks for businesses adopting circular models or regulations promoting recycled materials. (Bombonatti Filho, n.d.)Allocating funds for the development of recycling facilities and waste management systems is crucial to support businesses transitioning to circular models. Encouraging research and development through government grants and partnerships with academic institutions drives innovation in circular technologies. Policymakers can lead by example in circular procurement, favoring products from businesses following circular principles and creating a demand for such products. Finally, facilitating collaboration between businesses, NGOs, and government agencies through platforms for knowledge exchange can collectively address challenges and hasten the transition to a circular economy. For instance, The European Union introduces a "Circular Economy Tax Credit" that provides a 15% tax deduction for businesses that invest in product redesign, recycling infrastructure, or take-back programs.

C. Recommendations for Educators

Educators play a vital role in preparing future professionals for the circular economy. Integrating circular economy concepts into curricula, particularly in business, engineering, and environmental science programs, ensures that students are well-versed in circular principles. Encouraging interdisciplinary learning fosters a holistic understanding of the circular economy by promoting collaboration between different academic disciplines. Industry engagement through partnerships and internships with businesses practicing circular entrepreneurship provides students with real-world experiences. Hosting awareness campaigns, events, workshops, and seminars contributes to creating a culture of sustainability and responsible business practices among students and the wider community.(Brouwer & Thoden van Velzen, 2023) Educators should stay updated on industry trends, continuously refreshing their knowledge to ensure students receive relevant and up-to-date information, preparing them for the evolving landscape of sustainable business. These recommendations collectively empower educators to shape a new generation of professionals well-versed in the principles and practices of the circular economy. For instance, the Indian Institute of Technology Madras establishes a "Circular Economy Research Center," bringing together experts from materials science, manufacturing, and sustainability to conduct joint studies and pilot initiatives.

IX. FUTURE DIRECTIONS

As the circular economy continues to evolve, several key areas emerge as potential hotspots for innovation and growth. These future directions represent opportunities for entrepreneurs, policymakers, and educators to further advance the principles of circularity and create more sustainable business models.

1. **Advanced Materials and Design:** The development of new materials that are inherently more recyclable, biodegradable, or reusable will be crucial. Innovations in areas such as bio-based plastics, self-healing materials, and nano-materials could revolutionize product design and end-of-life management. For instance, research into materials that can be easily separated at the molecular level could significantly enhance recycling efficiency.

2. **Digital Technologies and the Internet of Things (IoT):** The integration of IoT and other digital technologies offers immense potential for tracking products throughout their lifecycle, optimizing resource use, and facilitating efficient take-back systems. Blockchain technology could be leveraged to create transparent and traceable supply chains, ensuring the authenticity of recycled materials and promoting trust in circular economy practices.
3. **Artificial Intelligence and Machine Learning:** AI and machine learning can play a crucial role in optimizing circular processes. These technologies can be used to predict maintenance needs, extending product lifespans, or to sort and process waste more efficiently. AI could also help in designing products for circularity by analyzing vast amounts of data on material properties and recycling processes.
4. **Circular Business Models in the Service Sector:** While much focus has been on manufacturing and consumer goods, there's significant potential for applying circular principles to the service sector. This could involve innovative models for sharing resources, optimizing energy use in buildings, or creating closed-loop systems for water and waste management in urban environments.
5. **Biomimicry and Regenerative Design:** Drawing inspiration from natural systems, biomimicry and regenerative design principles could lead to breakthrough innovations in circular economy practices. This approach could result in products and processes that not only minimize waste but actively contribute to ecosystem restoration.
6. **Cross-Industry Collaboration and Industrial Symbiosis:** The future of the circular economy lies in breaking down silos between industries. Encouraging collaboration where one industry's waste becomes another's raw material could lead to more efficient resource use across entire economic systems. Policy frameworks that incentivize such collaborations could accelerate this trend.
7. **Consumer Behavior and Education:** Innovations in how we educate and engage consumers will be crucial for the widespread adoption of circular economy practices. This could involve gamification of recycling processes, AR/VR experiences to visualize the impact of consumption choices, or community-based initiatives that make circular living more accessible and appealing.
8. **Circular Cities and Urban Planning:** As urbanization continues, there's immense potential in redesigning cities based on circular principles. This could involve innovations in waste management systems, shared mobility solutions, and urban agriculture that create closed-loop systems at the city level.
9. **Financial Innovations:** New financial instruments and models will be needed to support circular economy initiatives. This could include innovative insurance products for remanufactured goods, blockchain-based currencies that incentiv-

ize sustainable behaviors, or new metrics for assessing the long-term value of circular business models.

10. **Policy and Regulatory Frameworks:** Future innovations in policy could include more sophisticated extended producer responsibility schemes, tax systems that favor circular practices, or international agreements on the movement and processing of recyclable materials.

X. CONCLUSION

The circular economy represents a transformative shift from the traditional linear "take-make-dispose" model to a regenerative system where waste is minimized, and resources are reused and recycled. Entrepreneurs are key drivers of this change, developing innovative business models aligned with circular principles. The Circular PRISM Model in this paper provides a framework for entrepreneurs, covering product circularity, stakeholder engagement, and essential enablers.

Companies like Unilever and Patagonia showcase the successful application of circular economy principles, highlighting how these practices not only promote sustainability but also drive business growth, enhance brand loyalty, and create new revenue streams. Future innovation areas include advancements in materials science, digital technologies, AI, and biomimicry, all of which can enhance circularity across sectors. The development of circular cities, cross-industry collaborations, and new financial models will further accelerate the transition to a sustainable economic system. The transition to a fully circular economy faces challenges and requires collective effort from entrepreneurs, policymakers, educators, and consumers. Policymakers must create supportive regulatory frameworks, and educators need to raise awareness and equip the next generation with the necessary skills.

The circular economy offers a vision for a sustainable and resilient future, addressing environmental challenges while creating economic value and improving quality of life. Embracing circular principles, fostering innovation, and collaborating across sectors can lead to a healthier planet, stronger businesses, and better well-being for communities. As a blueprint for sustainable entrepreneurship and economic resilience, the circular economy is essential for the 21st century and beyond.

REFERENCES

Amaleshwari, U. A., & Jeevitha, R. (2023). Entrepreneurial orientation and circular business practices: A conceptual framework. *Journal of Management and Public Policy*, 14(2), 16–26.

Bombonatti Filho, O. (n.d.). CIRCULAR ECONOMY – A NEW MANAGEMENT MODEL FOR THE PLANET ECONOMIA CIRCULAR – UM NOVO MODELO DE GESTAO PARA O PLANETA. *19th CONTECSI International Conference on Information Systems and Technology Management*. DOI: 10.5748/19CONTECSI/PSE/SOC/6961

Brouwer, M., & Thoden van Velzen, U. (2023). *Multi-dimensional sustainability assessment of product-packaging combinations : MuDiSa: a calculation tool to assess the sustainability of product-packaging combinations in multiple dimensions of sustainability*. DOI: 10.18174/633072

Formentini, G., & Ramanujan, D. (2023). EXAMINING THE ROLE AND FUTURE POTENTIAL OF DESIGN FOR DISASSEMBLY METHODS TO SUPPORT CIRCULAR PRODUCT DESIGN. *Proceedings of the Design Society*, 3, 1735–1744. DOI: 10.1017/pds.2023.174

Grzymala, Z. (2023). *Circular Economy as a Sustainable Development Marketing Tool.*, DOI: 10.4018/978-1-6684-8681-8.ch015

Kaestner, L., Scope, C., Neumann, N., & Woelfel, C. (2023). SUSTAINABLE CIRCULAR PACKAGING DESIGN: A SYSTEMATIC LITERATURE REVIEW ON STRATEGIES AND APPLICATIONS IN THE COSMETICS INDUSTRY. *Proceedings of the Design Society*, 3, 3265–3274. DOI: 10.1017/pds.2023.327

Koval, V., Arsawan, I. W. E., Suryantini, N. P. S., Kovbasenko, S., Fisunenko, N., & Aloshyna, T. (2022). Circular Economy and Sustainability-Oriented Innovation: Conceptual Framework and Energy Future Avenue. *Energies*, 16(1), 243. DOI: 10.3390/en16010243 PMID: 35910686

Lisitsa, M., Khutieva, E., Doroshenko, O., Konareva, A., & Trifonova, L. (2022). *Circular Economy as an Alternative to Green Economy*. DOI: 10.2991/aer.k.220308.029

Maldonado Castro, A., Maldonado Castro, J., Yela Burgos, R., & Moreno Suqilanda, E. (2022). Circular economy and its impact on environmental sustainability. *Centro Sur*, 6(4). Advance online publication. DOI: 10.37955/cs.v6i4.286

Martino, B. (2023). Biomimicry in Building Architecture. *University of Colorado Honors Journal*, 118, 118. Advance online publication. DOI: 10.33011/cuhj20231867

Molchanova, R. V. (2023). CIRCULAR ECONOMY IN THE CONSTRUCTION INDUSTRY. *EKONOMIKA I UPRAVLENIE: PROBLEMY, RESHENIYA, 4/3*(136), 110–116. DOI: 10.36871/ek.up.p.r.2023.04.03.013

Mura, R., Vicentini, F., Botti, L. M., & Chiriacò, M. V. (2024). Achieving the circular economy through environmental policies: Packaging strategies for more sustainable business models in the wine industry. *Business Strategy and the Environment*, 33(2), 1497–1514. DOI: 10.1002/bse.3556

Ncube, A., Mtetwa, S., Bukhari, M., Fiorentino, G., & Passaro, R. (2023). Circular Economy and Green Chemistry: The Need for Radical Innovative Approaches in the Design for New Products. *Energies*, 16(4), 1752. DOI: 10.3390/en16041752

Özpolat, A., & Nakıpoğlu Özsoy, F. (Eds.). (2022). *Circular Economy in the Framework of Sustainable Development Policy*. Özgür Yayınları., DOI: 10.58830/ozgur.pub11

Popa, A. (2023). Circular economy as a strategy of regional and local development. *Strategii Si Politici de Management in Economia Contemporana*, 178–187. DOI: 10.53486/icspm2022.29

Roleders, V. V. (2023). CIRCULAR ECONOMY MODEL IN INDUSTRIAL ECOSYSTEMS. *The Actual Problems of Regional Economy Development*, 1(19), 243–254. DOI: 10.15330/apred.1.19.243-254

Santos -Corrada, M. D. L. M., Méndez-Tejeda, R., Flecha-Ortiz, J. A., & Lopez, E. (2024). An analysis of sustainable consumption practices through the role of the consumer behavior in the circular economy. *Journal of Consumer Behaviour*, 23(1), 229–242. DOI: 10.1002/cb.2183

Saranya, K. G., Hema, A., & Joanish Muthu, J. (2023). A review on sustainable biodiversity challenges and opportunities. *World Journal of Advanced Research and Reviews*, 17(1), 679–685. DOI: 10.30574/wjarr.2023.17.1.0069

Sehnem, S., Lara, A. C., Benetti, K., Schneider, K., Marcon, M. L., & da Silva, T. H. H. (2023). Improving startups through excellence initiatives: Addressing circular economy and innovation. *Environment, Development and Sustainability*, 26(6), 15237–15283. Advance online publication. DOI: 10.1007/s10668-023-03247-4 PMID: 37362985

Seier, M., Archodoulaki, V.-M., Koch, T., Duscher, B., & Gahleitner, M. (2023). Prospects for Recyclable Multilayer Packaging: A Case Study. *Polymers*, 15(13), 2966. DOI: 10.3390/polym15132966 PMID: 37447609

Shaikh, M. J., & Hyder, M. (2023). Green Packaging as a Positive Catalyst for Green Environment: Implementation in Emerging Markets around the Globe. *Pakistan Journal of Humanities and Social Sciences*, 11(1). Advance online publication. DOI: 10.52131/pjhss.2023.1101.0382

Soroka, A., Robinson, M., Gosling, J., Hoggins, L., Hall, J., & Naim, M. M. (2023). *Circular Economy Models in the Construction Sector: A Plastics Recycling Use Case.*, DOI: 10.1007/978-981-19-9205-6_14

Stoyanova-Koval, S., Slutskyi, Y., & Varhatiuk, M. (2023). CIRCULAR ECONOMY DEVELOPMENT TRENDS IN THE WORLD. *Economic Scope*. DOI: 10.32782/2224-6282/183-18

Taieb, A. H., & Ben Amor, M. (2023). Eco-design Design Strategy: Case Study Biomimicry Approach in Design Product Materials. *Asian Journal of Environment & Ecology*, 21(3), 1–20. DOI: 10.9734/ajee/2023/v21i3460

Timofei, O. (2023). Circular business models for increasing product usage. *Competitiveness and Innovation in the Knowledge Economy*, 74–78, 74–78. Advance online publication. DOI: 10.53486/cike2022.08

Yadav, C., & Garg, Ar. Y. (2023). DESIGN FOR DISASSEMBLY IN ARCHITECTURE. *INTERANTIONAL JOURNAL OF SCIENTIFIC RESEARCH IN ENGINEERING AND MANAGEMENT, 07*(04). DOI: 10.55041/IJSREM18950

Yang, D. (2023). Financial and Marketing Performance of P&G and Unilever. *BCP Business & Management*, 46, 49–57. DOI: 10.54691/bcpbm.v46i.5076

Zăpucioiu, L.-F., Sterie, M.-C., & Dimitriu, T. A. (2023). The Relevance of the Circular Economy in the Context of Sustainable Development. *Proceedings of the International Conference on Business Excellence, 17*(1), 1534–1543. DOI: 10.2478/picbe-2023-0138

Chapter 4
Environmental and Institutional Frameworks in Entrepreneurship Ecosystems

José G. Vargas-Hernandez
https://orcid.org/0000-0003-0938-4197
Tecnológico Nacional de México, ITSF, Mexico

Francisco J. González-Àvila
Tecnológico Nacional de México, ITSF, Mexico

Mario A. García-Camacho
https://orcid.org/0000-0002-9645-3199
Tecnológico Nacional de México, ITS Fresnillo, Mexico

Omar C. Vargas-González
https://orcid.org/0000-0002-6089-956X
Tecnológico Nacional de México, Ciudad Guzmán, Mexico

ABSTRACT

This study has the aim to analyze the environmental and institutional frameworks implications in entrepreneurship ecosystems. It is assumed that research on entrepreneurship ecosystem micro foundations are sensitive environmental and institutional factors including the agency of actors in their own local communities. The method used is the meta-analytical-reflective and descriptive based on conceptual, theoretical, and empirical literature reviews. It is concluded that the environmental and institutional factors are relevant in the formation and development of entrepreneurship ecosystems.

DOI: 10.4018/979-8-3693-4338-8.ch004

INTRODUCTION

Research on contextual particularities based on institutional environments for entrepreneurship and the formulation of specific policies to support the mechanisms should be applicable, even to least developed countries. The integration of institutional research into the activities of academic institutions has been the major transformation since the nineteenth century. The institutional environment of entrepreneurship ecosystems influences the construction and development of entrepreneurship, community, companies, and society. Institutions are patterns of social activities that shape collective and individual experience. Institutions form individuals in the various ways of behaving and relating to others.

In this sense, the business ecosystem perspective is a metaphorical holistic notion to analyze the economic groups of practices and activities in the growth of the company to emphasize the characteristics of the external environment that internal operations see reflected in their daily practices. For example: research on the nature of digital entrepreneurship ecosystems explores the impact in a broad environment to consolidate knowledge of ecosystems that are the basis of entrepreneurship.

Research on the multinational business environment focuses mainly on homogeneous institutions (Coviello and Jones 2004; Wielemaker & Gedajlovic, 2011; Busenitz et al., 2000; Kshetri, 2010; Kshetri, 2009). Entrepreneurship, like any other biological organism in environments, proliferates with institutions that promote its growth (Sobel, 2008; Fritsch, 2013; Bosma et al., 2018). Formal institutions, tasks, and environments can influence decisions and behaviors, especially women's serial entrepreneurship (Brush et al., 2009; Cetindamar et al., 2012).

The indeterminacy of research is the source of conditions and pressures for institutional change in situations of multiple equilibria beyond external institutional factors and shocks to establish problems as sources of changes in demographics, technology, etc., including new solutions, the abandonment of old practices, and stagnation (Dobbin, 1994; Greve, 1995). The adaptability of entrepreneurial ecosystems must address some tensions in research to analyze their evolutionary metamorphosis focused on environments and contexts, locations, places, actors, governance mechanisms, etc. (Molla, & Biru, 2023).

Research on institutional change for individual characters is significant (Bellah et al. 1991; Sullivan, 1995). Research on the process of institutional change explores the dynamics of institutional change identified in the dialectical relationship between actions, actors, practices, structures, and meanings, rather than focusing solely on macro-level structures and practices (Townley, 2002; Zilber, 2002). Sennett (1998) has conducted research on the interrelationships between institutional change and individual character within firms.

The construction of the research funding scheme for radical institutional change and incremental transformation can be the result of a compromise between relevant actors, including social partners and political parties involved in different institutional frameworks (Theobald and Hampel, 2013). Research on temporal institutional rootedness from the perspective of social movements provides insight into the sequence, pace, power, and momentum of institutional change.

From the contributions of Juma, et al (2023), the framing and prioritization of problems by regulatory agencies leads to opportunities for value creation and establishes agendas that involve resources and rules to reconfigure the limits of interaction with other agents and actors in the preservation of the environment. Resource-based theory and knowledge-based theory are inward-oriented focusing on the specific firm and serial entrepreneurship and its resources and knowledge, the analysis of the exit and re-entry strategies of entrepreneurship based on the contingencies of the environment, integrates institutional theory as a complementary approach (Carbonara et al., 2020; Cetindamar et al., 2012).

In this sense, the study asks: is the consolidation of entrepreneurial ecosystems related to or based on environmental and institutional frameworks? This study aims to analyze the implications of environmental and institutional frameworks on entrepreneurship ecosystems. Based on a meta-analytical-reflexive and descriptive development based on conceptual, theoretical and empirical reviews of the literature, of entrepreneurship ecosystems, environmental factors followed by institutional factors. Finally, some conclusions are presented.

ENTREPRENEURSHIP ECOSYSTEMS

Entrepreneurship ecosystems are the set of interconnected entrepreneurship institutions and organizations, actors, and entrepreneurship processes that come together formally and informally to connect, govern, and mediate performance within the local business environment (Brown & Mason, 2014). An entrepreneurship ecosystem is an interconnected set of potential and existing entrepreneurship actors, organizations such as companies and venture capital, institutions such as universities, business processes, that formally and informally mediate and govern performance within the local business environment (OECD, 2014).

Entrepreneurship ecosystems are understood as a complex model of emerging companies with a melting pot of cultures, infrastructure and services, information technologies, cultural and formal institutions, and demand domains, which capture the contextual characteristics of the socioeconomic, institutional, and information environment in cities (Perugini, 2023). The different models of entrepreneurial ecosystems depend on the environmental and emergent characteristics of the inserted ecosystems (Acs et al., 2014; Alvedalen & Boschma, 2017; Malecki, 2018; Cavallo et al., 2019; Kahle et al., 2020; Theodoraki & Catanzaro, 2021; Johnson et al., 2022).

The entrepreneurship ecosystem approach emerges as a transactional way to support the environment of high-growth enterprises (HGFs), including big blockbusters driven by entrepreneurship, recycling entrepreneurship by reinvesting their time, expertise, and money in supporting new entrepreneurship practices and activities in an accessible and information-rich environment. Entrepreneurial ecosystems as types of environments are conducive to the emergence of high-growth companies (HGFs) with the characteristics of growth dynamics.

Entrepreneurship ecosystems pose challenges in formulating policies that address enabling environments for start-ups given the scarcity of growing companies. Startups require supportive environments more than companies, which leads to new policy approaches (Brown & Mason, 2014). An adult startup is a possibility in the community for entrepreneurship and the potential rewards and positive spillover effects on the environment and impacts on the entrepreneurial ecosystem. Large corporate companies participate in local policymaking to create a friendly environment.

In short, the identification and development of entrepreneurial ecosystems requires its own customization through the combination of policies adapted to the unique characteristics of each ecosystem, promoting the quality of entrepreneurship to ensure the allocation of resources to productive use, and addressing the complexity of entrepreneurial ecosystems with a holistic policy approach. (Candeias & Sarkar, 2024). Highlighting the importance of environmental and institutional frameworks for the proliferation of entrepreneurship ecosystems in each context.

ENVIRONMENTAL FRAMEWORK

Identifying the characteristics of the environmental framework, it should be clarified that they are the external factors that affect entrepreneurs and companies; These can include economic, ecological, social, technological, cultural aspects, etc. Interconnecting potential and existing business actors, organizations (including companies), venture capitalists, business angels, banks, institutions (including universities), public sector agencies and financial bodies, and entrepreneurship processes such as the rate of company birth and growth, highly successful entrepreneurship levels, serial entrepreneurship, mindset within companies and entrepreneurial ambition, formal and informal merger.

Elements of entrepreneurship tend to create a friendly environment to identify the objectives of the entrepreneurship ecosystem's environment policy mixes (Kuckertz, 2019; Stam, 2018). A holistic consideration for policy intervention focuses on the actors of entrepreneurship ecosystems, the provision of ecosystem resources, and the connectors of the entrepreneurship ecosystem to the environment, resulting in a gradual shift towards growth-oriented entrepreneurship depending on contexts. Trust among the members of an entrepreneurial ecosystem is an essential element of a stable environment that favors the transfer of knowledge and skills (Iansiti and Levien, 2004; Theodoraki et al., 2018).

Early-stage entrepreneurial activity in underdeveloped institutional environments with insufficient resources and support from organizations in a top-down governance model in which the government has a critical role (Candeias & Sarkar, 2022). The dynamics of high-tech recycling entrepreneurship within entrepreneurial ecosystems is an appropriate context to create an institutional environment for the analysis of knowledge entrepreneurship in startup ecosystems (Corbett, 2007; Maravilla, 2013; Genoma, 2020). Connect, mediate, and govern performance within the local business environment. Venture capital is not a condition of the environment and goes beyond how it leads the emergence of entrepreneurial activities (Saxenian, 1994; Feldman, 2001; Mason et al, 2002; Garnsey & Heffernan, 2005).

Institutional intermediaries such as infrastructure provide public resources and business services (Armanios et al., 2017; Wei, 2022), addressing private organizational support in the general environment of entrepreneurship. Access to resources in the environment includes entrepreneurial actors, connectors, resource providers, entrepreneurial culture, etc. This conceptualization is used in data collection and analysis to explore emergent variance in the research model. The scarcity of resources in hostile environments promotes entrepreneurial ingenuity.

When comparing entrepreneurial environments, there are no specific rules about the determinants of developing the economics of entrepreneurial ecosystems, institutional entrepreneurship, performance indicators, related effects, and the nature of the changes that economies experience in institutional entrepreneurship. Some economies have significant differences in the business environment (Leong et al., 2008) that show multiple paths for the development of entrepreneurial ecosystems.

The institutional environment has effects on the development of entrepreneurship by focusing on the regulatory environment (Manolova et al., 2008). The regulatory environment, values, and culture with formal institutions are determinants of entrepreneurial activities, with effects that depend on entrepreneurial skills such as informal institutions (Li and Zahra, 2012). Cash entrepreneurship can be involved in creating and supporting practices and activities to improve the business environment by establishing and lobbying institutions and organizations.

Entrepreneurship ecosystems in developing countries should be explored taking into account the uncertainty surrounding the business environment that has an impact on business performance. Entrepreneurship must be analyzed from the uncertainty surrounding the organizational business environment that can seriously affect business performance in different countries (Al Saiqal et al., 2019). Entrepreneurship activities respond to the interrelationships of business organizations and environmental factors, focusing on the framework conditions of entrepreneurship, integrating variables in the Global Entrepreneurship Monitor (GEM) expressed in the entrepreneurial ecosystem model, which measures entrepreneurial activities and economic growth (Reynolds et al. 2005).

The interactions between entrepreneurship programs create a cohesive environment for entrepreneurship growth (Motoyama & Knowlton, 2016). Entrepreneurship activities require support programs designed and implemented based on the specific cultural characteristics of the environment (Jaén, Fernández-Serrano, & Liñan, 2013).

Entrepreneurship is the process of creating a business as a result of recognizing and taking advantage of opportunities in the environment characterized by uncertainty (Shane & Venkataraman, 2000). Development of the entrepreneurship ecosystem derived from digital technologies, ranging from new opportunities to alterations of existing businesses and changes in business models to account for digital environments (Kraus et al., 2018). The digital identification of entrepreneurship opportunities is characterized by the proliferation of risks to financial stability, changes in the regulatory environment (Autio et al., 2018; Anagnostopoulos, 2018; Li et al., 2020; Magnuson, 2018; Arner et al., 2015).

The transformation of business models is supported by saturated technology and pervasive environmental connections (Zaheer et al. 2019). Digital entrepreneurship is the search for opportunities used in digital media and other information and communication technologies in the digital context of network interactions and relationships that depend on the resources of the surrounding environment beyond the capabilities of entrepreneurship (Davidson y Vaast, 2010). A networking approach guides empirical research from a relational view of entrepreneurial ecosystems, enabling founders to have access to environmental resources (Aldrich and Zimmer, 1986).

The performance of the digital entrepreneurship ecosystem can be measured by the resulting and enabled digital unicorns and the core value propositions as a result of the ecosystem and an enabling environment that offers new possibilities, collaboration structures, means of participation, mediation tools, etc. (Acs et al., 2017; Torres y Godinho, 2022; Elia et al., 2020). The intention of entrepreneurship is affected by several factors, including traits and personalities, considering the interaction with the environmental factors of the entrepreneurial ecosystems (Alammari et al., 2019; Schmutzler et al., 2019). The interaction between personal attributes and the surrounding environment affects business development (Bird, 1988; Cavallo et al., 2019).

The entrepreneurship ecosystem approach creates an environment that involves alignment with individual motivations for moving toward entrepreneurship (Zhao & Seibert, 2006; Di Zhang & Bruning, 2011). Business motivations promote an environment that provides critical resources and capabilities, such as financing, knowledge, technology, skills, etc., to develop new business models and new products that enable the company's growth. Retraining occurs in the failure of the company and professional progression in a stable environment where entrepreneurship is a career that alternates between motivations for regrouping and expansion.

The examination of the factors that trigger the development of entrepreneurship, such as socio-intercultural and institutional-political environments, influence the development of entrepreneurship and entrepreneurial behavior (Chohra, 2019; Porras-Páez & Schmutzler, 2019). The socio-intercultural communication of entrepreneurship is supported by the mutual understanding of specific cultural and linguistic elements with diverse backgrounds that influence socio-cultural interactions between individuals that have an impact on the global business environment.

The characteristics of socio-intercultural entrepreneurship encourage the development and support of an area with socio-intercultural dimensions for social entrepreneurship that leads to improved performance of social economy activities. From the socio-intercultural perspective, socio-intercultural entrepreneurship is beyond the borders of its own culture, achieving a more global vision, considering social and environmental values, and satisfying needs that the economy cannot satisfy on its own. Sociocultural entrepreneurship develops in an environment of uncertainty avoidance.

Practicing socio-intercultural communication in global and international business is part of success in socio-intercultural entrepreneurship projects that require an open mind, without prejudices and paradigms, the ability to adapt behaviors and attitudes to different environments and contexts, and the ability to integrate differentiated socio-intercultural groups in diversity, plural communities, and inclusive identities. The critical analysis of the evaluation of socio-intercultural entrepreneurship highlights a fundamental issue of ethical identity in the business culture committed to the environment that becomes increasingly complex, uncertain and challenging due to expectations and different standards to be met, linguistic patterns, etc. (Chaney and Martin (2007).

The systemic entrepreneurship perspective holds that agents act on new perceived opportunities to mobilize and exploit environmental resources (Acs et al. 2014). Incubation serves to link entrepreneurship with the external environment to build ecosystems, dynamic capacities aimed at detecting and taking advantage of opportunities for reconfiguration. Incubation exploits the cognitive advantages of cross-cultural entrepreneurship aimed at detecting environmental opportunities, overcoming resource constraints, and increasing innovation to facilitate resource orchestration (Giudici et al., 2018; Lorenz et al., 2018; Autio, George & Alexy, 2011; Stahl & Maznevski, 2021).

An ecosystem is the union of localized cultural perspectives, social networks, investment capital, universities and research centers, and economic policies that create supportive environments for innovation-based ventures (Spigel, 2017). Innovation in serial entrepreneurship analyzes integration with capital theory and external environmental contingencies integrated with institutional theory. customs, traditions, etc., as the basis of business activities. The intrapreneur transforms dreams and ideas into projects focused on innovation and creativity to operate profitably within an organizational environment (Koontz, Weihrich, & Cannice, 2008). Open innovation stimulates serial entrepreneurship through outside-in and inside-out strategies that lead to the accumulation of human and social capital, to greater awareness and confidence in new opportunities in the external environment (Yun et al., 2019).

Enterprises behave adaptively to connect and interact with local environments. The entrepreneurship ecosystem framework explains the social interactions between actors and the entrepreneurship process and the local environment (Spigel & Harrison, 2018). Social entrepreneurship is aimed at solving social problems in its environment and creating added value to society in the cultural dimension of individualism - collectivism (Hofstede, 2001).

The management of social entrepreneurship evaluates the specificities and diversity of each culture (Zait, 2002) in order to achieve the socio-intercultural objectives of multinational organizations.

Social entrepreneurship has collective values such as the cultural dimension that leads to developing commitment to society by creating an environment that favors social activities. A clash of collective cultural values between the population and business groups can lead employees to real self-employment and vice versa (Baum et al., 1993). The promotion of social entrepreneurship is related to the level of uncertainty in the environment (Dancin et al., 2011).

Entrepreneurship benefits from conditions in high-income countries, such as professional entrepreneurship education, physical infrastructure and trade support services, low bureaucracy, government policies, and support. In addition, research and development transfers, entrepreneurial culture and social norms focused on entrepreneurial activities, foundation support, an open and dynamic market environment (Ahmad and Xavier, 2012; Doran et al., 2018; Guerrero et al., 2021; Rotefoss & Kolvereid, 2005).

Traditional or classic and student-based university models of entrepreneurship have different foundations. The traditional business model maximizes economic benefits and the student-oriented model tends to generate greater social, political, cultural, environmental, health, etc. benefits. Entrepreneurship-focused universities require a corporate entrepreneurship strategy that addresses institutional entrepreneurship initiatives and policymaking to provide knowledge and support entrepreneurial endeavors in a reduced-risk environment (Kirby, 2006; Woollard, 2010). The development of entrepreneurial ecosystems must combine bottom-up initiatives to improve the environment and top-down approaches. The entrepreneurial experience of the faculty moderates university ecosystems, facilitating connections between academia and the business environment, transmitting practical knowledge to students.

Private universities have higher levels of interaction with the market environment (Andrade, 2012; Barral et al., 2018). The entrepreneurial environment of the public university is more oriented towards academic and scientific production, which indicates a weak relationship with incentives for entrepreneurship (Ipiranga, Freitas, & Paiva, 2010). Universities must adapt to organizational needs and adapt to the changing environment to be more entrepreneurial and encourage intrapreneurship practices (Farrukh et al., 2019).

The experience of cross-cultural entrepreneurship can take advantage of opportunities in the environment that lead to better company performance (Wang, 2020; Yang & Yang, 2022). Macro-microenvironments link entrepreneurship, cross-cultural experience, and entrepreneurship ecosystem performance, contributing to dynamic capacity by uncovering the formation of dynamic ecosystem capabilities processes. The dynamics of ecosystem entrepreneurship creates an environment conducive to entrepreneurship (Stam, 2015). The relationship between business orientation and performance is influenced by contingent variables including organizational structure, culture, organizational resources, environment, industry characteristics, strategy, etc. (Slevin and Covin, 1990; Ostgaard & Birley, 1994; Eisenhardt & Schoonhoven, 1990; Stuart & Abetti, 1987; Covin & Slevin, 1989; Venkatraman, 1989).

Political decision-making should drive the dynamism and openness of domestic markets, which can lead to an unpredictable environment that can generate profitable business opportunities. Research on entrepreneurship in international markets examines the circumstances that foster entrepreneurial activities in different environments (Thomas and Mueller, 2000). In the context of low-income economies, the conditions of the business environment can be detrimental, even when launching new business organizations due to the limited orientation towards innovation as a driver of entrepreneurship (Guerrero et al., 2021). Business innovation fosters competitiveness in productive socio-organizational environments and consolidates the creation of organizations and companies that promote job creation in national, regional, and local contexts.

Research on the entrepreneurial ecosystem emphasizes the interconnections between elements of a regional economic and entrepreneurial environment (Spigel, 2017). Anexplicit focus on entrepreneurship activities in high-growth firms in local and regional settings generates and supports ambitious ventures. Financial environments that support entrepreneurship have a positive influence on national and regional economic growth (Gomes, et al. 2023). The favoured support of chaebols creates an unfavourable environment for small and medium-sized enterprises to access financial markets, playing a key role in boosting business activities.

An entrepreneurial culture respected by a society through the valuation of attitudes of entrepreneurship commitments, activities, and the type of institutional environment they influence (Guerrero et al., 2021). Entrepreneurship education in higher-income countries does not encourage entrepreneurship activities due to the multiple opportunities that education requires to adopt a relationship between environmental and institutional factors to foster entrepreneurial activities (Walter and Block, 2016). The transformation of entrepreneurial talent is a potential process for entrepreneurship ecosystems to find a social and contextual environment as independent cofactors (Steigertahl & Mauer, 2023). Business education is most effective if graduates move into environments conducive to entrepreneurship.

Exemplifying, the importance of entrepreneurial culture through a comparative review identified the distinctive characteristics of entrepreneurial ecosystems in the U.S. and Europe, to understand the complexities that drive innovation and economic growth. It establishes that as the global landscape continues to evolve, policies must be shaped, collaboration must be fostered, and the collective understanding of what drives successful entrepreneurship in diverse and dynamic contexts must be advanced (Tula, 2024). Studies on entrepreneurship ecosystems reveal that interactions between different actors, including customers, suppliers, institutions, governments, and universities, can result in a sustainable business ecosystem. (Chaudhary, 2023).

INSTITUTIONAL FRAMEWORK

Entrepreneurship ecosystems include the ability to identify greater opportunities using technology at both the individual and institutional levels. Entrepreneurship and ecosystems are linked by start-ups and new venture investments, including support from university spin-offs, institutions, human capital, government initiatives, and other elements of the ecosystem (Harrison and Leitch, 2010; Johnson et al., 2019; Jung et al., 2017; Öner & Kunday, 2016; Qian et al., 2013). Entrepreneurship ecosystems are more productive in contexts with inclusive and growth-enhancing institutions (Bosma et al., 2018; Sobel, 2008).

An integrative model of entrepreneurial ecosystems consists of interdependence and coevolution, includes institutional arrangements and elements of resourcing, bottom-up and bottom-up causalities of ecosystem quality outcomes (Stam and Van de Ven, 2021). Institutions are designed to solve problems that induce conventional relationships and practices that subsequently fuel recent problems, scarcity of resources, failures, leading to cycles of opportunism and increasing the benefits of institutional change (Leblebici et al., 1991; Abolafia, 1996). The dynamic feedback between institutional factors highlights the different aspects of institutionality due to changes in prices and the failures, efforts and failures of peripheral rivals to promote new institutional forms and models.

Economic, political, and ideological circumstances underlie conflicts of interest that generate susceptibility to institutional change, which alters the prominence of preferences and undermines the consent to compromise among these interests as the basis of the institutional balance of the system. Fundamental changes are triggered by external shocks and shocks rooted in dependence on the trajectory and institutional order and stability. External shocks can develop endogenously oriented institutional data to generate conditions for change. Endogenous and integrative institutional approaches lead to new conceptions and trajectories of change.

The dialectical perspective on institutional change suggests that institutions are susceptible to change by following a trajectory that examines the characteristics of the creation and persistence of institutions based on political arguments (Thelen, 2003). From a dialectical perspective, institutional stability is not always contingent on a renewed challenge of managing conflicts of interest. The dialectical trajectory accepts feedback mechanisms in the trajectory dependency approach.

Structural institutional arrangements should strengthen trust among institutional actors in academic and research institutions, supported by different methods and disciplines, to compete for resources (Shriberg, 2002). The assumption in a trajectory-dependent trajectory is that, depending on the trajectory chosen, adaptive institutional adjustments reduce the potential for conflict, increasing the price of change, an option that becomes less viable in the future. Positive feedback is a condition for the persistence of institutional arrangements, while others remain intact for extended periods due to prevailing conditions.

The configurations of entrepreneurship socio-ecosystems stimulate generic elements that affect institutional and physical infrastructure, startups, scaleups, and contrasting types such as gender entrepreneurship and high-growth firms (Hechavarría & Ingram, 2019; Sperber & Linder, 2019; Auerswald & Dani, 2017). The spatial nesting of contexts includes formal institutions in international, national, regional, municipal, and local conditions that make it difficult to delimit the spatial boundaries of causal mechanisms of entrepreneurial ecosystems. Entrepreneurship culture is an informal institution that reflects the value and prevalence of entrepreneurship in society (Fritsch & Wyrwich, 2014).

Endogenous and exogenous institutional circumstances provoke excessive interests and conflicts, moving the institution towards a new different equilibrium under an underlying dynamic of continuous relevance of options and, however, change is limited to unconstrained institutional actors. Endogenous and combined institutionalism confirms the centrality of politics and balances of power in coalition building, state policies, which are endogenous sources and trigger institutionally determined material and symbolic foundations, prevent and promote fundamental changes (Bartley and Schneiberg, 2002; Thornton, 2002). Institutional actors and stakeholders are embedded in institutions, changing prices and failures evoke fundamental and incremental institutional changes.

Exogenous mechanisms are relevant to institutional change and influence changing conditions for institutional equilibrium by increasing innate tensions and growing contradictions (Koreh and Shalev, 2009). The unbalanced distribution of institutional returns makes institutions susceptible to change based on informed compensatory measures. Conditions of change are created by existing institutions through incremental changes to deal with market failures, controversies, etc. Institutionalized ideas of market reform are being delegitimized.

Institutional pillars based on compromises between contradictory interests and preferences can be consolidated by simultaneously generating second-order preferences. The institutional options used by actors are limited to pursue their interests. Foundational contingencies, instead of increasing returns, maintain institutional continuity among the altered interests of the actors that result from the changing conditions between the costs of continuity and the price of change.

The institutions created solve a set of problems that are often imperfectly adapted for the management of others (Hollingsworth and Streeck, 1994). Actor- and stakeholder-developed institutions embody the coordination of problem-solving trade-offs that can produce cumulative price changes and new price failures, erosion of collective goods, hiring costs under incomplete and asymmetric information, and learning disabilities (Alchian and Demsetz, 1972; Ostrom, 1990; Powell et al., 1996).

Institutional construction and change respond to the problems of market failures, bilateral and exchange-based negotiation, and the implementation of agreements (Arrow, 1963; Heimer, 1985; Williamson, 1975) and the multi-actor producer of collective goods (Olson, 1971; Ostrom, 1990). A good example of institutions that produce market failures are natural gas companies, which have difficulties in price distribution that cause shortages and overinvestment in expensive solutions (Vietor, 1994). Institutions have benefits and costs related to new systems of institution-building and their impact on groups and stakeholders that emerge as price changes alter bargaining power and incentives, producing benefits for different alternatives and breaking equilibriums when the costs of change outweigh the benefits (Greif, 1998; Caballero, 2001; Norte, 1981).

Existing institutions generate symbolic and material conditions for transformation and incremental institutional change that results in failures and controversies. Institutions create mechanisms to shift the costs of failures, vested interests, sunk costs, and the veto of threats to innovative solutions (North, 1990; Vietor, 1994; Immergut, 1992; Wilson, 1980). Comparing periods and patterns of change provides data on the conditions for fundamental and incremental changes and transformations.

Institutional resilience increases the return to be distributed among the different institutional actors to resonate with first-order preferences.

The response of States may be to take ad hoc measures to achieve gradual fundamental institutional change with weak institutional coherence that may not last long, creating a base layer for social insurance (Doron, 1998; Gal, 2004). According to Marx, institutions are their own gravediggers.

Institutional reform makes the advantages of welfare state institutions depend on their contributions to their income and control of their expenditures (Koreh, & Shalev, 2009). Non-linearities and long-term lags as hypotheses focus on returns for welfare institutions (Blyth, 2001). The institutional framework of the Swedish model has effects with the collapse of financial institutions, since the business development institutionalized by the conservatives reduced the tasks of the state that it must perform.

Initiatives to scale up institutional reform through networking contribute to building trust among stakeholders in academic and research institutions in the recognition of transdisciplinary research aimed at fostering coordinated efforts to systematically modify institutional and structural arrangements. Causality between ephemeral phenomena is difficult to demonstrate, such as institutional and cultural structures with individual decisions. Elements of the entrepreneurship ecosystem can be measured by combining data from several specific sources and datasets from formal institutions and regional venture capital, combining variables for various dimensions of the elements that are more specifically measured, such as education level and entrepreneurial skills.

Institutional solutions create and develop new relationships, interests, and capacities for strategic behavior and learning that lead to empowering actors and stakeholders by functionally channeling the use of resources and competence (Noll & Owen, 1983; Vietor, 1994). Outdated interests should not be ignored when proclaiming innovative ideas because the unclear interests of the agents when institutions are being transformed. The ideal and material aspects of institutional transformation and change are analytical approaches to institutions. Institutional change and transformation should be conceived as complementary issues to mobilize ideas and material resources. Institutional ideas are essential components of institutional change considering the material alternative.

CONCLUSIONS

The analysis of this study on environmental and institutional frameworks and their implications in entrepreneurship ecosystems concludes that both environmental and institutional factors are relevant in the formation and development of entrepreneurial ecosystems. In essence, for an entrepreneurial ecosystem to be effective, it requires a harmonious combination of both frameworks: the environmental and the institutional. In order to create an environment where companies can be born, grow and succeed in a sustainable way.

An ecosystem is a set of interactions in a biotic community beyond its complex physical environment of living and non-living components. Entrepreneurship ecosystems are the set of interconnected potential and existing entrepreneurial actors, organizations, institutions, and processes that connect, mediate, and formally and informally govern performance within the local business environment. Entrepreneurship actors are crucial in the growth of ecosystems among interactions that positively impact individual perceptions through the indirect effects of entrepreneurship, including knowledge transfer, startup spirit, and environmental resources. Business ecosystems create an enabling environment for process-driven interactions between hierarchically independent, but mutually dependent actors in identifying opportunities and exploiting resources.

Financial environments that support entrepreneurship influence national and regional economic growth. Entrepreneurship ecosystems are beyond regional territories, with start-up creation defined by self-reinforcing connections and interrelationships between attributes, transforming cultural environments and perspectives. Spin-off processes drive the growth of entrepreneurial ecosystems facilitated by environmental attributes such as networks, talent, resources, knowledge, role models, mentoring, advice, etc.

New institutional forms interact in complex ways with existing institutional arrangements to create new structures and varied processes. The conceptualization of innovative ideas changes the definition of the agents that face problems in building and developing new institutional ideas. New forms of collaboration supported by governance mechanisms in novel environments lead to the emergence of entrepreneurship. Cooperation between organizations improves efficiency in the strategic approach to the changing environmental circumstances to create conditions of cooperation in evolving business ecosystems. A more favorable socio-ecological environment can be developed through a more humane orientation for people who accept their own mistakes and the failures of others without being criticized and encouraged to try again.

The policy model for the integration of socio-intercultural entrepreneurship must be based on the best collective practices of contribution in other socio-intercultural environments, considering the legal instruments to manage socio-cultural diversity and addressing conflicts. This model of policy integration of a socio-intercultural entrepreneurship approach should aim to facilitate the design, development and implementation of socio-intercultural entrepreneurship strategies.

The impact of the environment on the innovative capabilities of serial entrepreneurs needs to be further explored. The changing global business environment provides an opportunity to formulate policies to improve institutional support for social and serial entrepreneurship practices and activities, establishing the space for entrepreneurship as a digital nomad. Research on serial entrepreneurship may require different variables and units of analysis, such as the new venture, entrepreneur, personal attributes, career, age, business education and training, previous startups, family support, startup team, environmental influences, etc.

Research must find answers to the micro foundations of institutional change and its relationship to processes, routines, resources, and capacities. Research on the micro-foundations of the entrepreneurial ecosystem should be more sensitive to the agency of actors in their own communities rather than assuming the institutional and cultural imitations of complex systems.

REFERENCES

Abolafia, M. (1996). *Making Markets: Opportunism and Restraint on Wall Street*. Harvard University Press.

Acs, Z. J., Autio, E., & Szerb, L. (2014). National systems of entrepreneurship: Measurement issues and policy implications. *Research Policy*, 43(3), 476–494. DOI: 10.1016/j.respol.2013.08.016

Acs, Z. J., Stam, E., Audretsch, D. B., & O'Connor, A. (2017). The lineages of the entrepreneurial ecosystem approach. *Small Business Economics*, 49(1), 1–10. DOI: 10.1007/s11187-017-9864-8

Ahmad, S. Z., & Xavier, S. R. (2012). Entrepreneurial environments and growth: Evidence from Malaysia GEM data. *Journal of Chinese Entrepreneurship*, 4(1), 50–69. DOI: 10.1108/17561391211200939

Al Saiqal, N. Y., Ryan, J. C., & Parcero, O. J. (2019). Entrepreneurial intention and UAE youth: Unique influencers of entrepreneurial intentions in an emerging country context. *Journal of East-West Business*, 25(2), 144–165. DOI: 10.1080/10669868.2018.1536012

Alammari, A., Khalif, A. A., & DarougI, A. A. (2019). Restructuring the Libyan economy with available and unexploited resources of the tourism sector. *Volume II*, 398.

Alchian, A., & Demsetz, H. (1972). Production, information costs and economic organization. *The American Economic Review*, 62, 777–795.

Aldrich, H., & Zimmer, C. (1986). Entrepreneurship through social networks. In Sexton, D. L., & Smilor, R. W. (Eds.), *The art and science of entrepreneurship* (pp. 3–23). Ballinger.

Alvedalen, J., & Boschma, R. (2017). A critical review of entrepreneurial ecosystems research: Towards a future research agenda. *European Planning Studies*, 25(6), 887–903. DOI: 10.1080/09654313.2017.1299694

Anagnostopoulos, I. (2018). Fintech and regtech: Impact on regulators and banks. *Journal of Economics and Business*, 100, 7–25. https://doi.org/. 07. 003DOI: 10. 1016/j.jeconbus.2018

Andrade, J. A. (2012). Universidades empreendedoras e o contexto do nordeste brasileiro. *Revista Gestão & Tecnologia*, 12(2), 4–32. DOI: 10.20397/2177-6652/2012. v12i2.368

Armanios, D. E., Eesley, C. E., Li, J., & Eisenhardt, K. M. (2017). How entrepreneurs leverage institutional intermediaries in emerging economies to acquire public resources. *transformations and transitions*, 173-197. *Strategic Management Journal*, 38(7), 1373–1390. DOI: 10.1002/smj.2575

Arner, D. W., Barberis, J., & Buckley, R. P. (2015). The evolution of Fintech: A new post-crisis paradigm. *SSRN*, 47, 1271–1315. https://heinonline.org/HOL/LandingPage?handle=hein.journals/geojintl47&div=41&id=&page=. DOI: 10.2139/ssrn.2676553

Arrow, K. (1963). Uncertainty and the welfare economics of medical care. In *Essays in the Theory of Risk Bearing*: 117–219. Chicago: Markham, 1971.

Auerswald, P., & Dani, L. (2017). Economic ecosystems. In Clarke, G., Feldman, M., Gertler, M., & Wojcik, D. (Eds.), *New Oxford Handbook of Economic Geography*. Oxford University Press.

Autio, E., George, G., & Alexy, O. (2011). International Entrepreneurship and Capability Development—Qualitative Evidence and Future Research Directions. *Entrepreneurship Theory and Practice*, 35(1), 11–37. DOI: 10.1111/j.1540-6520.2010.00421.x

Autio, E., Nambisan, S., Thomas, L. D. W., & Wright, M. (2018). Digital affordances, spatial affordances, and the genesis of entrepreneurial ecosystems. *Strategic Entrepreneurship Journal*, 12(1), 72–95. DOI: 10.1002/sej.1266

Barral, M. R. M., Ribeiro, F. G., & Canever, M. D. (2018). Influence of the university environment in the entrepreneurial intention in public and private universities. *RAUSP Management Journal*, 53(1), 122–133. DOI: 10.1016/j.rauspm.2017.12.009

Bartley, T., & Schneiberg, M. (2002). Rationality and institutional contingency: The varying politics of economic regulation in the fire insurance industry. *Sociological Perspectives*, 45(1), 47–79. DOI: 10.1525/sop.2002.45.1.47

Baum, J. R., Frese, M., Baron, R. A., & Katz, J. A. (2007). Entrepreneurship as an area of psychology study: An introduction. *The Psychology of Entrepreneurship*, 1, 18.

Bellah, R. N., Madsen, R., Sullivan, W. M., Swidler, A., & Tipton, S. M. (1991). *The good society*. Knopf.

Bird, B. (1988). Implementing entrepreneurial ideas: The case for intention. *Academy of Management Review*, 13(3), 442–453. DOI: 10.2307/258091

Blyth, M. (2001). The Transformation of the Swedish Model: Economic Ideas, Distributional Conflict, and Institutional Change. *World Politics*, 54(1), 1–26. DOI: 10.1353/wp.2001.0020

Bosma, N., Content, J., Sanders, M., & Stam, E. (2018). Institutions, entrepreneurship, and economic growth in Europe. *Small Business Economics*, 51(2), 483–499. DOI: 10.1007/s11187-018-0012-x

Brown, R., & Mason, C. (2014). Inside the high-tech black box: A critique of technology entrepreneurship policy. *Technovation*, 34(12), 773–784. DOI: 10.1016/j.technovation.2014.07.013

Brush, C. G., De Bruin, A., & Welter, F. (2009). A gender-aware framework for women's entrepreneurship. *International Journal of Gender and Entrepreneurship*, 1(1), 8–24. DOI: 10.1108/17566260910942318

Busenitz, L. W., Gomez, C., & Spencer, J. W. (2000). Country institutional profiles: Unlocking entrepreneurial phenomena. *Academy of Management Journal*, 43(5), 994–1003. DOI: 10.2307/1556423

Candeias, J., & Sarkar, S. (2022). Entrepreneurial Ecosystems and distinguishing features of effective policies–an evidence-based approach. *Entrepreneurship and Regional Development*, 34(5-6), 343–375. DOI: 10.1080/08985626.2022.2045634

Candeias, J. C., & Sarkar, S. (2024). Entrepreneurial Ecosystems Policy Formulation: A Conceptual Framework. *The Academy of Management Perspectives*, 38(1), 77–105. DOI: 10.5465/amp.2022.0047

Carbonara, E., Tran, H. T., & Santarelli, E. (2020). Determinants of novice, portfolio, and serial entrepreneurship: An occupational choice approach. *Small Business Economics*, 55(1), 123–151. DOI: 10.1007/s11187-019-00138-9

Cavallo, A., Ghezzi, A., & Balocco, R. (2019). Entrepreneurial ecosystem research: Present debates and future directions. *The International Entrepreneurship and Management Journal*, 15(4), 1291–1321. DOI: 10.1007/s11365-018-0526-3

Cetindamar, D., Gupta, V., Karadeniz, E., & Egrican, N. (2012). What the numbers tell: The impact of human, family and financial capital on women and men's entry into entrepreneurship in Turkey. *Entrepreneurship and Regional Development*, 24(1–2), 29–51. DOI: 10.1080/08985626.2012.637348

Chaney, L. H., & Martin, J. (2007). *Intercultural Business Communication* (4th ed.). Pearson Prentice Hall.

Chaudhary, S., Kaur, P., Alofaysan, H., Halberstadt, J., & Dhir, A. (2023). Connecting the dots? Entrepreneurial ecosystems and sustainable entrepreneurship as pathways to sustainability. *Business Strategy and the Environment*, 32(8), 5935–5951. DOI: 10.1002/bse.3466

Chohra, M. (2019). A critical review of the academic entrepreneurial ecosystem in developing countries: The case of Algeria. *International Journal of Technology Management & Sustainable Development*, 18(3), 243–259. DOI: 10.1386/tmsd_00008_1

Corbett, A. C. (2007). Learning asymmetries and the discovery of entrepreneurial opportunities. *Journal of Business Venturing*, 22(1), 97–118. DOI: 10.1016/j.jbusvent.2005.10.001

Coviello, N. E., & Jones, M. V. (2004). Methodological issues in international entrepreneurship research. *Journal of Business Venturing*, 19(4), 485–508. DOI: 10.1016/j.jbusvent.2003.06.001

Covin, J. G., & Slevin, D. P. (1989). Strategic management of small firms in hostile and benign environments. *Strategic Management Journal*, 10(1), 75–87. DOI: 10.1002/smj.4250100107

Dancin, M. T., Dancin, D. A., & Tracey, P. (2011). Social Entrepreneurship: A Critique and Future Directions. *Organization Science*, 22(5), 1203–1213. DOI: 10.1287/orsc.1100.0620

Davidson, E., & Vaast, E. (2010). *Digital entrepreneurship and its sociomaterial enactment* 2010 43rd Hawaii International Conference on System Sciences, IEEE (2010), pp. 1-10

Di Zhang, D., & Bruning, E. (2011). Personal characteristics and strategic orientation: Entrepreneurs in Canadian manufacturing companies. *International Journal of Entrepreneurial Behaviour & Research*, 17(1), 82–103. DOI: 10.1108/13552551111107525

Dobbin, F. (1994). *Forging Industrial Policy*. Cambridge University Press. DOI: 10.1017/CBO9781139174183

Doran, J., McCarthy, N., & O'Connor, M. (2018). The role of entrepreneurship in stimulating economic growth in developed and developing countries. *Cogent Economics & Finance*, 6(1), 1442093. DOI: 10.1080/23322039.2018.1442093

Doron, A. (1998) The Introduction of Supplementary Means Tested Benefits: A Breach in the Universality of the National Insurance Old Age Pension System' (in Hebrew). In Ginosar, P. (ed) *Iyunim Betkumat Yisrael [Studies in Zionism, the Yishuv and the State of Israel: A Research Annual]* Vol. 8, Sede Boqer, The Ben Gurion Research Center, pp. 398 –423.

Eisenhardt, K. M., & Schoonhoven, C. B. (1990). Organizational growth: Linking founding team, strategy, environment, and growth among US semiconductor ventures, 1978-1988. *Administrative Science Quarterly*, 35(3), 504–529. DOI: 10.2307/2393315

Elia, G., Margherita, A. & Passiante, G. (2020). Digital entrepreneurship ecosystem: how digital technologies and collective intelligence are reshaping the entrepreneurial process. *Technol. Forecast. Soc. Chang.,* 150 (2020), Article 119791

Farrukh, M., Lee, J. W. C., & Shahzad, I. A. (2019). Intrapreneurial behavior in higher education institutes of Pakistan: The role of leadership styles and psychological empowerment. *Journal of Applied Research in Higher Education*, 11(2), 273–294. DOI: 10.1108/JARHE-05-2018-0084

Feldman, M. P. (2001). The entrepreneurial event revisited: Firm formation in a regional context. *Industrial and Corporate Change*, 10(4), 861–891. DOI: 10.1093/icc/10.4.861

Fritsch, M. (2013). New business formation and regional development: A survey and assessment of the evidence. *Foundations and Trends in Entrepreneurship*, 9(13), 249–364. DOI: 10.1561/0300000043

Fritsch, M., & Wyrwich, M. (2014). The long persistence of regional levels of entrepreneurship: Germany, 1925–2005. *Regional Studies*, 48(6), 955–973. DOI: 10.1080/00343404.2013.816414

Gal, J. (2004). *Social Security in Israel.* Magnes Press. (in Hebrew)

Giudici, A., Reinmoeller, P., & Ravasi, D. (2018). Open-system orchestration as a relational source of sensing capabilities: Evidence from a venture association. *Academy of Management Journal*, 61(4), 1369–1402. DOI: 10.5465/amj.2015.0573

Greif, A. (1998). Self-enforcing political systems and economic growth: Late medieval Genoa. In Bates, R., Greif, A., Levi, M., Rosenthal, J. L., & Weingast, B. (Eds.), *Analytical Narratives: 23–63.* Princeton University Press. DOI: 10.2139/ssrn.49207

Greve, H. (1995). Jumping ship: The diffusion of strategy abandonment. *Administrative Science Quarterly*, 40(3), 444–473. DOI: 10.2307/2393793

Guerrero, M., Liñán, F., & Cáceres-Carrasco, F. R. (2021). The influence of ecosystems on the entrepreneurship process: A comparison across developed and developing economies. *Small Business Economics*, 57(4), 1733–1759. DOI: 10.1007/s11187-020-00392-2

Harrison, R. T., & Leitch, C. (2010). Voodoo institution or entrepreneurial university? Spin-off companies, the entrepreneurial system and regional development in the UK. *Regional Studies*, 44(9), 1241–1262. DOI: 10.1080/00343400903167912

Hechavarría, D. M., & Ingram, A. E. (2019). Entrepreneurial ecosystem conditions and gendered national-level entrepreneurial activity: A 14-year panel study of GEM. *Small Business Economics*, 53(2), 431–458. DOI: 10.1007/s11187-018-9994-7

Heimer, C. (1985). *Reactive Risk and Rational Action: Managing Moral Hazard in Insurance Contracts*. University of California Press. DOI: 10.1525/9780520318465

Hofstede, G. (2001). *Cultures and Organizations*. Software of the Mind. McGraw-Hill.

Hollingsworth, J. R. & Wolfgang Streeck (1994). Countries and sectors: Concluding remarks on performance, convergence, and competitiveness. In J. R. Hollingsworth, P. Schmitter, and W. Streeck (eds.), *Governing Capitalist Economies*: 270–300. Oxford: Oxford University Press.

Immergut, E. (1992). The rules of the game: The logic of health policymaking in France, Switzerland, and Sweden. In S. Steinmo, Kathleen Thelen, and Frank Longstreth (eds.), *Structuring Politics*: 57–89. Cambridge, UK: Cambridge University Press.

Ipiranga, A. S. R., Freitas, A. A. F., & Paiva, D. (2010). O empreendedorismo acadêmico no contexto da interação universidade-empresa-governo. *Cadernos EBAPE*, 8(4), 676-693. https://doi.org/DOI: 10.1590/s1679-39512010000400000

Jaén, I., Fernandez-Serrano, J., & Francisco, L. (2013). Valores culturales, nivel de ingresos y actividad emprendedora. *Revista de Economía Mundial*, 35, 35–52.

Johnson, D., Bock, A. J., & George, G. (2019). Entrepreneurial dynamism and the built environment in the evolution of university entrepreneurial ecosystems. *Industrial and Corporate Change*, 28(4), 941–959. DOI: 10.1093/icc/dtz034

Johnson, D., Gianiodis, P., Harrison, R., & Bock, A. (2022). From laboratory to clinic: Science commercialization within university-centered entrepreneurial ecosystems. *R&D Management*. online first. DOI: 10.1111/radm.12535

Juma, N., Olabisi, J., & Griffin-EL, E. (2023). External enablers and entrepreneurial ecosystems: The brokering role of the anchor tenant in capacitating grassroots ecopreneurs. *Strategic Entrepreneurship Journal*, 17(2), 372–407. DOI: 10.1002/sej.1462

Jung, K., Eun, J.-H., & Lee, S.-H. (2017). Exploring competing perspectives on government-driven entrepreneurial ecosystems: Lessons from centres for creative economy and innovation (CCEI) of South Korea. *European Planning Studies*, 25(5), 827–847. . 2017.1282083DOI: <ALIGNMENT.qj></ALIGNMENT>10. 1080/ 09654313

Kahle, J. H., Marcon, É., Ghezzi, A., & Frank, A. G. (2020). Smart Products value creation in SMEs innovation ecosystems. *Technological Forecasting and Social Change*, 156, 120024. DOI: 10.1016/j.techfore.2020.120024

Kirby, D. (2006). Creating entrepreneurial universities in the UK: Applying entrepreneurship theory to practice. *The Journal of Technology Transfer*, 31(5), 599–603. DOI: 10.1007/s10961-006-9061-4

Knight, J. (2001). Explaining the rise of neoliberalism: The mechanisms of institu-tional change. In Campbell, J., & Perderson, O. (Eds.), *The Rise of Neoliberalism and the Institutional Analysis: 27-50*. Princeton University Press. DOI: 10.1515/9780691188225-006

Koreh, M., & Shalev, M. (2009, October). Dialectics of institutional change: The transformation of social insurance financing in Israel. *Socio-economic Review*, 7(4), 553–584. DOI: 10.1093/ser/mwp018

Kraus, S., Palmer, C., Kailer, N., Kallinger, F. L., & Spitzer, J. (2018). Digital entrepreneurship: A research agenda on new business models for the twenty-first century. *International Journal of Entrepreneurial Behaviour & Research*, 25(2), 353–375. DOI: 10.1108/IJEBR-06-2018-0425

Kshetri, N. (2009). Entrepreneurship in post-socialist economies: A typology and institutional contexts for market entrepreneurship. *Journal of International Entrepreneurship*, 7(3), 236–259. DOI: 10.1007/s10843-009-0039-9

Kshetri, N. (2010). Business perceptions of regulative institutions in Central and Eastern Europe. *Baltic Journal of Management*, 5(3), 356–377. DOI: 10.1108/17465261011079758

Kuckertz, A. (2019). Let's take the entrepreneurial ecosystem metaphor seriously! *Journal of Business Venturing Insights*, 11, e00124. DOI: 10.1016/j.jbvi.2019.e00124

Leblebici, H., Salancik, G., Copay, A., & King, T. (1991). Institutional change and the transformation of interorganizational fields: An organizational history of the U.S. broadcasting industry. *Administrative Science Quarterly*, 36(3), 333–363. DOI: 10.2307/2393200

Leong, B., Wee, A. K. S., & Yuen-Ping, H. (2008). Is an enterprise framework necessary for an entrepreneurial university? A comparison of technology start-ups in Singapore and Sweden. *Science & Public Policy*, 35(9), 647–656. DOI: 10.3152/030234208X287038

Li, J., Li, J., Zhu, X., Yao, Y., & Casu, B. (2020). Risk spillo-vers between FinTech and traditional financial institutions: Evidence from the US. *International Review of Financial Analysis*, 71, 101544. https://doi.org/. 101544DOI: 10. 1016/j.irfa.2020

Li, Y., & Zahra, S. A. (2012). Formal institutions, culture, and venture capital activity: A cross-country analysis. *Journal of Business Venturing*, 27(1), 95–111. DOI: 10.1016/j.jbusvent.2010.06.003

Lorenz, M. P., Ramsey, J. R., & Richey, R. G.Jr. (2018). Expatriates' international opportunity recognition and innovativeness: The role of metacognitive and cognitive cultural intelligence. *Journal of World Business*, 53(2), 222–236. DOI: 10.1016/j.jwb.2017.11.004

Magnuson, W. (2018). Regulating Fintech. *Vanderbilt Law Review*, 71(4), 1167-1226. https://heinonline. org/HOL/ Landi ngPage? handle= hein. journ als/ vanlr 71& div= 33&id=&page=

Malecki, E. J. (2018). Entrepreneurship and entrepreneurial ecosystems. *Geography Compass*, 12(3), e12359. DOI: 10.1111/gec3.12359

Manolova, T. S., Eunni, R. V., & Gyoshev, B. S. (2008). Institutional environments for entrepreneurship: Evidence from emerging economies in Eastern Europe. *Entrepreneurship Theory and Practice*, 32(1), 203–218. DOI: 10.1111/j.1540-6520.2007.00222.x

Marvel, M. R. (2013). Human capital and search–based discovery: A study of high–tech entrepreneurship. *Entrepreneurship Theory and Practice*, 37(2), 403–419. DOI: 10.1111/j.1540-6520.2011.00465.x

Mason, C., Cooper, S., & Harrison, R. (2002). Venture capital and high technology clusters: the case of Ottawa. In Oakey, R., During, W., & Kauser, S. (Eds.), *New Technology-Based Firms in the New Millennium* (Vol. II, pp. 261–278). Pergammon.

Molla, A., & Biru, A. (2023). The evolution of the Fintech entrepreneurial ecosystem in Africa: An exploratory study and model for future development, *Technological Forecasting and Social Change*, 186. *Technological Forecasting and Social Change*, 122123, 122123. Advance online publication. DOI: 10.1016/j.techfore.2022.122123

Motoyama, Y., & Knowlton, K. (2016). From Resource Munificence to Ecosystem Integration: The Case of GovernmentSponsorship in St. Louis. *Entrepreneurship and Regional Development*, 28(5–6), 448–470. DOI: 10.1080/08985626.2016.1186749

Noll, R., & Owen, B. (1983). *The Political Economy of Deregulation*. American Enterprise Institute.

North, D. (1981). *Structure and Change in Economic History*. W. W. Norton.

North, D. (1990). *Institutions, Institutional Change and Economic Performance*. Cambridge University. DOI: 10.1017/CBO9780511808678

OECD. (2014). *Entrepreneurial ecosystems and growth oriented entrepreneurship*. https://www.oecd.org/cfe/leed/Entrepreneurial-ecosystems.pdf

Olson, M. (1971). *The Logic of Collective Action*. Harvard University Press.

Öner, M. A., & Kunday, Ö. (2016). A study on Schumpeterian and Kirznerian entrepreneurship in Turkey: 2006–2013. *Technological forecasting and social change*, 102(2), 62–71. https://doi.org/. techfore.2015. 09. 005DOI: 10. 1016/ j

Ostgaard, T. A., & Birley, S. (1994). Personal networks and firm competitive strategy: A strategic or coincidental match? *Journal of Business Venturing*, 9(4), 281–305. DOI: 10.1016/0883-9026(94)90009-4

Ostrom, E. (1990). *Governing the Commons*. Cambridge, UK: Cambridge University Press. Perugini, F. (2023). Space–time analysis of entrepreneurial ecosystems. *The Journal of Technology Transfer*, 48(1), 240–291.

Porras-Paez, A., & Schmutzler, J. (2019). Orchestrating an entrepreneurial ecosystem in an emerging country: The lead actor's role from a social capital perspective. *Local Economy*, 34(8), 767–786. DOI: 10.1177/0269094219896269

Powell, W., Koput, k. & Smith-Doerr, L. (. (1996). Technological change and the locus of innovation: Networks of learning in biotechnology. *Administrative Science Quarterly*, 41, 116–145. DOI: 10.2307/2393988

Qian, H., Acs, Z. J., & Stough, R. R. (2013). Regional systems of entrepreneurship: The nexus of human capital, knowledge and new firm formation. *Journal of Economic Geography*, 13(4), 559–587. DOI: 10.1093/jeg/lbs009

Reynolds, P., Bosma, N., Autio, E., Hunt, S., De Bono, N., Servais, I., Lopez-Garcia, P., & Chin, N. (2005). Global entrepreneurship monitor: Data collection design and implementation 1998–2003. *Small Business Economics*, 24(3), 205–231. DOI: 10.1007/s11187-005-1980-1

Rotefoss, B., & Kolvereid, L. (2005). Aspiring, nascent and fledgling entrepreneurs: An investigation of the business start-up process. *Entrepreneurship and Regional Development*, 17(2), 109–127. DOI: 10.1080/08985620500074049

Saxenian, A. (1994). *Regional Competitive Advantage: culture and competition in Silicon Valley and Route* (Vol. 128). Harvard University Press.

Schmutzler, J., Andonova, V., & Diaz-Serrano, L. (2019). How context shapes entrepreneurial self-efficacy as a driver of entrepreneurial intentions: A multi-level approach. *Entrepreneurship Theory and Practice*, 43(5), 880–920. DOI: 10.1177/1042258717753142

Sennett, R. (1998). *The corrosion of character*. Norton.

Shane, S., & Venkataraman, S. (2000). The promise of entrepreneurship as a field of research. *Academy of Management Review*, 25(1), 217–226. https://www.jstor.org/stable/259271. DOI: 10.5465/amr.2000.2791611

Shriberg, M. (2002). Institutional assessment tools for sustainability in higher education: Strengths, weaknesses, and implications for practice and theory. *International Journal of Sustainability in Higher Education*, 3(3), 254–270. DOI: 10.1108/14676370210434714

Slevin, D. P., & Covin, J. G. (1990). New venture strategic posture, structure, and performance: An industry life cycle analysis. *Journal of Business Venturing*, 5(2), 123–135. DOI: 10.1016/0883-9026(90)90004-D

Sobel, R. S. (2008). Testing Baumol: Institutional quality and the productivity of entrepreneurship. *Journal of Business Venturing*, 23(6), 641–655. DOI: 10.1016/j.jbusvent.2008.01.004

Sperber, S., & Linder, C. (2019). Gender-specifics in start-up strategies and the role of the entrepreneurial ecosystem. *Small Business Economics*, 53(2), 533–546. DOI: 10.1007/s11187-018-9999-2

Spigel, B. (2017). The Relational Organization of Entrepreneurial Ecosystems. *Entrepreneurship Theory and Practice*, 41(1), 49–72. DOI: 10.1111/etap.12167

Spigel, B., & Harrison, R. (2018). Toward a process theory of entrepreneurial ecosystems. *Strategic Entrepreneurship Journal*, 12(1), 151–168. DOI: 10.1002/sej.1268

Stahl, G. K., & Maznevski, M. L. (2021). Unraveling the effects of cultural diversity in teams: A retrospective of research on multicultural work groups and an agenda for future research. *Journal of International Business Studies*, 52(1), 4–22. DOI: 10.1057/s41267-020-00389-9 PMID: 33487775

Stam, E. (2015). Entrepreneurial ecosystems and regional policy: A sympathetic critique. *European Planning Studies*, 23(9), 1759–1769. DOI: 10.1080/09654313.2015.1061484

Stam, E., & Van de Ven, A. (2021). Entrepreneurial Ecosystem Elements. *Small Business Economics*, 56(2), 809–832. DOI: 10.1007/s11187-019-00270-6

Steigertahl, L., & Mauer, R. (2023). Investigating the success factors of the Nordic entrepreneurial ecosystem – talent transformation as a key process. *International Journal of Entrepreneurship and Innovation*, 24(1), 7–18. DOI: 10.1177/14657503211051217

Stuart, R., & Abetti, P. A. (1987). Start-up ventures: Towards the prediction of initial success. *Journal of Business Venturing*, 2(3), 215–230. DOI: 10.1016/0883-9026(87)90010-3

Sullivan, W. M. (1995). *Work and integrity: The crisis and promise of professionalism in America.* HarperGoUins.

Thelen, K. (2003). How Institutions Evolve: Insights from Comparative-Historical Analy-sis. In Mahoney, J., & Rueschemeyer, D. (Eds.), *Comparative Historical Analysis in the Social Sciences* (pp. 208–239). Cambridge University Press. DOI: 10.1017/CBO9780511803963.007

Theobald, H., & Hampel, S. (2013). Radical Institutional Change and Incremental Transformation: Long-Term Care Insurance in Germany. In Ranci, C., & Pavolini, E. (Eds.), *Reforms in Long-Term Care Policies in Europe*. Springer., DOI: 10.1007/978-1-4614-4502-9_6

Theodoraki, C., & Catanzaro, A. (2021). Widening the borders of entrepreneurial ecosystem through the international lens. *The Journal of Technology Transfer*. Advance online publication. DOI: 10.1007/s10961-021-09852-7

Thomas, A. S., & Mueller, S. L. (2000). A case for comparative entrepreneurship: Assessing the relevance of culture. *Journal of International Business Studies*, 31(2), 287–301. DOI: 10.1057/palgrave.jibs.8490906

Thornton, P. (2002). The rise of the corporation in a craft industry: Conflict and conformity in institutional logics. *Academy of Management Journal*, 45(1), 81–101. DOI: 10.2307/3069286

Torres, P., & Godinho, P. (2022). Levels of necessity of entrepreneurial ecosystems elements. *Small Business Economics*, 59(1), 29–45. DOI: 10.1007/s11187-021-00515-3

Townley, B. (2002). The role of competing rationalities in institutional change. *Academy of Management Journal*, 45(1), 163–179. DOI: 10.2307/3069290

Tula, S. T., Ofodile, O. C., Okoye, C. C., Nifise, A. O. A., & Odeyemi, O. (2024). Entrepreneurial ecosystems in the USA: A comparative review with European models. *International Journal of Management & Entrepreneurship Research*, 6(2), 451–466. DOI: 10.51594/ijmer.v6i2.799

Venkatraman, N. (1989). The concept of fit in strategy research: Toward verbal and statistical correspondence. *Academy of Management Review*, 14(3), 423–444. DOI: 10.2307/258177

Vietor, R. (1994). *Contrived Competition: Regulation and Deregulation in America*. Belknap. DOI: 10.4159/harvard.9780674436794

Wei, Y. (2022). Regional governments and opportunity entrepreneurship in under-developed institutional environments: An entrepreneurial ecosystem perspective. *Research Policy*, 51(1), 104380. DOI: 10.1016/j.respol.2021.104380

Wielemaker, M., & Gedajlovic, E. (2011). Governance and capabilities: Asia's entrepreneurial performance and stock of venture forms. *Asia Pacific Journal of Management*, 28(1), 75–185. DOI: 10.1007/s10490-010-9221-9

Williamson, O. (1975). *Markets and Hierarchies*. Free.

Wilson, J. Q. (1980). The politics of regulation. In Wilson, J. Q. (Ed.), *The Politics of Regulation: 357-394*. Basic Books.

Woollard, D. (2010). Towards a theory of university entrepreneurship. *Industry and Higher Education*, 24(6), 413–427. DOI: 10.5367/ihe.2010.0017

Yang, F., & Yang, M. M. (2023). Examining motivation of IT vendors to share knowledge with clients. *International Journal of Information Management*, 71, 102646. DOI: 10.1016/j.ijinfomgt.2023.102646

Yun, J. J., Lee, M., Park, K., & Zhao, X. (2019). Open innovation and serial entrepreneurs. *Sustainability (Basel)*, 11(18), 5055. DOI: 10.3390/su11185055

Zaheer, H., Breyer, Y. & Dumay, J. (2019). Digital entrepreneurship: an interdisciplinary structured literature review and research agenda. *Technol. Forecast. Soc. Chang.*, 148 (2019), Article 119735.

Zaiţ, D. (2002). *Management intercultural. Valorizarea diferenţelor culturale*. Editura Economică.

Zhao, H., & Seibert, S. (2006). The big five personality dimensions and entrepreneurial status: A meta- analytical review. *The Journal of Applied Psychology*, 91(2), 259–271. DOI: 10.1037/0021-9010.91.2.259 PMID: 16551182

Zilber, T. (2002). Institutionalization as an interplay between actions meanings, and actors: The case of a rape crisis center in Israel. *Academy of Management Journal*, 45(1), 234–254. DOI: 10.2307/3069294

Chapter 5
Sustainable Social Entrepreneurship Development:
The Role of Artificial Intelligence

Akhilesh Chandra Prabhakar
https://orcid.org/0000-0002-1061-6509
University of Technology, Lae, Papua New Guinea

ABSTRACT

The intersection of social entrepreneurship and artificial intelligence (AI) presents a promising avenue for addressing pressing social and environmental challenges while fostering sustainable development. This abstract explores the evolving landscape of social entrepreneurship development and the transformative potential of AI in catalyzing positive change. By examining the role of AI in enhancing the effectiveness, scalability, and impact of social enterprises, this study aims to shed light on the opportunities and challenges inherent in leveraging AI for social good.

INTRODUCTION

Social entrepreneurship has become a powerful tool for driving social innovation and tackling long-standing societal issues. Unlike traditional businesses that prioritize profit above all else, social enterprises place equal importance on creating positive social or environmental impact while ensuring financial sustainability. However, scaling the impact of these enterprises can be challenging due to factors such as resource limitations, restricted market access, and scalability issues. Overcoming

DOI: 10.4018/979-8-3693-4338-8.ch005

these obstacles requires innovative solutions and collaborative efforts to maximize the reach and effectiveness of social entrepreneurship initiatives.

Artificial intelligence has indeed revolutionized the way social enterprises operate by leveraging technologies like machine learning, natural language processing, and predictive analytics. These tools can greatly enhance efficiency and effectiveness in areas such as impact measurement, resource allocation, market analysis, and stakeholder engagement. The potential for AI to drive positive change in the realm of social entrepreneurship is truly exciting.

AI-driven innovations have indeed opened up new possibilities for improving various aspects of society. By leveraging AI technology, social entrepreneurs can address complex challenges more effectively and create sustainable impact on a larger scale. From healthcare and education to agriculture and environmental conservation, AI-powered solutions are transforming the way essential services are accessed and decision-making processes are enhanced. This democratization of access and empowerment of marginalized communities are key benefits of integrating AI into social entrepreneurship efforts.

It is important to acknowledge the challenges and ethical considerations that come with integrating AI into social entrepreneurship. Algorithmic bias, data privacy concerns, and unequal access to AI technologies can indeed exacerbate disparities and hinder inclusive development outcomes. The high costs and technical expertise required for AI implementation also pose significant barriers for many social enterprises, especially those in resource-constrained settings. Addressing these issues will be crucial for ensuring that AI benefits all members of society equitably.

Taking a multi-stakeholder approach that emphasizes ethical AI development and collaboration among various groups is crucial in addressing these challenges. By investing in capacity-building initiatives, offering funding and mentorship opportunities, and forming partnerships with academia and the private sector, we can promote the adoption and integration of AI technologies in the social entrepreneurship sector. This inclusive approach will help drive innovation and create a positive impact in our communities.

The combination of social entrepreneurship and artificial intelligence has the potential to create a significant positive impact on a global scale. By utilizing AI technology, social entrepreneurs can drive innovation, increase their impact, and promote inclusive growth. It is crucial to address ethical, technical, and socio-economic factors to ensure that AI-driven solutions benefit all members of society. By carefully considering these aspects, we can work towards a more sustainable and equitable future.

AI has indeed revolutionized the landscape of social entrepreneurship by offering innovative solutions to complex societal challenges. Through data-driven insights and advanced technologies like machine learning and robotics, social entrepreneurs can enhance the effectiveness and scalability of their interventions. The democratization of AI tools has made them more accessible to grassroots organizations, empowering communities and fostering local innovation. However, it is crucial to address ethical and regulatory concerns such as data privacy and algorithmic bias to ensure that AI-driven initiatives uphold principles of fairness and inclusivity. By collaborating and sharing knowledge, social entrepreneurs can harness the power of AI responsibly to drive sustainable impact and advance inclusive development agendas.

AIMS & SCOPE

Social entrepreneurship is a field that focuses on addressing social, environmental, and economic challenges through innovative business models. While there are significant opportunities for positive impact, social entrepreneurs also encounter various obstacles in their efforts to create meaningful change. It is important to recognize and navigate these challenges to effectively drive positive social change.

Artificial Intelligence (AI) holds immense potential in transforming various sectors, including social entrepreneurship. The aims and scope of AI in social entrepreneurship encompass a wide range of objectives aimed at leveraging technology to address social, environmental, and economic challenges while creating sustainable and impactful solutions. Here's a closer look at the aims and scope:

Enhancing Efficiency and Effectiveness: AI technologies such as machine learning, natural language processing, and predictive analytics can enhance the efficiency and effectiveness of social entrepreneurship initiatives. By automating repetitive tasks, analyzing large datasets, and extracting insights, AI enables organizations to optimize their operations, allocate resources more efficiently, and make data-driven decisions.

Identifying and Understanding Social Problems: AI tools can help social entrepreneurs identify and understand complex social problems by analyzing diverse sources of data, including social media, government records, and sensor data. By applying techniques such as sentiment analysis and network analysis, AI can uncover hidden patterns, trends, and correlations, providing valuable insights into the root causes of social issues.

Designing Tailored Interventions: AI enables social entrepreneurs to design tailored interventions that are better aligned with the needs and preferences of their target beneficiaries. By analyzing individual preferences, behaviours, and socioeconomic characteristics, AI-powered systems can personalize services, recommendations, and support mechanisms, thereby increasing their relevance and impact.

Improving Access to Services: AI can improve access to essential services, such as healthcare, education, and financial inclusion, especially in underserved communities. Chatbots, virtual assistants, and mobile applications powered by AI technologies can provide personalized support, deliver educational content, and facilitate access to critical resources, overcoming barriers such as geographic distance and language barriers.

Facilitating Collaboration and Networking: AI platforms can facilitate collaboration and networking among social entrepreneurs, organizations, and stakeholders. By connecting individuals with similar interests, expertise, and resources, AI-powered platforms can foster knowledge sharing, collective problem-solving, and collaboration on joint initiatives, amplifying the impact of social entrepreneurship efforts.

Promoting Sustainability and Scalability: AI can help social entrepreneurs build sustainable and scalable solutions by optimizing resource utilization, predicting future trends, and identifying growth opportunities. By leveraging AI for impact measurement and evaluation, organizations can demonstrate their effectiveness, attract funding, and replicate successful models in new contexts, thereby expanding their reach and influence.

Ethical and Inclusive AI Deployment: Given the potential risks and ethical considerations associated with AI deployment, social entrepreneurs need to prioritize ethical and inclusive practices. This includes ensuring transparency, accountability, and fairness in AI algorithms and decision-making processes, as well as addressing biases and safeguarding privacy rights to promote trust and acceptance among beneficiaries and stakeholders.

The aims and scope of AI in social entrepreneurship are vast and multifaceted, ranging from enhancing operational efficiency and effectiveness to designing tailored interventions, improving access to services, fostering collaboration, promoting sustainability, and ensuring ethical deployment. By harnessing the power of AI technologies responsibly, social entrepreneurs can unlock new opportunities to address complex social challenges and create positive social change at scale.

STRATEGIES & METHODOLOGY OF SDGs

Facilitating international investment in small and medium-sized enterprises (SMEs) possesses the latent capacity to profoundly bolster the attainment of sustainable development goals (SDGs) by catalyzing economic growth, engendering job creation, fostering innovation, and fostering social inclusion. The avenues through which this unfolds are manifold:

- Economic Growth and Job Creation: SMEs serve as pivotal engines propelling economic growth and job generation, particularly within developing realms. International investment in SMEs catalyzes economic dynamism by affording access to capital, technology, and markets, thereby nurturing entrepreneurial endeavours, amplifying productive capacities, and engendering avenues for gainful employment. Sustainable economic expansion stands as a cornerstone in realizing SDG 8 (Decent Work and Economic Growth) and SDG 1 (No Poverty).
- Innovation and Technological Advancement: SMEs assume a pivotal role in propelling innovation and technological strides, thereby fostering heightened productivity, bolstering competitiveness, and sustainable development. International investment injects SMEs with the requisite resources and acumen to pioneer innovation and embrace novel technologies, thereby precipitating the emergence of sustainable solutions across sectors encompassing renewable energy, healthcare, agriculture, and education, thus championing the cause of SDG 9 (Industry, Innovation, and Infrastructure).
- Social Inclusion and Poverty Reduction: SMEs harbour the potential to engender social inclusion and abate poverty by affording opportunities to marginalized cohorts, comprising women, youth, and individuals with disabilities. International investment lends support to SMEs helmed or patronized by underrepresented demographics, facilitating access to financial resources, markets, and capacity-building endeavours. By fostering inclusive economic expansion and entrepreneurial pursuits, SMEs substantiate the aspirations enshrined in SDG 5 (Gender Equality) and SDG 10 (Reduced Inequalities).
- Environmental Sustainability: International investment channelled into SMEs serves as a harbinger of sustainable business practices and ecological stewardship, thereby furthering the objectives outlined in SDG 12 (Responsible Consumption and Production) and SDG 13 (Climate Action). By buttressing green SMEs and advocating for sustainable supply chains, investors can instigate strides toward resource efficiency, waste minimization, and the adoption of clean technologies, thus mitigating environmental repercussions and advancing sustainable development.
- Access to Finance and Markets: The pervasive dearth of access to financial resources poses a formidable obstacle for myriad SMEs, notably within developing spheres. International investment serves as a conduit, endowing SMEs with access to capital, financial services, and global markets, thereby enabling scale expansion, clientele diversification, and global competitiveness. Augmented access to financial capital and global markets underscores the aims enshrined in SDG 8 (Decent Work and Economic Growth) and SDG 9 (Industry, Innovation, and Infrastructure).

- Capacity Building and Knowledge Transfer: International investors oftentimes bring to the table a trove of expertise, networks, and best practices that can redound to the benefit of SMEs, spanning realms such as management, marketing, and technology. Through symbiotic partnerships, mentorship endeavours, and skill enhancement initiatives, international investors can bolster the capacity of SMEs, fortifying their resilience, competitive edge, and sustainability, thereby aligning with the tenets of SDG 4 (Quality Education) and SDG 17 (Partnerships for the Goals).

Promoting international investment in SMEs harbours the potential to profoundly advance the attainment of sustainable development goals by galvanizing economic growth, job creation, innovation, social inclusion, and environmental sustainability. By fortifying SMEs with access to financial capital, global markets, capacity-building initiatives, and technology infusion, international investors can unleash the transformative force of entrepreneurship, thereby imprinting a lasting positive impact on a global scale.

Mitigating the pervasive investment policy bias directed towards large multinational enterprise (MNE) groups, both in home and host countries, necessitates a multifaceted strategy incorporating policy interventions, regulatory frameworks, and collaborative efforts among stakeholders. Below are several strategies aimed at remedying this bias:

- Foster Fair Competition: Enforce policies and regulations geared towards fostering fair competition and establishing a level playing field for all enterprises, irrespective of their size. This could entail stringent enforcement of antitrust laws, curbing monopolistic practices, and ensuring transparency in government procurement procedures.
- Incentivize SME Investment: Introduce incentives, tax incentives, and financial support schemes specifically tailored to incentivize investment in small and medium-sized enterprises (SMEs). This might encompass offering grants, loans, or subsidies aimed at bolstering SME development, fostering research and innovation, or facilitating export initiatives.
- Streamline Regulatory Processes: Simplify and streamline regulatory procedures, licensing requirements, and administrative obligations for SMEs, thereby facilitating their establishment and operations both domestically and internationally. This may entail reducing bureaucratic hurdles, eliminating redundant paperwork, and enhancing access to vital information and resources.
- Enhance Access to Finance: Augment access to financial resources for SMEs by establishing specialized funding channels, venture capital pools, and microfinance initiatives tailored to the unique needs of small-scale enterprises.

This could involve instituting government-backed loan programs, guarantee schemes, or angel investor networks to furnish SMEs with the requisite capital.

- Facilitate Internationalization: Aid SMEs in expanding their footprint on the global stage by furnishing assistance with market research, export promotion, trade missions, and networking avenues. This may encompass establishing entities such as trade promotion agencies, export credit institutions, and business incubators geared towards facilitating SME entry into foreign markets.
- Cultivate Skills and Capacity: Invest in skills enhancement programs, training initiatives, and capacity-building endeavours aimed at enhancing SME competitiveness in the international arena. This might entail providing technical aid, management training, and mentorship programs to assist SMEs in enhancing their productivity, efficiency, and competitiveness.
- Advocate Responsible Business Practices: Encourage MNEs to embrace responsible business practices encompassing corporate social responsibility (CSR) initiatives, ethical supply chain management, and environmental sustainability measures. This could entail offering incentives for MNEs to exhibit dedication to social and environmental causes while holding them accountable for their actions.
- Foster Collaboration: Stimulate collaboration and synergies between MNEs and SMEs to leverage their respective strengths and resources. This could involve establishing supplier development schemes, technology transfer accords, and joint ventures between large corporations and smaller enterprises aimed at fostering innovation and knowledge exchange. By implementing these strategic imperatives, policymakers can endeavour to mitigate the entrenched investment policy bias towards large MNE groups, fostering a more conducive environment for SME development and expansion, both domestically and on the global stage. This, in turn, holds the potential to engender more inclusive and sustainable economic growth, spur job creation, and alleviate poverty.

The pivotal role of small and medium-sized enterprises (SMEs) in developing countries, and interregional foreign direct investment (FDI) is underscored by their substantive contributions to economic growth, job creation, technology dissemination, and regional cohesion. Several salient facets of their involvement merit attention:

- Driving Economic Growth: SMEs situated in burgeoning economies are increasingly assuming prominence as substantial conduits for FDI across regions. These entities often wield distinctive competitive advantages, epitomized by their nimbleness, adaptability, and nuanced grasp of local market dynamics, thereby affording them the acumen to discern and seize investment prospects within neighbouring jurisdictions or regional spheres.

- Fostering Regional Integration: SMEs serve as linchpins in bolstering regional economic amalgamation through the establishment of transnational alliances, collaborative ventures, and interlinked supply chains. By forging symbiotic ties with SMEs situated in adjacent territories or regional enclaves, enterprises can unlock access to nascent markets, pool resources, and harness economies of scale, thereby engendering a climate conducive to trade, investment, and economic synergy.
- Facilitating Technology Transfer: SMEs actively engaged in Global South,and interregional FDI channels serve as conduits for the transference of technology, expertise, and operational paradigms across national or regional borders. Through strategic investments in or partnerships with local enterprises, both multinational corporations (MNEs) and SMEs can effectuate the dissemination of cutting-edge technologies, managerial proficiencies, and innovative frameworks, thus fostering industrial upgradation, skill proliferation, and technology diffusion.
- Creating Employment Opportunities: SMEs constitute primary engines fueling employment generation in burgeoning economies, commanding a substantial share of aggregate employment across numerous jurisdictions. By venturing into novel markets or regional domains, SMEs can engender employment prospects, augment labour productivity, and contribute to poverty alleviation and societal advancement, particularly in rural hinterlands and marginalized enclaves.
- Promoting Sustainable Development: SMEs actively participating in South-South and interregional FDI initiatives wield the potential to underpin sustainable development agendas by championing inclusive growth, environmental stewardship, and corporate conscientiousness. Through adherence to ethical business precepts, adherence to local statutes, and proactive community engagement, SMEs can curtail adverse environmental and societal repercussions while accentuating positive economic and developmental outcomes.
- Enhancing Resilience and Diversification: SMEs embroiled in South-South and interregional FDI ventures can fortify the resilience and diversification of their operational frameworks by venturing into unexplored markets and mitigating reliance on singular markets or suppliers. By broadening their geographical footprint and clientele, SMEs can offset risks attendant to political volatility, economic downturns, or supply chain disruptions.
- Supporting Entrepreneurship and Innovation: SMEs enmeshed in South-South and interregional FDI endeavours can galvanize entrepreneurship and innovation by fostering a dynamic business ecosystem and propagating

knowledge spillage. Through strategic investments in research and development, technology assimilation, and market expansion, SMEs can catalyze innovation, entrepreneurial vigour, and economic dynamism across regional demarcations.

SMEs wield an indelible imprint on South-South and interregional foreign direct investment endeavours, propelling economic growth, nurturing regional cohesion, catalyzing technology dissemination, fostering employment, advocating sustainability, fortifying resilience and diversification, and nurturing entrepreneurial ingenuity and innovation. Policymakers, corporate leaders, and other stakeholders are enjoined to discern and harness the transformative potential of SMEs in driving inclusive and sustainable development across regional landscapes.

Maximizing the developmental impact of small and medium enterprises (SMEs) overseas investment necessitates a holistic approach that addresses myriad challenges while capitalizing on available opportunities. Below are several strategies delineating ways and means to realize this objective:

- Capacity Building: Facilitate support for capacity-building endeavours aimed at augmenting the competencies and competitiveness of SMEs endeavouring to venture overseas. This may entail provisioning training initiatives, technical aid, and mentorship programs to equip SMEs with the requisite acumen to navigate international markets adeptly, comprehend regulatory frameworks, and manage cross-border operations efficaciously.
- Access to Finance: Enhance SMEs' access to finance for overseas investment endeavours by instituting specialized funding mechanisms, venture capital pools, and financial instruments tailored to their distinct requirements. This might encompass extending loan guarantees, export credit insurance, or risk-sharing facilities to assuage apprehensions regarding perceived risks inherent in international expansion endeavours.
- Market Intelligence and Information: Facilitate access to market intelligence, information dissemination channels, and networking platforms to aid SMEs in identifying promising investment prospects and prospective collaborators in target markets. This could entail establishing trade promotion agencies, export assistance hubs, and digital platforms furnishing real-time market insights, business matchmaking services, and regulatory guidance.
- Policy Support: Cultivate an enabling policy milieu incentivizing and bolstering SMEs' overseas investment while remaining congruent with overarching developmental imperatives. This could encompass offering tax incentives, effecting regulatory reforms, and promulgating investment promotion initiatives aimed at encouraging SME involvement in sectors yielding high

developmental dividends, such as renewable energy, agriculture, healthcare, and infrastructure.

- Partnerships and Networking: Foster symbiotic partnerships and networking avenues between SMEs, multinational enterprises (MNEs), development agencies, and ancillary stakeholders to harness synergies, pool resources, and exchange expertise. This might entail fostering business consortia, industry clusters, and public-private collaborations that facilitate knowledge dissemination, technology transfer, and market penetration for SMEs.
- Corporate Social Responsibility (CSR) Initiatives: Encourage SMEs engaged in overseas investment to embed corporate social responsibility (CSR) precepts into their strategic frameworks and operational modalities. This could encompass supporting initiatives geared toward environmental sustainability, social inclusivity, and ethical business practices, spanning community development initiatives, equitable labour standards, and environmental conservation efforts.
- Risk Management: Furnish support for risk mitigation and management strategies to aid SMEs in navigating the vicissitudes and uncertainties inherent in overseas investment ventures. This might involve extending insurance products, political risk assurances, and dispute resolution mechanisms aimed at safeguarding SME investments and fortifying their resilience in foreign markets.
- Monitoring and Evaluation: Institute robust mechanisms for monitoring and evaluating the developmental impact of SMEs' overseas investments to engender accountability, transparency, and iterative learning. This could encompass conducting impact assessments, tracking key performance metrics, and soliciting stakeholder feedback to gauge the efficacy of support interventions and pinpoint areas warranting refinement. By deploying these stratagems, policymakers, development entities, and associated stakeholders can optimize the developmental impact of SMEs' overseas investments, thereby fostering inclusive and sustainable economic expansion, job creation, technology transfer, and poverty mitigation across both origin and destination nations.

SURVEY OF LITERATURE

An analysis of existing literature demonstrates an increasing number of studies delving into the merging of artificial intelligence with the advancement of social entrepreneurship.

The research conducted by Schulte, M., & Avgerou, C. (2017) highlights the crucial role of AI-driven analytics in evaluating and measuring the impact of social entrepreneurship initiatives. Utilizing AI-powered tools enables organizations to track outcomes, evaluate effectiveness, and improve accountability, ultimately enhancing their ability to create lasting social impact.

Furthermore, the literature emphasises the importance of innovation and solution design in addressing social challenges, as demonstrated in studies like that of Howaldt, J., & Schwarz, M. (2018). AI technologies such as machine learning and natural language processing present new opportunities for social entrepreneurs to develop scalable and adaptable solutions that meet the needs of underserved communities.

Inclusive access and empowerment are key themes in the literature, as shown in research by Ahuja, M., & Duggan, A. (2020). AI-powered technologies have the potential to bridge digital divides, increase access to essential services, and empower marginalized groups, leading to greater socio-economic inclusion and reduced disparities in resource access.

The ethical implications of integrating AI into social entrepreneurship are extensively discussed in the literature, with studies like that of Mittelstadt, B. D., & Floridi, L. (2016) emphasizing the importance of ethical guidelines and responsible AI practices. It is crucial to address biases, privacy concerns, and unintended consequences associated with AI algorithms, especially in contexts involving vulnerable populations.

Collaboration and ecosystem building are highlighted as essential components in utilizing AI for social entrepreneurship development, as indicated in research by Westley, F., & Antadze, N. (2017). Partnerships between social entrepreneurs, technology experts, policymakers, and other stakeholders can drive collective action, promote knowledge sharing, and facilitate systemic change, opening up new possibilities for tackling societal challenges.

The analysis of various writings on the intersection of Artificial Intelligence and Social Entrepreneurship Development emphasizes the significant impact AI can have on promoting sustainable social change. Through the ethical and collaborative utilization of AI technologies, social entrepreneurs have the opportunity to create innovative solutions, expand their reach, and tackle critical societal issues, ultimately fostering positive transformation and inclusive growth.

CONCEPTUAL FRAMEWORKS

Social entrepreneurship embodies a venture dedicated to the pursuit of social interests, intertwining production, distribution, and consumption processes in a manner where production, risks, and profits are communalized (Howaldt, 2018). It epitomizes a domain where entrepreneurs tailor their endeavours to directly align with the overarching aim of advancing societal welfare. Put differently, the primary objectives of social entrepreneurship entail fostering social equity alongside fostering self-reliance and sustainability (Schulte, 2017).

In the pursuit of capital accumulation and technological progress, particularly within developing nations, there has been a notable inclination toward incentivizing foreign direct investment (FDI) from multinational corporations (MNCs). However, MNCs often exhibit a failure to comprehend local dynamics, merely imposing their production schemes to maximize their profit margins, often falling short of optimal efficiency thresholds, thus accentuating the necessity for indigenous societal or entrepreneurial interventions. A widely accepted notion further suggests that for sustainable economic growth to materialize, resource allocation in production should be dictated by consumption priorities as revealed through the valuation of productive outputs.

Production frameworks reliant on institutional interventions necessitate resource consumption beyond that dedicated solely to goods and services production, thus manifesting inefficiencies over the long haul. From the economic doctrines espoused by Adam Smith to the theories propounded by Joseph Schumpeter, a consensus among economists prevails, asserting that privately-owned entrepreneurship operating within a framework of free competition, epitomized by laissez-faire conditions, serves as the primary engine propelling economic growth. This is achieved through the dual aims of capital formation and accumulation, which ultimately foster scientific and technological innovations, concurrently driving enhancements in production methodologies aimed at cost minimization and quality maximization, thereby optimizing individual profit margins. Within this trajectory of economic evolution, four principal trends emerge financialization, digitalization, privatization and corporatization, and marketization, along with the globalization of economies over the preceding three decades.

Technological advancement, especially within developing nations, transcends mere frontier innovation, extending to the adaptation of existing products and processes to achieve heightened productivity levels congruent with local contexts. Central to this process is the accessibility of technological knowledge by local enterprises, pivotal in shaping their capacity to deliver products and services essential for elevating living standards and fostering growth and competitiveness.

Economic development, often concentrated geographically and socially, tends to be urban-centric, accentuating pursuits primarily geared towards enhancing international trade for private corporate entities to maximize profits through enhanced competitiveness and liberalization. However, this oligopolistic-driven globalization has markedly exacerbated worldwide poverty, malnutrition, income disparities, unemployment, and environmental degradation.

Addressing poverty mandates a multifaceted strategy encompassing a focus on basic societal needs, human rights entitlements, sustainable natural resource management, and inclusive economic development across all sectors, spanning agriculture, manufacturing, and services, including healthcare and education. Only through the adoption of a multi-capability approach can employment opportunities be created, concurrently preserving individuals' freedoms and choices.

Contrarily, the Marxist school posits that the root cause of inequality, poverty, unemployment, underdevelopment, and unsustainability stems from the exploitation inherent in privately owned entrepreneurialism. In this context, social entrepreneurs assume a pivotal role in tackling critical social challenges, driven by their unwavering commitment to enhancing societal well-being. Within the local economy, the spectrum of occupations engaging the rural poor spans a diverse array, encompassing agriculture labour, small/marginal cultivators, and various artisanal pursuits. A network of collective enterprises, grounded in principles of worker cooperatives, epitomizes a potent avenue for empowering the rural poor, facilitating collective decision-making and surplus appropriation. Under competitive paradigms, self-employed small producers must coalesce not only to access resources but also to emerge as multi-sectoral collectives, fostering cooperative production endeavours. Recognizing the imperative of economies of scale in overcoming adverse competition, the rural poor must consciously amalgamate resources and capabilities to elevate the scale and scope of their collective production apparatus. Such a transformation is indispensable for surmounting barriers hindering the adoption of sophisticated technologies, thereby enhancing competitiveness within local markets.

The local economy, envisaged as a block-level, multi-sectoral network, necessitates the creation of community-based production units, fostering a symbiotic nexus encompassing production, distribution, and consumption at the grassroots level. This endeavour demands the establishment of viable large-scale production systems predicated on local resources, capabilities, and market dynamics through concerted organizational and scientific and technological endeavours, buttressed by active community participation spanning all facets of decision-making.

Strengthening interconnections among existing occupational cohorts and organizations represents a strategic imperative for advancing the local economy, premised on enhancing local value addition, entailing the linkage of primary and secondary production and the technological enhancement of extant occupations. To mitigate inter-producers' competition and augment resource and market access, concerted efforts must be directed towards organizing landless labourers, artisans, and impoverished peasants into area-based multi-sectoral large-scale production systems.

MAIN CHALLENGES

Resource Constraints: Limited access to funding, human capital, and infrastructure poses a significant challenge for social entrepreneurs. Unlike traditional for-profit ventures, social enterprises may struggle to attract investment due to perceived risks or lack of financial returns. This constraint can impede their ability to scale operations and reach underserved communities effectively.

- Sustainability: Balancing social impact with financial sustainability is a perennial challenge for social entrepreneurs. Achieving financial viability while prioritizing social or environmental objectives requires careful management of revenue streams, cost structures, and organizational priorities. Sustaining operations over the long term amidst fluctuating market conditions and funding landscapes adds complexity to the equation.
- Measuring Impact: Assessing and communicating the social impact of initiatives poses challenges due to the intangible nature of social outcomes and the lack of standardized metrics. Social entrepreneurs often struggle to demonstrate their effectiveness to stakeholders, including investors, donors, and beneficiaries, leading to difficulties in securing funding and support.
- Regulatory Hurdles: Social enterprises may encounter regulatory barriers and bureaucratic red tape that hinder their operations. Complex legal frameworks, licensing requirements, and compliance obligations can create administrative burdens and limit the scalability of innovative solutions, particularly in sectors such as healthcare, education, and finance.
- Market Dynamics: Competing in established markets dominated by traditional profit-driven enterprises can be daunting for social entrepreneurs. Limited brand recognition, distribution channels, and market penetration may pose challenges in gaining traction and achieving market competitiveness, especially in sectors with entrenched incumbents.

OPPORTUNITIES

Innovation: Social entrepreneurship thrives on innovation, offering opportunities to develop novel solutions to pressing societal challenges. By leveraging technology, creative business models, and collaborative approaches, social entrepreneurs can pioneer transformative solutions that address unmet needs and create positive social change.

- Partnerships & Collaboration: Collaborative partnerships with governments, NGOs, corporations, and community stakeholders can amplify the impact of social entrepreneurship initiatives. By leveraging complementary resources, expertise, and networks, social entrepreneurs can scale their impact, access new markets, and drive systemic change more effectively.
- Market Demand: Growing consumer awareness and demand for socially responsible products and services present opportunities for social entrepreneurs to tap into emerging markets. Increasingly, consumers are seeking products and brands that align with their values, creating market opportunities for ethical and sustainable businesses that prioritize social impact alongside profitability.
- Policy & Advocacy: Social entrepreneurs can leverage advocacy and policy initiatives to create an enabling environment for social innovation and entrepreneurship. By advocating for supportive policies, regulatory reforms, and funding mechanisms, they can address systemic barriers, mobilize resources, and catalyze broader societal change.
- Impact Investing: The rise of impact investing and socially responsible finance offers new avenues for funding social entrepreneurship ventures. Impact investors, philanthropic foundations, and social finance institutions are increasingly allocating capital to enterprises that generate measurable social and environmental returns alongside financial profitability, unlocking funding opportunities for social entrepreneurs.

While social entrepreneurship faces myriad challenges, it also presents abundant opportunities for driving positive change and creating sustainable impact (Ahuja, 2020). By embracing innovation, collaboration, and advocacy, social entrepreneurs can overcome obstacles, leverage market dynamics, and unlock transformative solutions to address some of the world's most pressing challenges.

AI IMPLICATIONS FOR SUSTAINABLE DEVELOPMENT

There is a vast potential for Artificial Intelligence to advance sustainable development goals. AI can indeed offer innovative solutions to complex challenges in environmental conservation, social equity, and economic prosperity. Some ways AI can contribute to sustainable development include optimizing resource management, predicting and mitigating environmental risks, enhancing healthcare access, and promoting inclusive economic growth.

- Environmental Conservation and Resource Management: AI technology has the potential to revolutionize environmental monitoring and conservation efforts by providing valuable insights and predictions based on data analysis. By leveraging AI algorithms to analyze satellite imagery, track deforestation, monitor wildlife populations, and assess changes in ecosystems, we can better understand and protect our environment. Additionally, smart resource management systems powered by AI can optimize energy consumption, water usage, and waste management, leading to more efficient and sustainable utilization of resources in both urban and rural areas. This innovative use of AI can help us make more informed decisions and take proactive steps towards a greener and more sustainable future.
- Climate Change Mitigation and Adaptation: AI technologies like machine learning play a crucial role in analyzing climate data and informing climate change mitigation strategies. By utilizing AI-driven climate models, policymakers, businesses, and communities can develop adaptive measures and resilience-building strategies to address the challenges posed by climate change. Additionally, AI-enabled precision agriculture techniques can assist farmers in optimizing crop yields, reducing inputs, and mitigating the environmental impact of agriculture, ultimately contributing to climate-smart agricultural practices. It's exciting to see how AI is being leveraged to tackle such important global issues.
- Renewable Energy Integration: AI algorithms play a crucial role in optimizing the integration of renewable energy sources like solar and wind power into existing energy grids. By forecasting energy demand, optimizing energy production, and improving grid stability, AI-driven energy management systems help facilitate the transition to a low-carbon energy system. This technology is essential in creating a more sustainable and efficient energy infrastructure for the future.
- Social Equity and Inclusive Development: AI-powered tools have the potential to revolutionize access to essential services in underserved communities. By leveraging technologies like telemedicine platforms, personalized learn-

ing systems, and mobile banking solutions, we can bridge the digital divide and promote inclusive development. Additionally, initiatives like chatbots for mental health support and job-matching platforms for marginalized populations can play a crucial role in addressing social inequalities and empowering individuals to access opportunities for economic and social advancement.

- Economic Growth and Innovation: AI-driven innovation indeed has the potential to bring about significant positive impacts on economic growth, job creation, and social entrepreneurship (Mittelstadt, 2016). By leveraging AI technologies, startups and technology hubs can foster innovation ecosystems that attract investment, talent, and expertise, ultimately supporting sustainable development initiatives. Additionally, the optimization of business processes and enhancement of productivity through AI can lead to the unlocking of new markets, further contributing to sustainable economic development while minimizing environmental impact.
- Data-driven Decision Making and Governance: AI-enabled data analytics have the potential to revolutionize decision-making processes and governance across different sectors by providing valuable insights from large datasets. It's crucial to address ethical and regulatory challenges to ensure that AI-driven initiatives uphold principles of fairness and transparency. By using AI responsibly and collaboratively, stakeholders can leverage its transformative power to advance sustainable development goals and create a more equitable and resilient future for everyone. AI has the capability to transform social entrepreneurship in rural areas by providing innovative solutions to complex problems and promoting sustainable development. By leveraging AI technologies, social entrepreneurs can access valuable insights, optimize resource allocation, and create impactful initiatives that benefit local communities. The potential for AI to revolutionize social entrepreneurship in rural areas is truly exciting and holds great promise for driving positive change.
- **Data Analysis and Decision Making:** AI plays a crucial role in empowering social entrepreneurs to make informed decisions and create impactful solutions for rural communities. By leveraging AI technology to collect and analyze data from various sources, entrepreneurs can gain valuable insights that can drive positive change and address the specific needs of rural areas. This data-driven approach not only enhances efficiency but also enables more targeted and effective resource allocation. Overall, AI serves as a powerful tool for social entrepreneurs to make a meaningful difference in rural communities.
- **Precision Agriculture:** Precision agriculture is indeed a field where AI is making remarkable progress. By harnessing the power of AI tools like drones, sensors, and predictive analytics, farmers can enhance their crop yields, re-

duce resource wastage, and better manage risks related to weather variability. AI algorithms play a crucial role in analyzing soil conditions, tracking crop development, and offering valuable recommendations to farmers. This not only boosts agricultural productivity but also fosters sustainable farming practices in rural communities. It's exciting to see how AI is revolutionizing the agricultural sector for the betterment of all involved.

- **Access to Healthcare:** AI-driven telemedicine platforms have the potential to greatly improve healthcare accessibility in rural areas with limited access to traditional healthcare facilities. By leveraging AI-powered diagnostic tools and chatbots, patients can receive timely medical advice and support from healthcare professionals remotely. This not only helps in accurate diagnosis and treatment planning but also reduces disparities in healthcare delivery, ultimately leading to better health outcomes for individuals in remote areas.
- **Education and Skill Development:** AI-based educational technologies have the potential to revolutionize education in rural communities by providing personalized learning experiences and skill development opportunities. Virtual tutors and adaptive learning platforms can help bridge the gap in access to quality education, while AI-driven skill development programs can empower rural youth to thrive in their communities. By leveraging these technologies, we can indeed democratize education and create more opportunities for economic growth and development in rural areas.
- **Environmental Conservation:** AI technology has indeed revolutionized the way we can monitor and protect natural resources in rural areas. By leveraging AI-powered systems to analyze satellite imagery, we can effectively track deforestation, detect illegal logging activities, and assess wildlife habitats. This real-time environmental insight allows conservation organizations and policymakers to implement targeted interventions and sustainable land management practices, ultimately safeguarding biodiversity and ecosystem services for rural communities dependent on natural resources. It's truly remarkable how AI can contribute to the preservation of our planet's precious resources.
- **Financial Inclusion:** AI-powered fintech solutions have the potential to greatly benefit rural areas by providing tailored banking services, assessing creditworthiness through alternative data sources, and offering personalized financial advice through chatbots and mobile apps. By leveraging AI in a responsible and culturally sensitive manner, social entrepreneurs can drive inclusive growth and empower underserved populations to participate in the formal economy. It's essential to consider the unique dynamics of rural communities to ensure that AI initiatives truly make a positive impact on financial inclusion and overall development outcomes. Artificial Intelligence (AI) is

increasingly playing a pivotal role in strengthening social entrepreneurship in China, particularly in addressing societal challenges, fostering economic development, and promoting equality.

PERFORMANCE & EFFICIENCY

AI-driven social entrepreneurship initiatives in China have demonstrated high performance by effectively addressing social challenges with innovative solutions. For instance, platforms like Ant Financial's Sesame Credit utilize AI algorithms to assess creditworthiness, enabling efficient lending to individuals and small businesses. Efficiency is enhanced through automation and optimisation of processes in sectors such as healthcare, finance, and logistics. AI-powered systems streamline operations, reduce manual labour, minimize errors, and increase productivity.

COMPETITIVENESS

Chinese social entrepreneurship leveraging AI has enhanced the competitiveness of domestic firms in both local and global markets. Companies like Tencent, Alibaba, and Baidu have developed AI technologies and platforms that rival those of international counterparts. AI-driven innovations enable Chinese enterprises to offer cutting-edge products and services, gaining a competitive edge in various industries such as e-commerce, fintech, and telecommunications.

- Welfare and Contribution to GDP: AI-driven social entrepreneurship contributes to improving the welfare of Chinese citizens by providing access to essential services, enhancing healthcare outcomes, and promoting financial inclusion. The contribution of AI-driven social entrepreneurship to China's GDP is significant, as these initiatives drive economic growth through increased productivity, innovation, and value creation across various sectors.
- Exports: Chinese AI companies are increasingly exporting AI technologies, products, and services to global markets. For instance, companies like Huawei, SenseTime, and DJI have expanded their international presence by exporting AI-powered solutions in areas such as telecommunications, facial recognition, and drones. AI-driven social entrepreneurship enhances China's export competitiveness by offering advanced technologies and innovative solutions that cater to global demand.
- Income Generation and Employment Creation: AI-driven social entrepreneurship initiatives (Westley, 2017) generate income opportunities for in-

dividuals and businesses by creating new markets, facilitating e-commerce, and enabling innovative business models. Moreover, AI adoption stimulates demand for skilled labour, driving employment growth in technology-related fields such as software development, data analysis, and AI research.

Social entrepreneurship leveraging AI in China has demonstrated strong performance, efficiency, competitiveness, and welfare enhancement. These initiatives make significant contributions to Chinese GDP and exports while generating income and creating employment opportunities, thereby driving sustainable economic and social development. Continued support and investment in AI-driven social entrepreneurship are crucial for furthering China's innovation capabilities and promoting inclusive growth. China has witnessed a burgeoning ecosystem of social entrepreneurship, with numerous organizations and initiatives dedicated to addressing various social and environmental challenges while also pursuing sustainable business models.

Some of the existing social entrepreneurship ventures are in China across different sectors:

- Xiaohongshu (Little Red Book): Xiaohongshu is a social commerce platform that combines user-generated content with e-commerce. It allows users to discover and purchase products recommended by other users, influencers, and brands. The platform focuses on lifestyle, fashion, beauty, and travel, empowering users to share their experiences and recommendations.
- Leping Social Entrepreneur Foundation: Leping Social Entrepreneur Foundation supports social entrepreneurship in China by providing funding, mentorship, and networking opportunities to social enterprises. It aims to foster innovation and sustainable development while addressing social and environmental challenges.
- Yihaodian: Yihaodian is an e-commerce platform that specializes in selling groceries and daily necessities online. It focuses on providing convenient and affordable access to quality products, particularly in underserved areas. Yihaodian also emphasizes environmental sustainability by promoting green packaging and eco-friendly products.
- Mingyian: Mingyian is a social enterprise that promotes rural development and poverty alleviation through agricultural initiatives. It works with farmers to improve agricultural productivity, quality standards, and market access. Mingyian also provides training and support to empower rural communities and enhance their livelihoods.
- BabyTree: BabyTree is a parenting and family-focused online platform that provides information, resources, and community support to parents. It offers content on pregnancy, childcare, education, and health, catering to the needs

of new and expecting parents. BabyTree also features e-commerce services for baby products and services.

- Xinhehui (New Farmers' Club): Xinhehui is a social enterprise that promotes sustainable agriculture and rural development in China. It operates community-based agricultural cooperatives that engage farmers in organic farming practices, agricultural training, and cooperative marketing. Xinhehui aims to improve farmers' incomes and living standards while promoting environmental conservation.
- Taobao Village: Taobao Village is an initiative by Alibaba Group that supports rural e-commerce development in China. It empowers rural entrepreneurs and farmers to sell their products online through Alibaba's e-commerce platforms, such as Taobao and Tmall. Taobao Village revitalizes rural economies, creates employment opportunities, and fosters inclusive growth.
- Robin Hood Army China: Robin Hood Army China is a volunteer-driven organization that addresses food insecurity and hunger by redistributing surplus food to those in need. Volunteers collect excess food from restaurants, hotels, and events and distribute it to homeless shelters, orphanages, and low-income communities. The organization operates in multiple cities across China, leveraging technology and community partnerships to maximize impact.
- Green Monday China: Green Monday China promotes sustainable and plant-based eating habits to improve health and reduce environmental impact. It offers vegetarian and vegan food options, educational programs, and advocacy campaigns to raise awareness about the benefits of plant-based diets. Green Monday China collaborates with restaurants, schools, and corporate partners to promote healthier and more sustainable food choices.
- BaishanCloud: BaishanCloud is a tech-driven social enterprise that provides cloud computing and content delivery services while prioritizing environmental sustainability. It leverages renewable energy sources and energy-efficient infrastructure to minimize its carbon footprint. BaishanCloud also supports environmental conservation projects and initiatives to address climate change.

These are just a few examples of the diverse and innovative social entrepreneurship ventures in China. They demonstrate the growing trend of leveraging business models for social impact, addressing pressing social and environmental issues, and contributing to sustainable development in the country. However, social entrepreneurship plays a significant role in China's economy by addressing social issues while also contributing to economic development. While exact figures on GDP share may not be readily available, we can understand the impact of social entrepreneurship in China by looking at various sectors where it operates:

- Healthcare: Social enterprises in China are addressing gaps in healthcare access and affordability. They provide medical services, healthcare products, and innovative solutions to improve health outcomes, contributing indirectly to economic productivity by keeping the workforce healthy.
- Education: Social entrepreneurship in education focuses on improving access to quality education, especially in rural and underserved areas. Initiatives include educational technology platforms, tutoring programs, and scholarships, which contribute to human capital development and long-term economic growth.
- Environmental Sustainability: Social enterprises in China are tackling environmental challenges such as pollution, resource depletion, and climate change. By promoting sustainable practices, developing clean technologies, and raising awareness, they contribute to environmental conservation, which has economic benefits in terms of resource efficiency and resilience.
- Financial Inclusion: Social enterprises in China are working to expand access to financial services for underserved populations, including rural communities and small businesses. By providing microfinance, mobile banking, and insurance products, they promote financial inclusion and empower individuals to participate more fully in the economy.
- Employment Generation: Social enterprises create job opportunities, particularly for disadvantaged groups such as women, minorities, and people with disabilities. By offering vocational training, skills development, and employment placement services, they contribute to poverty reduction and social stability, which in turn supports economic growth.

While the exact contribution of social entrepreneurship to China's GDP may be challenging to quantify, its impact on various aspects of economic and social development is significant. As social entrepreneurship continues to grow and evolve in China, it is expected to play an increasingly important role in shaping the country's economic future and promoting sustainable development.

SOCIAL ENTREPRENEURSHIP: CASE STUDY OF PAPUA NEW GUINEA

Social entrepreneurship has emerged as a viable alternative to traditional entrepreneurship, presenting a platform for societal advancement and the empowerment of marginalized sections of society and economic sectors in Papua New Guinea. Multi-sectoral Social Entrepreneurship transcends mere philanthropy, emphasizing the utilization of local resources at their origin by indigenous populations.

This approach aims to minimize unnecessary transportation costs while fostering community-driven development.

CHALLENGES & OPPORTUNITIES OF SOCIAL ENTREPRENEURSHIP IN PNG

Throughout history, physical and human resources have often been exploited by the elites of society, leading to imbalances and challenges. In Papua New Guinea (PNG), the intricate ecosystems comprising sea water, forestry land, agricultural land, livestock, and people are intricately intertwined, particularly in mountain farming systems. However, burgeoning population growth and the marginalization of agroecosystems have placed immense pressure on natural resources, compelling local communities to sustain themselves. To address these challenges, it is imperative to disseminate technologies about natural resource utilization and conservation, particularly in the agricultural sector. Research institutions, including the prominent University of Technology (UoT) in Papua New Guinea, play a pivotal role in developing such technologies. However, effective extension programs are necessary to ensure the accessibility of these technologies to marginalized farmers. Feedback from stakeholders regarding social acceptability, financial viability, replicability, and region-specific modifications is crucial for the success of these initiatives.

Rural areas in PNG encounter a myriad of obstacles including poor institutional support, lack of skills, inadequate infrastructure, and environmental degradation. Government-led development programs often adopt a top-down planning approach, lacking participatory mechanisms and quality control measures necessary for sustainable impact. Agriculture, livestock, fisheries, and forests form the backbone of Papua New Guinean societies, providing sustenance and livelihoods to rural communities. The symbiotic relationship between these sectors cannot be overstated, with agriculture serving as a form of mixed farming and forests serving as a vital resource for fuel, fodder, and construction materials. The existing socio-economic-cultural institutions in Papua New Guinea are deeply intertwined with customary tenure-based land ownership systems. Leveraging these social institutions forms the foundation of social entrepreneurship initiatives. Strengthening Multi-sectoral Production Systems Networks through existing social institutions facilitates community acceptance and adoption of these initiatives.

The analysis of farming systems in project areas reveals a pattern of constraints and opportunities. Poor institutional support and skills, inadequate water management practices, and degradation of forest health are among the key challenges faced by rural communities. Collective action, efficient resource management, and innovative solutions are imperative to overcome these obstacles and promote sustainable rural development in Papua New Guinea.

Social entrepreneurship in Papua New Guinea (PNG) presents an intriguing paradigm of innovative strategies geared towards tackling social, environmental, and economic hurdles while fostering positive impacts. Delving into the realm of social entrepreneurship in PNG unveils a profound narrative, exemplified by a notable case study:

CASE STUDY: THE PNG TRIBAL FOUNDATION

The PNG Tribal Foundation stands as a prominent exemplar of social entrepreneurship in Papua New Guinea. Established by Gary Juffa, a Papua New Guinean luminary in politics and conservation, the foundation is dedicated to safeguarding the cultural legacy and ancestral wisdom of PNG's indigenous tribes, all the while championing sustainable development and environmental stewardship.

- Mission and Objectives: At the core of the PNG Tribal Foundation lies a mission to empower indigenous communities through avenues such as education, healthcare, and economic prospects, while safeguarding their cultural essence and natural endowments. Endeavouring to mitigate a myriad of challenges confronting indigenous populations, ranging from poverty and educational disparities to health inequities and environmental degradation, the foundation strives for holistic upliftment.
- Initiatives and Impact: Cultural Preservation: A cornerstone of the foundation's endeavours lies in the preservation and propagation of the rich cultural tapestry of PNG's indigenous tribes. This entails initiatives encompassing the documentation of traditional wisdom, revitalization efforts for indigenous languages, and the orchestration of cultural exchange platforms. By venerating and conserving indigenous heritage, the foundation fosters communal resilience and fosters a sense of identity.
- Education and Capacity Building: The PNG Tribal Foundation extends educational opportunities and capacity-building initiatives to bolster the agency of indigenous youth and communities. This encompasses scholarships, vocational training initiatives, and literacy campaigns aimed at enhancing educational accessibility and augmenting livelihood prospects.
- Healthcare Access: Recognizing the healthcare exigencies prevailing in remote indigenous enclaves, the foundation spearheads initiatives aimed at enhancing healthcare accessibility. These endeavors encompass the establishment of medical facilities, mobile health brigades, and health education

programs, thereby catalyzing improved health outcomes and enhancing quality of life.

- Environmental Conservation: In tandem with indigenous communities, the PNG Tribal Foundation remains steadfast in its commitment to environmental conservation and sustainable development. This translates into endeavors aimed at biodiversity preservation, ecosystem restoration, and the advocacy for sustainable land management practices, thereby fortifying both cultural and ecological resilience.

Challenges and Opportunities:

- Resource Constraints: The PNG Tribal Foundation, akin to myriad social enterprises, grapples with resource constraints, spanning funding limitations and logistical hurdles in reaching remote outposts.
- Cultural Sensitivity: Navigating the delicate equilibrium between preserving cultural legacies and fostering contemporary development mandates meticulous engagement with cultural nuances and community sensibilities.
- Policy and Advocacy: To amplify its impact, the foundation actively engages in policy advocacy and forges partnerships with governmental entities, non-governmental organizations, and international stakeholders, endeavouring to address systemic impediments and cultivate an ecosystem conducive to social entrepreneurship and community development in PNG.

In essence, the PNG Tribal Foundation epitomizes the transformative potential of social entrepreneurship in effectuating positive change across Papua New Guinea. By addressing multifaceted challenges and empowering indigenous communities whilst safeguarding cultural heritage, the foundation underscores the pivotal role of social entrepreneurship in steering sustainable development and inclusive growth in PNG, thereby exemplifying a beacon of hope amidst complex socio-economic landscapes.

AN OVERVIEW OF COCOA PRODUCTION & CHOCOLATE MANUFACTURING IN PNG

Cocoa production and chocolate manufacturing in Papua New Guinea (PNG) represent a significant sector of the country's economy, offering opportunities for economic development, rural livelihoods, and value addition.

- **Cocoa Production:** Cocoa is one of PNG's major agricultural commodities, with the country being renowned for producing high-quality cocoa beans.

The majority of cocoa production in PNG takes place in the East Sepik, Madang, Morobe, and East New Britain provinces. Smallholder farmers, often in rural areas, cultivate cocoa on small plots of land using traditional farming methods.

- **Quality and Flavor Profiles:** PNG cocoa is known for its unique flavour profiles, characterized by fruity, floral, and nutty notes. This distinctive taste is attributed to the country's diverse microclimates, fertile soils, and genetic diversity of cocoa varieties, including Criollo, Trinitario, and Forastero.
- **Sustainability Initiatives:** Various initiatives are underway to promote sustainable cocoa production in PNG, including certification programs such as Fairtrade and Rainforest Alliance. These programs aim to improve farmer livelihoods, promote environmental conservation, and ensure ethical labour practices within the cocoa supply chain.
- **Government Support:** The PNG government provides support to the cocoa sector through policy interventions, research and extension services, and infrastructure development. Efforts are made to enhance productivity, quality, and market access for cocoa farmers, including the establishment of cocoa fermentaries and drying facilities.
- **Challenges:** Despite its potential, the PNG cocoa sector faces several challenges, including ageing cocoa trees, limited access to agricultural inputs, pest and disease pressures (such as cocoa pod borer), inadequate infrastructure, and market volatility. These challenges can hinder productivity, quality, and competitiveness in the global cocoa market.
- **Chocolate Manufacturing:** While cocoa production is well-established in PNG, chocolate manufacturing is relatively nascent. However, there is growing interest in adding value to cocoa beans domestically by processing them into chocolate products. Some local companies and cooperatives are involved in chocolate manufacturing, producing artisanal and premium chocolates for both domestic and export markets.
- **Economic Opportunities:** The development of a local chocolate manufacturing industry holds the potential for creating additional economic opportunities, generating employment, and capturing more value along the cocoa value chain. By processing cocoa beans domestically, PNG can retain more of the economic benefits within the country and diversify its agricultural exports.
- **Market Access:** Accessing international markets for PNG chocolate products may require investments in branding, marketing, and distribution channels to differentiate products and meet consumer preferences. Leveraging PNG's reputation for high-quality cocoa beans can be a strategic advantage in marketing PNG chocolate products globally.

Cocoa production and chocolate manufacturing in Papua New Guinea represent important sectors with significant potential for economic development and value addition. By addressing challenges and seizing opportunities along the cocoa value chain, PNG can further harness the benefits of its cocoa industry for sustainable growth and rural livelihood improvement.

Figure 1. Entrepreneurs standing with cocoa

SOCIAL ENTREPRENEURSHIP: CASE STUDY OF BRAZIL

Social entrepreneurship in Brazil has gained significant momentum in recent years, driven by a growing recognition of the role of business in addressing social and environmental challenges. Brazil, with its vast economic disparities and complex social issues, has become fertile ground for innovative solutions that combine profit generation with positive social impact. Here's an overview of the social entrepreneurship landscape and performance in Brazil:

- Addressing Inequality and Poverty: Brazil faces significant challenges related to inequality, poverty, and access to basic services. Social entrepreneurs in the country are addressing these issues through various initiatives focused on economic inclusion, education, healthcare, and housing. For example, enterprises like Gerando Falcões work to empower marginalized communities through education and job training programs, helping individuals break the cycle of poverty and achieve economic self-sufficiency.

- Environmental Conservation and Sustainable Development: Brazil is home to the Amazon rainforest, a vital ecosystem that plays a crucial role in global climate regulation. Social entrepreneurs in Brazil are leading efforts to promote environmental conservation and sustainable development in the region. Initiatives such as Instituto Socioambiental (ISA) work with indigenous communities to protect their land rights and preserve biodiversity, while startups like ReciclAção focus on waste management and recycling to reduce environmental impact.
- Promoting Entrepreneurship and Innovation: Brazil has a vibrant startup ecosystem, with social enterprises playing an increasingly important role in driving entrepreneurship and innovation. Organizations like Artemisia and Ashoka support social entrepreneurs through mentorship, funding, and networking opportunities, fostering a culture of innovation and impact-driven business models in the country.
- Community-Led Development and Empowerment: Social entrepreneurship in Brazil often emphasizes community-led development and empowerment, with initiatives focusing on participatory approaches and collaboration with local stakeholders. Projects such as Banco Palmas, a community bank in the outskirts of Fortaleza, empower residents to access financial services, create businesses, and revitalize the local economy through microcredit and social currency programs.
- Tech-Driven Solutions for Social Impact: Brazil's tech-savvy population and growing digital infrastructure have paved the way for tech-driven solutions to social challenges. Social entrepreneurs are leveraging technology to address issues such as healthcare access, education quality, and financial inclusion. Platforms like Descomplica provide affordable online education to students from low-income backgrounds, while startups like Nubank offer financial services to the unbanked population through mobile banking apps.
- Policy Advocacy and Collaboration: Social entrepreneurs in Brazil actively engage in policy advocacy and collaboration with government agencies, civil society organizations, and corporate partners to scale their impact and drive systemic change. Platforms such as Sistema B advocate for legal frameworks that support social enterprises and promote business practices aligned with environmental and social sustainability.

- Global Influence and Collaboration: Brazilian social entrepreneurs are increasingly engaged in global networks and collaborations to share knowledge, resources, and best practices. Organizations like Yunus Social Business Brazil collaborate with international partners to incubate and scale social enterprises, amplifying their impact and creating opportunities for cross-border collaboration and learning. Social entrepreneurship in Brazil is thriving, with a diverse range of initiatives making significant strides in addressing social, environmental, and economic challenges. By combining business acumen with a commitment to social impact, Brazilian social entrepreneurs are driving positive change and shaping a more inclusive and sustainable future for the country. To effectuate the implementation of any ideas or models, adherence to fundamental parameters is indispensable, ensuring their seamless integration within the fabric of society. These parameters delineate a holistic framework, encapsulating the multifaceted dimensions of societal, technological, financial, administrative, judicial, emotional, and environmental considerations.

Firstly, any proposed initiative must garner political acceptance, embodying principles and policies amenable to the prevailing governance structures. This necessitates alignment with the overarching political ethos, fostering harmony and cooperation across diverse ideological spectra.

Secondly, the societal desirability of the proposed model is imperative, necessitating its resonance with the collective aspirations, values, and norms of the populace. Such resonance engenders societal cohesion, fostering inclusivity and fostering a sense of ownership among stakeholders.

Technological feasibility constitutes a cornerstone criterion, requiring alignment with prevailing technological capabilities and advancements. Integration with cutting-edge technologies ensures efficacy, scalability, and adaptability, thereby facilitating seamless implementation and operation.

Financial viability is a pivotal consideration, mandating a comprehensive evaluation of cost implications, revenue streams, and economic sustainability. Fiscal prudence is paramount, ensuring prudent allocation of resources and optimal utilization of financial capital.

Administrative feasibility underscores the pragmatic aspect of implementation, entailing streamlined processes, efficient resource allocation, and effective coordination among stakeholders. Administrative efficacy is indispensable for the successful execution and management of the proposed endeavour.

Judicial tenability is imperative, necessitating compliance with extant legal frameworks, statutes, and regulations. Adherence to legal norms ensures the legitimacy and enforceability of the proposed model, mitigating legal risks and fostering regulatory compliance.

Emotional relatability embodies a profound connection with the human experience, encapsulating empathy, compassion, and resonance with the emotional psyche of individuals. Emotional resonance cultivates trust, engendering a sense of empathy and solidarity among stakeholders.

Lastly, environmental sustainability underscores the imperative of ecological stewardship, necessitating a conscientious appraisal of environmental impacts and mitigation strategies. Harmonizing human activities with ecological imperatives ensures the preservation of environmental integrity and the long-term viability of ecosystems. Adherence to these foundational parameters engenders a synergistic convergence of diverse considerations, facilitating the seamless implementation of ideas and models while fostering societal well-being, technological progress, economic prosperity, and environmental sustainability.

REFERENCES

Ahuja, M. (2020). Promoting inclusive access and empowerment through AI in social entrepreneurship. *The Journal of Development Studies*, 56(4), 789–806.

Howaldt, J. (2018). Harnessing AI for innovation in social entrepreneurship. *Technology Innovation Management Review*, 8(1), 12–20.

Mittelstadt, B. D. (2016). Ethical considerations in AI deployment for social entrepreneurship. *Ethics and Information Technology*, 18(4), 249–267.

Schulte, M. (2017). AI-driven analytics for impact assessment in social entrepreneurship. *Journal of Social Entrepreneurship*, 8(1), 89–106.

Westley, F. (2017). Collaboration and ecosystem building in AI-driven social entrepreneurship. *Stanford Social Innovation Review*, 15(3), 76–88.

Chapter 6
Redefining Fashion Sustainability for Industry 5.0:
Sustainability

Shruti Tiwari
https://orcid.org/0009-0003-8592-5642
Parul University, India

Palak Patel
Parul University, India

ABSTRACT

The fashion industry is undergoing a shift towards sustainability, with recycling playing a crucial role. Upcycling garments extends their life and promotes a culture of reuse, while downcycling may destroy the original design and aesthetics of garments. Balancing downcycling and upcycling is essential to minimize environmental impact while maintaining design integrity. Consumer behaviors and technological innovations also shape the fashion recycling landscape. Effective sustainability strategies must balance the benefits and challenges of both upcycling and downcycling, fostering a holistic approach to textile and garment recycling. Understanding these processes will guide fashion towards a more sustainable, circular, and innovative future.

DOI: 10.4018/979-8-3693-4338-8.ch006

1. INTRODUCTION

1.1. The Environmental Cost of Fashion

Fast fashion has significant environmental and social costs. The industry's impacts on pollution, water consumption, carbon emissions, human rights, and gender inequality are becoming more apparent. Organizations globally, including those in Geneva, are working together to reform the fashion industry and promote international cooperation on these issues.

Figure 1. Negative Impact Areas of The Apparel Industry

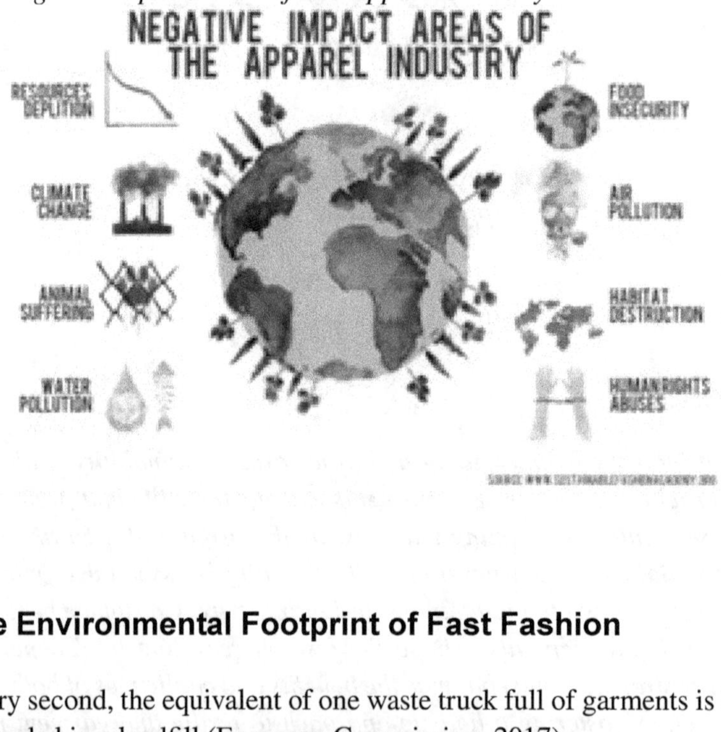

1.2. The Environmental Footprint of Fast Fashion

- Every second, the equivalent of one waste truck full of garments is burned or discarded in a landfill (European Commission, 2017).
- Plastic accounts for approximately 60% of all materials used in the fashion industry.
- Washing garments releases 500,000 tons of microfibers into the ocean annually, equivalent to 50 billion plastic bottles.
- The fashion industry is responsible for 8-10% of global carbon emissions, surpassing international aviation and marine shipping combined. If current trends continue, its carbon budget contribution could increase to 26% by 2050 (Ellen MacArthur Foundation, 2017).

- The industry consumes 93 billion cubic meters of water annually, enough to meet the needs of five million people, contributing to water scarcity in some areas.
- Approximately 20% of industrial wastewater pollution worldwide originates from the fashion industry.

1.3. What is sustainable fashion?

Sustainable fashion considers environmental, social, and economic impacts. It involves making clothing, accessories, and other fashion items in an environmentally responsible manner, respecting worker rights, and ensuring fair wages and safe working conditions. This includes using eco-friendly materials, reducing waste and carbon footprint, promoting ethical sourcing and production, and supporting circular fashion practices like recycling and upcycling. Sustainable fashion aims to create a more responsible and ethical industry with a positive social and environmental impact.

Figure 2. Sustainable Fashion

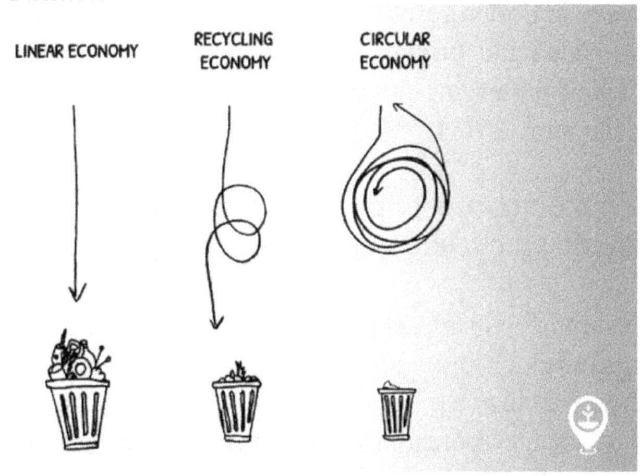

The fashion industry is under increasing pressure to address these issues, leading to a focus on sustainability with recycling playing a critical role. This study explores the impact of various recycling methods on consumer behavior and environmental sustainability in the fashion sector.

1.3.1. Upcycling Garments: Extending the Life of Fashion Items

Upcycling is emerging as a promising method for extending the life of garments while preserving craftsmanship and design integrity. This study examines the potential of upcycling to encourage "thrifting" behaviors among consumers, reducing fashion waste and enhancing sustainability (Aus, 2011).

1.3.2. Recycling Garments: Balancing Upcycling and downcycling

While upcycling preserves the essence of fashion items, traditional downcycling can unintentionally "destroy" the original design and aesthetics of garments. Balancing these two approaches is crucial, considering the unique properties of textiles and garments (Fletcher, 2008).

1.3.3. The Distortion of Shapes and Patterns: A Consequence of Recycling

Downcycling often results in the loss of intricate shapes and patterns, diminishing the value and originality of fashion pieces. This research highlights the importance of preserving the visual and design appeal of recycled fashion items (Gam & Banning, 2011).

1.3.4. Environmental Implications: Energy-Intensive down cycling vs. Circular Upcycling

The environmental impact of fashion recycling is significant. While downcycling reduces the need for virgin resources, it can have a higher environmental footprint due to energy-intensive processes. In contrast, upcycling promotes the cyclical use of existing resources, potentially requiring innovative techniques to minimize energy use (Fischer & Pascucci, 2017).

1.3.5. Consumer Behaviours and Technological Innovations

Consumer behaviors and technological advancements greatly influence the fashion recycling landscape. This study explores how consumer choices and preferences can drive sustainable practices in the fashion industry. Additionally, it examines technological innovations that enable more efficient and eco-friendly recycling processes (Gazzola et al., 2020).

2. AIMS AND OBJECTIVES:

The primary aim of this research is to investigate the effect of upcycling on fashion recycling, proposing a balanced approach that integrates both upcycling and downcycling methods. This study aims to evaluate the environmental impact of these processes while analyzing the influence of consumer behaviors and technological innovations on sustainable practices in the fashion industry. To achieve these aims, the objectives include conducting a comprehensive literature review and empirical research, assessing the environmental footprints of upcycling and downcycling, and developing practical guidelines for sustainable fashion recycling. Ultimately, this research seeks to contribute to the ongoing dialogue on fashion sustainability, providing insights and recommendations to support a more environmentally friendly and innovative approach to recycling in the fashion sector.

2.1. Aims:

1. Investigate the effect of upcycling on fashion recycling.
2. Propose a balanced approach to upcycling and downcycling.
3. Evaluate the environmental impact of upcycling and downcycling.
4. Analyze the impact of consumer behaviors and technological innovations.

2.2. Objectives:

1. Conduct a comprehensive literature review.
2. Conduct empirical research.
3. Evaluate environmental footprints.
4. Develop guidelines for sustainable fashion recycling.
5. Contribute to the ongoing dialogue on fashion sustainability.

3. REVIEW OF LITERATURE:

Sustainable fashion and recycling have emerged as critical areas of research in the rapidly changing fashion business. This study synthesizes available material to shed light on the complicated link between sustainability and recycling practices in fashion.

3.1. Sustainable Fashion:

A corpus of literature highlights the evolution of sustainable fashion, stressing the industry's transition to ecologically conscientious methods. Authors such as Fletcher (2008) investigate the theoretical foundations of sustainable fashion, highlighting the problems and possibilities that come with incorporating ecological and social factors into design and manufacturing processes (Fletcher, 2008).

3.2. Recycling in Fashion:

Researchers, like Birtwistle and Moore (2007), have investigated the various ways of recycling in the fashion sector. This encompasses both upcycling and downcycling tactics, emphasizing the environmental and economic benefits of recycling materials and prolonging the life cycle of clothing (Ellen MacArthur Foundation, 2017).

3.3. Upcycling and Its Impact:

Upcycling, a popular method in sustainable fashion, has received significant attention. Muthu (2019) and Ballesteros et al. (2020) highlight how upcycling repurposes abandoned textiles, helping to preserve workmanship and design integrity. The ability of upcycling to affect consumer behavior, particularly in promoting thrifting habits, is a recurring subject (Aus, 2011; Fischer & Pascucci, 2017).

3.4. Downcycling Challenges:

Choi and Holbrook (2007) investigate the disadvantages of downcycling methods. The unexpected consequences, such as the destruction of original ideas and the loss of exquisite forms and patterns, are addressed, emphasizing the importance of striking a precise balance between upcycling and downcycling (Kim & Damhorst, 1998).

3.5. Environmental Footprint:

The environmental impact of fashion recycling processes is an important consideration. Nielsen and Glans (2018) present information on the life cycle assessments of various recycling techniques. They explore how, while downcycling reduces demand for virgin materials, it can occasionally increase the environmental impact owing to energy-intensive operations (Gazzola et al., 2020; Pol, 2010).

If nothing is done, the fashion sector would emit an estimated 2.7 billion tons of CO2 equivalent (CO2e) by 2030. Currently, 70% of CO2e emissions occur during the production and processing stages, with 20% occurring during the utilization phase (European Commission, 2017; Ellen MacArthur Foundation, 2017).

Figure 3. Environmental Effects of the Clothing Industry

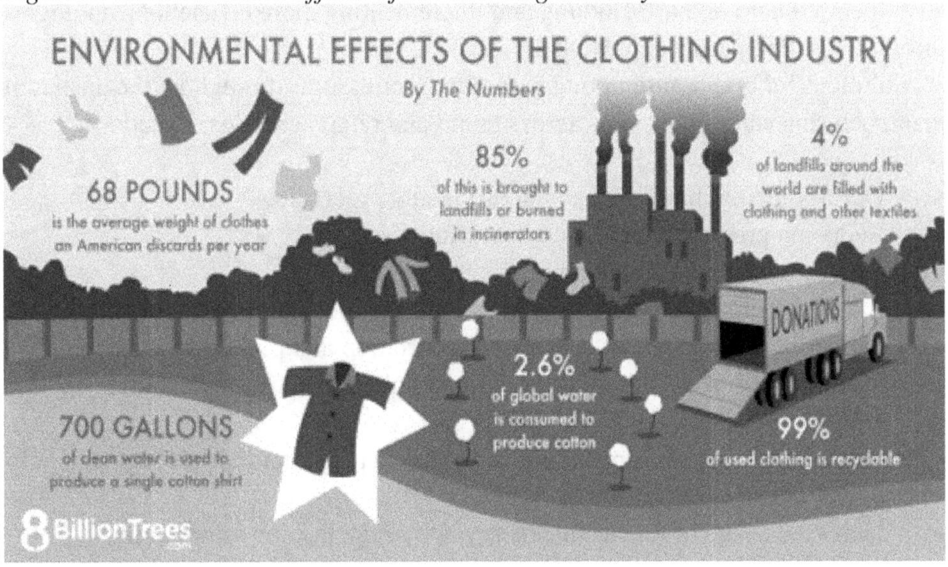

3.6. Consumer Behaviors and Technology:

Scholars, like Shen et al. (2021), are studying the roles of consumer behaviors and technology advancements in creating the fashion recycling landscape. Understanding how customers interact with sustainable fashion choices and how technology enables circular practices is critical to the industry's future.

3.6.1. How Consumers and Brands Can Slow Down Fashion's Carbon Footprint:

Sufficient actions customers may take to minimize the fashion industry's carbon footprint include:

- Reducing new clothes purchases

- Moving towards more sustainable clothing options (e.g., buying secondhand items)
- Increasing usage times.
- Minimizing washing and drying.
- Responsible disposal.

Adopting a circular business strategy focused on recycling, upcycling, and reuse can help firms minimize their CO2e emissions. These strategies include allowing customers to share or lease clothing and implementing more efficient technologies throughout a company's supply chain.

Solutions for brands attempting to minimize emissions throughout the upstream manufacturing stage, as well as across brand and retail activities, include:

- Decarbonizing material manufacturing and processing
- Reducing production and manufacturing waste
- Decarbonizing clothing manufacture
- Efficiency enhancements, such as switching to less carbon-intensive fibers
- Increase the usage of sustainable transportation and packaging.
- Minimizing returns to reduce emissions linked with transportation
- Decarbonizing Retail Operations
- Optimizing demand forecasting and stock management technology can help reduce overproduction.
- Increased usage of renewable energy across the fashion value chain.

Figure 4. Carbon Footprint

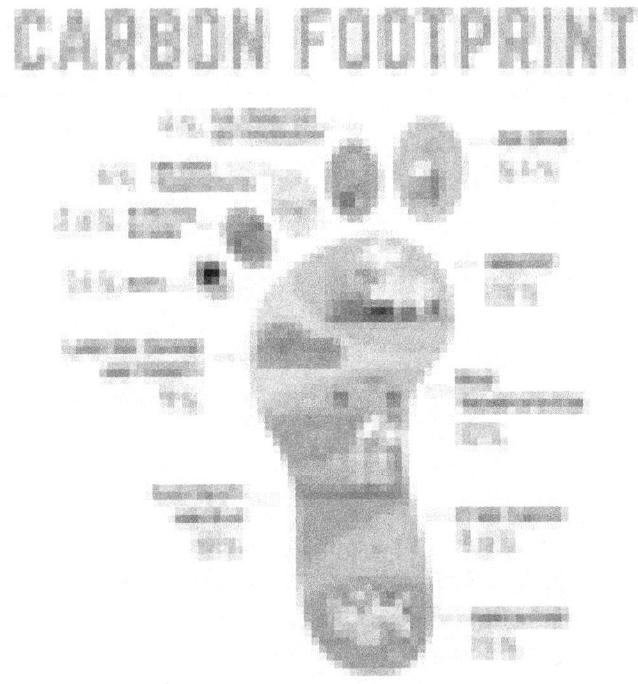

If decarbonization efforts are intensified, global emissions from upstream production, brand and retail activities might be cut by 1.3 billion tons.

3.7. Holistic Approaches:

The need for a holistic approach to textile and garment recycling is emphasized in works like Laitala et al. (2020). Integrating social, economic, and environmental considerations, researchers advocate for comprehensive sustainability strategies that address the complexities of the fashion supply chain (Laitala et al., 2020).

3.8. International Cooperation on Sustainable Fashion:

Because fashion value chains are worldwide and the industry has a substantial influence on achieving the United Nations Sustainable Development Goals (SDGs), international cooperation is critical to promoting sustainable fashion.

Figure 5. Impact of the fashion industry on the SDGs (UNECE, 2018)

The UN Alliance for Sustainable Fashion, founded at the fourth United Nations Environment Assembly (UNEA-4), seeks to abolish fashion's environmentally and socially harmful practices. The Alliance strengthens collaboration across UN agencies by assessing their efforts to make fashion more sustainable, identifying solutions and gaps in existing activities, and presenting the findings to governments to influence policy. Additionally, the Forests for Fashion Initiative, led by UNECE, FAO, and partners, encourages inventive fashion solutions made from sustainable forest-based products (UN Alliance for Sustainable Fashion, 2019).

4. METHODOLOGY

'Exploratory research' is used to explore problems that have been uncovered but not properly defined in the past, like sustainable fashion from the customer's perspective has not been thoroughly studied.

As a result, this type of study seldom produces a compelling conclusion. For study goals, both qualitative and quantitative data were collected. A questionnaire/ survey was utilized to collect quantitative data, which was then evaluated to develop and draw a numerical and statistical correlation between the factors that influence customer attitudes toward sustainable fashion.

4.1 Upcycling:

Upcycling involves reusing old materials to create products of higher value or quality compared to traditional recycling. This process can include transforming plastic bottles into new shoes or repurposing reclaimed wood to craft high-quality furniture. Upcycling supports a circular economy, where products are reused multiple times instead of being discarded after a single use. This sustainable approach maximizes the use of existing resources, reducing the need for new products made from fresh materials (Aus, 2011; Ellen MacArthur Foundation, 2017; European Commission, 2017).

Figure 6. UpCycling

4.2 Recycling:

In the fashion industry, recycling entails finding new uses for existing garments or converting waste textiles into reusable materials. This process often involves garments re-entering the retail phase of their lifecycle, with items being reintroduced to the market through charities and collection points. Textile recycling can also mean breaking down high-quality materials into their purest raw forms or substrates. Recycling technologies are essential in addressing raw material shortages and provide companies with additional methods for managing their raw material supplies (Fletcher, 2008; Gam & Banning, 2011; GFA & BCG, 2017).

Figure 7. Recycling

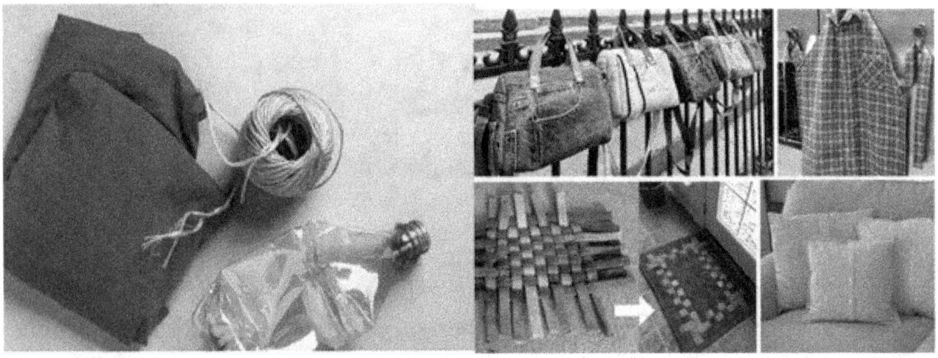

4.3 Downcycling:

Downcycling is defined as recycling an item in such a way that the resulting product is of lower value than the original. Unlike upcycling, which creates products of higher value, downcycling typically results in a decrease in value. This process is more closely related to repurposing but results in a product with diminished value and a new form. Downcycling differs from reuse because it involves a transformation that decreases the item's value (Fischer & Pascucci, 2017; Gazzola et al., 2020; Kim & Damhorst, 1998).

Figure 8. Downcycling

This study employs both descriptive research design and experimental survey research. Its primary objective is to gather survey data reflecting the ideas, behaviors, and attitudes of 100 respondents towards the fashion industry. The study aims to establish the roles of upcycling, recycling, and downcycling in promoting sustainability within the industry (Gam & Banning, 2011; GFA & BCG, 2017).

5. RESULT AND DISCUSSION

The data of the respondents was collected under three variables A) Idea B) Purchase Behaviour C) Attitude through Google form and analysed statistically with the help of pie charts.

1. IDEA –

Figure 9 Idea of Upcycling, Downcycling, Recycling

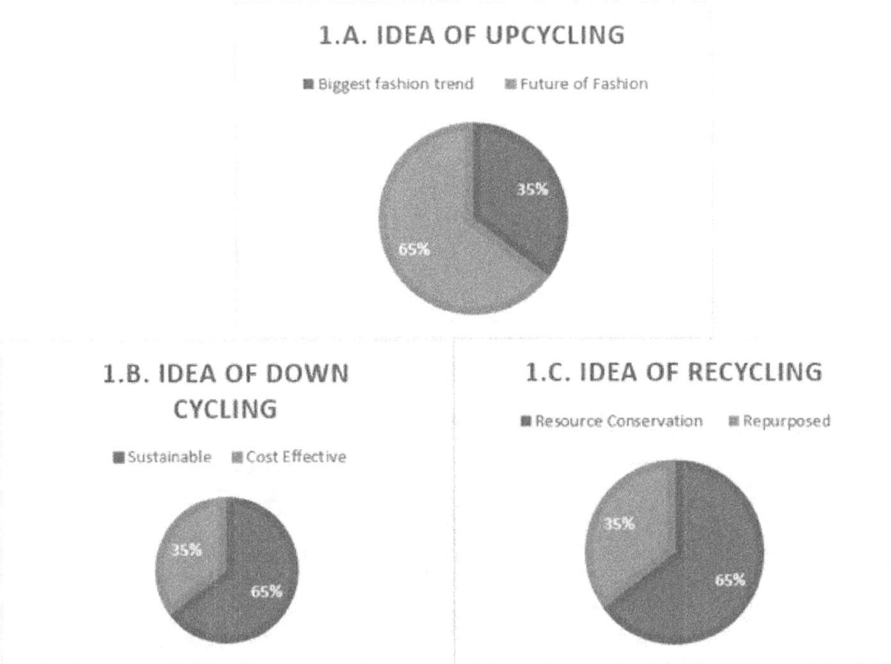

The above chart depicts the percentage distribution of responses about the idea of upcycling. 35% (blue) respondents described it as the Biggest fashion trend whereas 65%(orange) take it as the future of fashion. For down cycling 65% (blue) respondents denote it as sustainable, whereas 35% (orange) respondents finds it cost effective. 65% (blue) respondents finds the idea of recycling as resource conservation, where as 35%(orange) respondents finds it as repurposed.

2. PURCHASE BEHAVIOUR -

Figure 10. Purchase behavior regarding Upcycling, Downcycling, and Recycling

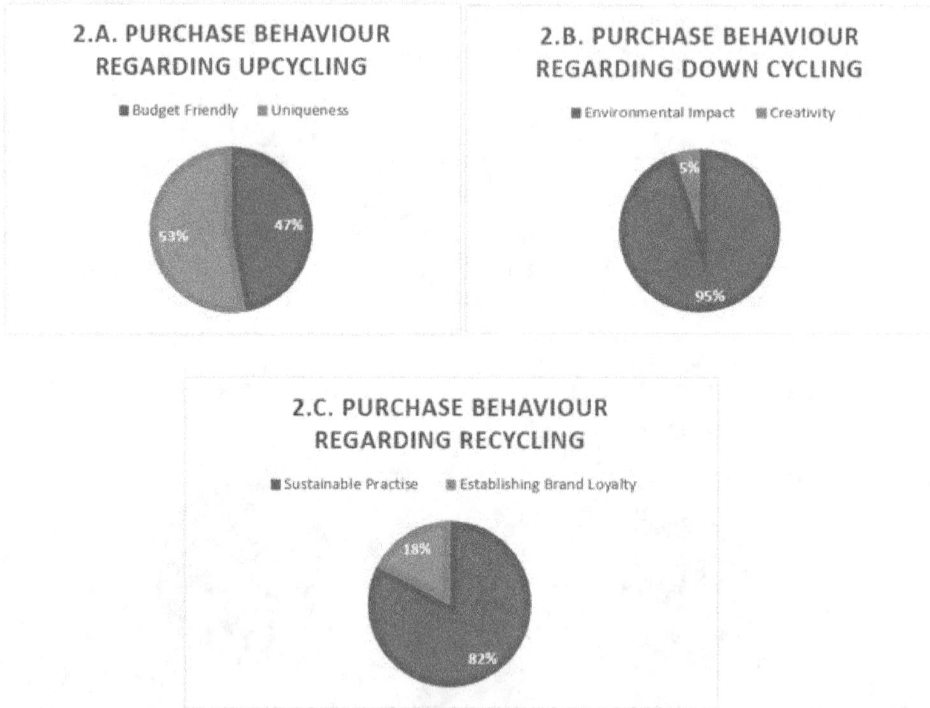

The above charts show the purchasing behavior of respondents regarding Upcycled, down-cycled, and recycled garments, 47% (blue) respondents included upcycled garments in their wardrobe due to budget-friendliness, whereas 53% (orange) respondents found them unique. Being a conscious and responsible citizen 95% (blue) of respondents believe that adding downcycling to their purchase behavior will help create a positive environmental impact. However, 5% (orange) of respondents find it creative. 82% (blue) of respondents find recycling a sustainable practice, whereas 18% (orange) of respondents consider it as establishing brand loyalty.

3. ATTUTUDE

Figure 11. Attitude towards Upcycling, Downcycling and Recycling

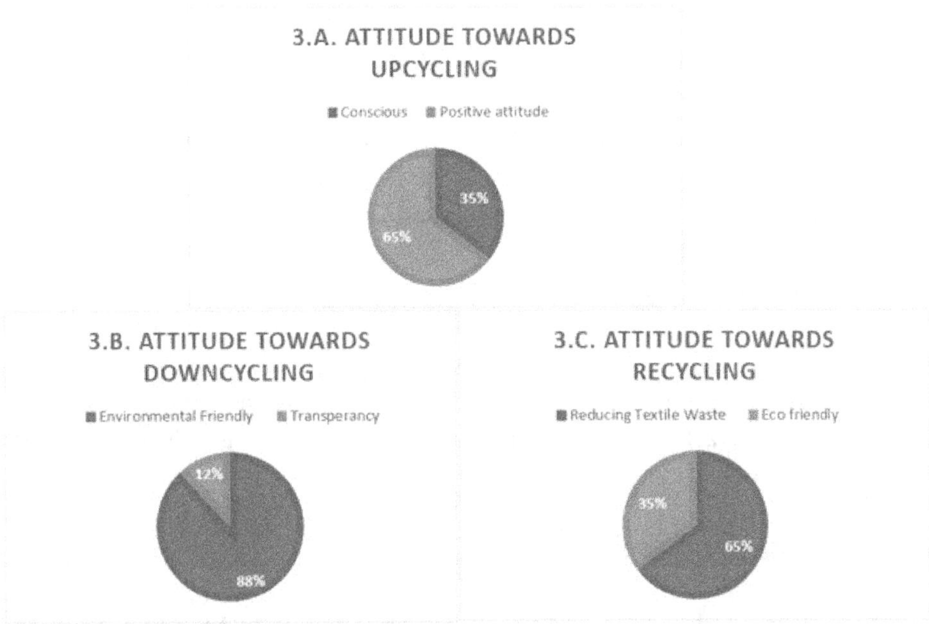

It is being observed from the above chart that the attitude of 35% (blue) respondents towards upcycling are conscious, whereas 65% (orange) of respondents are found positive. Regarding down cycling 88% (blue) of respondents finds it environmental friendly, whereas 12% (orange) of respondents consider it transparent. 65% (blue) of respondents consider that recycling is helpful in reducing textile waste, whereas 35% (orange) of respondents finds it eco – friendly.

6. SUGGESTIONS

6.1. How Designers Can Help Companies Design for the Circular Economy

By creating adaptable clothing for various situations and styles, the fashion industry can significantly reduce the production of new garments and their environmental impact. Producing fewer new garments leads to reduced resource consumption and less waste generation (Gazzola et al., 2020).

6.2. How Can Designers Become Change-Makers?

6.2.1. Zero-Waste Patterns: Revolutionizing Fashion by Eliminating Waste

In today's sustainability-driven era, the fashion industry faces a significant challenge: reducing waste. Traditional fashion design processes produce considerable fabric waste during cutting and sewing, exacerbating environmental issues and depleting resources. Zero-waste patterns, however, offer a groundbreaking approach to transforming the industry's stance on waste (Gam & Banning, 2011).

6.2.2. Rethinking Traditional Design

Conventional fashion design often views fabric as a disposable resource, creating patterns with little consideration for leftover scraps and offcuts, leading to substantial textile waste. This wasteful method not only damages the environment but also strains industry resources (Aus, 2011).

6.2.3. A Sustainable Solution

Zero-waste patterns mark a significant shift from unsustainable practices. These patterns are carefully crafted to utilize every inch of fabric, leaving no scraps behind. This approach ensures that each piece of fabric contributes to the final garment, minimizing waste from the start. Imagine a puzzle where every piece fits perfectly without gaps; this is the essence of zero-waste patterns. Designers develop intricate and innovative patterns that allow efficient cutting and assembly of garments, ensuring each piece of fabric is used purposefully. The result is both aesthetically pleasing and environmentally responsible (Fletcher, 2008).

6.2.4. Cradle-to-Cradle Design: Closing the Material Loop

Cradle-to-cradle (C2C) design principles promote products that are not only sustainable but also regenerative. In the fashion industry, C2C design involves creating garments that can be safely returned to the ecosystem or repurposed as raw materials for new products without harming the environment. This approach ensures that the fashion industry becomes part of the solution rather than a source of pollution (Ellen MacArthur Foundation, 2017).

6.3. Five Principles of Humanity-Centered Design

Humanity-centered design goes beyond traditional human-centered design by including all of humanity and our ecosystems. Don Norman outlines five principles of humanity-centered design, highlighting the importance of inclusive and sustainable design practices (Fischer & Pascucci, 2017).

6.4. Sustainable Fashion vs. Fast Fashion

The fashion industry is one of the largest polluters globally, with significant environmental impacts. Today, we consume 400 times more clothing than 20 years ago. Sustainable fashion aims to mitigate these negative impacts by implementing practices that reduce waste, pollution, and the use of non-renewable resources. In recent years, global research and thought leadership panels have identified the best strategies for reducing the fashion industry's carbon footprint. Here are some immediate opportunities fashion brands can consider to become more sustainable (European Commission, 2017; GFA & BCG, 2017).

Figure 12. Latest R's

6.5. Designing for a Circular System with a Focus on Physical Durability

In a predominantly linear fashion industry, the average fast fashion garment made from fossil fuels lasts only a few washes. Designing garments for longevity is a straightforward way for brands to be more environmentally conscious. Sustainable fashion brands should aim to create garments that fit within a circular model, intended to be passed along to multiple owners. Brands that produce durable clothing excel on resale platforms like TheRealReal and Trove. Consumers are willing to pay more and show increased loyalty to brands known for producing long-lasting garments (Gazzola et al., 2020).

Figure 13. Circular economy system

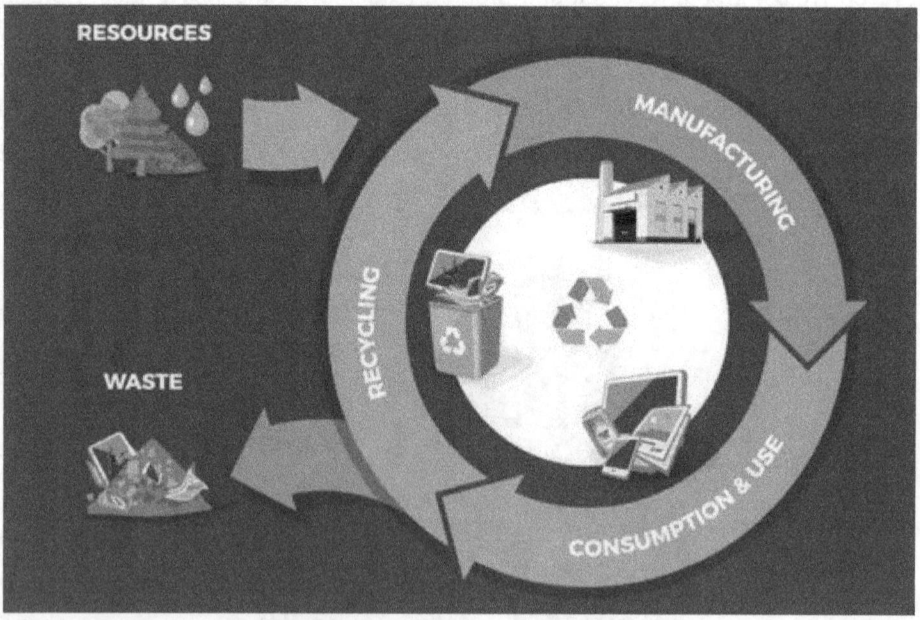

6.5.1. Design with Emotional Durability in Mind

Many of us have owned clothing items that made us happy and were worn until they completely wore out. While not every garment can carry such emotional value, fashion brands can design with emotional durability in mind. Brands can encourage consumers to fall in love with high-quality pieces that are timeless, modular, or versatile. The growing consumer value of buying less but buying better can be addressed by focusing on these principles. Though it might seem counterintuitive from a commercial perspective, as it reduces purchase frequency, it builds brand trust. This strategy has been successful for industry leaders like Patagonia and new sustainable brands like AYR, which has doubled in size every year since its 2014 inception by selling only high-quality basics (Aus, 2011).

Figure 14. The circular economy butterfly diagram by the Ellen MacArthur Foundation illustrates how we can minimize waste using both renewable and non-renewable materials

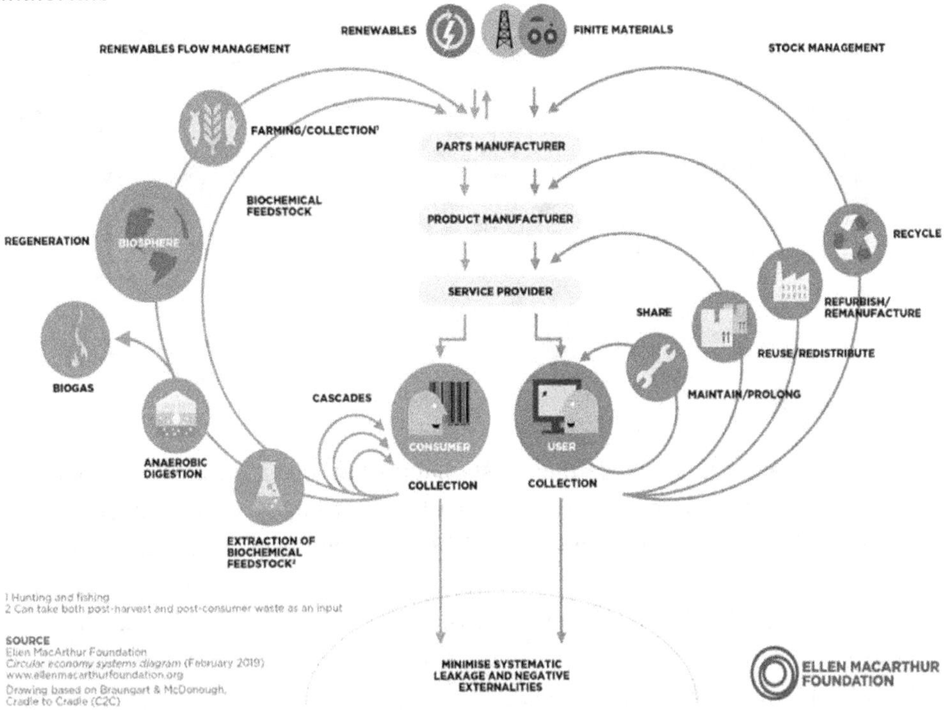

6.5.2. Consider bio-derived or recycled ingredients

A significant portion of a fashion brand's carbon footprint occurs indirectly through its value chain. By choosing renewable sustainable materials such as organic cotton and bamboo, brands can reduce their products' carbon footprints. Consumers are willing to pay more for such materials. Recycled polyester, derived from open-loop recycling of PET bottles, also reduces environmental impact and is available at scale. New sustainable innovations are entering the fiber market, such as The LYCRA Company's fiber made from annually renewable field corn instead of fossil fuels, and Rubi Laboratories' carbon-negative viscose fiber. These innovations can be incorporated without altering the manufacturing process (Ellen MacArthur Foundation, 2017).

Figure 15. Kapok Biolight yarn, fabric and Ternua SEAL L/S t-shirt in UYN's Bio Lab at ISPO 2022

6.6. Afterlife

Fashion brands can enhance their sustainability by adopting practices that prioritize the reuse, recycling, and repurposing of their products. Using biodegradable materials in their designs and supporting clear consumer disposal instructions these goals. Brands can also implement in-house recycling programs, like Madewell's denim recycling initiative, which allows customers to exchange pre-loved jeans for store credit. The collected jeans are then repurposed for residential insulation by Habitat for Humanity (Fletcher, 2008).

Figure 16. Residential insulation by Habitat

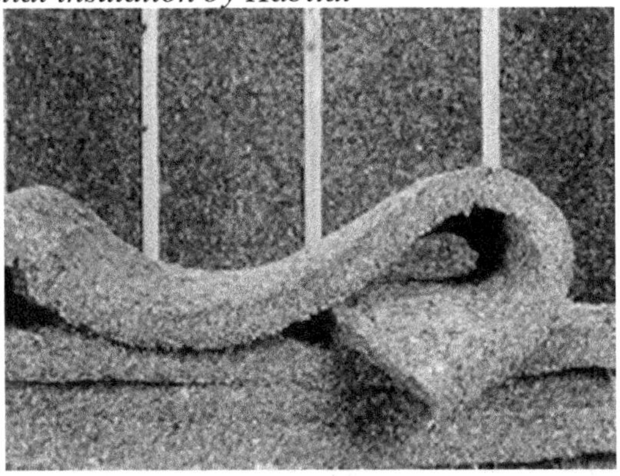

6.7. Adopting Sustainable Fashion Practices

6.7.1. Shop at Thrift and Vintage Stores

Thrift and vintage clothing stores often offer new, unworn designer items. Shopping at these stores extends the life of clothing and provides unique pieces, making it a sustainable choice.

6.7.2. Choose Natural Materials and Sustainable Fabrics

Avoid synthetic fabrics like polyester, which constitute more than half of all clothing worldwide, are derived from fossil fuels, and take years to degrade. Instead, opt for natural textiles such as organic cotton and linen. Organic cotton is preferable to conventional cotton, which requires significant water and energy to produce and uses hazardous pesticides (Gazzola et al., 2020; Ellen MacArthur Foundation, 2017).

6.7.3. Invest in Sustainable Fashion Brands

Many fashion brands are now embracing sustainability. Although fast fashion is still prevalent, increased consumer demand for eco-friendly clothing will drive the production of more sustainable options (Fischer & Pascucci, 2017).

6.7.4. Consider Your Water Footprint

The textile industry consumes over 24,000 gallons of water per year. To reduce your water footprint, consider the fabrics you purchase. Organic cotton uses significantly less water than conventional cotton, and low-water dyes further minimize water usage. Investing in bamboo bed sheets, pillowcases, and duvet covers from sustainable brands is another effective way to reduce your water footprint (Fletcher, 2008).

6.7.5. Buy High-Quality Clothing

Many people buy new clothes when their current ones lose shape or appeal, perpetuating the fast fashion cycle. By choosing higher-quality clothing, we encourage brands to improve garment quality. Higher-quality clothing lasts longer, which benefits the environment (Gam & Banning, 2011).

6.7.6. Stop Throwing Old Clothes Away

Think twice before discarding your favorite jeans or classic white shirt. Throwing clothes in the garbage contributes to overflowing landfills (European Commission, 2017).

6.7.7. Alternatives to Throwing Away Clothes

- **Mending:** Items with rips, tears, or small holes can often be easily repaired.
- **Donating:** Depending on their condition, give your items to friends, relatives, neighbors, or charities.
- **Reselling:** Many websites and consignment stores resell quality clothing in good condition.
- **Recycling:** Some clothing brands accept worn items, or you can take worn-out clothing to a textile recycling container. Textiles can be recycled to create new garments (Gazzola et al., 2020; Aus, 2011).

6.7.8. Rent Clothes for Single-Use Occasions

Clothes rental is a rapidly growing, ethical business model. It is an excellent option for garments that you will not wear for long periods or special occasions. Some businesses also offer monthly subscriptions, allowing customers to regularly update their wardrobes (GFA & BCG, 2017).

6.7.9. Care for Clothes Well

Extending the life of your clothes minimizes your environmental footprint and reduces clothing waste. Proper laundering is crucial to increasing their longevity. Use cold water, a gentle wash cycle, and air dry your clothes to help them retain their like-new appearance longer. Proper storage is also essential; protect your clothing from sun exposure, pests, and dust by storing them in high-quality garment bags (Fletcher, 2008).

6.7.10. Embrace Circular Fashion

The circular fashion industry aims for a system where all items can be reused, recycled, or returned to the environment (if biodegradable or compostable). While the fashion industry still has a long way to go, supporting items that can be reused or recycled advances the sustainable movement (Ellen MacArthur Foundation, 2017).

7. CONCLUSION

Pathways to Sustainability:

The literature underscores that sustainable fashion and recycling offer distinct pathways toward a more environmentally responsible industry. It is crucial to grasp the nuanced implications of various recycling processes, consumer behaviors, and technological interventions to guide the fashion industry toward a circular and innovative future. This research contributes to the ongoing discourse, providing valuable insights to foster positive change within fashion sustainability.

In conclusion, the fashion industry is at a pivotal juncture, with upcycling and downcycling presenting unique sustainability approaches. These methods influence how we “upcycle garments,” “recycle garments,” and promote “thrifting,” while also challenging and “distorting” traditional fashion norms. Understanding the complex implications of these processes is essential for steering the fashion industry towards a more sustainable, circular, and innovative future. This research enhances the ongoing dialogue on fashion sustainability, offering insights to drive positive change within the industry.

REFERENCES

E3S Web of Conferences. (2024). Sustainable fashion and textile recycling.

Aus, R. (2011). Trash to trend: Using upcycling in fashion design [Unpublished doctoral dissertation]. Estonian Academy of Arts.

Ellen MacArthur Foundation. (2017). A new textiles economy: Redesigning fashion's future.

European Commission. (2017). *Circular economy in practice—reducing textile waste*. EASME.

Finnish Standard Association. (1983). *Hospital textiles. Sheet polyester-cotton; SFS 2945*. Finnish Standard Association.

Finnish Standard Association. (2010). *Quantitative chemical analysis. Part 1: General principles of testing; SFS 1833-11*. Finnish Standard Association.

Fischer, A., & Pascucci, S. (2017). Institutional incentives in circular economy transition: The case of material use in the Dutch textile industry. *Journal of Cleaner Production*, 155, 17–32. DOI: 10.1016/j.jclepro.2016.12.038

Fletcher, K. (2008). *Sustainable fashion and textiles: Design journeys*. Earthscan/ James & James.

IEEE Future Directions. (2022). Wrapping up the year: Sustainability in fashion.

Gam, H. J., & Banning, J. (2011). Addressing sustainable apparel design challenges with problem-based learning. *Clothing & Textiles Research Journal*, 29(3), 202–215. DOI: 10.1177/0887302X11414874

Gazzola, P., Pavione, E., Pezzetti, R., & Grechi, D. (2020). Trends in the fashion industry. The perception of sustainability and circular economy: A gender/generation quantitative approach. *Sustainability (Basel)*, 12(7), 2809. DOI: 10.3390/su12072809

GFA & BCG. (2017). *Pulse of the fashion industry*. Global Fashion Agenda and the Boston Consulting Group.

Green Hermitage. (n.d.). The circular economy in fashion

Hamilton, J. A. (2024). *Textile recycling—A review*. ResearchGate.

SAGE Journals. (2022). Sustainable fashion practices.

Kim, H., & Damhorst, M. L. (1998). Environmental concern and apparel consumption. *Clothing & Textiles Research Journal*, 16(3), 126–133. DOI: 10.1177/0887302X9801600303

Martin, M., & Parsapour, A. (2012). Upcycling wastes with biogas production: An energy and economic analysis. In Proceedings of the Venice 2012: International Symposium on Energy from Biomass and Waste, Venice, Italy, 12–15 November 2012.

National Center for Biotechnology Information. (2020). Environmental impacts of fashion.

Pol, V. G. (2010). Upcycling: Converting waste plastics into paramagnetic, conducting, solid, pure carbon microspheres. *Environmental Science & Technology*, 44(12), 4753–4759. DOI: 10.1021/es100243u PMID: 20481621

ResearchGate. (n.d.). A terminology for downcycling. • Grounded. (n.d.). Sustainable fashion: 4 ways fashion brands can be more sustainable.

ResearchGate. (n.d.). Achieving sustainability through zero waste fashion—a review.

ScienceDirect. (n.d.). A review on textile recycling processes.

ScienceDirect. (n.d.). Environmental impacts of textile recycling.

ScienceDirect. (n.d.). Recycling processes in the textile industry.

SpringerLink. (2020). Sustainable fashion: Concepts and practices of.

SSRG International Journals. (2023). Achieving sustainability through zero waste fashion—A review. *International Journal of Humanities and Social Science*, 10(1), 105.

Textile Exchange. (n.d.). Downcycling.

Textiles & Clothing Sustainability. (2015). Sustainable fashion. *RE:view*.

IEEE Xplore. (2023). Sustainable fashion: The future directions.

IEEE Xplore. (n.d.). Sustainable textile innovations.

IEEE Xplore. (n.d.). Recycling in the fashion industry.

IEEE Xplore. (n.d.). Sustainable fashion practices for the future.

Chapter 7
Reviewing Opportunities and Challenges of Sustainable Entrepreneurship in Sri Lanka

H. M. T. S. Herath
University of Kelaniya, Sri Lanka

H. A. K. N. S. Surangi
https://orcid.org/0000-0002-2671-2212
University of Kelaniya, Sri Lanka

Mohamed Mihilar Shamil
https://orcid.org/0000-0002-5533-5129
Hong Kong Metropolitan University, Hong Kong

ABSTRACT

In response to significant societal issues, sustainable entrepreneurship has surfaced as a potential means of solving ecological and social problems. However, most recent studies on sustainable entrepreneurship have been phenomenon-driven, with context-specific findings and a relatively implicit theoretical relationship. Thus, the main goals of this chapter are to investigate the opportunities and challenges of sustainable entrepreneurship in Sri Lanka. The method used was a qualitative, multiple-case investigation. Two cases from Sri Lanka were examined. Semi-structured interviews were conducted with co-founders. The results showed that sustainable entrepreneurship in the two firms revolved around four key areas: 1) a process view,

DOI: 10.4018/979-8-3693-4338-8.ch007

2) a triple bottom line focused value creation 3) the centrality of opportunities, and 4) triple bottom line solutions. The findings of this study have significance for existing and future entrepreneurs, policymakers, and entrepreneurship education. The chapter also contribute to sustainable entrepreneurship research opportunities, and challenges.

INTRODUCTION

Sustainable entrepreneurship is an emerging subfield of entrepreneurship (Genus, 2021) that is in its nascent stage, with limited empirical studies available (Belz & Binder, 2015; Bonfanti et al., 2024). Sustainable entrepreneurship is an interdisciplinary (Bonfanti et al., 2024) and transformative field that lies at the intersection of entrepreneurship and sustainability. Sustainable entrepreneurship is a paradigm shift from a conventional entrepreneurial focus on creating economic value (Vuorio et al., 2018) to creating non-economic values, such as social and environmental value, for enterprises. The entrepreneurial pursuit of profit and consumerism has caused imbalances in the social-environment-economic spheres. This has resulted in trade-offs between economic gains, social well-being, and environmental sustainability. Intergovernmental organisations, governments, corporate leaders, entrepreneurs, and social leaders have engaged in dialogue aimed at creating a better future through a variety of sustainability-focused initiatives.

'Sustainability' is derived from the notion of sustainable development encapsulated in the Brundtland Commission's report (1992). The report's definition of sustainable development has modelled our understanding of various concepts linked to sustainability or sustainable development. Woodfield et al. (2017) argue for a micro-level conceptualisation of sustainable development, given its macro definition, to enhance understanding and implementation of sustainability at individual and organizational levels. Elkington's Triple Bottom Line (TBL) approach laid the foundation for operationalising the concept of sustainability at the organizational level (1994). The TBL approach combines three dimensions of sustainability (economic, environmental, and social) and calls on organisations to balance the outcomes of all three dimensions and eliminate tradeoffs (Wesseh et al., 2023). More contemporary sustainability-based frameworks such as Environment-Social-Governance (ESG) have emerged as an alternative to the TBL. Sustainability in the management and business disciplines has largely emphasised sustainability practices that advocate addressing social-environmental-economic issues. Hooi et al. (2016) emphasis that sustainability should primarily be about creating a better quality of life for both current and future generations, rather than solely addressing the socio-environmental challenges faced by mankind. Thus, sustainable entrepreneurship has emerged as a holistic concept that aims to create a more sustainable future by linking sustainability with entrepreneurs and enterprises.

Table 1. Definitions of Sustainable Entrepreneurship

Cohen and Winn (2007, p. 35)	"entrepreneurship as a scholarly field seeks to understand how opportunities to bring into existence "future" goods and services are discovered, created, and exploited, by whom, and with what consequences"
Pinkse and Groot (2015, p. 634)	"the discovery, creation, and exploitation of entrepreneurial opportunities that contribute to sustainability by generating social and environmental gains for others in society"
Hockerts and Wustenhagen, (2010, p. 482)	"the discovery and exploitation of economic opportunities through the generation of market disequilibria that initiate the transformation of a sector towards an environmentally and socially more sustainable state"
Maaßen et al. (2023, p.2)	"Sustainable entrepreneurship stands for alternative business models that create social and environmental value"
Shepherd and Patzelt (2011, p. 142)	"the preservation of nature, life support, and community in the pursuit of perceived opportunities to bring into existence future products, processes, and services for [...] economic and non-economic gain to individuals, the economy, and society"
Johnson and Schaltegger (2020, p. 1142)	"the discovery, creation, and exploitation of opportunities for (future) goods and services that simultaneously sustain the natural and social environment and provide economic and noneconomic gain for others"

Several definitions of sustainable entrepreneurship can be found in the extant literature (see Table 1). Shabbir (2023) regards sustainable entrepreneurship as an all-encompassing strategy for addressing sustainability issues. Haldar (2019) posits that sustainability-focused entrepreneurs or corporate leaders establish and operate businesses to create social, environmental, and economic value from the outset. Sustainable entrepreneurship involves more than just compliance with social and environmental laws; rather it calls on entrepreneurs to embrace a proactive (strategic) approach to 'sustainability' (McWilliams et al., 2006; Wesseh et al., 2023). Entrepreneurs adopting a strategic approach to sustainability also means the necessity to go beyond meeting current societal expectations for legitimacy, because future society's expectations may differ and evolve. Sustainable entrepreneurship positions the entrepreneur at the centre of the sustainability agenda for enterprises beyond the discourse on sustainability practices and processes. Entrepreneurship, as stated by Shane et al. (2003), involves human agency and is the result of individuals acting to pursue opportunities. Thus, entrepreneurs are called upon to develop sustainability-oriented entrepreneurial behaviour and ventures with the long-term aim of securing a sustainable future.

This chapter aims to review opportunities and challenges for sustainable entrepreneurship in Sri Lanka. The questions guiding this chapter are: (1). What are the main opportunities for sustainable entrepreneurship in Sri Lanka? (2). What challenges do sustainable entrepreneurs face? (3). How can policy frameworks be improved to support sustainable entrepreneurship? In fact, the chapter attempts to provide insights and recommendations to foster sustainable entrepreneurship in Sri Lanka.

The rest of the chapter is structured as follows. The next section discusses the theoretical background including a conceptual schema. Subsequently, the opportunities and challenges for sustainable entrepreneurship in Sri Lanka is discussed. This is followed by a brief methodology and two case studies. The latter sections of the chapter entail a section on policy recommendations for promoting sustainable entrepreneurship in Sri Lanka and a conclusion with future research directions.

COUNTRY CONTEXT

Sri Lanka is a lower-middle income country in South Asia. It embraced open economic policies prior to many Asian economies, and was the first South Asian economy to embark on such a path (Sahoo, 2006). Nevertheless, its progressive economic initiatives were short-lived, as the country endured war lasting almost three decades. Ending the war in 2009 spurred economic growth for a few years; however, incoherent economic policies and reforms, socio-political upheavals and the Covid-19 pandemic have precipitated the worst economic crisis since its independence. The economy has suffered multiple shocks since 2019, and the government yearned to return its economy on the recovery path. Despite embracing open economic policies, Sri Lanka's economy has never experienced double-digit growth. Given Sri Lanka's lacklustre economic performance, entrepreneurship can be viewed as an important driver of economic growth and response to economic downturns (Lewis et al., 2024). The International Labour Organization (ILO) (2023) identifies entrepreneurship development as an area for policy intervention in Sri Lanka to address economic crises and future shocks.

As for the 2019 edition of the Global Entrepreneurship Index (GEI), Sri Lanka, was ranked 90th (GEDI, 2019). Sri Lanka occupies the 89th position in the 2024 iteration of the Global Innovation Index and is positioned 12th among lower middle-income economies and 5th among central and south Asian economies (WIPO, 2024). Thus, Sri Lanka ranked lower in global entrepreneurship, and innovation indices are an indication of its state of business ecosystem. The Sri Lanka Startup Report 2019 identified a resurgence in startups in Sri Lanka (SLASSCOM, 2019). Nevertheless, the contemporary startup ecosystem in Sri Lanka is likely to differ significantly amidst the economic recovery from a crisis and in the aftermath of the pandemic. Moreover, most startups in Sri Lanka seem to be in the technology industry, and little is known about the extent to which they cater to sustainability entrepreneurship.

Sri Lanka's socio-political-economic landscape is rooted in its rich agrarian and hydraulic civilisation (Jayasena & Selker, 2004). Environmental sustainability has been part of Sri Lanka's agrarian societies, as they have adopted different crops, farming methods, and water management according to the islands' geographical landscape. Sri Lanka's ancient irrigation system comprises a Tank Cascade System for harvesting and distributing rainwater. Moreover, Buddhism, as the main religion of the country, has instilled a notion of sustainability throughout its ancient civilisation and continues to shape the sustainability stances and views of individuals (Abeydeera et al., 2016). Contemporary Sri Lanka depends on hydropower plants for renewable and affordable electricity. More recently, Sri Lanka launched a floating solar power plant and plans to initiate a few more in the years to come. Sri Lanka also had launched a rooftop solar power generation project with funds from the Asian Development Bank for domestic and commercial users. Thus, reflecting a focus on renewable energy as the need of the hour. Sustainability is engrained in the Sri Lankan society and continues to evolve as the country faces newer challenges. There is an urgent need to map the sustainability and entrepreneurship landscape in Sri Lanka to address its chronic socio-economic issues. Aligning with this view, the report on Sustainable Sri Lanka 2030 Vision and Strategic Path makes recommendations on promoting entrepreneurship that focuses on agriculture and green technologies (Presidential Expert Committee, 2019).

THEORETICAL BACKGROUND AND LITERATURE REVIEW

The importance of sustainable entrepreneurship can be viewed from both macro and micro lenses. From a macro perspective, sustainable entrepreneurship contributes to sustainable development within an economy. The UN's 2030 agenda for Sustainable Development, comprising the Sustainable Development Goals (SDGs), provides a comprehensive framework for entrepreneurs to contribute to sustainable development. At the micro level, entrepreneurs can seek to capitalise on sustainability-related niche opportunities and transform existing traditional ventures to become more sustainable. An individual who engages in entrepreneurial activities aimed at fostering sustainable development and building sustainable ventures can receive rent to improve social, environmental, and economic conditions (Cohen & Winn, 2007). Thus, it is important to bridge organizational-level sustainability-driven entrepreneurial activities with macro-level sustainability goals (i.e. SDGs).

The macro-view echoes the impact of sustainable entrepreneurship outside the organizational boundary in a broader external environment. For example, Ecomaximus is a business entity in Sri Lanka which won the BBC World Challenge in 2006 for making environmental-friendly paper using Elephant dung. The company's production facilities are in rural areas and provide employment for rural youth in Sri Lanka. It is evident that Ecomaximus uses naturally available resources to reduce its impact on the earth's ecosystem while simultaneously attempting to alleviate poverty among rural folk. While the business is being sustainable through its materials and processes, it also contributes to achieving national SDGs. Similarly, Vega Innovations a sustainable mobility solutions provider in Sri Lanka is manufacturing electric three wheelers as it caters for a larger segment of the market. Such technological innovations are an attempt to address sustainability needs of the country. Pastran et al. (2021) claims that MSMEs can play a pivotal role in accelerating the implementation of SDGs. However, mapping the impact of sustainable entrepreneurship on sustainable development is both challenging and complex.

The micro-view emphasises sustainable entrepreneurial activities which may involve sustainable products and services, business processes, and business ventures. Sustainable entrepreneurship entails the identification and exploitation of opportunities that generate social and environmental value at the individual and organizational levels. This viewpoint underscores the entrepreneurial process, which encompasses the identification of opportunities, resource mobilization, and value creation; it also emphasizes the role of individual entrepreneurs in the advancement of sustainability (Cohen & Winn, 2007; Patzelt & Shepherd, 2011). The micro-level view can be connected to the process approach of entrepreneurship which emphasis on identifying entrepreneurial opportunities and it encompasses that sustainability-oriented entrepreneurs may attempt to launch truly sustainable business ventures or transform existing traditional businesses to be more sustainable (Sreenivasan & Suresh, 2023). Eller et al. (2020) presented a theoretical model for identifying sustainability opportunities. Patzelt and Shephered (2011) asserted that identifying sustainable development opportunities requires individuals to be knowledgeable about the changes in the social, natural, and economic environments in which they live. Dean and McMullen (2007) suggest that sustainability opportunities may emerge from environmentally related market failures where entrepreneurs should be viewed as the catalyst that transform such market flaws into viable and enduring business prospects. Such transformation often involves turning challenges into opportunities. For example, finding new uses for old materials, creating energy from renewable sources, and meeting societal requirements with new products that enhance people's quality of life. Sustainable entrepreneurs typically seek out these opportunities where traditional businesses may see obstacles (Parrish, 2010). Sustainability can help entrepreneurs distinguish themselves in the market, draw environmentally and socially concerned customers, and create resilient businesses that support long-term societal goals. Entrepreneurial ventures that emphasize fair trade practices and environmental stewardship often gain customer loyalty and brand reputation, which can translate into long-term business success (Hall et al. 2010).

Thus, it is evident that entrepreneurs and their opportunity-seeking behaviour are central to the micro-view.

THE INTEGRATED FRAMEWORK

Macro-micro views are not independent but integrative, and calls on entrepreneurs go beyond the conventional profit-centric business narrative to embed sustainability into an organisation's business model with the aim of contributing positively to sustainable development. Eller et al. (2020) argued that solving sustainable development issues requires system-wide changes, and micro-level sustainability initiatives are the starting point to bring about changes at the macro-level.

Figure 1 shown below comprehends how integrating the macro and micro level perspectives of sustainable entrepreneurship may align with broader sustainability goals. Sustainable opportunities stem from macro environment and may be seized by the entrepreneur resulting in sustainability focused activities. Kiran et al. (2024) claims that ESG framework can be applied to evaluate sustainable business opportunities and ventures. The intent of such entrepreneurial action is to minimize negative externalities at organizational level and contribute to sustainable development at national level which is mapped by the SDGs. Sustainable entrepreneurs may face challenges from the macro and micro level perspectives. Essentially, the outcomes of sustainable entrepreneurship activities should transcend beyond the organizational boundary to have an accumulated effect at national level. The role of the institutions and agents in the macro environment is to drive such sustainable entrepreneurship and facilitate its activities to align with national sustainability development priorities.

Figure 1. Conceptual Schema

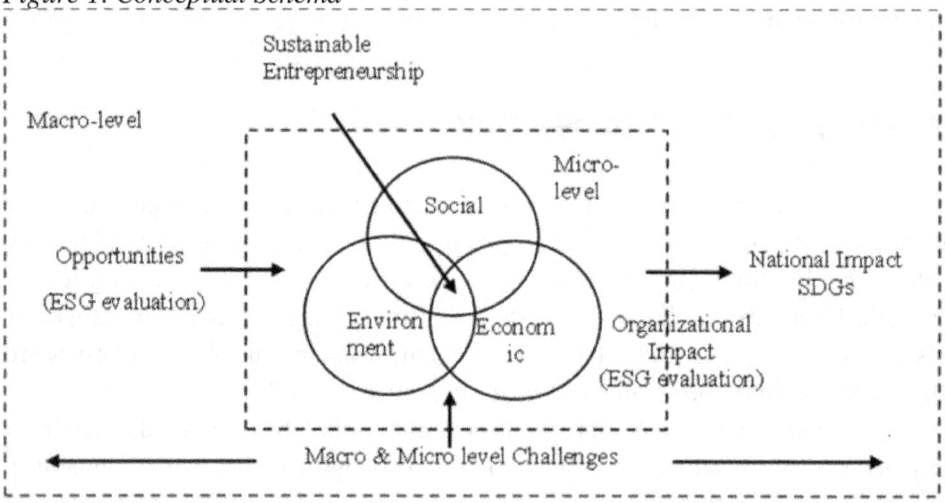

Source: Authors' conception

OPPORTUNITIES FOR SUSTAINABLE ENTREPRENEURSHIP IN SRI LANKA

Sri Lanka has a conducive climate for sustainable entrepreneurship, with opportunities spanning various promising sectors and a supportive policy framework. Entrepreneurs who are innovative and passionate about sustainability in their business models are well-positioned to capitalize on these opportunities, contributing to the country's economic, social, and environmental well-being. Here are some key opportunities available for sustainable entrepreneurs in the country.

NATURAL RESOURCE ABUNDANCE AND BIODIVERSITY:

Sri Lanka's biodiversity and natural beauty present potential for eco-tourism, with sustainable practices attracting eco-conscious tourists and generating economic benefits, as noted by the World Travel and Tourism Council (WTTC, 2018). The country's fertile land and climate also provide opportunities for organic farming and sustainable practices, attracting entrepreneurs to the growing global organic market. The International Federation of Organic Agriculture Movements highlights this growth, creating opportunities (IFOAM, 2017). Renewable energy sources, such as solar, wind, and hydropower, can contribute to energy security and promote sustainable development (ADB, 2016).

GROWING CONSUMER AWARENESS OF SUSTAINABLE CONSUMPTION

Sri Lankan consumers are becoming more conscious of health, wellness, and environmental and social issues,, leading to a growing market for eco-friendly products and services (Weeraratne, 2016). Increasing consumer awareness and demand for sustainable products create new market opportunities in sectors like organic food, natural health products, and wellness tourism (Global Wellness Institute, 2018).

GOVERNMENT INCENTIVES AND SUPPORT PROGRAMS

The Sri Lankan government is key in promoting sustainable entrepreneurship. Fiscal and monetary policies like tax exceptions, grants, subsidies, interest and exchange rates, and other incentives are favourably used to ensure a conducive business environment. Also, government authorities like the Ministry of Industry and Commerce, Export Development Board, and Board of Investment provide several supportive programs, workshops, and other assistance. These policy initiatives help to promote innovation, competitiveness, and sustainability in the SMW sector. But still, several challenges exist.

Tourism is among the top three sources of foreign exchange in Sri Lanka. In 2018, international tourist arrivals to Sri Lanka exceeded 2.3 million and post-Covid arrivals were on the up and yet to reach the peaks of 2015 to 2019 (Sri Lanka Tourism Development Authority, 2023). The prior Government of Sri Lanka focused on increasing tourist arrivals to five million per year. This would result in an increase in the carbon footprint of Sri Lanka's tourism industry and potentially lead to additional negative externalities. The Strategic Plan for Sri Lanka Tourism 2022 – 2025 proposes to earn foreign exchange of US $ 5 billion from the tourism industry (World Bank, 2022). This can't be achieved without increasing tourist arrivals and placing stress on natural resources in the island nation. Thus, the strategic plan recognises the importance of guidelines and certifications to transform the industry into a more sustainable one. This advertently calls upon existing tourism entities and new entrants to embrace a sustainable pathway and The Strategic Plan for Sri Lanka Tourism 2022 – 2025 recommends a sustainable and resilient model of tourism (World Bank, 2022). Hence, the government with its agencies may provide necessary policy directions, incentives, and support to promote sustainable entrepreneurship targeting the tourism industry.

TECHNOLOGICAL ADVANCEMENTS AND INNOVATION POTENTIAL

Advancements in technology and innovation provide opportunities for sustainable entrepreneurship in areas such as renewable energy, waste management, and sustainable agriculture. The increasing adaptation of digital technologies also supports the growth of sustainable business models for entrepreneurs (ICTA, 2020). Entrepreneurs can leverage these technologies to create innovative solutions that address environmental challenges. However, several improvements are yet to be addressed.

EDUCATION AND CAPACITY BUILDING

Sustainable business education and research and development are crucial for fostering a new generation of business leaders committed to sustainability. Reasonable opportunities are available in the country to develop educational programs and training workshops focused on sustainable business practices, though many challenges exist. For instance, The National Science Foundation of Sri Lanka supports research and innovation in sustainable technologies, enabling entrepreneurs to collaborate with academic institutions and research organizations.

SOCIAL RESPONSIBILITY INITIATIVES

Large corporations invest largely in sustainability-focused CSR initiatives, allowing entrepreneurs to partner with them to address social and environmental issues. The Global Reporting Initiative (GRI) emphasizes the importance of CSR in corporate strategies (GRI, 2016). Also, social entrepreneurs – those who seek to address social issues by means of commercial solutions – are attracting attention. Entrepreneurs can launch businesses with an eye toward environmental preservation, healthcare, and education, therefore producing social impact in addition to profits.

CHALLENGES FACING SUSTAINABLE ENTREPRENEURS IN SRI LANKA

Access to Finance and Investments

Sustainable entrepreneurs in Sri Lanka face challenges in securing funding because of perceived risks and limited investor awareness. Traditional financial institutions may be reluctant to invest in sustainable projects, limiting entrepreneurs' access to capital (UNCTAD, 2018). Often, funding in underdeveloped financial and capital markets comes at higher costs and interest rates, which restricts sustainable entrepreneurs from accessing funds. High borrowing costs can significantly impact the financial viability of new and small-scale sustainable enterprises (CBSL, 2019). Making it more difficult, many investors lack awareness and understanding of the potential returns from sustainable investments. This can result in a lower propensity to fund sustainable projects, further limiting the financial resources available to entrepreneurs (GIZ, 2018).

Moreover, the ambiguity surrounding the return for investments in sustainable entrepreneurial efforts and high costs (Mansouri & Momtaz, 2022), may discourage investors from comprehending the sustainability impact on society and environment. Although ESG frameworks provides a comprehensive guide to understand sustainability impact of an organization, it is lagging in developing and emerging markets compared to the developed markets resulting in limited ESG focused funds for sustainable entrepreneurs.

LACK OF INFRASTRUCTURE AND TECHNOLOGICAL SUPPORT

Infrastructure and technological support limit the ability of entrepreneurs to implement and scale sustainable solutions. At present, the available infrastructure facilities in Sri Lanka, including transportation, energy, and waste management systems, are not up to a satisfactory level and may not always support sustainable business operations. Also, access to advanced technologies and innovative solutions is often restricted due to high costs and limited availability. Sustainable entrepreneurs may struggle to acquire the technology needed to implement sustainable practices and improve efficiency (ICTA, 2020).

REGULATORY AND POLICY BARRIERS

Despite the policy provisions, the inconsistent enforcement of environmental and business regulations can create uncertainty for entrepreneurs and demotivate them (OECD, 2017). Also, the present complex bureaucratic procedures, lengthy approval processes, and lack of coordination between government agencies create significant administrative burdens, increase costs and hinder business operations (World Bank, 2019). Sustainable entrepreneurs may find it challenging to navigate these disparate regulations and align their business practices with all relevant policies (ADB, 2016).

LIMITED ENTREPRENEURIAL SKILLS AND EDUCATION

There is a lack of entrepreneurial skills and education in Sri Lanka, hindering sustainable entrepreneurship growth. Many entrepreneurs lack the necessary expertise to develop and manage sustainable business models, secure funding, and navigate regulatory environments (GEM, 2018). Also, the country is critically lacking in training programs focused on sustainable entrepreneurship. Educational institutions and professional training centres need to incorporate sustainability into their curricula to prepare future entrepreneurs better (UNDP, 2018).

SOCIO-CULTURAL BARRIERS AND RESISTANCE TO CHANGE

Socio-cultural barriers and resistance to change present significant challenges for sustainable entrepreneurs (Mair & Marti, 2009). Traditional mindsets and practices can impede the adoption of innovative and sustainable approaches. There is often a lack of awareness about the benefits of sustainable business practices among the general population and business community. This can result in low consumer demand for sustainable products and services, making it difficult for entrepreneurs to achieve market acceptance (Weeraratne, 2016). In some cases, local communities may resist sustainable projects due to mistrust or misunderstanding of the benefits. Effective communication and community engagement are crucial to overcoming this resistance and gaining local support for sustainable initiatives (UNDP, 2018).

The challenges facing sustainable entrepreneurs in Sri Lanka are multifaceted and require concerted efforts from various stakeholders, including the government, financial institutions, educational bodies, and entrepreneurs themselves. By addressing these barriers, Sri Lanka can create a more supportive environment for sustainable businesses, fostering innovation, economic growth, and environmental sustainability.

CASE STUDIES OF SUCCESSFUL SUSTAINABLE ENTREPRENEURSHIP

Methodology

To identify sustainable entrepreneurs' experiences, a qualitative investigation was conducted using a multiple-case study method. Research using case studies provides deep insights into the phenomenon and access to the unique characteristics of the unit under study. Thus, cases are often sampled intentionally to provide data-rich insights. We deliberately chose entrepreneurial firms (cases) that, by preset selection criteria, 1) had recognised a sustainable opportunity that generates economic, ecological, and social value; 2) had been in operation for more than ten years; and 3) had been the push behind the identification, development, and utilisation of the opportunity. Two cases were selected for the study. Dilmah is a large company with various ventures; its principal enterprise is a tea plantation. Another small business representing the food and agriculture sectors is called Ranbath Organic. Semi-structured interviews were conducted to gather the data. Documents and information from the company websites were also used. The (co-)founders, who have first-hand experience with the entrepreneurial process from ideation to market launch, are the primary informants. Interviews were conducted in June 2024 in Sri Lanka. They usually lasted thirty to forty-five minutes. All interviews were audio recorded. A thematic analysis was used to examine the data.

Case I: Dilmah PLC

Sri Lanka is replete with examples of sustainable entrepreneurship. Dilmah Ceylon Tea Corporation PLC, also known as Dilmah, is a beverage corporation in Sri Lanka. The process of sustainable entrepreneurship may involve problem identification, opportunity recognition, and development of a triple-bottom-line solution.

Identify business opportunities and provide triple-bottom-line solutions

In Sri Lanka, women are less likely than men to engage in entrepreneurial activity. In Sri Lanka, the patriarchal nature of society continues to pose a challenge in terms of gender discrimination, causing fewer women to pursue entrepreneurship. Dilmah Company is therefore committed to empowering women to have a better future. For instance, Dilmah's women's development program has led to an innovative bakery venture. Located near Moratuwa, Swashakthi Bakery and Tea Room provide a range of healthy meals at reasonable prices. Recent additions include juice bars and food orders for events hosted jointly or independently by enterprising women. The bakery set up an activity station and hopper stand on Fridays, serving a range of freshly made local foods. Dilmah provided unemployed women several job opportunities through this venture.

Dilmah identifies the ecological and social issues and offers creative fixes for them. Unfair pay practices and female unemployment have been identified as social issues.

> *"Social problems are mostly caused by economic issues, particularly those related to unemployment. It frequently stands in the way of worthwhile endeavours."*

As a result, Dilmah opened a new cashew-processing facility as part of a green effort with Dilmah Conservation, and the firm planted one million cashew plants in 2010 in one of the most impoverished regions of Sri Lanka. This program helped approximately 20,000 households by providing them with an extra source of income.

Dilmah also identified problems with the underprivileged. For instance, the North of Sri Lanka suffered greatly from the almost three-decade-long ethnic conflict, which also had a negative impact on the region's development, economy, government, and peace. The Dilmah-led programmes in the North of Sri Lanka aim to support and facilitate the Northern region's post-war reconstruction. As per the cofounder words,

> *"I have not forgotten my promise, and as Dilmah has expanded, so too has its earnings, which goes towards supporting the MJF Charitable Foundation's initiatives. Our Foundation has transformed numerous thousands of lives—I say "our" because every person who drinks Dilmah tea is a member of the MJF Foundation. Its aid work will keep expanding in cycle with Dilmah."*

Dilmah established the Charitable Foundation, which has always aimed to combat prejudice against people with disabilities. In order to give these people the support and care they need to grow into contributing members of society and lead independent lives, numerous comprehensive programs have been put in place. The company gave people access to new business opportunities and the required facilities for launching and operating their enterprises.

Additionally, Dilma strives to empower the underprivileged by providing education and career training so that men, women, and young people can obtain stable jobs, live strong and dignified lives, and escape dependency. The only culinary school in Sri Lanka with World Chefs certification is Dilmah's Empower Culinary and Hospitality School. This social effort with an industry focus gives underprivileged children opportunities and training.

Dilmah's Small Entrepreneurs Programme (SEP) gives underprivileged women and men the tools they need to launch profitable businesses, enhancing their sense of value and dignity. The SEP project, one of the first Foundation initiatives to launch immediately after the December 2004 tsunami, has helped nearly 2,000 small business owners and their families in an effort to rebuild self-sufficient communities.

Dilmah concentrates on sustainable farming. As per Mr. Fernando, Dilmah's co-founder,

"I wanted to bring my country's tea – the finest in the world – garden fresh and ethically produced. Regrettably, most companies are not taking proactive steps to find answers and do not perceive the necessity to address environmental effects. Businesses must take into account how their production methods, product life cycles, and supply chains may affect the environment. As a co-founder of the business, I constantly share my environmental concerns with staff members through awareness and training initiatives."

They believe that organic, naturally produced agriculture without chemical pesticides, fertilisers, and genetically engineered organisms has a future and a market. These values permeate every farming method that Dilmah uses and the people with whom they collaborate. Among the hurdles facing sustainable entrepreneurship are issues that constitute the "main problems for opportunity identification" (Torfing & Ansell, 2017), which are best addressed through forms of governance incorporating partnerships and multi-actor networks (Hofstad & Torfing, 2016). Concerning the owner,

"Businesses, governments, and individuals must work together to address the worldwide effects of environmental challenges. Working together, companies and environmental groups can promote creativity, information exchange, and the creation of long-term solutions."

The quotation reveals that these problems can be effectively addressed through collaborative relationships, which calls for the constructive integration of partners' differences and resources and the development of novel solutions that challenge accepted practices.

Case II: Ranbath Organic

Ranbath Organic, which was established in Sri Lanka by Janaki Kathiriarachchi, is another excellent example of a sustainable enterprise. There is a widespread perception that food cooked and cultivated at home is healthier than food purchased from the market. A few decades ago, before chemical fertilisers and pesticides were widely employed, Sri Lankans grew the necessary fruits and vegetables in their backyard gardens. They relied entirely on natural pest control techniques and compost fertilisers produced in their gardens. This cultivation strategy was appropriate because it was performed in small-scale home gardens rather than in large-scale commercial production. After Sri Lanka's independence, its social dynamics changed, and its population was concentrated in its cities. The nation transitioned to commercial agriculture at the same time, growing crops on a large scale and necessitating the use of chemical pesticides and fertilisers. However, Sri Lankans have always loved homemade food that has been passed down through generations. Furthermore, with the rise in non-communicable diseases, including cancer, diabetes, and cardiovascular diseases, the need to return to indigenous cuisine using locally grown ingredients has gained prominence.

In this setting, Ranbath Organic began cultivating fruits and vegetables organically in this environment, which proved to be successful in the long run. Consequently, Ranbath Organic Foods were founded. The owner went one step further from home-grown to entirely organic food farming. Her business received scientific certification that it is organic, which is no small feat. She launched her company 20 years ago by bringing a novel product consisting of cleansed, washed, and chopped green leaves to the market. Not because she wanted to start a business in the traditional sense, but rather because she wanted to give people healthy food. She devised a simple method to accomplish this, and then decided to expand it as a mission to help other people, especially since many mothers also have to balance office jobs. She started collaborating with farmer cooperatives, farming using only natural ways, and producing fertiliser that was entirely organic. Along with accreditation from the Netherlands Control Union, they also received more stringent organic certification attesting to the organic status of the agricultural fields.

Identifying business opportunities through problems

Ranbath highlighted this issue as an increased prevalence of non-communicable diseases and poor dietary habits. Furthermore, farmers' income is insufficient to support their families' food and educational expenses. As the owner explains

"Farmers' high-quality agricultural products sell well at huge retail chains, but their income is insufficient to support their families and send their kids to school"

This issue led to Ranbath's power to recognise the commercial prospects presented by this gap and to produce agricultural products based on organic principles that are safe for humans and the environment, and to try to improve the farmers' living standards, provide job opportunities, and contribute to rural development. She also had to deal with the issues of waste and excessive consumption in her company. She began to become irritated with *the amount of food waste*. She takes advantage of the increased demand for organic goods today to open a restaurant that solely serves organic meals. The co-founders recognised an opportunity to process and market organic agricultural products, which represent a Lifestyle of Health and Sustainability, to the target Asian market in Europe and export them from Sri Lanka.

Even though Sri Lankan business owners are able to recognize profitable entrepreneurial opportunities, they encounter numerous contextual and institutional obstacles when attempting to execute. As the owners explained,

"The main reason for the countless social issues that exist today is corruption. It frequently stands in the way of worthwhile endeavours. Additionally, there is a lack of appropriate coordination between the Sri Lankan organisations that assist entrepreneurs. Obtaining the environmental certificate was my goal. I visited numerous organisations and was dissatisfied with the assistance I received."

She further explained, "*we can easily take any certificate without rigorous evaluation if we have a personal connection.*"

According to the above quotation, the owner has long expressed concerns about the effect of not having proper regulations on businesses. Certain industries have regulations requiring new entrants to acquire government approval before they can operate, but some businesses take advantage of their political clout to get licenses and certifications more quickly.

Developing a triple-bottom-line solution

Ranbath constantly considers ecological value in terms of affordability, openness, and quality of service. Fair and direct trading are highly valued in Ranbath. The founders chose to buy organic goods cultivated in forest gardens exclusively without pesticides as they continued to develop their sustainable company strategy.

"The aims are the same even when the means are different. Additionally, I oppose fossil fuels and favour switching to alternative energy sources. Changing society through awareness and education and bringing these challenges to light are important components of our endeavour. the company should be the first to raise awareness of this, followed by society".

These findings are in line with the micro and macro perspectives of sustainable entrepreneurship, which state that an organisation should initiate sustainable business initiatives at the micro level within the company before disseminating the information to outside parties, which explains the macro perspective. Furthermore, validated emission reduction certificates were used to offset the CO_2 emissions of transportation operations from Sri Lankan farmers to German consumers.

The company is constantly looking for ways to enter sustainable markets. The final stage of the entrepreneurial process is market creation or entry.

"Regarding internet use and a new Fair-Trade model, we consider Ranbath to be a trailblazer. Consumers who want transparency from businesses and who place increasing trust in online buying"

Ranbath also puts much emphasis on transparency and trust. The company entered the European online market in September 2018. The focus was on sustainable products. This is the point in time when environmentally friendly innovation is made available to the market and becomes commercialised. Consumers who want transparency from businesses and who place increasing trust in online buying helped Ranbath Organic's entry into the European market. It distributes sustainable agricultural products directly to end-users who appreciate the product's quality, bypassing traditional sellers.

POLICY RECOMMENDATIONS FOR PROMOTING SUSTAINABLE ENTREPRENEURSHIP

To enhance the policy framework for sustainable entrepreneurship, the following recommendations are proposed. These measures aim to create a supportive environment that encourages the growth of sustainable businesses, contributing to Sri Lanka's long-term economic, social, and environmental sustainability.

IMPROVING ACCESS TO FINANCE

The case study's findings have brought to light several financial issues, including low agricultural income, unequal compensation methods, and a high rate of unemployment among women in the community. Therefore, improving access to finance is crucial for the growth and sustainability of entrepreneurial ventures in Sri Lanka. By developing innovative funding mechanisms such as green bonds and impact investing, expanding microfinance and credit facilities along with credit guarantee schemes, promoting green banking, leveraging international funding sources, and fostering public-private partnerships, Sri Lanka can create a supportive financial ecosystem for sustainable entrepreneurs. Mansouri & Momtaz (2022) states that the lack financing opportunities for sustainable entrepreneurial ventures is matter of public policy and governments should step forward in providing subsidies and assistance for such sustainable entrepreneurial exercises.

INVESTING IN INFRASTRUCTURE

As this study has shown, companies aid in the provision of infrastructure amenities, such as the post-war reconstruction of the northern region and the reconstruction of communities through infrastructure following the tsunami. Investing in infrastructure is vital for supporting sustainable entrepreneurship in Sri Lanka. By focusing on renewable energy, waste management, water management, transportation, digital infrastructure, and innovation facilities, the country can create an enabling environment for sustainable businesses. In support, corporations can collaborate with innovation hubs by means of funding, mentorships, and collaborative projects. Also, research and development centres can invest in to drive innovation and support the commercialization of sustainable products and services. Academic collaborations are also encouraged to promote applied research and innovation.

ENHANCING REGULATORY FRAMEWORK

The primary issue, as the case study's respondents made evident, is that culture discourages sustainable entrepreneurship, and many developing nations like Sri Lanka lack robust regulatory frameworks for entrepreneurs. Enhancing the regulatory framework is crucial for fostering sustainable entrepreneurship in Sri Lanka. By streamlining processes, ensuring policy consistency, incentivizing sustainable practices, strengthening institutions, and implementing robust monitoring and evaluation systems, Sri Lanka can create a supportive environment that encourages the growth of sustainable businesses. Digitalization of government services is also a needed priority that can enhance efficiency, transparency, and accessibility, making it easier for entrepreneurs to comply with regulations (ICTA, 2020). A robust and supportive regulatory framework can help overcome many of the challenges faced by entrepreneurs and promote the growth of sustainable businesses.

DEVELOPING ENTREPRENEURIAL SKILLS AND EDUCATION

Based on the narratives of the interviewees in the selected organizations, it appears that many businesses in Sri Lankan society are not as concerned about sustainable entrepreneurship. Developing entrepreneurial skills and education is essential for nurturing a generation of sustainable entrepreneurs in Sri Lanka. Gupta and Matharu (2022) states that entrepreneurship education should include sustainability concepts which will facilitate sustainable innovation and business ventures in the future. By implementing comprehensive training programs, integrating sustainability into educational curricula, promoting innovation and creativity through innovation hubs and incubators, and launching public education campaigns to increase public awareness and community engagement, Sri Lanka can create a robust ecosystem that supports sustainable entrepreneurship.

To make these possible, collaborative research projects between research and regular funding mechanisms for research and development are needed.

ENCOURAGING PRIVATE-PUBLIC PARTNERSHIP

This study's findings demonstrated that networking would be a practical way to find long-term opportunities and lessen the difficulties experienced by entrepreneurial organisations. Encouraging public-private partnerships is essential for promoting sustainable entrepreneurship in Sri Lanka. By fostering collaboration in policy development, infrastructure investment, capacity building, financing, and the promotion of sustainable practices, public-private partnerships can create a supportive environment for sustainable businesses. These partnerships leverage the strengths of both sectors, driving innovation, economic growth, and environmental sustainability

CONCLUSION AND FUTURE RESEARCH DIRECTIONS

Sustainable entrepreneurship is an emerging interdisciplinary field that focuses on creating social, environmental, and economic value. Sustainable entrepreneurship involves a transformation from entrepreneurship's general focus on economic value to balancing outcomes across the triple bottom line dimensions. From a macro perspective, sustainable entrepreneurship contributes to sustainable development within an economy, aligning with the UN's Sustainable Development Goals (SDGs). At the micro level, entrepreneurs can capitalize on sustainability-related niche opportunities and transform existing ventures to become more sustainable. Two case studies of sustainable entrepreneurship in Sri Lanka were examined to understand the phenomenon of sustainable entrepreneurship. Sri Lanka offers a conducive climate for sustainable entrepreneurship, with opportunities spanning various sectors and an improving institutional environment.

The discussion opens the door for prospective entrepreneurs by showing them how to create opportunities that focus on various value improvements at the same time, rather than just profit. These real-world ramifications enable entrepreneurs to achieve social and environmental value by fusing profit and purpose. Policymakers could, for example, encourage triple-bottom-line focus, create entrepreneurial ecosystems, and offer infrastructure, financial, and other forms of support to sustainable businesses. Policymakers should take sustainable entrepreneurship into serious consideration when promoting sustainable lifestyles since the results of this study indicate that it has the potential to be a transformative force. The findings are useful for entrepreneurship education because they inform students about the potential for generating triple-bottom-line value and give teachers a foundation for establishing courses that centre on the unique area of sustainable entrepreneurship. The study highlights the source of entrepreneurial potential found in social and ecological concerns, which holds relevance for (prospective) entrepreneurs in addition to promoting research on sustainable entrepreneurship.

Although qualitative research offers deep insights into poorly understood phenomena, it frequently has limitations regarding generalisability. Simultaneously, alternative criteria—credibility, transferability, dependability, and confirmability—as put forth by Guba and Lincoln (1994) are a proper way to assess qualitative data. To maintain the focus on gaining deep insights into the phenomenon of sustainable entrepreneurship, these were taken into consideration during the design and execution of the study. It is also important to reiterate that qualitative approaches offer a promising starting point for the quantitative investigation of the phenomenon. This chapter's main goal was to highlight "how" opportunities for sustainable development are identified, nurtured, and taken advantage of. Switching from a process model to a change model, including both macro- and micro-level dimensions (such as the founder's identity and external environment) is a relevant direction for future research. How the entrepreneurial process embeds sustainability in different stages should be examined in more detail.

REFERENCES

Abeydeera, S., Kearins, K., & Tregidga, H. (2016). Does Buddhism Enable a Different Sustainability Ethic at Work? *Journal of Corporate Citizenship*, 62(62), 109–130. https://www.jstor.org/stable/90003767. DOI: 10.9774/GLEAF.4700.2016.ju.00013

ADB. (2016). *Renewable Energy in Asia: The Role of the Private Sector*. Asian Development Bank.

ADB. (2018). *Asian Development Outlook 2018: How Technology Affects Jobs*. Asian Development Bank.

Belz, F. M., & Binder, J. K. (2017). Sustainable Entrepreneurship: A Convergent Process Model. *Business Strategy and the Environment*, 26(1), 1–17. DOI: 10.1002/bse.1887

Bonfanti, A., De Crescenzo, V., Simeoni, F., & Loza Adaui, C. R. (2024). Convergences and divergences in sustainable entrepreneurship and social entrepreneurship research: A systematic review and research agenda. *Journal of Business Research*, 170, 114336. DOI: 10.1016/j.jbusres.2023.114336

Brundtland, G. (1987). *Report of the World Commission on Environment and Development: Our Common Future*. United Nations General Assembly document A/42/427.

Central Bank of Sri Lanka. (2019). *Annual Report 2019*. Central Bank of Sri Lanka.

Cohen, B., & Winn, M. I. (2007). Market imperfections, opportunity and sustainable entrepreneurship. *Journal of Business Venturing*, 22(1), 29–49. DOI: 10.1016/j.jbusvent.2004.12.001

Dean, T. J., & McMullen, J. S. (2007). Toward a theory of sustainable entrepreneurship: Reducing environmental degradation through entrepreneurial action. *Journal of Business Venturing*, 22(1), 50–76. DOI: 10.1016/j.jbusvent.2005.09.003

Elkington, J. (1994). Towards the Sustainable Corporation: Win-Win-Win Business Strategies for Sustainable Development. *California Management Review*, 36(2), 90–100. DOI: 10.2307/41165746

Eller, F. J., Gielnik, M. M., Wimmer, H., Tholke, C., Holzapfel, S., Tegtmeier, S., & Halberstadt, J. (2020). Identifying business opportunities for sustainable development: Longitudinal and experimental evidence contributing to the field of sustainable entrepreneurship. *Business Strategy and the Environment*, 29(3), 1387–1403. DOI: 10.1002/bse.2439

GEM. (2018). *Global Entrepreneurship Monitor 2018/19 Global Report*. GEM Consortium.

Genus, A. (2021). Sustainable entrepreneurship research in the 2020s: An introduction. *Business Strategy and the Environment*, 30(3), 1419–1422. DOI: 10.1002/bse.2705

GIZ. (2018). *Comparative Analysis of SME Policies in South Asia*. Deutsche Gesellschaft für Internationale Zusammenarbeit (GIZ).

Global Entrepreneurship Development Institute (GEDI). (2019). *Global Entrepreneurship Index 2019*. Global Entrepreneurship Development Institute.

Global Wellness Institute. (2018). *Global Wellness Economy Monitor*. Global Wellness Institute.

GRI. (2016). *Sustainability Reporting Guidelines*. Global Reporting Initiative.

Guba, E. G., & Lincoln, Y. S. (1994). Competing paradigms in qualitative research. In Denzin, N. K., & Lincoln, Y. S. (Eds.), *Handbook of qualitative research* (pp. 105–117). Sage Publications, Inc.

Gupta, N., & Matharu, M. (2022). Examining the enablers of sustainable entrepreneurship – an interpretive structural modelling technique. *Journal of Entrepreneurship in Emerging Economies*, 14(5), 701–726. DOI: 10.1108/JEEE-10-2021-0416

Haldar, S. (2019). Towards a conceptual understanding of sustainability-driven entrepreneurship. *Corporate Social Responsibility and Environmental Management*, 26(6), 1157–1170. DOI: 10.1002/csr.1763

Hall, J. K., Daneke, G. A., & Lenox, M. J. (2010). Sustainable Development and Entrepreneurship: Past Contributions and Future Directions. *Journal of Business Venturing*, 25(5), 439–448. DOI: 10.1016/j.jbusvent.2010.01.002

Hockerts, K., & Wustenhagen, R. (2010). Greening Goliaths versus emerging Davids — Theorizing about the role of incumbents and new entrants in sustainable entrepreneurship. *Journal of Business Venturing*, 25(5), 481–492. DOI: 10.1016/j.jbusvent.2009.07.005

Hofstad, H., & Torfing, J. (2016). Collaborative innovation as a tool for environmental, economic and social sustainability in regional governance. *Scandinavian Journal of Public Administration*, 19(4), 49–70. DOI: 10.58235/sjpa.v19i4.14992

Hooi, H. C., Ahmad, N. H., Amran, A., & Rahman, S. A. (2016). The functional role of entrepreneurial orientation and entrepreneurial bricolage in ensuring sustainable entrepreneurship. *Management Research Review*, 39(12), 1616–1638. DOI: 10.1108/MRR-06-2015-0144

IFOAM. (2017). *The World of Organic Agriculture: Statistics and Emerging Trends 2017*. International Federation of Organic Agriculture Movements.

Information and Communication Technology Agency (ICTA). (2020). *Digital Economy Strategy of Sri Lanka*. Information and Communication Technology Agency.

International Labour Organization (ILO). (2023). *Impact of multiple crises on Sri Lanka's micro, small and medium-sized enterprises*. International Labour Organization.

Jayasena, H. A. H., & Selker, J. S. (2004). Thousand Years of Hydraulic Civilization Some Sociotechnical Aspects of Water Management. *Proceedings of the Workshop on Water and Politics: Understanding the Role of Politics in Water Management*. World Water Council.

Johnson, M. P., & Schaltegger, S. (2020). Entrepreneurship for Sustainable Development: A Review and Multilevel Causal Mechanism Framework. *Entrepreneurship Theory and Practice*, 44(6), 1141–1173. DOI: 10.1177/1042258719885368

Kiran, P. R., Chaubey, A., & Shastri, R. K. (2024). Incorporating the ESG framework to analyse entrepreneurial opportunities among tribal people. *Management of Environmental Quality*, 35(2), 249–269. DOI: 10.1108/MEQ-08-2023-0247

Lewis, D., Bowers, R., Heslop, L., & Tawfic, S. (2024). From Ecosystems to Advicescapes: Business, Development and Advice in Sri Lanka and Bangladesh. *Journal of South Asian Development*, 0(0), 345–363. Advance online publication. DOI: 10.1177/09731741241239120

Maaßen, C., Rovira, R., & Urbano, D. (2023). A Process Model for Sustainable Entrepreneurship: Evidence from a Highly Entrepreneurial European Region. *Journal of Social Entrepreneurship*, in press, 1–32. DOI: 10.1080/19420676.2023.2221262

Mansouri, S., & Momtaz, P. P. (2022). Financing sustainable entrepreneurship: ESG measurement, valuation, and performance. *Journal of Business Venturing*, 37(6), 106258. Advance online publication. DOI: 10.1016/j.jbusvent.2022.106258

McWilliams, A., Siegel, D. S., & Wright, P. M. (2006). Corporate Social Responsibility: Strategic Implications. *Journal of Management Studies*, 43(1), 1–18. DOI: 10.1111/j.1467-6486.2006.00580.x

Ministry of Industry and Commerce. (2017). *National Policy Framework for Small and Medium Enterprise (SME) Development*. Government of Sri Lanka.

NSF. (2019). *National Science Foundation of Sri Lanka*. National Science Foundation.

OECD. (2017). *Enhancing the Contributions of SMEs in a Global and Digitalised Economy*. Organisation for Economic Co-operation and Development.

Parrish, B. D. (2010). Sustainability-driven entrepreneurship: Principles of organization design. *Journal of Business Venturing*, 25(5), 510–523. DOI: 10.1016/j.jbusvent.2009.05.005

Pastran, A., Colli, E., & Poclaba, C. (2021). Sustainable entrepreneurship: A new way of doing business. *Journal of the International Council for Small Business*, 2(2), 147–158. DOI: 10.1080/26437015.2021.1882915

Patzelt, H., & Shepherd, D. A. (2011). Recognizing Opportunities for Sustainable Development. *Entrepreneurship Theory and Practice*, 35(4), 631–652. DOI: 10.1111/j.1540-6520.2010.00386.x

Pinkse, J., & Groot, K. (2015). Sustainable Entrepreneurship and Corporate Political Activity: Overcoming Market Barriers in the Clean Energy Sector. *Entrepreneurship Theory and Practice*, 39(3), 633–654. DOI: 10.1111/etap.12055

Presidential Expert Committee. (2019). *The report on Sustainable Sri Lanka 2030 Vision and Strategic Path*. Presidential Secretariat, Government of Sri Lanka.

Sahoo, P. (2006). *Foreign Direct Investment in South Asia: Policy, Trends, Impact and Determinants*. ADB Institute Discussion Paper No 56. Asian Development Bank Institute.

Shabbir, M. S. (2023). Exploring the relationship between sustainable entrepreneurship and the United Nations sustainable development goals: A comprehensive literature review. *Sustainable Development (Bradford)*, 31(4), 3070–3085. DOI: 10.1002/sd.2570

Shane, S., Locke, E. A., & Collins, C. J. (2003). Entrepreneurial motivation. *Human Resource Management Review*, 13(2), 257–279. DOI: 10.1016/S1053-4822(03)00017-2

Shepherd, D. A., & Patzelt, H. (2011). The New Field of Sustainable Entrepreneurship: Studying Entrepreneurial Action Linking "What is to be Sustained" with "What is to be Developed". *Entrepreneurship Theory and Practice*, 35(1), 137–163. DOI: 10.1111/j.1540-6520.2010.00426.x

Sreenivasan, A. & Suresh, M. (2023). Exploring the contribution of sustainable entrepreneurship toward sustainable development goals: A bibliometric analysis. *Green Technologies and Sustainability*, 3(1).

Sri Lanka Association of Software and Service Companies (SLASSCOM). (2019). *Sri Lanka Startup Report 2019*. Sri Lanka Association of Software and Service Companies.

Sri Lanka Tourism Development Authority (SLTDA). (2023). *Annual Statistical Report 2023*. Sri Lanka Tourism Development Authority. https://www.sltda.gov.lk/en/annual-statistical-report

Torfing, J., & Ansell, C. (2017). Strengthening political leadership and policy innovation through the expansion of collaborative forms of governance. *Public Management Review*, 19(1), 37–54. DOI: 10.1080/14719037.2016.1200662

UNCTAD. (2018). *World Investment Report 2018: Investment and New Industrial Policies. United Nations Conference on Trade and Development.*

UNDP. (2018). *Promoting Inclusive and Sustainable Economic Growth*. United Nations Development Programme.

Vuorio, A. M., Puumalainen, K., & Fellnhofer, K. (2018). Drivers of entrepreneurial intentions in sustainable entrepreneurship. *International Journal of Entrepreneurial Behaviour & Research*, 24(2), 359–381. DOI: 10.1108/IJEBR-03-2016-0097

Weeraratne, B. (2016). Sustainable Consumption and Production in Sri Lanka. *Sri Lanka Journal of Social Sciences*, 39(1), 1–8.

Wesseh, P. K.Jr, Lin, B., Zhang, Y., & Wesseh, P. S. (2024). Sustainable entrepreneurship: When does environmental compliance improve corporate performance? *Business Strategy and the Environment*, 33(4), 3203–3221. DOI: 10.1002/bse.3657

Woodfield, P., Woods, C., & Shepherd, D. (2017). Sustainable entrepreneurship: Another avenue for family business scholarship? *Journal of Family Business Management*, 7(1), 122–132. DOI: 10.1108/JFBM-12-2015-0040

World Bank. (2019). *Doing Business 2020: Comparing Business Regulation in 190 Economies*. World Bank Group.

World Bank. (2022). *Strategic Plan for Sri Lanka Tourism 2022 – 2025*. The World Bank. https://www.sltda.gov.lk/en/download-2

World Intellectual Property Organization (WIPO). (2024). *Global Innovation Index 2024: Unlocking the Promise of Social Entrepreneurship*. Geneva: WIPO. DOI: 10.34667/tind.50062

WTTC. (2018). *Travel and Tourism Economic Impact 2018*. World Travel and Tourism Council.

Chapter 8
Role of Social Entrepreneurship in Sustainable Development:
Perspectives From Business Experts

A. Ayyoob
https://orcid.org/0009-0003-2839-3598
University of Calicut, India

Aparna Sajeev
https://orcid.org/0000-0001-5642-5460
University of Calicut, India

ABSTRACT

In today's world, social entrepreneurship offers innovative solutions to global challenges, addressing societal and environmental issues. This abstract explores the impact and challenges of social entrepreneurship, focusing on its role in sustainable development. Drawing on business experts' insights, it examines drivers, barriers, and effective strategies. The study employs mixed methods, including qualitative and quantitative analyses, to uncover the pivotal role of social entrepreneurship in addressing societal, economic, and environmental challenges. Despite obstacles, social entrepreneurs leverage effective business models to create social and environmental value, emphasizing collaboration, innovation, and social responsibility. Recommendations include fostering cross-sector partnerships and promoting adaptability within organizations to advance sustainability goals. These insights provide practical guidance for policymakers and practitioners seeking to prioritize sustainability while achieving organizational success and positive societal impact.

DOI: 10.4018/979-8-3693-4338-8.ch008

1. INTRODUCTION

Social entrepreneurship emerges as a pivotal force in driving sustainable development, intricately intertwining social and environmental imperatives through innovative business models and collaborative partnerships. By addressing pressing social and environmental challenges, social entrepreneurs are crucial in advancing the Sustainable Development Goals (Bataineh et al., 2023; Viktoriia Ilchenko, 2023; Kalendzhjan & Kadol, 2022). They adeptly navigate the entrepreneurial ecosystem, engaging with diverse stakeholders across finance, politics, law, and academia to nurture the growth of social enterprises (Wagner & Kabalska, 2023). Through their endeavours, social entrepreneurs generate social value and harness innovation to tackle complex societal issues, fostering positive economic, social, and environmental impacts (Lubberink, 2019). Moreover, these socially involved startups actively collaborate with their stakeholders, co-creating and capturing value while navigating the intricate dynamics of value exchange, thus showcasing social entrepreneurship's multifaceted nature and transformative potential. By understanding the intricacies of social entrepreneurship and drawing insights from successful practices, the researchers gain valuable guidance for shaping future initiatives in this realm, thus fostering sustainable development and societal progress.

In an era marked by unprecedented global challenges, the concept of social entrepreneurship has emerged as a beacon of hope, offering innovative solutions to address pressing societal and environmental issues while fostering sustainable development. Social entrepreneurs, driven by a profound sense of purpose and a commitment to positive change, leverage entrepreneurial principles to tackle complex problems and create lasting impact. With their unique blend of business acumen and social mission, they stand at the forefront of a movement towards a more inclusive, equitable, and sustainable world. Against this backdrop, this study explores the multifaceted landscape of social entrepreneurship and its pivotal role in promoting sustainable development. By delving into the intricate interplay between business innovation, social impact, and environmental stewardship, the researchers seek to uncover the underlying mechanisms that drive the success of social entrepreneurship ventures in creating meaningful change. By integrating theoretical frameworks with empirical evidence, the researchers endeavour to deepen our understanding of the dynamics shaping the field of social entrepreneurship and chart a course toward a more prosperous and equitable future. As the researchers navigate the intricacies of social entrepreneurship, they are reminded of the transformative power inherent in the entrepreneurial spirit, which is the power to challenge the status quo, inspire collective action, and catalyse positive change. In this study, the researchers explore the untapped potential of social entrepreneurship to drive sustainable development and create a brighter tomorrow for all. This introduction sets the stage for the study, emphasizing the importance of social entrepreneurship in addressing global challenges and promoting sustainable development. It captures the essence of the research endeavour and invites readers to embark on a journey of exploration and discovery into the world of social entrepreneurship.

1.1 Statement of the Problem:

In recent years, there has been a growing recognition of the pivotal role that social entrepreneurship plays in fostering sustainable development worldwide. Social entrepreneurs leverage innovative business models to address pressing social and environmental challenges while generating economic value. However, despite the increasing prominence of social entrepreneurship, there remains a need to comprehensively understand its impact, effectiveness, and challenges from the perspective of business experts. The problem lies in the existing gap in the literature regarding the nuanced insights and perspectives of business experts on the intersection of social entrepreneurship and sustainable development. While numerous studies have explored various aspects of social entrepreneurship, there is a lack of in-depth understanding of how business experts perceive the role of social entrepreneurship in contributing to sustainable development goals, the effectiveness of different business models employed by social entrepreneurs, and the challenges faced by social enterprises in achieving sustainable impact. Furthermore, as the global community grapples with complex social and environmental issues, there is an urgent need to identify best practices, strategies, and opportunities for enhancing the effectiveness and scalability of social entrepreneurship initiatives. Without a thorough understanding of the perspectives and experiences of business experts in this field, policymakers, investors, and practitioners may lack the necessary insights to support and foster the growth of social entrepreneurship as a catalyst for sustainable development.

Therefore, this study aims to address the following research questions:

- How do business experts perceive the role of social entrepreneurship in promoting sustainable development?
- What are the key drivers and barriers to the success of social entrepreneurship initiatives in achieving sustainable impact?
- What are social entrepreneurs' most effective business models, strategies, and practices to create social and environmental value?
- What opportunities exist for collaboration and investment in social entrepreneurship ventures to maximize their contribution to sustainable development goals?

- How can policymakers, investors, and practitioners better support and promote the growth of social entrepreneurship as a means to address global social and environmental challenges?

1.2 Significance of the Study

The exploration of sustainable entrepreneurship within this chapter holds profound significance, aligning closely with its objectives and intended audience. Through a comprehensive approach, synthesizing theoretical frameworks and practical strategies from diverse fields such as entrepreneurship, sustainability, business, and environmental studies, this chapter advances multidisciplinary understanding. Offering actionable insights into fostering sustainable entrepreneurship ecosystems is a guiding beacon for policymakers and practitioners, empowering them with holistic insights essential for effective decision-making and action. Furthermore, by examining the impact of sustainable entrepreneurship on economic, social, and environmental dimensions, this chapter inspires future research endeavors and scholarship, encouraging scholarly inquiry and stimulating dialogue around emerging topics and trends. Academics, researchers, and graduate students in relevant fields will find a rich tapestry of ideas, theories, and empirical findings that invigorate their intellectual curiosity and shape their scholarly pursuits. As sustainable entrepreneurship emerges as a potent force for positive change, this chapter catalyzes collective action toward a more sustainable and equitable future. By fostering collaboration among stakeholders and emphasizing the transformative potential of collaborative approaches, policymakers, government officials, and entrepreneurs are provided with a wealth of knowledge to inform strategies and initiatives. In essence, this study represents a pivotal contribution to the ongoing discourse on sustainable entrepreneurship, offering a roadmap for navigating the complexities of the 21st century with foresight, purpose, and resilience.

1.3 Objectives of the Study

1. Understand business experts' perceptions of the role of social entrepreneurship in promoting sustainable development
2. Identify key drivers and barriers to the success of social entrepreneurship initiatives in achieving sustainable impact
3. Determine effective business models, strategies, and practices social entrepreneurs employ to create social and environmental value.

1.4 Conceptual Model

Figure 1. Social and environmental value creation

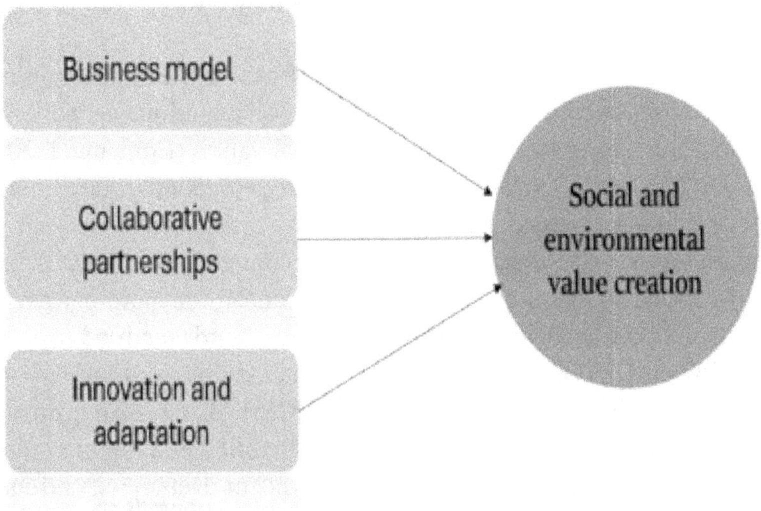

1.5 Variables for the Study

Dependent variable:

- Social and environmental value creation: This variable encompasses the overall impact of social entrepreneurship ventures, including both social and environmental outcomes.

Independent variables:

- Business model: This variable refers to the type of business model social entrepreneurs adopt, such as hybrid models, traditional profit-making models, or non-profit models.
- Collaborative partnerships: This variable relates to the extent and effectiveness of partnerships established by social entrepreneurs with stakeholders, including local communities, governments, NGOs, and businesses.
- Innovation and adaptation: This variable captures the degree of innovation and adaptability demonstrated by social entrepreneurship ventures in response to changing market dynamics, stakeholder needs, and environmental challenges

2. REVIEW OF LITERATURES

2.1 Key Drivers And Barriers To The Success Of Social Entrepreneurship Initiatives In Achieving Sustainable Impact

Key drivers for the success of social entrepreneurship initiatives in achieving sustainable impact encompass factors such as collaboration, networking, and a steadfast commitment to social and environmental values (Emmanuel, 2023). Furthermore, environmental considerations, societal perceptions, social networking, effective social impact measurement, and access to financial resources are catalysts for enhancing social entrepreneurs' performance (Bataineh et al., 2023). Conversely, barriers to success entail challenges such as a need for more partnerships and networking opportunities with fellow social entrepreneurs, inadequate engagement with corporate entities, lack of government collaboration, and limited utilization of social networking platforms (Abdul et al., 2023). Additionally, impediments, including stringent government regulations, difficulties in adopting cutting-edge technology, restricted access to funding, low levels of awareness, and inadequate social impact measurement methodologies, constrain the efficacy of social entrepreneurship initiatives (Inalegwu & Mpele, 2022).

Various factors contribute to the success of social entrepreneurship initiatives in achieving sustainable impact, reflecting the intricate interplay between environmental conditions, societal attitudes, social networks, and access to financial resources. These elements are pivotal drivers, empowering social entrepreneurs to enhance their performance and contribute meaningfully to sustainable development. The environmental context within which social entrepreneurship operates significantly influences its effectiveness. Factors such as resource availability, ecological resilience, and climate dynamics shape the landscape social entrepreneurs navigate, influencing both the challenges they face and the opportunities they seize. Moreover, societal perceptions play a critical role in determining the acceptance and adoption of social entrepreneurship initiatives. Positive attitudes towards social innovation and community empowerment can foster an environment conducive to the success of such ventures.

Equally crucial are the social networks that social entrepreneurs cultivate. These networks serve as conduits for knowledge exchange, collaboration, and support, enabling entrepreneurs to leverage diverse perspectives and resources to pursue their objectives. Strong social ties within communities and strategic partnerships with other organizations amplify the impact of social entrepreneurship initiatives and enhance their sustainability. Access to financial resources remains a cornerstone of success for social entrepreneurs. Adequate funding facilitates program implementation, scalability, and long-term sustainability. Whether through grants, investments, or other financial instruments, securing adequate resources empowers social entrepreneurs to innovate, experiment, and adapt their approaches to address evolving social and environmental challenges. However, despite these drivers, social entrepreneurship faces formidable barriers that hinder its success and impact. Challenges such as limited partnerships and networking opportunities inhibit collaboration and resource mobilization, constraining the scalability and effectiveness of initiatives. Insufficient engagement with corporate entities and government agencies further restricts access to resources, expertise, and regulatory support necessary for sustainable growth. Overcoming these barriers necessitates concerted efforts to foster an enabling ecosystem for social entrepreneurship characterized by enhanced collaboration, supportive policies, and increased access to financial and non-financial resources. In conclusion, addressing social and environmental challenges through social entrepreneurship requires a holistic approach that leverages critical drivers while mitigating barriers to success. Social entrepreneurs can drive meaningful change and contribute significantly to sustainable development, even in challenging contexts like South Africa's townships, by harnessing environmental conditions, societal perceptions, social networks, and financial resources.

2.2 Effective business models, strategies, and practices employed by social entrepreneurs to create social and environmental value

Social entrepreneurs leverage innovative business models and strategies to catalyse positive social change (Kreutzer, 2022). They prioritize reinvesting profits into social causes, emphasizing the generation of earned income over personal enrichment. Central to the success of social enterprises are the intricate interactions among various components of their business models, which concurrently create both social and economic value while aligning internal operations, market dynamics, and financial management with the organization's mission (Oham & Okeoma John-Paul Okeke, 2022). Corporate social entrepreneurship, a fusion of corporate social responsibility (CSR) and social entrepreneurship principles, strategically balances economic and social value among stakeholders, exemplified by initiatives like the Sido Muncul partnership program (Neessen et al., 2021). These practices entail activities such as problem identification, resource allocation, network establishment, mentorship, innovation, and performance evaluation, ultimately resulting in the enhancement of farmers' welfare through knowledge dissemination, product innovation, marketing initiatives, and market guarantees (Hani & Yustina, 2022)

Social entrepreneurs are at the forefront of a transformative movement, utilizing innovative business models and strategies to forge a path toward social and environmental progress. Unlike traditional entrepreneurs driven solely by profit motives, these visionaries prioritize creating societal value over personal gain. Their ventures are not just about generating revenue; they are about catalyzing positive change and addressing pressing issues that affect communities worldwide. One of the most significant contributions of social entrepreneurship lies in its alignment with sustainable development goals. By tackling issues like poverty, inequality, and environmental degradation, social enterprises serve as powerful agents for change. They introduce holistic solutions that alleviate immediate hardships and lay the groundwork for long-term resilience and prosperity. What sets social enterprises apart is their unique approach to business. They integrate their mission into every aspect of their operations, from product development to marketing and financial management. This alignment ensures that every decision serves social and economic objectives, fostering a symbiotic relationship between profit-making and societal impact.

In recent years, we have witnessed the emergence of corporate social entrepreneurship, a strategic blend of corporate social responsibility and social entrepreneurship. This hybrid model seeks to leverage the resources and influence of large corporations to drive positive change in communities. By harnessing the power of business for good, corporate social entrepreneurship benefits the bottom line and creates value for society at large. Furthermore, social businesses play a crucial role in promoting social inclusion by breaking down barriers to access. By offering affordable products and services, they democratize essential resources for low-income populations, empowering them to lead healthier, more dignified lives. In doing so, they address immediate needs and stimulate economic activity and job creation within underserved communities. In essence, social entrepreneurship represents a fundamental shift in how we perceive business. It is not just about making money but about making a difference. Through their innovative spirit and unwavering commitment to social and environmental causes, social entrepreneurs pave the way for a more equitable, sustainable, and inclusive future for all.

2.3 Barriers and Contextual Influences

Barriers and contextual influences play a significant role in shaping the effectiveness of social entrepreneurship in sustainable development. While social entrepreneurship embodies innovation and altruism, it faces key challenges such as regulatory barriers, bureaucracy, and the inability of the formal sector to absorb labor, hindering its growth and impact (Inggang et al., 2023). The success of sustainable social entrepreneurship is influenced by factors like motivation, creativity, leadership, family support, and community relationships, emphasizing the importance of individual, social, and political elements in fostering impactful initiatives (Latifah et al., 2023). Additionally, the theoretical framework presented underscores the critical role of contextual and structural factors in mediating and moderating the sustainability of entrepreneurial development projects, emphasizing the need to align project implementation models with the dynamic realities of entrepreneurship for sustainable outcomes (Nicasio & Samuel, 2024). Local policies, economic conditions, and cultural attitudes significantly impact social entrepreneurship, where supportive local policies and stable economic conditions can create an enabling environment, while adverse political climates and economic instability pose significant challenges. Regional and cultural variations necessitate a localized approach to address unique obstacles effectively, as challenges faced by social entrepreneurs vary significantly across different contexts. Understanding the influence of political climates and economic stability on social ventures is crucial, as these elements shape the operational landscape for social entrepreneurs, affecting their ability to scale and sustain their initiatives. By comprehending these barriers and contextual influences, stakeholders can develop more effective strategies to support social entrepreneurship, ensuring it can thrive and contribute meaningfully to sustainable development across diverse settings.

3. RESEARCH METHODOLOGY

For this study on sustainable entrepreneurship, an empirical research design was employed, chosen for its suitability in accommodating the dynamic nature of the field. This approach facilitated data collection and analysis flexibility, enabling a comprehensive understanding of sustainable entrepreneurship across diverse contexts. Data were gathered through a variety of methods. A rigorous literature review was conducted, providing a foundational understanding of critical concepts and identifying gaps in existing research. Additionally, an interview was conducted with a purposive sample of stakeholders using a structured questionnaire. 182 business experts were interviewed for the collection of data. These interviews offered qualitative insights into the lived experiences and perspectives of individuals involved in sustainable entrepreneurship. This quantitative approach allowed for assessing prevalent practices and attitudes towards sustainability within the broader entrepreneurial community. Furthermore, document analysis of relevant reports and policy documents provided additional context and insights into the ecosystem of sustainable entrepreneurship.

Data analysis involved both qualitative and quantitative approaches. A thematic analysis based on the literature will be conducted to identify recurring patterns and themes. In contrast, a statistical analysis of survey data will generate descriptive statistics and reveal correlations and regressions. Ethical considerations were paramount throughout the research process. Participants were provided clear information about the study's purpose and rights, and informed consent was obtained before data collection. Measures were implemented to ensure participant confidentiality and data protection in compliance with relevant regulations.

4. FINDINGS AND DISCUSSIONS

4.1 Thematic analysis

4.1.1. Innovative Strategies and Practical Implementation

In the realm of sustainable development, the role of social entrepreneurship is pivotal in driving innovative strategies and practical implementation for positive societal impact. Social entrepreneurship, characterized by innovative, sustainable, and impact-driven solutions to societal challenges, aligns closely with the Sustainable Development Goals (SDGs) agenda, emphasizing the interconnectedness between social entrepreneurship and sustainable development (Rekha, 2024). Furthermore, green entrepreneurship models have shown success in addressing environmental issues while promoting economic growth and community well-being through creative business strategies, technology adoption, and strategic partnerships (Prokopenko et al., 2024). Additionally, the intersection of entrepreneurship, innovation, and sustainability highlights the essential role of innovation in driving sustainable development, showcasing how entrepreneurs can lead change towards a more sustainable and equitable future (Khan, 2024). By integrating entrepreneurship education within higher education institutions, students are equipped with the knowledge, skills, and mindset necessary to address complex social and environmental challenges, fostering a culture of responsible entrepreneurship and contributing to the UN Sustainable Development Goals (Patricia, 2024). Analyzing case studies of both successful and unsuccessful ventures provides valuable insights into the practical implementation of social entrepreneurship. Successful ventures often illustrate the effective use of innovative business models and strategic partnerships to achieve social and environmental goals, while examining unsuccessful ventures helps identify common pitfalls and challenges, offering lessons on what to avoid and how to overcome obstacles.

Digital platforms and technological advancements play a critical role in scaling social impact; technologies such as mobile applications, blockchain, and data analytics can enhance the efficiency and reach of social enterprises. For instance, mobile apps can facilitate better access to services for underserved populations, while blockchain can ensure transparency and accountability in social projects. The use of technology in social entrepreneurship not only enhances operational efficiency but also helps in reaching a wider audience and creating a larger impact. Implementing practical strategies for integrating social entrepreneurship into sustainable development involves leveraging innovative approaches and fostering strategic collaborations. Key strategies include adopting sustainable business models that are economically viable, socially responsible, and environmentally sustainable; building strategic partnerships with governments, non-profits, and private sector organizations to amplify the impact of social entrepreneurship initiatives; and utilizing impact measurement tools and frameworks to measure and evaluate the impact of social initiatives, thereby demonstrating effectiveness and attracting investment. By exploring these innovative strategies and practical implementations, social entrepreneurs can significantly contribute to sustainable development, balancing the potential and challenges of social entrepreneurship, and providing a comprehensive understanding of its role in driving positive societal change.

4.1.2 Collaborative Partnerships and Financial Strategies

Collaborative partnerships and financial strategies play pivotal roles in the realm of social entrepreneurship and sustainable development, as highlighted in various research papers. The role of social entrepreneurship in sustainable development emphasizes the instrumental role of social entrepreneurs as catalysts for change, fostering collaborations between communities and governance structures (Inggang et al., 2023). The interconnectedness between social entrepreneurship and sustainable development goals underscores the need for greater support and integration of social entrepreneurship within broader development frameworks to accelerate progress towards sustainability (Rekha, 2024). Additionally, the study on bibliographic mapping of social entrepreneurship publications suggests the necessity for authors to collaborate and for practitioners to leverage the existing synergy between research areas, emphasizing the importance of collaborative efforts in advancing the field (Abdullahi & Abubakar, 2023). Financial aspects, such as funding challenges, impact investing, and sustainable financing options, are critical for the success of social enterprises. Social entrepreneurs often face significant funding challenges, requiring innovative financial strategies to secure necessary resources. Impact investing and sustainable financing options are increasingly recognized as viable solutions to these challenges, providing essential support for scaling social impact. A comparative analysis of traditional versus social entrepreneurship models reveals that social enterprises, while often yielding lower financial returns, offer substantial social returns that contribute to sustainable development goals.

4.1.3 Social entrepreneurship in promoting sustainable development

Social entrepreneurship stands at the nexus of societal progress, economic vitality, and environmental stewardship, serving as a dynamic catalyst for sustainable development. Within this realm, social entrepreneurs wield innovative solutions to address a spectrum of pressing challenges, from poverty alleviation and human rights advocacy to environmental conservation and energy security. These ventures operate on the principle that profit-making and social impact are not mutually exclusive; they are intertwined elements of a broader mission to drive positive change. Its inherent capacity to transcend traditional boundaries and forge collaborative partnerships among diverse stakeholders sets social entrepreneurship apart. Governments, businesses, civil society organizations, and local communities converge under social entrepreneurship, leveraging collective expertise and resources to tackle complex societal issues. Social entrepreneurs amplify their impact through this collaborative approach, creating a ripple effect that extends far beyond individual initiatives. At the core of social entrepreneurship lies a commitment to the triple bottom line: people, planet, and profit. Social entrepreneurs redefine the essence of business success by prioritizing social and environmental considerations alongside financial objectives. This integrated approach optimizes resource allocation and addresses systemic inequities and environmental degradation, laying the groundwork for a more sustainable future.

Moreover, the proliferation of social entrepreneurship contributes significantly to the resilience and competitiveness of national economies. Governments and policymakers play a pivotal role in fostering an enabling environment that nurtures the growth of social enterprises, incentivizing innovation and social impact. In doing so, they bolster economic diversification, enhance social cohesion, and promote inclusive growth, advancing the broader agenda of sustainable development. Social entrepreneurship embodies the ethos of responsible business practices and transformative change. Its impact extends far beyond the confines of traditional business models, permeating communities, industries, and global landscapes. As we navigate the complexities of the 21st century, social entrepreneurship emerges as a beacon of hope, a vehicle for driving positive change and forging a more equitable, inclusive, and sustainable world for future generations.

4.2 Empirical Analysis

4.2.1 Sample profile of the experts

Table 1 presents a comprehensive overview of the demographic profile of the study participants, highlighting key variables such as years of experience, generational cohorts, and level of education.

Table 1. Sample profile

Variable	Attributes	Frequency	Percent
Year of Experience	Less than 5 Years	92	50.5
	5 Years or more	90	49.5
	Total	182	100.0
Generations	Generation X	47	25.8
	Millennials	82	45.1
	Generation Z	53	29.1
	Total	182	100.0
Level of Education	Higher secondary or below	48	26.4
	Degree	96	52.7
	P.G. or above	38	20.9
	Total	182	100.0

Source: Field data, 2024

The data illustrates a balanced distribution across various attributes, reflecting the diverse composition of the sample. Regarding professional experience, approximately half of the participants (50.5%) have less than 5 years of experience, while the remaining half (49.5%) possess 5 years or more. This indicates a mix of early-career professionals and individuals with more extensive experience, contributing to a varied perspective pool. Generational categorization reveals a substantial representation of Millennials (45.1%), followed closely by Generation Z (29.1%) and Generation X (25.8%). This generational diversity underscores the inclusion of participants from different age groups, each potentially offering unique insights shaped by their generational experiences and values.

Regarding educational background, most participants hold a degree (52.7%), while a significant portion have education up to higher secondary or below (26.4%). Additionally, a notable percentage of participants (20.9%) possess a postgraduate degree or higher qualification. This diverse educational landscape suggests a mix of academic backgrounds, enriching the study with varied perspectives and expertise. Overall, Table 1 provides a comprehensive snapshot of the study participants' demographic composition, highlighting the sample's breadth and diversity across key demographic dimensions.

4.2.2 Business model

Table 2 presents descriptive statistics related to various aspects of the business model in the context of social entrepreneurship and sustainable development. The table provides insights into participants' perceptions and beliefs regarding social entrepreneurship initiatives' roles, challenges, and essential components.

Table 2. Descriptive statistics

	N	Mean	Std. Deviation
Social entrepreneurship plays a significant role in promoting sustainable development.	182	4.05	.654
I believe that social entrepreneurship initiatives can effectively address pressing social and environmental issues.	182	3.68	1.141
Social entrepreneurship initiatives face substantial challenges in achieving sustainable impact.	182	3.23	1.071
Lack of access to funding is a significant barrier to the success of social entrepreneurship initiatives.	182	3.67	.964
Government policies and regulations have a significant impact on the success of social entrepreneurship ventures.	182	3.78	1.095
Collaboration with government agencies and NGOs is crucial for the success of social entrepreneurship initiatives.	182	3.20	1.101
Innovative business models are essential for social entrepreneurship ventures to create sustainable social and environmental impact.	182	3.60	.786
Effective marketing and communication strategies are vital for raising awareness and gaining support for social entrepreneurship initiatives.	182	3.81	.957
Measuring social and environmental impact is challenging but essential for the success of social entrepreneurship ventures.	182	3.93	1.161
Adopting sustainable business practices, such as ethical sourcing and waste reduction, is integral to the success of social entrepreneurship ventures.	182	3.82	.947
Business model	182	3.6780	.51278

Source: Field data, 2024

The mean scores reflect the average agreement level among participants, ranging from 1 (strongly disagree) to 5 (strongly agree). Overall, participants demonstrate relatively high agreement with statements affirming the significance of social entrepreneurship in promoting sustainable development. For instance, the mean score for "Social entrepreneurship plays a significant role in promoting sustainable development" is 4.05, indicating a strong consensus among participants.

Similarly, participants expressed confidence in the effectiveness of social entrepreneurship initiatives in addressing pressing social and environmental issues, as evidenced by the mean score of 3.68 for the corresponding statement. However, participants also acknowledge challenges facing social entrepreneurship ventures, such as limited access to funding (mean score: 3.67) and the complexity of measuring social and environmental impact (mean score: 3.93). These findings highlight the multifaceted nature of sustainability challenges and the need for innovative solutions. Moreover, participants recognize the importance of collaboration with government agencies and NGOs (mean score: 3.20) and the adoption of sustainable business practices (mean score: 3.82) for the success of social entrepreneurship ventures.

This underscores the significance of partnerships and ethical considerations in achieving sustainable impact. Overall, the descriptive statistics presented in Table 2 offer valuable insights into participants' perceptions of the business model aspects of social entrepreneurship and their role in advancing sustainable development goals. These findings can inform strategic decision-making and policy formulation to support and promote social entrepreneurship initiatives.

4.2.3 Collaboration and partnership

Table 3 provides descriptive statistics related to collaboration and partnership aspects within organizations. The table presents participants' perceptions and attitudes toward collaboration with external stakeholders and the importance of partnerships in achieving organizational goals. Mean scores, ranging from 1 (strongly disagree) to 5 (strongly agree), indicate the average level of agreement among participants with each statement. Overall, participants demonstrate a strong consensus on the significance of collaboration and partnership for organizational success and impact. The mean score for the statement "Collaboration with other organizations is essential for achieving our organization's goals" is 3.97, indicating high agreement among participants regarding the importance of collaboration. Similarly, participants express a commitment to seeking partnerships with external stakeholders to enhance organizational impact, as evidenced by the mean score of 3.80 for the corresponding statement. Additionally, participants emphasize the value of effective communication, mutual trust, and transparency in fostering successful partnerships, with mean scores ranging from 3.72 to 3.82.

Table 3. Descriptive statistics

	N	Mean	Std. Deviation
Collaboration with other organizations is essential for achieving our organization's goals.	182	3.97	.696
Our organization actively seeks partnerships with external stakeholders to enhance our impact.	182	3.80	1.043
We prioritize building long-term collaborative relationships with our partners.	182	3.43	1.016
Collaborating with diverse stakeholders enriches our projects and initiatives.	182	3.87	.929
Effective communication and mutual trust are critical for successful partnerships.	182	3.82	.959
Our organization values transparency and openness in our collaborative efforts.	182	3.72	1.079
We regularly evaluate and assess the effectiveness of our partnerships.	182	3.80	.945
We actively engage in cross-sector partnerships to address complex challenges.	182	4.13	.626
We are open to exploring innovative partnership models to achieve our objectives.	182	3.53	.784
Our organization recognizes the importance of shared values and common goals in fostering successful collaborations.	182	3.55	1.000
Collaboration and partnership	182	3.7637	.48137

Source: Field data, 2024

Furthermore, participants recognize the importance of cross-sector partnerships in addressing complex challenges, as indicated by the high mean score of 4.13 for the statement, "We actively engage in cross-sector partnerships to address complex challenges." These findings underscore the importance of collaboration and partnership strategies in driving organizational effectiveness and addressing societal challenges. They also highlight the need for organizations to prioritize relationship-building, transparency, and innovation in their collaborative efforts to maximize impact. Overall, the descriptive statistics presented in Table 3 offer valuable insights into participants' perspectives on collaboration and partnership within organizations and their role in achieving organizational goals and societal impact.

4.2.4 Innovation and adaptation

Each statement is rated on a scale of 1 (strongly disagree) to 5 (strongly agree), with mean scores indicating the average level of agreement among participants with each statement. Overall, participants demonstrate a positive outlook on innovation and adaptation within their organizations, with a mean score of 3.8385 for this category. Participants strongly value innovation as a driver of positive change and growth, as evidenced by the mean score of 3.77 for the statement, “Our organization values innovation as a driver of positive change and growth.” Additionally, they indicate a supportive environment for innovation, with mean scores ranging from 3.70 to 4.04 for statements such as “We encourage and support employees to propose and implement innovative ideas” and “We actively seek out new technologies and methodologies to improve our processes.”

Table 4. Descriptive statistics

	N	Mean	Std. Deviation
Our organization values innovation as a driver of positive change and growth.	182	3.77	1.107
We encourage and support employees to propose and implement innovative ideas.	182	3.84	.926
We actively seek out new technologies and methodologies to improve our processes.	182	4.04	.915
Our organization fosters a culture of experimentation and learning from failure.	182	4.04	1.050
We adapt quickly to changing market conditions and emerging trends.	182	3.77	.970
We invest in research and development to stay ahead of the competition.	182	3.70	.982
We prioritize creativity and out-of-the-box thinking in problem-solving.	182	3.20	1.048
We regularly review and update our strategies to respond to evolving challenges.	182	4.32	.806
We embrace change as an opportunity for growth and improvement.	182	3.76	1.119
Our organization continuously seeks ways to innovate and stay relevant in our industry.	182	3.94	1.042
Innovation and adaptation	182	3.8385	.48452

Source: Field data, 2024

Furthermore, participants emphasize the importance of adaptability and flexibility in responding to changing market conditions and emerging trends, as reflected in statements such as “We adapt quickly to changing market conditions and emerging trends” (mean score of 3.77) and “We embrace change as an opportunity for growth and improvement” (mean score of 3.76). The high mean score of 4.32 for “We regularly review and update our strategies to respond to evolving challenges” indicates a strong emphasis on strategic flexibility and the proactive nature of organizational adaptation. Overall, the descriptive statistics presented in Table 4 highlight participants' recognition of the importance of innovation, adaptability, and continuous improvement in driving organizational success and staying relevant in a dynamic business environment.

4.2.5 Social and environmental value creation

Table 5 provides descriptive statistics on social and environmental value creation within organizations. Participants' perceptions and attitudes toward integrating social and environmental considerations into business activities are examined through various statements, each rated on a scale from 1 (strongly disagree) to 5 (strongly agree). The mean scores reflect the average level of agreement among participants with each statement, indicating the extent to which organizations prioritize social and environmental value creation. Key findings include commitment to social impact alongside financial returns, transparency in reporting social and environmental performance, and engagement in initiatives supporting biodiversity conservation and ecosystem preservation. However, there are areas for improvement, such as minimizing environmental footprint and enhancing collaboration with local stakeholders for community impact.

Table 5. Descriptive statistics

	N	Mean	Std. Deviation
Our organization places a high priority on creating positive social impact alongside financial returns.	182	3.66	1.177
We actively measure and track the social and environmental outcomes of our business activities.	182	3.52	.984
Our products/services are designed to address specific social or environmental needs in our community.	182	3.81	.998
We collaborate with local stakeholders to ensure our operations have a positive impact on the community.	182	3.19	1.088
We strive to minimize our environmental footprint by implementing sustainable practices in our operations.	182	3.05	1.021
Our organization is committed to transparency in reporting our social and environmental performance.	182	4.05	.606
We engage in initiatives that support biodiversity conservation and ecosystem preservation.	182	4.41	.800
We invest in renewable energy sources to reduce our carbon footprint and combat climate change.	182	3.57	.816
We prioritize fair labor practices and ethical sourcing in our supply chain.	182	3.68	1.107
We support social enterprises and initiatives that promote economic empowerment and equality.	182	3.86	1.088
We actively seek feedback from stakeholders to improve our social and environmental practices.	182	3.94	1.176

continued on following page

Table 5. Continued

	N	Mean	Std. Deviation
Our organization is committed to creating shared value for all stakeholders through our business activities.	182	3.56	1.021
Social and environmental value creation	182	3.6909	.50373

Source: Field data, 2024

These findings underscore the importance of integrating social and environmental considerations into business practices to create shared value for all stakeholders.

4.2.6 Year of Experiences and social and environmental value creation

Table 6 presents findings from an independent samples t-test comparing social and environmental value creation scores between two groups based on years of experience. Individuals with less than 5 years of experience had a mean score of 3.4303, while those with 5 years or more had a higher mean of 3.9574. Levene's test revealed no significant difference in variances between the groups, ensuring the validity of the subsequent t-test. The t-test indicated a highly significant difference in mean scores ($p < 0.001$), with more experienced individuals scoring significantly higher.

Table 6. Independent sample t test

Year of Experiences	N	Mean	Std. Deviation	Levene's Test for Equality of Variances		t-test for Equality of Means			Remarks
				F	Sig.	t	df		Equal variances assumed
Less than 5 Years	92	3.4303	.44634	1.154	.284	-8.269	180	.000	
5 Years or more	90	3.9574	.41267						

Source: Field data, 2024

This suggests that as individuals accumulate more extended experience, they exhibit greater proficiency in integrating social and environmental considerations into their work. This finding underscores the importance of experience in fostering values aligned with sustainability and social responsibility within organizations. Further research could explore the specific mechanisms driving this relationship and investigate strategies for promoting such values across diverse levels of experience within the workforce.

4.2.7 Generations and Social and environmental value creation

Table 7 provides descriptive statistics and the outcomes of a one-way ANOVA analyzing social and environmental value creation scores across three generational cohorts: Generation X, Millennials, and Generation Z. The table displays the number of participants (N), mean scores, and standard deviations within each group. Levene's Test for Homogeneity of Variances assesses the equality of variances across the groups, with a non-significant result indicating that this assumption is met. The subsequent ANOVA reveals highly significant differences in mean scores among the generational groups ($p < 0.001$). Specifically, Generation Z exhibits the highest mean score, followed by Millennials and Generation X.

Table 7. Descriptive statistics and one way ANOVA

	N	**Mean**	**Std. Deviation**	**Test of Homogeneity of Variances**		**ANOVA**		**Remarks**
				Levene Statistic	Sig.	F	Sig.	
Generation X	47	3.0621	.35503	.764	.468	127.891	.000	One way ANOVA
Millennials	82	3.8130	.29588					
Generation Z	53	4.0597	.34022					
Total	182							

Dependent variable: Social and environmental value creation Source: Field data, 2024

Table 8 Multiple Comparisons

(I) Generations	**(J) Generations**	**Mean Difference (I-J)**	**Std. Error**	**Sig.**
Generation Z	Millennials	-.75095	.05946	.000
	Generation X	-.99769	.06512	.000
Millennials	Generation Z	.75095	.05946	.000
	Generation X	-.24674	.05728	.000
Generation X	Generation Z	.99769	.06512	.000
	Millennials	.24674	.05728	.000

Dependent Variable: Social and environmental value creation Tukey HSD
The mean difference is significant at the 0.05 level. Source: Field data, 2024

This suggests potential generational disparities in attitudes and behaviors toward social and environmental responsibility within organizational contexts. Further research could explore the underlying factors driving these differences and inform strategies for promoting inclusive sustainability initiatives tailored to each generational cohort's values and preferences. Understanding and addressing these disparities are essential for fostering collaboration and advancing sustainable practices across generations within organizations.

Table 8 provides insights from multiple comparisons using Tukey's Honestly Significant Difference (HSD) test. It focuses on the dependent variable "Social and environmental value creation" across Generation X, Millennials, and Generation Z. The table presents mean differences between pairs of generational groups along with standard errors and significance levels.

Results indicate significant differences in mean scores among all generational pairs. Generation Z exhibits lower scores than Millennials and Generation X, with mean differences of -0.75095 and -0.99769, respectively ($p < 0.001$). Millennials also score higher than Generation X, with a mean difference of -0.24674 ($p < 0.001$). These findings underscore recognizing and addressing generational disparities in promoting social and environmental responsibility within organizational contexts. Customized strategies may be necessary to engage and empower each generation effectively in sustainability initiatives.

4.2.8 Level of education and Social and environmental value creation

Table 9 presents descriptive statistics and the outcomes of a one-way ANOVA examining social and environmental value creation scores across three educational attainment levels: Higher secondary or below, Degree, and P.G. or above. The table includes the number of participants (N), mean scores, standard deviations, and results of Levene's Test for Homogeneity of Variances. Findings reveal that individuals with higher education levels tend to score higher in social and environmental value creation. Specifically, participants with a P.G. or above exhibit the highest mean score, followed by those with a degree and individuals with a Higher secondary education or below.

The absence of significant differences in variances across education level groups ensures the validity of the subsequent ANOVA analysis, which indicates highly significant differences in mean scores among the groups. These results suggest that higher education equips individuals with the knowledge and skills necessary to engage in activities promoting social and environmental value creation. Policymakers and organizations could leverage these insights to design interventions and educational programs to foster sustainability practices within communities and workplaces. Further research could delve into the underlying mechanisms through which education influences attitudes and behaviours related to social and environmental responsibility, contributing to developing more targeted and effective strategies.

Table 9. Descriptive statistics and one way ANOVA

	N	Mean	Std. Deviation	Test of Homogeneity of Variances		ANOVA		Remarks
				Levene Statistic	Sig.	F	Sig.	
Higher secondary or below	48	3.1840	.38167	2.213	.112	75.436	.000	One way ANOVA
Degree	96	3.7604	.39427					
P.G. or above	38	4.1557	.29900					
Total	182	3.6909	.50373					

Dependent Variable: Social and environmental value creation Source: Field data, 2024

Table 10. Multiple Comparisons

(I) Generations	(J) Generations	Mean Difference (I-J)	Std. Error	Sig.
Higher secondary or below	Degree	-.57639	.06596	.000
	P.G. or above	-.97167	.08102	.000
Degree	Higher secondary or below	.57639	.06596	.000
	P.G. or above	-.39529	.07151	.000
P.G. or above	Higher secondary or below	.97167	.08102	.000
	Degree	.39529	.07151	.000

Dependent Variable: Social and environmental value creation Tukey HSD
The mean difference is significant at the 0.05 level. Source: Field data, 2024

Table 10 illustrates the outcomes of multiple comparisons conducted through Tukey's Honestly Significant Difference (HSD) test for the dependent variable "Social and environmental value creation" across three educational attainment levels: Higher secondary or below, Degree, and P.G. or above. The table displays mean differences between pairs of educational groups, along with standard errors and significance levels. Results reveal significant disparities in mean scores among all pairs of educational levels. Individuals with Higher secondary education or below score notably lower in social and environmental value creation compared to those with a degree and those with a P.G. or above, with mean differences of -0.57639 and -0.97167, respectively ($p < 0.001$). Moreover, individuals with a degree also score significantly lower than those with a P.G. or above, with a mean difference of -0.39529 ($p < 0.001$). These findings underscore the influence of education on fostering values and behaviours aligned with sustainability and social responsibility. They highlight the need for tailored interventions and educational programs to promote sustainable practices, considering individuals' varying levels of educational attainment.

4.2.9 Relationship between Social and environmental value creation with Business model, Collaboration and partnership, and Innovation and adaptation

Table 11 presents the outcomes of multiple correlation analysis among key variables: Social and environmental value creation, Business model, Collaboration and partnership, and Innovation and adaptation. Descriptive statistics provide insights into the mean and standard deviation for each variable. The correlation coefficients reveal significant positive relationships between Social and environmental value creation and the other variables: Business model ($r = 0.900$, $p < 0.01$), Collaboration and partnership ($r = 0.787$, $p < 0.01$), and Innovation and adaptation ($r = 0.881$, $p < 0.01$).

Table 11. Multiple correlation

	Mean	Std. Deviation	N	Pearson Correlation	Sig. (2-tailed)
Social and environmental value creation	3.6909	.50373	182		
Business model	3.6780	.51278	182	.900	.000
Collaboration and partnership	3.7637	.48137	182	.787	.000
Innovation and adaptation	3.8385	.48452	182	.881	.000

Correlation is significant at the 0.01 level (2-tailed). Source: Field data, 2024

These findings suggest that a robust business model, effective collaboration and partnership initiatives, and a culture of innovation and adaptation are closely associated with increased social and environmental value creation within organizations. Understanding these correlations can inform strategic decision-making aimed at promoting sustainability and social responsibility while simultaneously driving business success.

4.2.10 Multiple regression

Table 12 presents the outcomes of a multiple regression analysis aimed at predicting Social and environmental value creation based on three key predictors: Innovation and adaptation, Collaboration and partnership, and Business model. The model summary indicates a strong relationship between the predictors and the dependent variable, with an R Square value of 0.863, suggesting that these predictors can explain approximately 86.3% of the variance in Social and environmental value creation. The significant positive correlation coefficients between the predictors and the dependent variable indicate that higher levels of Innovation and adaptation, Collaboration and partnership, and an effective Business model are associated with increased levels of social and environmental value creation. These findings underscore the importance of these factors in driving sustainability and social responsibility initiatives within organizations. However, the moderate positive autocorrelation detected by the Durbin-Watson statistic suggests the presence of some residual pattern in the data that warrants further investigation.

Table 12. Model Summary[b]

Model	R	R Square	Adjusted R Square	Std. Error of the Estimate	Durbin-Watson
1	.929[a]	.863	.860	.18818	1.635

a. Predictors: (Constant), Innovation and adaptation, Collaboration and partnership, Business model
b. Dependent Variable: Social and environmental value creation
Source: Field data, 2024

Table 13 presents the outcomes of an analysis of variance (ANOVA) for the regression model predicting Social and environmental value creation based on Innovation and adaptation, Collaboration and partnership, and Business model. The ANOVA results indicate that the regression model significantly predicts Social and environmental value creation, as evidenced by the highly significant F-statistic ($F = 372.995$, $p < 0.001$).

Table 13. ANOVA[a]

Model		Sum of Squares	df	Mean Square	F	Sig.
1	Regression	39.624	3	13.208	372.995	.000[b]
	Residual	6.303	178	.035		
	Total	45.928	181			

a. Dependent Variable: Social and environmental value creation
b. Predictors: (Constant), Innovation and adaptation, Collaboration and partnership, Business model
Source: Field data, 2024

This suggests that combining these predictors explains a substantial portion of the variance in Social and environmental value creation.

Table 14. Coefficients[a]

Model		Unstandardized Coefficients		Standardized Coefficients	t	Sig.
		B	Std. Error	Beta		
1	(Constant)	-.019	.122		-.156	.876
	Business model	.474	.070	.482	6.765	.000
	Collaboration and partnership	.073	.057	.070	1.276	.204
	Innovation and adaptation	.441	.054	.424	8.189	.000

a. Dependent Variable: Social and environmental value creation Source: Field data, 2024

The sum of squares for the regression (39.624) dramatically exceeds that of the residuals (6.303), underscoring the model's overall significance in explaining the observed variance. These findings underscore the critical role of Innovation and adaptation, Collaboration and partnership, and an effective Business model in driving social and environmental value creation within organizations. By recognizing and leveraging these predictors, organizations can strategically enhance their sustainability efforts, contributing to their success and broader societal well-being.

Table 14 provides the coefficients for a regression model predicting Social and environmental value creation based on the predictors: Business model, Collaboration and partnership, and Innovation and adaptation. The results reveal several significant findings. Firstly, the constant term is not statistically significant, suggesting it does not significantly contribute to predicting Social and environmental value creation. However, both the Business model and Innovation and adaptation coefficients are statistically significant ($p < 0.001$), indicating their positive association with Social and environmental value creation. Specifically, a one-unit increase in the Business model is associated with a 0.474-unit increase, and a one-unit increase in innovation and adaptation is associated with a 0.441-unit increase in Social and environmental value creation.

On the other hand, while positive, the Collaboration and partnership coefficient is not statistically significant, suggesting it may not significantly contribute to predicting Social and environmental value creation after controlling for other predictors. These findings underscore the importance of prioritizing business models, innovation, and adaptation initiatives to drive organizations' creation of social and environmental value. By focusing on these areas, organizations can better align their strategies with sustainability goals, ultimately contributing to broader societal well-being.

5. RECOMMENDATIONS

Promoting social entrepreneurship education within educational institutions and training programs is essential for equipping individuals with the necessary knowledge and skills to engage in activities that create social and environmental value. Organizations and governments should invest in capacity-building initiatives that empower social entrepreneurs to effectively address sustainability challenges. Policymakers need to formulate policies that create an enabling environment for social entrepreneurship, including access to funding, regulatory support, and incentives for sustainable practices. Encouraging cross-sector collaboration between government agencies, NGOs, businesses, and academia can leverage diverse expertise and resources to address complex societal challenges. Additionally, the adoption of innovative technologies and methodologies can improve the effectiveness and scalability of social entrepreneurship initiatives. Developing standardized frameworks and tools for measuring and reporting social and environmental impact will enhance the transparency, accountability, and credibility of social entrepreneurship ventures. Promoting diversity and inclusion within social entrepreneurship ecosystems ensures representation from diverse demographic groups and perspectives. Providing training and resources for social entrepreneurs to effectively evaluate and monitor the impact of their initiatives enables continuous learning and improvement. Encouraging the adoption of sustainable business models that prioritize social and environmental value creation alongside financial returns fosters long-term sustainability. Facilitating knowledge-sharing and networking opportunities for social entrepreneurs allows for the exchange of best practices, lessons learned, and innovative solutions. Allocating resources for research and development in social entrepreneurship generates evidence-based insights that inform policy and practice. Engaging youth in social entrepreneurship initiatives through mentorship, training, and funding opportunities taps into their creativity, energy, and passion for social change. By implementing these recommendations, stakeholders can create a supportive ecosystem for social entrepreneurship, unlocking its potential to drive sustainable development and address pressing societal and environmental challenges.

6. THEORETICAL AND PRACTICAL IMPLICATIONS

6.1 Theoretical Implications

Understanding the role of social entrepreneurship in sustainable development is critical for advancing theoretical frameworks in this field. The study sheds light on business experts' perceptions, which contribute to a deeper understanding of how social entrepreneurship can drive societal and environmental well-being. This understanding is essential for framing social entrepreneurship within the broader context of sustainable development. By exploring how social entrepreneurs leverage innovative strategies, business models, and technologies to address sustainable development challenges, the study provides valuable insights into the potential and challenges of social entrepreneurship (Rekha, 2024). These insights help build a more robust theoretical foundation, demonstrating the interconnectedness between social entrepreneurship and the Sustainable Development Goals. Identifying the key drivers and barriers to the success of social entrepreneurship initiatives enriches theoretical frameworks by providing nuanced insights into the factors that facilitate or hinder the achievement of sustainable impact. The research highlights various challenges such as regulatory barriers, economic conditions, and cultural attitudes that significantly influence the success of social ventures. Understanding these barriers is crucial for developing theoretical models that accurately reflect the complexities of social entrepreneurship. The study also emphasizes the importance of individual, social, and political elements in fostering impactful initiatives, providing a comprehensive view of the contextual influences on social entrepreneurship (Inggang et al., 2023; Latifah et al., 2023).

The findings of the study highlight effective business models, strategies, and practices that social entrepreneurs employ to create social and environmental value. These findings offer theoretical insights into the mechanisms through which social entrepreneurship drives sustainable development. By examining case studies of successful and unsuccessful social ventures, the study illustrates the practical application of these models, emphasizing the role of innovation, technology, and cross-sector partnerships in scaling impact (Abdullahi & Abubakar, 2023). This practical evidence strengthens theoretical frameworks, showcasing how innovative business strategies and technological advancements can enhance the effectiveness of social entrepreneurship in achieving sustainable outcomes.

6.2 Practical Implications

The insights from this study can significantly impact strategic decision-making within organizations. By understanding the key drivers and barriers to the success of social entrepreneurship initiatives, organizations can design more effective strategies and interventions to promote social entrepreneurship and advance sustainable development goals. The study provides practical guidance on leveraging innovative strategies, digital platforms, and cross-sector partnerships to scale social impact (Rekha, 2024). This information is invaluable for organizations looking to make informed decisions that align with sustainable development objectives. Policymakers can use the study's findings to formulate policies and programs that support and incentivize social entrepreneurship, fostering an enabling environment for sustainable development. Addressing regulatory challenges, providing financial support mechanisms, and creating a conducive policy environment are essential steps for promoting social ventures (Nicasio Gicovi Njue & Samuel Nduati Kariuki, 2024). The study underscores the importance of local policies, economic conditions, and cultural attitudes in shaping the success of social entrepreneurship, providing policymakers with the necessary insights to develop targeted interventions that address these contextual factors.

Understanding the significance of collaboration and partnership is another key practical implication of the study. Organizations can prioritize building partnerships with government agencies, NGOs, and other stakeholders to enhance the impact of social entrepreneurship ventures. Collaborative efforts are essential for scaling social impact and achieving sustainable development (Rekha, 2024). The study highlights the role of cross-sector partnerships in enhancing social impact, providing practical examples of how these collaborations can be effectively managed to maximize outcomes. Fostering a culture of innovation and adaptability within organizations is crucial for responding effectively to changing market conditions and emerging trends. The study emphasizes the importance of embracing technological advancements and innovative business models to drive sustainable impact (Garg & Kumar, 2023). Organizations can use these insights to cultivate an environment that encourages continuous improvement and responsiveness to societal challenges, thereby enhancing their capacity to create social and environmental value.

Policymakers and educational institutions can design interventions and educational programs to equip individuals with the knowledge and skills necessary to engage in activities that promote social and environmental value creation. Integrating entrepreneurship education within higher education institutions is essential for fostering a culture of responsible entrepreneurship (Patricia, 2024). The study provides practical guidance on how to design educational programs that prepare individuals for the complexities of social entrepreneurship, ensuring that they are equipped to address complex social and environmental challenges. Tailoring sustainability initiatives to address generational and educational disparities is crucial for ensuring inclusivity and effectiveness across diverse demographics. Organizations can use the study's findings to design initiatives that are equitable and accessible to all, promoting inclusivity in sustainable development efforts (Latifah Hanum et al., 2023). This approach ensures that sustainability initiatives are effective across different demographic groups, contributing to a more inclusive and equitable future. Finally, organizations can prioritize adopting effective business models identified in the study to maximize social and environmental value creation while ensuring long-term sustainability. By leveraging successful strategies and practices, businesses can enhance their impact and contribute to sustainable development (Abdullahi

& Abubakar Sadiq Sallau, 2023). The study provides practical insights into the mechanisms through which social entrepreneurship drives sustainable outcomes, offering valuable guidance for optimizing business models to achieve greater social and environmental impact.

REFERENCES

Abdullahi, M., & Sallau, A. S. (2023). Social Entrepreneurship as Panacea for Sustainable Community Development. [CIJDS]. *Caleb International Journal of Development Studies*, 06(01), 55–61. DOI: 10.26772/cijds-2023-06-01-03

Bataineh, M. J., Marcuello, C., Sánchez-Sellero, P., & Universidad de Zaragoza. (2023). Toward sustainability: the role of social entrepreneurship in creating social-economic value in renewable energy social enterprises. *REVESCO. Revista de Estudios Cooperativos*. DOI: 10.5209/reve.85561

Bataineh, M. J., Marcuello, C., Sánchez-Sellero, P., & Universidad de Zaragoza. (2023). Toward sustainability: the role of social entrepreneurship in creating social-economic value in renewable energy social enterprises. *REVESCO. Revista de Estudios Cooperativos*. DOI: 10.5209/reve.85561

Emmanuel Inalegwu Akoh. (2023). *Social entrepreneurship as a tool for sustainable development in the townships in KwaZulu-Natal province*. https://doi.org/DOI: 10.51415/10321/4826

Garg, M., & Kumar, P. (2023). Social Entrepreneurship and Sustainable Development: A Bibliometric Analysis. *Colombo Business Journal*, 14(2), 99–131. DOI: 10.4038/cbj.v14i2.159

Hanum, L., Noor, I., & Wahyudi, L. E. (2023). Individual and Social Influence on the Sustainable Social Entrepreneurs Development. *Jurnal Ilmu Sosial Dan Humaniora*, 12(2), 288–295. DOI: 10.23887/jish.v12i2.62081

Viktoriia Ilchenko. (2023). Social Entrepreneurship as a Tool to Achieve the Goals of Sustainable Development. *Ринкова економіка: сучасна теорія і практика управління, 21*(3(52)), 114–126. DOI: 10.18524/2413-9998.2022.3(52).275788

Inalegwu Akoh, E., & Mpele Lekhanya, L. (2022). Social entrepreneurship and networking challenges: Impact on sustainable development in South Africa. *Problems and Perspectives in Management*, 20(4), 195–209. DOI: 10.21511/ppm.20(4).2022.15

Kalendzhjan, S. O., & Kadol, N. F. (2022). *Social entrepreneurship as a catalyst for sustainable socio-economic development*. https://doi.org/DOI: 10.56199/dpcsebm.kvzv9880

Khan, M. A. I., Syed, A. J., & Azharuddin, S. (2023). Social Entrepreneurship: Driving Change and Creating Positive Societal Impact. Social Entrepreneurship: Driving Change and Creating Positive Societal Impact.

Khan, S. (2024). Innovation and Sustainable Development in Entrepreneurship. *SMS Journal of Entrepreneurship & Innovation*, 10(1), 69–81. DOI: 10.21844/smsjei.v10i01.30006

Kreutzer, K. (2022). Social Enterprises. *Edward Elgar Publishing Limited EBooks*, 121–123, 121–123. Advance online publication. DOI: 10.4337/9781800375499.social.enterprises

Lubberink, R. (2019). Social Entrepreneurship and Sustainable Development. *Methods in Molecular Biology (Clifton, N.J.)*, 1965, 1–11. DOI: 10.1007/978-3-319-71058-7_47-1

Neessen, P. C. M., Voinea, C. L., & Dobber, E. (2021). Business Models of Social Enterprises: Insight into Key Components and Value Creation. *Sustainability (Basel)*, 13(22), 12750. DOI: 10.3390/su132212750

Njue, N. G., & Kariuki, S. N. (2024). Contextual and Structural Factors, Project Modelling and Sustainability of Entrepreneurial Development Projects: A Conceptual Framework. *European Journal of Business Management and Research*, 9(2), 35–42. DOI: 10.24018/ejbmr.2024.9.2.1713

Nuralam, I. P. SE, M., & Putri, N. V. W. (2023). Fostering Sustainable Entrepreneurship in Emerging Market: an Interdisciplinary Perspective.

Oham, C. A. (2022). *Okeoma John-Paul Okeke*. Advances in Business Strategy and Competitive Advantage Book Series. Strategic Formulation and Implementation of Social Entrepreneurs., DOI: 10.4018/978-1-7998-7724-0.ch001

Patricia, P. (2024). The Role Of Entrepreneurship Education In Universities To Pursue Sustainable Development Goals. *Feedforward*, 4(1), 23–23. DOI: 10.19166/ff.v4i1.8129

Prokopenko, O., Chechel, A., Koldovskiy, A., & Kldiashvili, M. (2024). Innovative Models of Green Entrepreneurship: Social Impact on Sustainable Development of Local Economies. Ekonomìka, Ekologìâ. *Socìum*, 8(1), 89–111. DOI: 10.61954/2616-7107/2024.8.1-8

Sirine, H., & Yustina, E. P. D. (2022). Business Model Canvas: The Implementation Method of Corporate Social Entrepreneurship. *Jagaditha: Jurnal Ekonomi & Bisnis*, 9(2), 176–184. DOI: 10.22225/jj.9.2.2022.176-184

Wagner, R., & Kabalska, A. (2023). Between Involvement and Profit: Value (Un-) Captured by a Born-Social Start-Up. *Journal of Social Entrepreneurship*, •••, 1–26. DOI: 10.1080/19420676.2023.2199765

Chapter 9
Sustainable Entrepreneurship: Lessons From Emerging Economies

Quazi Tafsirul Islam
https://orcid.org/0000-0003-3451-1346
North South University, Bangladesh

Rayed Rahman
https://orcid.org/0009-0000-6130-8197
North South University, Bangladesh

Md. Shamim Talukder
North South University, Bangladesh

Muhammad Faisol Chowdhury
https://orcid.org/0000-0002-2221-6174
North South University, Bangladesh

ABSTRACT

This article explores the role of sustainable entrepreneurship in emerging economies, showing how sustainable practices drive economic growth while addressing social and environmental challenges. It discusses sustainability and the UN's Sustainable Development Goals (SDGs), which guide entrepreneurs in aligning their businesses with global targets. Highlighting both challenges and opportunities, the article pushes entrepreneurs towards innovative, eco-friendly business models. Through case studies, it demonstrates how sustainable entrepreneurship alleviates poverty, unemployment, and environmental degradation, leveraging local knowledge for long-term solutions. Addressing challenges like finance access and infrastructure

DOI: 10.4018/979-8-3693-4338-8.ch009

limitations, the article suggests regulatory reforms, incentives, and better ESG rating systems to foster sustainable entrepreneurship. Ultimately, it calls for support from policymakers, investors, and entrepreneurs to scale sustainable practices and position emerging economies as key players in the global sustainability agenda.

INTRODUCTION TO SUSTAINABILITY & SDGS AND HOW THAT AFFECTS ENTREPRENEURS

Driven by urgent issues worldwide, sustainability has come to the forefront of conversation. Sustainability refers to the consideration of economic, social and environmental resources for the usage of current generations and conservation for the future (Brundtland, 1987). In recent years the United Nations SDG goals have emerged as a comprehensive framework for addressing global sustainability challenges. (United Nations, 2015). Giovannoni & Fabietti (2013) posits that sustainability is a multifaceted concept and that sustainable development requires an integrated approach at various levels and from different parties involved.

The SDGs comprise of 17 interconnected goals covering a plethora of issues including poverty alleviation, climate change, responsible consumption and production (United Nations, 2015). These goals give us a guideline to achieve sustainability and an equitable world by 2030. The 2030 agenda for sustainable development was adopted in 2015 by all United Nations members. The SDG goals were created with an aim of peace and prosperity for humans and the planet. Each goal has about 8-12 targets which need to be matched in order to realize these goals.

For entrepreneurs, SDGs offer both challenges and opportunities. Entrepreneurs are increasingly facing pressure to align their business processes with SDG guidelines to demonstrate social and environmental responsibility (Schaltegger & Wagner, 2011). Consumers are also becoming more aware of the changing environment and prefer sustainable products to those produced unsustainably. This can also be an opportunity for entrepreneurs to gain a competitive advantage over their competitors using sustainability as a spearhead to expand their business and bring a positive impact on the environment (Schaltegger & Burritt, 2018).

The push towards sustainability has led to the rise of new business models and entire new markets that champion long term environmental, economic and social goals. These new entrepreneurs who integrate SDG goals into their business strategies can access new customer segments who are increasingly in favor of sustainable goods and services. Incorporating such practices into marketing efforts can also increase brand awareness and reputation which help them to be seen as leaders in sustainability. This attracts not only environmentally conscious consumers but also investors and future employees and collaborators who are serious about leaving a positive social impact (Kim & Mauborgne, 2014).

Emerging economies often suffer from various chronic conditions such as staleness in new ways to increase growth, unused labor, and high environmental degradation due to unrefined economic activity. According to Hall et al. (2010), sustainable business practices can help these countries in overcoming challenges such as poverty, unemployment, and environmental degradation. Entrepreneurs in these places are confronted with limited resources, but they can use local knowledge and context-specific tactics to create long-term solutions (Seelos & Mair 2005). Furthermore, sustainable entrepreneurship can contribute to inclusive economic growth by creating jobs and fostering innovative problem solutions (Dean & McMullen, 2007).

Because of the growing global demand for environmentally friendly products and services, emerging economies provide unique potential for sustainable entrepreneurs. Governments and international organizations are increasingly supporting sustainable development initiatives by providing capital and market access for such firms. This assistance can assist entrepreneurs in emerging economies in overcoming financial and infrastructure constraints and scaling their sustainable companies (Bruton et al. 2015).

Furthermore, sustainable entrepreneurship in emerging nations can help to meet global sustainability goals by tackling local environmental and social challenges. By focusing on renewable energy, sustainable agriculture, and waste management, entrepreneurs can create solutions that reduce the effects of climate change and enhance resource efficiency (Korhonen et al. 2018). This integration with the sustainable development goals not only strengthens local communities, but also establishes these economies as essential players in the global sustainability agenda. In the next section we talk about sustainable entrepreneurs and how they impact emerging economies.

SUSTAINABLE ENTREPRENEURSHIP & ITS IMPLICATIONS FOR EMERGING ECONOMIES

Sustainable entrepreneurship has emerged as quite the game changer in the entrepreneurship sphere and as a focal point in the business world. Billed as green or social entrepreneurship, sustainable entrepreneurship seeks to create value to a variety of stakeholders involved from the shareholders, customers, employees, communities and the environment while ensuring long term viability (Hockerts, 2017).

Central to this concept of sustainable entrepreneurship is the idea that integration of sustainable measures at every possible aspect of the business, from product design, raw materials, production, marketing, operations and stakeholder management

(Seelos & Mair, 2017). This holistic approach requires entrepreneurs to consider not only the profitability of their business, but also the social and environmental implications of their actions ; the aim is to balance long term profits with long term sustainability (Dean & McMullen, 2017). Sustainable entrepreneurs also strive to strike a balance between economic, social and environmental sustainability.

Sustainable business can be extremely important in emerging nations when it comes to solving environmental and socioeconomic problems. Sustainable business methods can help these economies overcome problems including poverty, unemployment, and environmental degradation (Hall, Daneke, & Lenox, 2010). In these areas, sustainable business owners have the power to promote inclusive economic growth through generating jobs, enhancing livelihoods, and encouraging creative problem-solving.

Entrepreneurs in developing nations, however, also face formidable obstacles. Due to investors' reluctance to fund projects with longer payback times and higher perceived risks, financing is difficult to come by (Bruton, Khavul, Siegel, & Wright, 2015). Inadequate transport networks and unstable energy sources are two more infrastructural flaws that might impede the expansion of sustainable firms.

Emerging economies can gain an increased competitive edge in the international trade market with funding towards sustainable services and products ever increasing. Subsidizing and promoting the sustainable development sector and its contemporaries can foster innovation which goes on to produce unique products. These companies and products can play a major part in exports and services improving the trade balance of companies. Many countries worldwide are currently starting state sponsored sustainable startup incubators hoping to spur innovation and sustainable products services. With such backing it is easier for entrepreneurs to follow green practices. These innovations with good ESG scores can attract high amounts of FDI which turns into a positive feedback cycle. This inflow of FDI can leverage local resources and address local needs thereby allowing sustainable entrepreneurs to generate employment opportunities and drive inclusive economic development. Sustainable businesses are often seen as less risky with long term potential, making them ideal investments to impact investors and investment funds related to socially responsible causes (Mair & Marti, 2006).

These sustainable entrepreneurs can bring forth positive change in their communities. For example, SELCO Solar Light Pvt. Ltd. based in Bangalore, India have changed the lives of a large number of poor rural households with the power of solar energy. Solar energy is a well researched sustainable and green energy source which was the base of SELCO in providing solar energy based interventions such as solar lighting, thermal water heaters and inverter systems. These technologies are offered at affordable prices which explains their success over the years. They have through a unique solution brought solutions to various different consumer segments such as vendors, farmers and households. These areas received little or otherwise expensive energy supplies which were unaffordable by the masses. They have since partnered with microfinance organizations, philanthropic organizations and financial institutions to extend these last mile solar powered energy solutions for the rural masses in India. We now talk about social and environmental challenges that sustainable entrepreneurs seem to face in their journey towards a greener earth.

SOCIAL AND ENVIRONMENTAL CHALLENGES

When pursuing a sustainable future while engaging in sustainable entrepreneurship, entrepreneurs face a myriad of challenges which stem from social and environmental issues that demand innovative developments. These challenges can stem from various places such as the socio economic environment of particular countries including but not limited to poverty, inequality, inadequate infrastructure, climate change and environmental degradation (UNDP, 2020). In emerging economies which do not necessarily promote sustainable development or uphold to the highest standards the sustainability practices it is often the case that entrepreneurs struggle to access financial resources. Green businesses have uncertain futures as these entrepreneurs do not have a blueprint or a walkthrough to their business processes. These can lead to higher upfront costs and longer payback periods. Most traditional investors require short payback periods and invest little compared to the higher upfront costs one might need in this economy. These payback periods also vary. A car for instance has a lifespan of about say 20 years but replacing such inefficient and carbon emitting vehicles to greener alternatives such as electric vehicles can take a long time not to mention this new technology costing a fortune to many consumers. Where do all of these existing cars go? A wide and intense shift in consumer demand towards sustainable products will be required.

Marginalized communities often face socio economic inequalities when accessing resources, education and opportunities (Bhattacharya & Kharas, 2010). Entrepreneurs pushing to greener practices often cannot keep up with policy changes from inconsistent regulatory bodies and market fluctuations. COVID-19 and the conflicts going on in eastern europe threaten an ever present recession stricken market.Subject to different markets, locations and scale of operations, sustainable entrepreneurs often encounter administrative obstacles such as obscure taxation regulations, compliance issues and licensing requirements which can eat up a significant amount of time before a business can be operational. Climate change is proving to be the most pressing issue of this decade exacerbating existing vulnerabilities which can potentially harm businesses and communities in emerging economies (IPCC, 2014). Post

COVID lock downs have seen a shift in favor of sustainable products in emerging markets which is a good sign amidst all the noise.

In countries with higher percentage shares of emissions like China and India, we have to consider the impact of climate change. These places are subject to worsening climate change related disasters and rising sea levels. The air quality indices are also at alarming rates which poses the question of who takes the blame? These conditions can affect economic productivity and pose costs to all stakeholders. The scarcity of resources, namely natural capital, is another concern. Global populations are expected to rise causing shortages to natural capital. See these are local concerns and another question remains, who will take steps to internalize these negative externalities? For now, these costs are distributed disproportionately to lower socioeconomic communities in terms of living expenses, pollution induced illnesses and others. The government also takes on some costs via repairing infrastructure which have been damaged by extreme weather conditions.

Among other challenges faced by entrepreneurs are cultural and political resistance, market inefficiencies and a general lack of education. Entrepreneurs who are working on sustainable business models are often faced with adversaries of those industries they are trying to disrupt. This causes friction and agitation from established players in the market who target often politically and economically these budding entrepreneurs trying to make a difference. This acts as a discouraging barrier often seen through predatory activities by larger corporations trying to keep a firm grip on their market share. Some companies even go as far as to implement loss leader pricing models to keep and capture market share and hence these markets have high barriers to entry. Market inefficiencies such as information asymmetry can damage efforts towards sustainability. Consumers and businesses may lack information about the benefits of sustainable products and practices leading to under appreciation and adoption. Inefficiencies such as negative externalities also exist and the question of who takes the blame and who bears the cost is discussed later on in the chapter. Despite these market inefficiencies, entrepreneurs are making strides to overcome these barriers. We talk about four companies later on as case studies in this chapter who are tackling unique problems through their guile and champion the essence of sustainability.

Entrepreneurs are developing innovative solutions to these real time problems and continue to adapt to this ever changing world. Adopting renewable energy can reduce dependence on fossil fuels and lower greenhouse gas emissions. Sustainable agriculture can also improve food security while not harming natural resources. (Pretty et al., 2018). Food security is an urgent issue in developing countries and adopting sustainable agriculture to feed a growing population not only saves the environment from harm but promotes a way of life that is sustainable. Circular economy models are also being explored that emphasize waste reduction and efficiency in resource allocation, thereby creating production and consumption patterns that are increasingly sustainable (Korhonen, Nuur, Feldmann & Brikie, 2018). This transition from linear models to circular economy models require extensive planning, innovative product/service design, customer input and business strategies. This can only be achieved through policy changes and a combined effort of private and public entities. We now look at some of the theoretical foundations behind sustainable entrepreneurship.

THEORETICAL FOUNDATIONS

The Triple Bottom Line (TBL) approach, conceptualized by Elkington in 1998, has become a fundamental framework for businesses aiming to achieve sustainability. The TBL framework emphasizes three pillars: economic, social, and environmental performance, often referred to as the three Ps - Profit, People, and Planet. Elkington (2018) reinforced the importance of these dimensions, urging businesses to go beyond traditional financial metrics to incorporate social and environmental impacts in their performance evaluations.

The economic dimension of the TBL approach focuses on financial performance and economic viability. It emphasizes profitability, cost-saving, and economic growth, ensuring that businesses remain economically sustainable. By integrating economic sustainability, businesses can attract investment, achieve competitive advantage, and foster long-term growth (Elkington, 2018).

The social dimension of the TBL approach addresses the impact of business operations on society. It includes aspects such as fair labor practices, community engagement, and contribution to social equity. Social sustainability ensures that businesses act ethically and contribute positively to society, which can enhance their reputation, build customer loyalty, and improve employee satisfaction (Elkington, 2018).

The environmental dimension of the TBL approach focuses on minimizing the ecological footprint of business activities. It includes reducing waste, conserving resources, and mitigating environmental impacts. Environmental sustainability is crucial for preserving natural resources and ensuring the long-term viability of ecosystems. Businesses that prioritize environmental performance can achieve regulatory compliance, reduce operational costs, and appeal to environmentally conscious consumers (Elkington, 2018).

Elkington's TBL approach advocates for an integrated view of sustainability, where economic, social, and environmental dimensions are interdependent. Businesses adopting this approach are better equipped to address the complex challenges of sustainable development and create value for all stakeholders. The TBL framework encourages businesses to think holistically and strategically, fostering innovation and resilience in an increasingly dynamic and resource-constrained world.

To expand on the Triple Bottom Line (TBL) approach as introduced by John Elkington, it's essential to examine both its foundational principles and how recent adaptations and critiques have refined this model. TBL, encapsulating economic, social, and environmental pillars—often termed as Profit, People, and Planet—presents a holistic framework that pushes organizations to consider the broader impacts of their activities beyond mere financial performance. Below, I elaborate on TBL's core components, the nuances of implementing TBL in various industries, and its evolving relevance, incorporating recent insights and potential areas for further research.

ECONOMIC DIMENSION: PROFIT AND LONG-TERM VIABILITY

The economic dimension of TBL, while traditionally focused on profitability, is increasingly recognized as a pillar supporting sustainable economic growth rather than short-term financial gains. This perspective advocates that economic sustainability is more than just profit maximization; it is about fostering stable, long-term economic conditions that contribute to overall societal welfare. Companies aligning with TBL are thus encouraged to consider financial strategies that support sustainable development goals, including responsible investments, cost-efficiency improvements, and resilient business models that can withstand economic uncertainties.

Recent studies have further developed tools to quantify and compare economic contributions within TBL, such as using Data Envelopment Analysis (DEA) to measure and benchmark companies' economic efficiency within a sustainable context (Cortes, 2017). This allows companies, especially within high-impact industries like fast fashion and consumer goods, to evaluate their operational efficiencies against sustainability metrics, offering a pathway to economic sustainability that aligns with reduced resource consumption and minimized environmental degradation (Cortes, 2017).

SOCIAL DIMENSION: PEOPLE AND SOCIAL RESPONSIBILITY

The social pillar emphasizes an organization's responsibility to various stakeholders, including employees, customers, and the broader community. This dimension urges companies to engage in ethical labor practices, foster community welfare, and uphold social equity. Within TBL, social sustainability involves fair wages, safe working conditions, and opportunities for personal and professional growth for employees. Community-wise, social responsibility could mean supporting local development, investing in community education programs, or participating in social initiatives that alleviate societal issues.

Some scholars argue that the social pillar has historically received less focus than economic and environmental aspects, particularly in terms of measurable impact (Fifka & Idowu, 2013). There is a growing call for methodologies that integrate social metrics into standard reporting frameworks, addressing gaps in the analysis of social outcomes. For instance, integrating social sustainability into value stream mapping could better align internal and external stakeholders in achieving shared social goals (Mora, Akinci, & Alarcón, 2019). Thus, enhancing social sustainability as part of TBL aligns companies' operations with broader societal needs, building long-term trust with stakeholders (Fifka & Idowu, 2013), (Mora et al., 2019).

ENVIRONMENTAL DIMENSION: PLANET AND ECOLOGICAL FOOTPRINT

The environmental pillar emphasizes the need to minimize the ecological impact of business activities. This aspect focuses on reducing waste, conserving resources, and adopting sustainable practices to mitigate environmental impacts. Companies prioritizing environmental sustainability take steps to manage resources responsibly, invest in green technology, and adopt circular economy practices, where waste is minimized through the continuous use of resources.

The circular economy, in particular, has emerged as an extension of the environmental pillar, encouraging businesses to transition from linear "take-make-waste" models to circular models that prioritize reuse, recycling, and renewable inputs. Case studies, such as those in the fashion industry, reveal how adopting TBL can drive paradigm shifts in resource management (Connell & Kozar, 2017). By incorporating circular practices, organizations reduce their environmental footprint and ensure compliance with increasingly stringent environmental regulations, which is both a regulatory requirement and a consumer expectation (Connell & Kozar, 2017).

INTEGRATED VIEW: THE SYNERGY OF THE THREE PILLARS

Elkington's TBL approach advocates that economic, social, and environmental aspects are interdependent, urging businesses to adopt a balanced approach to sustainability. Businesses implementing TBL holistically benefit from reduced costs, improved community relations, and enhanced brand reputation, which collectively contribute to a resilient competitive advantage. However, integrating TBL is complex, with inherent tensions between each pillar. For instance, achieving environmental goals may increase short-term costs, impacting economic outcomes. Similarly, maintaining fair wages and investing in social initiatives could constrain financial resources.

Several recent studies propose that TBL's potential lies in its adaptability and scalability, meaning businesses can tailor TBL principles based on their industry, size, and geographic context. For instance, airport projects, as seen with Los Angeles World Airports, employ TBL in planning to achieve a "win-win-win" across all three dimensions by optimizing operations to reduce environmental impact while boosting social and economic benefits (Lemaster & Jackson, 2009). Such cases exemplify how the TBL can be an adaptive framework for sustainability in industries with distinct social and environmental pressures (Lemaster & Jackson, 2009).

EVOLUTION OF TBL AND EMERGING PERSPECTIVES

Despite its success, some scholars argue that TBL's traditional three-pillar structure might be limiting when applied to today's multifaceted sustainability challenges. To address these, researchers have proposed augmenting TBL with additional dimensions. For instance, adding "health" as a fourth pillar has been suggested to recognize the intersection of social, environmental, and economic factors with human health, which is central to sustainable communities (Semenza, 2012). Other scholars argue for a fifth pillar focusing on governance or political considerations, acknowledging that sustainable outcomes often require strong governance frameworks to address complex regulatory landscapes (Semenza, 2012).

Furthermore, Elkington himself has critiqued the limitations of TBL, suggesting that the framework requires rethinking to remain relevant in modern business contexts. He noted that many businesses have implemented TBL in a superficial manner, treating sustainability efforts as an extension of traditional profit-driven practices without fully integrating social and environmental considerations (Loviscek, 2021). To overcome these limitations, there is a growing emphasis on shifting TBL from a reporting tool to a strategic model that encourages genuine sustainability transformation (Loviscek, 2021).

FUTURE DIRECTIONS AND IMPLICATIONS FOR RESEARCH

The future of TBL research and application lies in addressing these critiques by refining the framework to better align with today's sustainability landscape. Areas for further exploration could include developing robust quantitative metrics for TBL's social and environmental dimensions, as these remain challenging to measure compared to financial outcomes. Examining how emerging technologies, like artificial intelligence and blockchain, can support TBL objectives, particularly in tracking environmental and social impacts across supply chains. Researching TBL's application in various sectors, such as tech, healthcare, and energy, each of which faces unique sustainability challenges. Incorporating governance as a fourth pillar ensures that sustainability strategies receive adequate support from regulatory bodies and align with broader societal goals.

In summary, the TBL approach remains a foundational sustainable model, advocating for a balance between economic, social, and environmental responsibilities. As businesses adopt TBL, an adaptation of the framework, such as adding additional pillars or enhanced quantitative metrics, could help address modern challenges and more accurately reflect the interconnected nature of global sustainability. The TBL model is thus evolving from a static reporting tool into a dynamic strategic approach, fostering resilience, innovation, and holistic growth. This progression reflects TBL's enduring relevance and adaptability in a world increasingly committed to sustainable development.

THEORY OF PLANNED BEHAVIOR

The Theory of Planned Behavior (TPB), developed by Ajzen (1991), has been widely applied to understand the factors influencing individual behavior. Vuorio, Puumalainen, and Fellnhofer (2018) extended this theory to explore how personal values, environmental awareness, and perceived behavioral control influence sustainable entrepreneurship. Their research provides insights into the psychological and cognitive processes that drive entrepreneurs to adopt sustainable practices.

Personal values play a significant role in shaping sustainable entrepreneurship. Vuorio et al. (2018) found that individuals with strong pro-environmental values are more likely to engage in sustainable business practices. These values influence their intentions and behaviors, driving them to create businesses that align with their ethical and environmental beliefs. Entrepreneurs with high environmental values prioritize sustainability and are motivated to develop eco-friendly products and services.

Environmental awareness is another crucial factor influencing sustainable entrepreneurship. Vuorio et al. (2018) highlighted that individuals who are aware of environmental issues and their impact on the planet are more likely to adopt sustainable practices. This awareness can be fostered through education, media, and personal experiences. Entrepreneurs who understand the importance of environmental sustainability are more likely to incorporate green practices into their business models and operations.

Perceived behavioral control, which refers to an individual's perception of their ability to perform a behavior, also influences sustainable entrepreneurship. Vuorio et al. (2018) found that entrepreneurs who believe they have the necessary skills, resources, and opportunities to implement sustainable practices are more likely to do so. This perception of control is influenced by factors such as access to finance, support networks, and regulatory frameworks. Entrepreneurs who feel confident in their ability to overcome barriers are more likely to pursue sustainable business ventures.

The TPB framework, as applied by Vuorio et al. (2018), underscores the importance of aligning personal values, environmental awareness, and perceived behavioral control to promote sustainable entrepreneurship. By understanding these factors, policymakers and educators can design interventions to support and encourage entrepreneurs to adopt sustainable practices. This approach can lead to the development of innovative solutions that address environmental challenges and contribute to sustainable development.

RESOURCE-BASED VIEW

The Resource-Based View (RBV) of the firm, articulated by Hart and Dowell (2011), posits that sustainable resources can provide a competitive advantage. This theory emphasizes that firms with valuable, rare, inimitable, and non-substitutable resources are more likely to achieve and sustain competitive advantage. In the context of sustainable entrepreneurship, the RBV highlights the strategic importance of integrating sustainability into business operations to enhance long-term competitiveness.

Hart and Dowell (2011) argue that sustainable resources, such as eco-efficient technologies, renewable energy, and sustainable supply chains, can create significant competitive advantages. These resources are not only valuable for reducing costs and improving operational efficiency but also for meeting regulatory requirements and addressing stakeholder expectations. Firms that invest in sustainable resources can differentiate themselves in the market and attract environmentally conscious customers and investors.

The RBV also emphasizes the importance of organizational capabilities in leveraging sustainable resources. Hart and Dowell (2011) highlight that firms need to develop capabilities such as innovation, collaboration, and strategic planning to effectively utilize sustainable resources. These capabilities enable firms to adapt to changing market conditions, identify new opportunities, and create sustainable business models. Firms with strong organizational capabilities can continuously improve their sustainability performance and maintain a competitive edge.

Moreover, the RBV suggests that sustainable resources can lead to reputational benefits. Hart and Dowell (2011) argue that firms that are recognized for their sustainability efforts can enhance their brand reputation and build trust with stakeholders. A strong reputation for sustainability can attract customers, investors, and talented employees, creating a virtuous cycle of competitive advantage. Firms that prioritize sustainability can also mitigate risks associated with environmental and social issues, further strengthening their competitive position.

The integration of sustainable resources into the RBV framework underscores the strategic importance of sustainability in achieving and sustaining competitive advantage. Hart and Dowell (2011) provide a theoretical foundation for understanding how firms can leverage sustainable resources to create long-term value. This perspective encourages firms to invest in sustainable technologies, develop organizational capabilities, and build strong reputations to enhance their competitiveness in a rapidly evolving market landscape.

CIRCULAR ECONOMY MODEL

The Circular Economy (CE) model, as discussed by Geissdoerfer et al. (2017) and Kirchherr, Reike, and Hekkert (2017), represents a paradigm shift from the traditional linear economy to a more sustainable and regenerative economic system. The CE model focuses on closing the loop of product lifecycles through strategies such as reducing, reusing, recycling, and recovering materials. This approach aims to minimize waste, reduce resource consumption, and create a sustainable economy (Islam et al, 2022; Islam & Akif, 2024).

Geissdoerfer et al. (2017) emphasize that the CE model is essential for sustainable entrepreneurship as it offers numerous opportunities for innovation and value creation. By adopting circular business models, entrepreneurs can develop products and services that are designed for longevity, repairability, and recyclability. This shift not only reduces environmental impact but also creates new business opportunities in areas such as remanufacturing, refurbishment, and recycling.

Kirchherr, Reike, and Hekkert (2017) further highlight the relevance of the CE model to sustainable entrepreneurship by discussing its potential to drive economic, social, and environmental benefits. The CE model encourages businesses to rethink their value chains and adopt sustainable practices that can lead to cost savings, resource efficiency, and competitive advantage. For instance, businesses that implement circular practices can reduce material costs, improve supply chain resilience, and enhance product quality.

The CE model also promotes collaboration and innovation across industries and sectors. Geissdoerfer et al. (2017) argue that circular business models require collaboration between manufacturers, suppliers, customers, and policymakers to create closed-loop systems. This collaboration can lead to the development of new technologies, business models, and regulatory frameworks that support the transition to a circular economy. Entrepreneurs who embrace this collaborative approach can drive systemic change and contribute to the broader sustainability agenda.

Kirchherr, Reike, and Hekkert (2017) also address the challenges and barriers to implementing the CE model. They note that transitioning to a circular economy requires significant changes in business practices, consumer behavior, and policy frameworks. Entrepreneurs must navigate these challenges by developing innovative solutions, engaging stakeholders, and advocating for supportive policies. Despite these challenges, the CE model offers a promising pathway for sustainable entrepreneurship and long-term economic resilience.

The CE model, as discussed by Geissdoerfer et al. (2017) and Kirchherr, Reike, and Hekkert (2017), provides a comprehensive framework for sustainable entrepreneurship. By adopting circular principles, entrepreneurs can create value while minimizing environmental impact and contributing to a sustainable economy. This approach encourages innovation, collaboration, and systemic change, making it a powerful tool for achieving sustainability goals and fostering economic growth.

The following 4 cases of sustainable entrepreneurship in different areas. We now look at CYCLO in the fashion industry, Code Effort in their journey of recycling cigarette buds, Loop Biotech and their disruption to the traditional funeral market and finally Krill Design repurposing agro waste and combating food waste. These four companies have exemplified each in different industries how to use sustainable practices to create new markets, jobs and reduce the strain on our environment.

CASE 1

CYCLO

When it comes to pioneers of closed loop production systems to upcycle pre consumer textile waste, no other company in Bangladesh comes close to CYCLO. Having worked with fashion industry giants such as H&M, Zara, Jack & Jones, KOHL's and Primark, CYCLO continues to innovate and practice sustainable development for the betterment of society. All of the yarn produced by CYCLO is at least 50% recycled cotton (CYCLO Recycled Fibers, 2022).

What started as a low quality yarn manufacturer used mostly to produce cleaning materials has evolved into CYCLO recycled fibers that produce high quality yarn that is commercially applicable and recognised internationally as a sustainable alternative (Brishty et al., 2025). Their business process starts from sourcing raw materials from garment manufacturers to find and then sort fibers by color and quality as they do not dye the fibers, reducing waste. This way the color of the waste materials collected determines the final color of the yarn. The fibers are recycled using machines where the yarns are shredded into recycled cotton fiber and is then blended with other fibers to ensure color matching and fiber strength. The blended fibers are then spun into yarn and delivered to customers who can then create a variety of products.The whole process is done without the use of water, dyes or chemicals and uses less energy per kg (lower CO_2 emissions) as opposed to traditional ring spinning. The usage of open end spinning machines is a practical strategy that many factories could consider using. The Bangladesh RMG industry is perhaps its greatest asset which through exporting to most major countries supports millions of workers and their families. The government also provides special incentives to this export heavy industry. CYCLO is one of the few players in this industry to take up such uniquely sustainable practices. It goes without saying that it will inspire others in the industry to follow suit to gain not only a unique market proposition but also a greater market share and recognition.

The fashion industry also produces millions of tonnes of waste each year which contribute to the detriment of the environment. These waste come in the form of garment waste from cutting shapes, carbon-di-oxide, and other harmful chemicals. Nearby land and rivers are increasingly filled with waste. CYCLO in this sense has a unique proposition to the market that they produce yarn from ready made garment waste consuming no externally added chemicals or dyes. The fashion industry for years has been about consumer demand and how it sways products, production houses, the people in the industry and the raw materials it consumes to meet ever increasing demand. Amidst all the chaos of seasonal trends, micro trends and influencer marketing, consumers and producers often forget the impact they have on the environment. Reports show that sustainable fashion is at an all time high and is only going to continue going up. Brands are increasingly conscious about sustainable practices and are using it as a marketing tool to capture new segments of consumers. This is a result of consumers being sustainable conscious and pushing demand. The cycle of sustainable fashion is not limited to just the creation process to be sustainable but from materials to manufacturing, working conditions of workers and equitable pay is of equal importance. As global awareness rises, consumers are shifting from businesses with poor sustainability practices to those who put sustainability at the forefront of their value proposition. As a result these brands are likely to see positive results in their businesses.

CASE 2

Code Effort

Established by Noida-based entrepreneurs Naman Gupta and Vipul Gupta in 2018, Code Effort is an Indian startup aiming to revolutionize cigarette waste management. Code Effort focuses on collecting discarded cigarette butts through strategically placed V-bins (value bins) at cigarette vendors. The collected waste butts go through a five-step process consisting of manual separation, paper recycling, fiber recycling, composting, and wastewater recycling to produce reusable paper and fibers as end products (Islam et al., 2025).

Code effort processes the extracted paper by combining it with an organic binder to manufacture mosquito repellent. The extracted fibers are chemically processed to neutralize their toxicity and used as stuffing in various products, such as pillows, cushions, and keychains. The firm has plans to manufacture products such as air purifiers and eyewear using reclaimed cigarette butt components in the near future (Anuj Ramatri, 2020).

The global cigarette market is massive with big tobacco companies luring in consumers at large scales despite taxes and bans across the globe. Smokers go through packs of cigarettes a day to regulate their nicotine levels as they fear withdrawals if they stop. Certain people are also using it as a means of mood modulation. It is the largest preventable risk factor for morbidity across countries. Although smoking is increasingly dealt with by social disapproval, a large number of people including the youth are addicted to nicotine. The body isn't the only thing that is being affected through smoking, the environment is increasingly become a litter for smokers who throw out the remainder of the cigarette stick after they are done with their business. These cigarette buds are then a part of plastic pollution making its way to landfills worldwide. These buds also secrete toxins that can kill fish and other sea creatures. Code Effort have collaborated with waste pickers in collection of cigarette buds and have paid them per kilo of waste collected. Aside from producing cushions, pillows, and mattresses they also have also produced in collaboration with Lee Cooper - jeans made from cigarette butts! This goes to show the range and scope of this sustainable business and how many entrepreneurs can take advantage of such waste in the environment around us to make a positive impact and reduce the damage we cause (Ali et al., 2024).

Code Effort has become India's largest cigarette waste management and recycling firm, recycling and repurposing over two billion cigarette butts to date. Resulting in over a hundred billion liters of water being saved, over a hundred local women being empowered through work, and the direct reduction of GHG emissions as well as boosting the local economy, promoting a circular economy and green innovation (Code Effort Private Limited, 2023; Dia et al, 2025).

CASE 3

Loop Biotech

Bob Hendrikx and Lonneke Westhoff conceived Loop Biotech during their graduation project at Delft University of Technology. The duo pondered on and explored ways to incorporate nature and sustainability into people's daily lives (Loop Biotech, 2024). They found their answer with Mycelium, an underground root network of mushrooms responsible for converting organic dead matter and pollutants into nutrients and nourishment for the environment (Loop Biotech, 2023). With patented technology and strong market positioning, Loop Biotech is a prime example of innovation while using the earth's resources sustainably and offering consumers an innovative product.

With a mission to restore nature and secure a positive ecological footprint for future generations, Loop Biotech invented the first-ever "living coffin." These coffins are fully biodegradable, manufactured solely from upcycled hemp fibers and local species of mushrooms grown in seven days at the company's facilities in Delft, Netherlands. Loop Biotech currently offers three different coffins: the "Loop Living Cocoon™," "Loop EarthRise,™" and "Loop ForestBed™," along with a host of eco-friendly accessories ranging from biodegradable paint to sustainable shrouds and linings (Loop Biotech, 2024). Aside from coffins, they have expanded to biodegradable paint, sustainable wading and interior lining for their coffins.

They solve an interesting problem of biodegradable options for funerals. These sustainable coffins unleash the potential of mycelium which are used to grow the coffin in 7 days and are absorbed by nature in 45 days. Traditional coffins degrade slower and might contain chemicals that are harmful for the environment when absorbed eventually. Wooden coffins are expensive and require chopping trees are only becoming pricier worldwide as trees become scarcer. This alternative not only solves the problem but has a huge impact on the environment. It is projected that the funeral market will be worth about $189 billion by 2030 (Nowshin, 2024). With a market which is going to be worth that much it remains to be seen as to how much the founders of Loop Biotech can scale the business and expand to different markets across the globe.

CASE 4

Krill Design

Krill Design, an innovative Italian startup, champions sustainability with its circular economy model, converting organic waste into useful products. Ivan Calimani, Martina Lamperti, and Yack H. Di Maio, all architects by profession, founded the company in 2018 with the goal of bridging the gap between agro-food waste and consumer products in a sustainable method.

Food waste is a major cause of concern for the world. As millions of people go hungry each day, millions more are wasting food at an alarming rate. This food is not only not being used to solve hunger, but producing waste as a byproduct of production and consumption which degrades the environment. Food in landfills breakdown to form methane which is a greenhouse gas contributing to global warming.

Krill Design's sustainability strategy is based on the circular economy paradigm, which transforms waste into resources. They collect organic waste, such as orange peels, and process it into bioplastics. These bioplastics are used to make environmentally friendly, compostable products, which reduces landfill waste and reliance on fossil fuels. Their flagship product, the Ohmie Lamp, is a prime example, made entirely of orange peels and demonstrating the potential of reclaimed materials. Krill Design's commitment to sustainability is evident in their diverse product offerings, which include packaging, furniture, and home decor. These products are not only biodegradable; but also serve aesthetic and functional purposes. The Ohmie Lamp, for example, combines natural materials with a sleek design, demonstrating that sustainability and quality are compatible. Their influence goes beyond product innovation as they actively promote sustainability through community engagement and education, emphasizing the importance of circular economy practices. By converting waste into valuable materials, they help to reduce environmental impact and promote social change. Furthermore, Krill Design invests heavily in R&D, constantly improving their bioplastic technology. The material they use is called Rekrill which is patented and 100% biodegradable and compostable. They claim that "1 kg of ReKrill corresponds to 1 kg of CO2 offset!" (Krill Design, n.d). This dedication to innovation positions them as green tech industry leaders, encouraging broader adoption of sustainable practices and creating new market opportunities. Krill Design is poised for significant expansion, with plans to increase production capacity and investigate new applications for their biopolymers. Their vision includes creating a complete line of home furnishings and decor aimed at reducing waste and increasing sustainability. They use crowdfunding to not only secure financial support and also to build a community of environmentally conscious consumers who are in the know and truly support this venture.

Krill Design exemplifies how innovation and sustainability can work together to drive meaningful change. Their method for converting organic waste into high-quality products provides a viable solution to environmental issues. As they continue to innovate and expand, Krill Design is poised to play a critical role in shaping a sustainable future, demonstrating that eco-design is more than a trend, but a necessary evolution in the design world.

CASE 5

M-KOPA Solar: Enabling Energy Access in Kenya

M-KOPA Solar has revolutionized energy access in Kenya by providing affordable, solar-powered home systems to low-income households in rural, off-grid areas. Leveraging a pay-as-you-go model, M-KOPA's business approach allows customers to make incremental payments through mobile money platforms, a system particularly suited for low-income populations with irregular income flows (Rastogi, 2018). M-KOPA's model not only enables these households to access sustainable energy but also reduces reliance on kerosene, which poses health risks and contributes to greenhouse gas emissions (Wyche et al., 2018). By targeting communities with limited infrastructure, M-KOPA has created a scalable solution for bridging the energy gap in Kenya, which aligns with Sustainable Development Goal 7, aimed at providing universal energy access.

Studies have shown that M-KOPA's approach has led to significant social and environmental benefits. Households using solar systems reported improved air quality, reduced expenditure on energy sources, and better educational outcomes, as students could study after dark with safe lighting (Pailman et al., 2015). M-KOPA exemplifies how technology, financial innovation, and sustainability principles can merge to foster positive change in underserved communities, while building a profitable enterprise (Wyche et al., 2018); (Rastogi, 2018); (Pailman et al., 2015; Rafi et al., 2024).

CASE 6

Xinca: Advancing Circular Economy in Argentina

Xinca, an Argentine company, addresses environmental waste through its production of sustainable footwear made from recycled materials, such as scrap rubber and industrial waste. Founded in 2013, Xinca operates with a clear mission to reduce landfill waste while providing employment opportunities for marginalized communities, including individuals from economically disadvantaged backgrounds and prison inmates (Connell & Kozar, 2017). Xinca exemplifies a circular economy model, as it repurposes waste materials into valuable products, reducing the environmental footprint of the fashion industry, which is traditionally associated with high levels of waste and pollution.

Xinca's impact extends beyond environmental sustainability. By employing individuals from marginalized communities, the company fosters social equity, an important aspect of the Triple Bottom Line approach. The social benefits of Xinca's operations highlight how sustainable entrepreneurship can address both environmental and social issues, offering a holistic approach to sustainability. Xinca has garnered attention across Latin America and has become a model for integrating sustainable practices within manufacturing, contributing to a shift towards greener practices in the region's fashion industry (Connell & Kozar, 2017).

DISCUSSION AND POLICY IMPLICATIONS

The underlying factors and discussions on sustainable development and most importantly sustainable entrepreneurship yields several key findings and sheds light on various practical strategies and policy implications based on theoretical foundations.

The idea that sustainable entrepreneurship and sustainability in general is a multifaceted process requiring intricate interactions between society, businesses and the environment leads us to realize that it requires eliminating tensions and effectively integrating all three factors at play (Giovannoni & Fabietti, 2013). In the case of emerging economies, the case studies of sustainable entrepreneurship spotlight the different approaches and practical strategies that are being used to address societal and environmental issues while keeping processes sustainable (Dutta et al, 2016). A common theme across the case studies is the importance of stakeholder management. To manage each and every stakeholder across production levels and consumer bases while fostering collaboration and feedback only promotes sustainable practices further (Dacin et al, 2010).

Policy is paramount to any endeavor undertaken by any entity and sustainable entrepreneurship is no different, key policy changes such as a regulatory reforms and incentivising policy to enable sustainable entrepreneurship can foster more growth in the sector. Placing progressive taxes on carbon emissions and waste emissions would also steer the boat towards more sustainable practices. Policies that encourage innovation, access to finance and entrepreneurship education can amplify the development of scalable sustainable businesses (Banerjee & Duflo, 2019). Gender equality and social inclusion for marginalized groups can also be promoted by effective policies which can give rise to better entrepreneurs who can help to achieve sustainable development goals (Sarkis et al, 2010).

ESG rating systems like credit rating systems are needed to improve. The established quality of credit ratings are taught in finance classes and rightfully so, as the determinants of worthiness and transparency is well looked after. Current ESG ratings are nowhere near the quality and precision of credit ratings. Most people use rudimentary ESG ratings and simple filters to determine whether companies are worth investing in. Companies and rating agencies are both required to improve upon their practices and provide transparency to the people. Our suggestions would be constructed based on solid quant based systems, portfolios of sustainable firms. However current ESG ratings when taken into account have to be taken with a grain of salt and used as a gateway to skip some information search times in order to make decisions in investment. Firms from emerging markets tend to have higher ESG scores and are cheaper than counterparts from developed countries. Turkish company Arçelik issued about 350 million euros in green bonds and received a massive response in the form of a 500% over subscription. This shows a clear demand for such ESG focused activities.

From recycled fibers with little to no waste, cigarette buds being repurposed to make paper, organic waste matter to be made into coffins, and food waste being repurposed we see a range of different case uses of sustainable practices. These businesses and entrepreneurs are redefining standard business processes and industry norms to find the finest possible solution to each problem in their own contexts. The resilience, creativity and adaptability of these sustainable entrepreneurs lead the way for practitioners, policymakers and researchers to follow suit and make a difference.

CONCLUSION

The Sustainable Development Goals (SDGs) play a pivotal role in shaping sustainable entrepreneurship by providing a comprehensive framework for addressing global sustainability challenges. Entrepreneurs are encouraged to align their business strategies with the SDGs, fostering innovation and sustainable practices that contribute to economic, social, and environmental goals. This alignment not only enhances the sustainability of their businesses but also supports the broader global agenda for achieving a sustainable and equitable world by 2030 (Horne et al., 2020).

The SDGs offer a roadmap for sustainable entrepreneurship by highlighting specific targets that entrepreneurs can address through innovative business models. Entrepreneurs who integrate SDG principles into their operations can create significant value by addressing pressing global issues such as poverty, climate change, and responsible consumption. This alignment provides a dual benefit of promoting sustainability while unlocking new business opportunities (Pomare, 2018).

In emerging economies, sustainable entrepreneurs face unique benefits and challenges. These economies often grapple with issues such as resource scarcity, environmental degradation, and socio-economic inequalities. Sustainable entrepreneurship can address these challenges by leveraging local knowledge and context-specific strategies to create long-term solutions. However, entrepreneurs in these regions also face significant barriers such as limited access to finance, inadequate infrastructure, and regulatory hurdles (Ashari et al., 2021).

Sustainable entrepreneurship presents numerous economic opportunities. Entrepreneurs can tap into new markets and customer segments that prioritize sustainable products and services. By focusing on sustainability, businesses can enhance their brand reputation, attract investment, and achieve long-term growth. Additionally, sustainable practices can lead to cost savings through resource efficiency and waste reduction (Schmiedeknecht, 2019).

Environmental benefits are also significant. Sustainable entrepreneurs contribute to reducing the ecological footprint of their operations by adopting green technologies, renewable energy, and circular economy principles. These practices help mitigate climate change impacts, conserve natural resources, and promote biodiversity. Furthermore, sustainable entrepreneurship supports the transition to a low-carbon economy, which is crucial for achieving global climate goals (Günzel-Jensen et al., 2020).

Social impact is another critical aspect. Sustainable entrepreneurs can create inclusive economic growth by generating employment, improving livelihoods, and fostering social equity. By addressing social issues such as poverty and inequality, these businesses contribute to the overall well-being of communities. This approach aligns with the broader objectives of the SDGs, which aim to ensure that no one is left behind in the pursuit of sustainable development (Fukuda-Parr & Muchhala, 2020).

Despite the benefits, sustainable entrepreneurs in emerging economies face several challenges. Access to finance is a significant barrier, as many investors are reluctant to fund projects with longer payback periods and higher perceived risks. Innovative financing mechanisms, such as impact investing and green bonds, are needed to support these ventures (Metawea, 2020).

Infrastructural limitations, such as inadequate transport networks and unreliable energy supplies, also hinder the growth of sustainable businesses. Governments and international organizations must invest in infrastructure development to create an enabling environment for sustainable entrepreneurship (Ganesh et al., 2019).

Socio-economic inequalities present additional challenges. Marginalized communities often lack access to resources, education, and opportunities, making it difficult for sustainable entrepreneurs to thrive. Policies promoting social inclusion and equal access to resources are essential to overcome these barriers (Seikkula-Leino et al., 2021).

In conclusion, the integration of SDGs into entrepreneurial activities offers a pathway to sustainable development, particularly in emerging economies. While the potential benefits are substantial, addressing the challenges requires concerted efforts from entrepreneurs, policymakers, and stakeholders. By fostering an enabling environment and supporting innovative solutions, sustainable entrepreneurship can drive inclusive and sustainable growth, contributing significantly to the achievement of the SDGs.

REFERENCES

Ajzen, I. (1991). The theory of planned behavior. *Organizational Behavior and Human Decision Processes*, 50(2), 179–211. DOI: 10.1016/0749-5978(91)90020-T

Anuj Ramatri. (2020, January 20). *The man who Recycled our Cigarette Waste | Anuj Ramatri* [Video]. YouTube. https://www.youtube.com/watch?v=qVuRu1c6PIs

Ashari, H., Abbas, I. K. A., Abdul-Talib, A. N., & Mohd Zamani, S. N. (2021). Entrepreneurship and Sustainable Development Goals: A Multigroup Analysis of the Moderating Effects of Entrepreneurship Education on Entrepreneurial Intention. *Sustainability (Basel)*, 14(1), 431. DOI: 10.3390/su14010431

Banerjee, A. V., & Duflo, E. (2019). *Good Economics for Hard Times*. PublicAffairs.

Brishty, S. P., Islam, Q. T., Alam, S. R. & Akif, A. (2025). Cyclo Fibers: Pioneering Sustainable Textile Production in Bangladesh. SAGE Publications: SAGE Business Cases Originals.

Brundtland, G. H. (1987). *Our common future: The World Commission on Environment and Development*. Oxford University Press.

Bruton, G., Khavul, S., Siegel, D., & Wright, M. (2015). New financial alternatives in seeding entrepreneurship: Microfinance, crowdfunding, and peer–to–peer innovations. *Entrepreneurship Theory and Practice*, 39(1), 9–26. DOI: 10.1111/etap.12143

Code Effort Private Limited. (2023). *Code Effort*. Retrieved March 22, 2024, from https://www.codeefforts.com/about

Connell, K. Y. H., & Kozar, J. (2017). Introduction to special issue on sustainability and the triple bottom line within the global clothing and textiles industry. *Fashion and Textiles*, 4(1), 1–3.

Connell, K. Y. H., & Kozar, J. (2017). Introduction to special issue on sustainability and the triple bottom line within the global clothing and textiles industry. *Fashion and Textiles*, 4, 1–3.

Connell, K. Y. H., & Kozar, J. M. (2017). Introduction to special issue on sustainability and the triple bottom line within the global clothing and textiles industry. *Fashion and Textiles*, 4(1), 1–3.

Cortes, A. (2017). A Triple Bottom Line Approach for Measuring Supply Chains Sustainability Using Data Envelopment Analysis. *European Journal of Sustainable Development*, 6(3), 119–128. DOI: 10.14207/ejsd.2017.v6n3p119

Dacin, P. A., Dacin, M. T., & Matear, M. (2010). Social entrepreneurship: Why we don't need a new theory and how we move forward from here. *The Academy of Management Perspectives*, 24(3), 37–57.

Dean, T. J., & McMullen, J. S. (2007). Toward a theory of sustainable entrepreneurship: Reducing environmental degradation through entrepreneurial action. *Journal of Business Venturing*, 22(1), 50–76. DOI: 10.1016/j.jbusvent.2005.09.003

Dia, R. R., Akif, A., Islam, Q. T., Hossain, M. A. (2025). Interactive Cares Bangladesh: Empowering Bangladesh's Future Through Education and the SDGs. SAGE Publications: SAGE Business Cases Originals.

Dutta, S., Lanvin, B., & Wunsch-Vincent, S. (2016). *Global innovation index 2016: Winning with global innovation*. Cornell University, INSEAD, and the World Intellectual Property Organization (WIPO).

Elkington, J. (2018). 25 Years ago I coined the phrase "Triple Bottom Line." Here's why it's time to rethink it. Harvard Business Review. Retrieved from https://hbr.org/2018/06/25-years-ago-i-coined-the-phrase-triple-bottom-line-heres-why-im-giving-up-on-it

Fifka, M., & Idowu, S. (2013). Sustainability and Social Innovation. In Idowu, S., & Capaldi, N. (Eds.), *Encyclopedia of Corporate Social Responsibility* (pp. 309–315).

Fukuda-Parr, S., & Muchhala, B. (2020). The Southern origins of sustainable development goals: Ideas, actors, aspirations. *World Development*, 126, 104706. DOI: 10.1016/j.worlddev.2019.104706

Ganesh, U., Sinha, S., Gokhale, A., Kaushal, A., Gupta, A., & Thukral, C. (2019). Innovations for Scaling Green Sectors.

Geissdoerfer, M., Morioka, S. N., de Carvalho, M. M., & Evans, S. (2018). Business models and supply chains for the circular economy. *Journal of Cleaner Production*, 190, 712–721. DOI: 10.1016/j.jclepro.2018.04.159

Giovannoni, E., & Fabietti, G. (2013). What is sustainability? A review of the concept and its applications. *Integrated reporting: Concepts and cases that redefine corporate accountability, 21-40.*

Günzel-Jensen, F., Siebold, N., Kroeger, A., & Korsgaard, S. (2020). Do the United Nations' Sustainable Development Goals matter for social entrepreneurial ventures? A bottom-up perspective. Journal of Business Venturing Insights.

Hall, J. K., Daneke, G. A., & Lenox, M. J. (2010). Sustainable development and entrepreneurship: Past contributions and future directions. *Journal of Business Venturing*, 25(5), 439–448. DOI: 10.1016/j.jbusvent.2010.01.002

Hart, S. L., & Dowell, G. (2011). A natural-resource-based view of the firm: Fifteen years after. *Journal of Management*, 37(5), 1464–1479. DOI: 10.1177/0149206310390219

Hockerts, K. (2017). Determinants of social entrepreneurial intentions. *Entrepreneurship Theory and Practice*, 41(1), 105–130. DOI: 10.1111/etap.12171

Horne, J., Recker, M., Michelfelder, I., Jay, J., & Kratzer, J. (2020). Exploring entrepreneurship related to the sustainable development goals - mapping new venture activities with semi-automated content analysis. *Journal of Cleaner Production*, 242, 118052. DOI: 10.1016/j.jclepro.2019.118052

IPCC. (2014). [*Impacts, Adaptation, and Vulnerability. Part A: Global and Sectoral Aspects*. Contribution of Working Group II to the Fifth Assessment Report of the Intergovernmental Panel on Climate Change.]. *Climatic Change*, •••, 2014.

Islam, Q. T., & Akif, A. (2024). Paperman Foundation India: Driving Sustainability through Circular Economy and Creating Impact. SAGE Publications: SAGE Business Cases Originals.

Islam, Q. T., Talukder, M. S., & Haque, K. L. (2022). Sustainable Development Through the Circular Economy: Experience From Emerging Economies. In Redefining Global Economic Thinking for the Welfare of Society (pp. 75-93). IGI Global.

Islam, Q. T., Zabir, F., Singh, T. (2025). Code Effort's Model: A Case Study in SDG-Driven Environmental Entrepreneurship. SAGE Publications: SAGE Business Cases Originals.

Kim, W. C., & Mauborgne, R. A. (2014). *Blue ocean strategy, expanded edition: How to create uncontested market space and make the competition irrelevant*. Harvard business review Press.

Kirchherr, J., Reike, D., & Hekkert, M. (2017). Conceptualizing the circular economy: An analysis of 114 definitions. *Resources, Conservation and Recycling*, 127, 221–232. DOI: 10.1016/j.resconrec.2017.09.005

Korhonen, J., Nuur, C., Feldmann, A., & Birkie, S. E. (2018). Circular Economy as an Essentially Contested Concept. *Journal of Cleaner Production*, 175, 544–552. DOI: 10.1016/j.jclepro.2017.12.111

Krill Design. (n.d.). Krill Design. https://en.krilldesign.net/

Lemaster, K., & Jackson, V. F. (2009). Sustainable Airport Projects: Going Beyond LEED. *Airport Magazine*, 20.

Loop Biotech. (2023, May 22). *The inventors of the World's First Living Coffin | Loop Biotech* [Video]. YouTube. https://www.youtube.com/watch?v=uQXOls5Mefs

Loop Biotech. (2024, March 4). About us - *Bob Hendrikx & Lonneke Westhoff.* https://loop-biotech.com/about-us/

Loviscek, V. (2021). Triple Bottom Line toward a Holistic Framework for Sustainability: A Systematic Review. *Revista de Administração Contemporânea.*

Mair, J., & Marti, I. (2006). Social entrepreneurship research: A source of explanation, prediction, and delight. *Journal of World Business*, 41(1), 36–44. DOI: 10.1016/j.jwb.2005.09.002

Metawea, M. (2020). The role of financial institutions in supporting entrepreneurial success: Case of Egypt. American Journal of Business and Operations Research.

Mora, M., Akinci, B., & Alarcón, L. (2019). Integrating Social Sustainability in Value Stream Mapping: Panelized Post-Disaster Temporary Housing Case Study. *Proceedings of the 36th International Symposium on Automation and Robotics in Construction (ISARC).* DOI: 10.22260/ISARC2019/0076

Nowshin, S. (2024, May 6). *Magical mushrooms: How mycelium is changing industries beyond food.* Sifted. https://sifted.eu/articles/mushroom-tech-mycelium-loop-biotech

Pailman, W., Kruger, W., & Prasad, G. (2015). Mobile payment innovation for sustainable energy access. *2015 International Conference on the Domestic Use of Energy (DUE)*, 39-44.

Pomare, C. (2018). *A Multiple Framework Approach to Sustainable Development Goals (SDGs) and Entrepreneurship.* Entrepreneurship and the Sustainable Development Goals. DOI: 10.1108/S2040-724620180000008006

Pretty, J., Benton, T. G., Bharucha, Z. P., Dicks, L. V., Flora, C. B., Godfray, H. C. J., Goulson, D., Hartley, S., Lampkin, N., Morris, C., Pierzynski, G., Prasad, P. V. V., Reganold, J., Rockström, J., Smith, P., Thorne, P., & Wratten, S. (2018). Global assessment of agricultural system redesign for sustainable intensification. *Nature Sustainability*, 1(8), 441–446. DOI: 10.1038/s41893-018-0114-0

Rafi, S., Dia, R. R., Gazi, M. A., & Islam, Q. T. (2024). Fairphone: The Phone That Protects the Planet. SAGE Publications: SAGE Business Cases Originals. Ali, K. S., Islam, Q. T., Zabir, F., & Hossain, M. A. (2024). SWAP: A Sustainable Solution to Our E-Waste Problem. SAGE Publications: SAGE Business Cases Originals.

Rastogi, C. (2018). M-Kopa Solar: Lighting up the Dark Continent. *South Asian Journal of Business and Management Cases*, 7(1), 93–103. DOI: 10.1177/2277977918774648

Recycled Fibers, C. Y. C. L. O. (2022, May 18). *About - CYCLO® Recycled Fibers*. CYCLO® Recycled Fibers. https://www.cyclofibers.com/about/

Sarkis, J., Gonzalez-Torre, P., & Adenso-Diaz, B. (2010). Stakeholder pressure and the adoption of environmental practices: The mediating effect of training. *Journal of Operations Management*, 28(2), 163–176. DOI: 10.1016/j.jom.2009.10.001

Schaltegger, S., & Burritt, R. (2018). *Contemporary environmental accounting: Issues, concepts and practice*. Routledge.

Schaltegger, S., & Wagner, M. (2011). Sustainable entrepreneurship and sustainability innovation: Categories and interactions. *Business Strategy and the Environment*, 20(4), 222–237. DOI: 10.1002/bse.682

Schmiedeknecht, M. (2019). Social Innovation and Entrepreneurship Supporting the Sustainable Development Goals (SDGs)–Fostering Social Value Creation. The Future of the UN Sustainable Development Goals.

Seelos, C., & Mair, J. (2017). *Innovation and scaling for impact: How effective social enterprises do it*. Stanford University Press.

Seikkula-Leino, J., Jónsdóttir, S., Håkansson-Lindqvist, M., Westerberg, M., & Eriksson-Bergström, S. (2021). Responding to Global Challenges through Education: Entrepreneurial, Sustainable, and Pro-Environmental Education in Nordic Teacher Education Curricula. Sustainability.

Semenza, J. (2012). Creating Sustainable Communities: The Quadruple Bottom Line. *EcoHealth*, 9(4), 499–501. DOI: 10.1007/s10393-012-0795-1

UNDP. (2020). *Human Development Report 2020: The Next Frontier*. Retrieved from https://hdr.undp.org/sites/default/files/hdr2020.pdf

United Nations. (2015). *Transforming our world: The 2030 Agenda for Sustainable Development*. Retrieved from https://sustainabledevelopment.un.org/post2015/transformingourworld

Vuorio, A., Puumalainen, K., & Fellnhofer, K. (2018). Drivers of entrepreneurial intentions in sustainable entrepreneurship. *International Journal of Entrepreneurial Behaviour & Research*, 24(2), 359–381. DOI: 10.1108/IJEBR-03-2016-0097

Wyche, S., Chidziwisano, G. H., Uwimbabazi, F., & Simiyu, N. (2018). Defamiliarizing the Domestic: Exploring "M-Kopa Solar" and Sustainable Practices in Rural Kenyan Households. *Proceedings of the 1st ACM SIGCAS Conference on Computing and Sustainable Societies*, 21. DOI: 10.1145/3209811.3211888

Chapter 10
Sustainable Entrepreneurship in Emerging Economies (BRICS): Unveiling Opportunities Amid Challenges

Sachin Prakash Srivastava
https://orcid.org/0000-0003-1577-4132
Dr. Vishwanath Karad MIT World Peace University, India

Sonali Srivastava
https://orcid.org/0000-0003-0551-8442
Symbiosis Centre for Management Studies, Symbiosis International University, India

Himanshu Varshney
https://orcid.org/0000-0001-5706-6148
Netaji Subhas University of Technology, New Delhi, India

Supriya Paigude
https://orcid.org/0000-0003-0564-0421
Dr. Vishwanath Karad MIT World Peace University, India

ABSTRACT

Emerging economies often face challenges of suboptimal resource allocation, socioeconomic disparities, and deficiencies in healthcare and social welfare provisions. India's journey to become the third-largest start-up ecosystem globally

DOI: 10.4018/979-8-3693-4338-8.ch010

clearly demonstrates how entrepreneurship has successfully tackled these difficulties. Nevertheless, using sustainable business concepts in entrepreneurial activities is crucial for sustainably addressing these challenges. Conventional business beliefs chase only profit motives, but sustainable entrepreneurship promotes a fundamental change in the belief that businesses may achieve financial gain while safeguarding the environment by focusing on people, profit, and the planet. This chapter has elucidated the significance of sustainable entrepreneurship in alleviating social and economic inadequacies in developing nations. Additionally, it explores the growing opportunities that arise from implementing circular economy and SDG objectives.

INTRODUCTION

Emerging economies often face challenges such as ineffective distribution of resources, disparities in wealth distribution, and deficiencies in healthcare and social services. India's ascent to become the third-largest start-up ecosystem globally has been efficiently tackled by entrepreneurship (Bothra, 2024; Singh et al., 2020). Nevertheless, enduring resolutions to these issues are yet to be offered until companies opt to incorporate sustainable business principles into their operational practices. Sustainable development holds paramount importance for rising economies and the global community as a whole. Let's examine the case of infrastructure. Developed economies have recently reached saturation regarding the growth and development of their infrastructure and industrial industries. Nevertheless, the nascent economy is presently transitioning towards attaining developed nation status, yet it still possesses a substantial amount of infrastructure development yet to be accomplished. These economies make up about 75% of the global economy. The world will encounter environmental challenges if growing economies depend on outdated methods. Hence, achieving sustainable growth in rising economies is paramount (Chaparro-Banegas et al., 2024; Zakari & Oluwaseyi Musibau, 2024).

Sustainable entrepreneurship advocates a paradigm shift in that enterprises can prosper economically while ensuring environmental preservation. It prioritizes individuals, financial gain, and the environment. The significance of individuals as stakeholders in sustainable business lies in their commitment to prioritizing the well-being and interests of the people (Figge et al., 2002). Entrepreneurs strongly dedicated to sustainability eschew traditional business practices, processes, and protocols, opting instead for goods and services that exhibit superior social and environmental attributes. According to (Bonfanti et al., 2024), In this hypothetical situation, traditional market structures, production techniques, products, and consumption habits that are associated with unsustainable practices are replaced with more sustainable alternatives. Sustainable entrepreneurship is closely associated with the circular economy framework, introduced as part of the 17 objectives of the United Nations' sustainable development goals (SDGs) in 2015. Scholars and professionals from several countries have also expressed their endorsement of sustainable entrepreneurship as a viable strategy for addressing these sustainability objectives. India has also recognized the significance of entrepreneurial pursuits in addressing intricate societal challenges. India's rapid economic growth has fostered a prosperous entrepreneurial climate, with several new businesses emerging across various sectors. In addition to sustainable businesses launched by individuals, the participation of the community is vital in accomplishing sustainable development goals. Communities must undergo transformation to address the Sustainable Development Goals (SDGs) inside society. Relying just on the government is inadequate for successfully implementing the SDGs. A community-centric strategy can facilitate the adoption of sustainable business ideas by individuals, especially if society as a whole recognizes it as necessary for the betterment of society (Satsangi & Dhir, 2024)

Nevertheless, this upward trend in growth is accompanied by enduring social, economic, and environmental obstacles that require prompt and enduring resolutions. Although philanthropy has been a longstanding practice in India, there is a growing interest in utilizing economic strategies to achieve sustained social impact (Sörensson & Ghannad, 2024). This chapter analyses the opportunities and challenges related to advancing sustainable entrepreneurship in India, recognizing the simultaneous potential of the social and sustainable enterprise (SSE) in promoting economic inclusivity and generating employment opportunities. The author has also introduced a theoretical framework that utilizes an antecedent and consequence model to examine the phenomenon of sustainable entrepreneurship in emerging economies.

How is sustainable entrepreneurship different from Social Entrepreneurship?

According to Terán-Yépez et al (2020),

"With the emergence of sustainable development goals, the scope of entrepreneurship has broadened from generating wealth to solving societal and environmental issues in a sustainable manner. Sustainable entrepreneurship is how individuals identify, cultivate, and capitalize on possibilities to create future goods and services that yield economic, social, and ecological benefits [...]."

The existing body of literature does not elucidate the demarcation between social and sustainable entrepreneurship. The notion of social entrepreneurship has existed since the 1950s, and the definition of social entrepreneurship is still ambiguous, and its boundaries with other areas of study are unclear (Bonfanti et al., 2024; Saebi et al., 2019). The distinction between social and sustainable entrepreneurship is rooted in the enterprise's vision and business model. There are two viewpoints to consider. Entrepreneurs may choose to produce either a general or sustainable product utilizing sustainable raw materials. This strategic decision is driven by the current trend of sustainable products and their significant market demand. By capitalizing on this opportunity, entrepreneurs can effectively sell sustainable products. The second approach involves the utilization of an innovative business model to provide a sustainable solution for addressing social and environmental challenges. Therefore, sustainable entrepreneurship advocates for a paradigm shift in the notion that enterprises can attain economic prosperity while preserving the natural environment. It prioritizes individuals, financial gain, and the environment. Individuals are seen as significant stakeholders in sustainable business because they believe in the principles of being for and by the people (Figge et al., 2002; Halberstadt et al., 2024).

According to (Kamaludin et al., 2024),

"A social enterprise places a significant emphasis on its social mission as a fundamental aspect of its corporate existence while also prioritizing the pursuit of profitability in another segment of the corporation to ensure the continuity of its operations [...]."

Social entrepreneurship offers a viable way to address social and environmental concerns that cannot effectively and economically resolve through state-sponsored welfare initiatives. Both profit and nonprofit orientations can be observed in social enterprises (Kamaludin et al., 2024). Large corporations or multinational enterprises (MNCs) actively engage in social causes and address the issue by leveraging their resources (Kickul & Lyons, 2020). (Mair & Marti, 2006) provide a definition of a social enterprise, a company engaged in economic operations to achieve social goals. In the past, numerous corporations have allocated a specific division to focus on social entrepreneurship. One instance of such a firm is Narayana Hinduyalaya Ltd., a publicly traded Indian corporation that offers cost-effective and significantly subsidized healthcare services to persons residing in impoverished conditions. (Kickul & Lyons, 2020) define social entrepreneurship (SE) as the engagement of individuals and business entities in entrepreneurial activities oriented explicitly toward achieving social objectives. An illustrative case is Janani Foods Private Limited, a social enterprise founded by a marketing specialist that offers extensive agricultural services to economically disadvantaged farmers in India (Gupta et al., 2020). Prior studies have established a connection between social entrepreneurship and corporate social responsibility (CSR) within organizations. Studies have determined that social entrepreneurship is a comprehensive form of CSR, wherein CSR is regarded as a tool to accomplish the goals of social entrepreneurship (Buendía-Martínez & Carrasco Monteagudo, 2020; García-Jurado et al., 2021).

Objectives

The objectives of this chapter are as follows:

A. To elucidate the current state of sustainable entrepreneurship in emerging economies.
B. To investigate the potential opportunities for sustainable entrepreneurial ventures in developing economies.
C. To delve into the challenges faced by sustainable entrepreneurship in emerging markets and suggest possible remedies for their mitigation.

Outline of the Chapter

The chapter is organized as follows: Section 2 offers a comprehensive overview of the historical context encompassing sustainable entrepreneurship in emerging economies. Section 3 explores a comparative synthesis of the current state of sustainable entrepreneurial practices in emerging economies. Section 4 explores the potential opportunities for sustainable entrepreneurial initiatives in emerging economies. Section 5 discusses various challenges sustainable entrepreneurship faces in emerging economies and suggests ways to address them. Section 6 highlights the successful case studies related to sustainable entrepreneurship. Section 7 presents a theoretical framework that uses an antecedent and consequence model to analyze the phenomenon of sustainable entrepreneurship in emerging economies. In Section 8, the chapter presents recommendations and practical implications, and finally, section 9 concludes with a discussion on the potential for future scope.

Historical Background of Sustainable Entrepreneurship in Emerging Economies

The notion of sustainable business has long been widely recognized as the ability of a company's business model to endure over a prolonged duration. The emergence of the phrase "sustainable entrepreneurship" occurred after the implementation of sustainable development goals. Therefore, it is necessary to do an initial examination of sustainable development before delving into the subject of sustainability within the realm of entrepreneurship. The global recognition of the notion of sustainable development occurred during the United Nations Conference on the Human Environment in Stockholm in 1972. The Brundtland Commission's report, titled "Our Common Future" and released in late 1987, introduced the notion of sustainable development as a viable remedy for environmental degradation and socioeconomic challenges. The United Nations Conference on Environment and Development, held in Rio de Janeiro in 1992, was ultimately rooted in sustainable development. The summit served as a platform for a worldwide endeavor to formulate action plans and strategies to transition toward a more sustainable economic trajectory. In 2015, the United Nations officially approved seventeen Sustainable Development Goals

(SDGs), ratified on January 1, 2016 (Mikhailova et al., 2024; Sorooshian, 2024). Since its inception by Elkington in 1997, the triple bottom line concept has played a crucial role in shaping environmentally conscious company strategy.

The triple bottom line (TBL) is a theoretical framework that encompasses evaluating a company's performance across its financial, social, and environmental dimensions (Jamgade et al., 2024; Kamaludin et al., 2024). Scholars have advanced the concept of sustainable entrepreneurship through the integration of conventional entrepreneurial methodologies with the incorporation of environmental and societal concerns. As a consequence, the notion has been formulated. Despite being a relatively recent concept, it has seen substantial advancements in recent years. A sustainable environment refers to a strategic approach business use to promote the advancement of social, environmental, and economic objectives that align with the needs of the current generation while safeguarding future generations' well-being. This is achieved by guaranteeing the sustainability of the environment (Baporikar, 2021). Given the novelty of sustainable entrepreneurship in emerging economies, it is imperative to engage in further scholarly deliberations regarding the intersection and divergence of sustainable entrepreneurship and social entrepreneurship and categorizing its underlying factors (Avelar et al., 2024).

The academic literature has generated two separate historical views on sustainable entrepreneurship. The initial perspective pertains to the incorporation of sustainable business practices inside their operational framework, whereas the subsequent viewpoint revolves around addressing social, economic, and environmental challenges by employing profit-driven sustainable firms. Both perspectives provide distinct challenges. The present chapter examines the BRICS countries, namely Brazil, Russia, India, China, and South Africa, as a point of reference for emerging nations.

The first perspective is the incorporation of environmentally friendly business practices into the existing operations of a firm. The aforementioned action was seen as their contribution towards social and environmental causes, as it was the sole requirement mandated by the governing bodies. Nevertheless, throughout the course of time, regulatory measures have become increasingly rigorous, resulting in heightened corporate responsibility for addressing social and environmental issues. Throughout history, commercial firms operating in emerging nations have been motivated by the objective of maximizing financial gains. Consequently, they have allocated a predefined portion of their resources towards corporate social responsibility initiatives, with the aim of addressing various social and environmental issues. Consequently, they included ecologically conscious business methods into their operational framework. Notable instances of sustainable adoption include the use of recycled ecologically acceptable raw materials, the adoption of advanced technology with less pollution, and the construction of a natural supply chain. An additional perspective that lends validity to the concept of a circular economy is presented here. Elucidate The Securities and Exchange Board of India (SEBI) has implemented a requirement for the top 100 listed companies in India, as determined by their market capitalization, to adhere to environmental, social, and governance (ESG) reporting criteria. Starting from 2015, the leading 500 companies have been required to provide data on environmental, social, and governance aspects.

The second viewpoint entails the creation of novel sustainable enterprises that are based on the triple bottom-line framework, intending to tackle social and economic challenges (Sarma et al., 2024; Shahid et al., 2023). Historically, several instances exist where entrepreneurs initiated the establishment of firms from their inception to address prevailing societal challenges. The concept of a circular economy was adopted, wherein treated waste from various operations is utilized as a primary resource and then transformed into a useful product (Diacono & Baldacchino, 2024; Klofsten et al., 2024) The vendor of waste materials has the opportunity to generate supplementary revenue via the implementation of this business plan. The air quality in the surrounding regions was adversely affected due to the necessity for farmers in India to incinerate the residual stubble following paddy harvesting. The municipal authorities administered the air quality index (AQI) to indicate worsening consequences such as respiratory illness. Many emerging enterprises have been developed to address the issue in an environmentally friendly manner.

Present Status of Sustainable Entrepreneurship in BRICS Economies: Comparative Synthesis

The BRICS countries serve as an exemplary illustration of growing economies owing to their potential for growth facilitated by the substantial demographic dividend. During the early 2000s, Jim O'Neill, a prominent economist, identified the four rapidly expanding economies that are projected to significantly influence the world economy by the year 2050 (Mulibana & Tshikovhi, 2024). These economies were called the BRIC, encompassing Brazil, Russia, India, and China. After careful consideration, South Africa was identified as a potential and strategically significant rising economy, including it in the BRIC countries in 2010. The "17 Sustainable Development Goals (SDGs)" were established during the UN General Assembly Summit in September 2015. The five BRICS nations must contribute to achieving the Sustainable Development Goals (SDGs) due to their affiliation with the United Nations (UN).

Brazil

Austrian writer Stefan Zweig highlighted the potential of Brazil in his book Land of the Future because of its enviable natural resources (Amazon Forest), population, and geographical location in South America. It is the 10th largest economy in the world with $ 2.126 trillion and the largest producer of coffee. Brazil's SME (Small and medium enterprises) industry accounts for 30% and 54.5% of GDP and formal employment, and Brazil's government has promoted the spirit of sustainable development in SMEs while encouraging entrepreneurship in the country. Sebrae (Support Service for Micro and Small Enterprises) is one agency, a non-profit private entity that plays a crucial role in the sustainable development of SMEs in Brazil. However, starting a new venture in Brazil is not easy as Brazil currently stands in the 124th position in the world with ease of doing business ranking. Despite this, in 2023, Brazil witnessed a surge in registered startups, with an estimated 13,400, representing a significant growth of 244 percent compared to the previous year's figure of fewer than 4,000 firms. In 2021, the infusion of capital into startup ventures in Brazil attained an unprecedented sum of US$ 9.4 billion, representing a roughly threefold increase compared to the preceding year and a tenfold expansion within 10 years (Statista, 2014).

Russia

The Global Entrepreneurship Monitoring data reveals that entrepreneurial activity in Russia is comparatively weaker than in other nations undergoing economic transition (Mordovets et al., 2022). The ranking of Russia in terms of ease of doing business has experienced a notable boost, positioning it at the 28th position out of 190 nations. This growth may be attributed to a series of steps implemented by the Russian government (Economics, 2024). According to the NAFI research center data, the business environment for small and medium-sized enterprises (SMEs) in Russia is currently unfavorable. Entrepreneurs' primary challenges include high tax rates, tariffs, insurance premiums, and non-tax payments. Additionally, there is a decrease in demand for goods and services, intense competition from the informal sector, administrative obstacles, and difficulty securing loans (Parshutina et al., 2019). Russia is dedicated to achieving sustainable development goals and has made significant progress in promoting sustainable enterprise. The Russian government has started the National Green Investment Regulatory Policy to provide adequate investment towards sustainable entrepreneurship related to agriculture, climate, and eco-friendly solutions to socio-economic challenges. The government-enabled structure is also supported by non-governmental bodies; for instance, GreenTech is a prominent annual initiative in Russia that seeks to identify and provide assistance to technology companies to enhance environmental conditions, mitigate negative environmental consequences, and promote sustainable development. This initiative receives funding from many governmental entities in the Russian Federation, including the Ministry of Natural Resources and Environment, the Ministry of Construction, Housing and Utilities, and the Ministry of Energy. Russia has also emphasized the role of the construction industry in the economy as well as environmental protection, as most manufacturing industries directly or indirectly depend on the real estate sector. If green practices are promoted in the real estate sector, they will eventually be transmitted to related industries due to the incorporation of green practices requirements in products. For instance, the Russian Green Building Council (RuGBC) does the same thing and is responsible for fostering green construction practices by collaborating with different stakeholders.

India

In the last decade, India has seen tremendous growth in sustainable entrepreneurship. This rise of sustainable entrepreneurship in India is propelled by factors such as enhanced environmental consciousness, rising demand for ethical goods and services, and governmental efforts to foster sustainable development. An observable increase in the quantity of environmentally conscious startups in India is evident, with a particular emphasis on renewable energy, waste management, water conservation, sustainable agriculture, and eco-friendly products.

Some notable sustainable entrepreneurship businesses are Phool, Ather Energy, BluSmart, and Just Organik. According to the National Chemical Laboratory (NCL) and PET Packaging Association for Clean Environment (PACE), the projected value of the recycled Polyethylene Terephthalate (PET) plastic business in India ranges from around US$ 400-550 million. PET recycling in India is over 90%, surpassing the recycling rates in Japan (72%), Europe (48%), and the United States (31%). Hence, India has significant prospects for implementing a circular economy (IBEF, 2024). These firms utilize cutting-edge technology and business approaches to tackle environmental concerns and create economic value. The Indian government has implemented various initiatives to promote sustainable entrepreneurship, such as the Startup India campaign, the Atal Innovation Mission, and several renewable energy and sustainability programs. Policy initiatives such as the National Solar Mission and Swachh Bharat Abhiyan are designed to foster the use of renewable energy sources and enhance sanitation and waste management protocols. Internationally, sustainable entrepreneurs have attracted significant investment, totaling $700 billion, from various new financing instruments focused on social, green, and sustainability initiatives. India's financial sector has also seen improvements in funding for sustainable entrepreneurs, with investments in renewable energy, waste recycling, and e-mobility businesses. The World Bank is introducing a credit guarantee scheme worth $100 million to support India's rooftop solar program (George, 2021). Niti Aayog set up a circular economy cell (CE Cell) in 2022, which has prepared a roadmap for scrapping vehicles and other used automated products that will be transformed into usable material and can be used as input raw material in many of the manufacturing processes (Aayog, 2024).

China

As the largest developing country globally, the Chinese government introduced the notion of "mass entrepreneurship and innovation" in its 2015 government work report. This initiative aims to foster integrated job creation and entrepreneurial activity among various demographic groups, including young graduates and migrant workers. After the 18th National Congress of the Communist Party of China, the government has been improving service reform. It has become the national venture capital guidance fund for emerging industries and has strengthened the importance of enterprise innovation and entrepreneurship. The data indicates that China has contributed 31% to global growth over the past decade. At present, China is confronted with significant hurdles in the form of environmental degradation and a deceleration in economic growth. The Chinese government has expedited the process of "green development". Therefore, sustainable entrepreneurship holds greater significance for the government in attaining its objectives. In China, crowdfunding has emerged as a promising means of financing sustainable-oriented enterprises. Crowdfunding has the ability to effectively address environmental and social challenges by compensating sustainable enterprises for their shortage of financial resources.

South Africa

Despite being underdeveloped, the South African economy has significant potential and ample access to enormous natural and other resources (GEM, 2020). South Africa possesses the most advanced economy on the African continent, with a value of $401.47 billion, and holds a prominent position in various areas. Micro, small, and medium enterprises (MSMEs) constitute over 2 million entities, representing 98% of the official business sector. However, their contribution to formal employment is less than one-third (UNCTAD, 2023). South Africa has struggled to progress in fostering entrepreneurship as a prominent catalyst for economic advancement, employment generation, and societal integration. Currently, South Africa occupies the 84th position in the rating of ease of doing business, indicating a considerable potential for future improvement. South Africa has demonstrated considerable potential in achieving sustainable development goals through the implementation of various policies and initiatives, including the Renewable Energy Independent Power Producer Procurement Programme (REIPPPP), the Green Economy Accord, and the establishment of the Small Enterprise Development Agency (SEDA) (UNCTAD, 2023). Another notable advantage is the involvement of private funds and foundations, such as the SAB Foundation, Izibulo SME Fund, GreenCape, and Sustainable Livelihoods Foundations (SLF), in facilitating the establishment of enterprises at the grassroots level. The scarcity of hygienic water in rural regions is a significant issue in Africa. I-drop is a noteworthy sustainable business that offers an affordable drinking water system that can be handled remotely. The following table presents a tabular depiction of the current state of sustainable entrepreneurship in the BRICS countries. It includes comprehensive information on prominent governmental and non-governmental projects, as well as important sustainable startups.

Table 1. Tabular representation of the present status of sustainable entrepreneurship in BRICS countries

Country	Major Govt Initiatives	Major Non-Governmental Initiatives	Notable Sustainable Startups
Brazil	Startup Brasil, Agenda Brasil +Sustentavel, ESG reporting, PRONATEC (Vocational education and training)	Instituto Quintessa, Brazilian Micro and Small Business Support Service (SEBRAE), Artemisia	Green Studio, SuperOpa Brasil, We. Flow, Nextron Energia
Russia	Climate Russia Portal, National Green Investment Regulatory Policy	Green Tech Startup Booster (Skolkovo Foundation), CleanTech Russia, Russian Green Building Council (RuGBC)	Biocad, EkoTerra, Greenwise
India	Startup India Seed Fund Scheme (SISFS), National initiatives for Developing and Harnessing Innovations (NIDHI), Startup India Scheme, Make in India, Atal innovation Mission	Sankalp Forum, Acumen India, Ashoka Fellowship, Impact Investors Council (IIC).	Phool, Ather Energy, BluSmart, Just Organik
China	Beautiful China	Crowdfunding Platform: Kickstarter.	BYD, GEM
South Africa	Renewable Energy Independent Power Producer Procurement Program (REIPPPP), Green Economy Accord, Small Enterprise Development Agency (SEDA)	SAB Foundation, Izibulo SME Fund, GreenCape, Sustainable Livelihoods Foundations (SLF)	Kudoti, I-Drop Water, Wildcards.world

OPPORTUNITIES OF SUSTAINABLE ENTREPRENEURSHIP IN EMERGING ECONOMIES

Emerging nations hold great potential for participating in entrepreneurial endeavors that prioritize the triple bottom-line framework, which encompasses the aspects of people, profit, and the planet. Identifying opportunities in sustainable entrepreneurship may vary from those of profit-driven business concepts. "SE opportunities emerge when investment is needed to generate positive social impact or simply to create social value"(Nayak & Pillai K, 2024). Sustainable entrepreneurship is driven by certain societal requirements, which can also be linked to the personal needs of entrepreneurs (Halberstadt et al., 2024). In the present section, sector-wise opportunities are presented;

Agriculture

The agricultural sector in numerous emerging economies is considered the least developed. An optimal condition of the agricultural sector guarantees both food security and environmental sustainability in the country through the conservation of natural resources. Sound agriculture has a crucial role in sustaining rural livelihoods. Many developing nations face societal and environmental challenges due to their adherence to unsustainable practices (Sarma et al., 2024).

Recycling of Agricultural Proceed Waste

Stubble burning, entailing the elimination of paddy crop residues, has been noted to exert adverse effects on the air quality index (AQI) in northern India, particularly in Haryana and the NCR region, before winter. An efficacious approach to addressing this issue entails the conversion of rice crop residue into a sustainable commodity. Moreover, this initiative offers farmers a supplementary source of revenue. Furthermore, this opportunity fosters the principles of a circular economy.

Food Preservation, Processing, and Packaging

The unorganized structure of storage facilities is a significant barrier to food preservation in emerging economies. According to the data obtained from the RTI of the Food Corporation of India (FCI), an estimated 1628 metric tonnes of grains were wasted during the period of 2022-2023. The utilization of substandard preservatives is contributing to the emergence of food safety concerns in developing nations. The issue is further exacerbated by the insufficient funds allocated for the development of indigenous preservatives. The limited knowledge among rural populations regarding the quality of preservatives has presented a favorable circumstance for sustainable entrepreneurs to enter the food preservation and processing industries, offering practical solutions to policymakers.

Floriculture

The floriculture industry offers profitable prospects for entrepreneurs, as demonstrated by the substantial increase in the cultivation area dedicated to floriculture in India, which rose from 54,000 hectares in 1994-95 to 2,50,000 hectares in 2016-17. (Kumar, 2020). The global market for agricultural products is experiencing a consistent upward trend, and India has the potential to emerge as a significant participant due to its diverse agro-climatic conditions. These conditions encompass fertile soil, a favorable atmosphere, abundant water supplies, cost-effective labor, and a skilled workforce. These elements play a crucial role in the growth of different flower species throughout the year. The cultivation of floricultural crops necessitates substantial labor. In a nation such as India, the floriculture industry holds immense promise for generating valuable employment opportunities in both rural and urban regions.

Renewable Energy

From the investing and business points of view, the prospect of owning and operating a renewable energy power generation facility is attractive. This fact makes it most appealing to emerging economies, as there is generally an abundance of sunlight in such countries. The latest technology makes solar power, Wind energy, biomass, etc., even more attractive, allowing isolated communities to generate their own electricity without needing expensive power lines and a connection to a large-scale plant. This can be very cost-effective. The aggregate quantity of commercially viable electricity derived from wind energy surpasses the current utilization of human power from all accessible sources. Solar power is a significant form of renewable energy, and its technologies may be roughly classified as either passive solar or active solar based on their methods of capturing and distributing solar energy or converting it into solar power.

Transportation And Mobility

Transportation and mobility have innumerable effects on the planet and its people, causing environmental degradation and social and cultural change. Transportation accessibility is a key driver of economic development and increased opportunities, so rather than discourage transportation improvement in developing countries, these entrepreneurs propose sustainable alternatives. Electric vehicles are being promoted in many parts of the developed world to reduce emissions and fuel dependence. Unfortunately, electric vehicles' high cost and maintenance make them an impractical choice for many in developed countries with established gasoline infrastructure. However, the lower maintenance and fuel costs of electric vehicles may make them a more feasible choice in developing nations, provided that the proper infrastructure for recharging and maintenance can be provided.

Affordable Healthcare

Affordable health care is a remarkable burden for several developing countries worldwide and is often deemed an intractable problem. Yet entrepreneurs have an extraordinary opportunity to turn health care into good care at a cost that won't break the bank. According to the World Health Organisation (2010), health is a fundamental human right, and equal access to medical services is vital for individuals to realize their full potential. With a slew of technologies and delivery system innovations to spur from it, entrepreneurs can disrupt the high-cost, low-results status quo that permeates the entire world. Whether it's a tech startup or a new way to do business, the healthcare system can serve as an incubator for new businesses and a testing ground for established overseas markets.

Waste Management and Recycling

Waste generation is a global concern, and the problem is more convoluted in emerging countries. Waste management is considered inefficient in most countries, and over time, people have begun to recognize the importance of waste management and its far-reaching effects. Recycling is considered an investment sector, and social entrepreneurs are making large-scale efforts to gather the threats around local communities' environment that improve the standard of living through recycling. In many developing countries, sustainable waste management is critical in minimizing current environmental concerns, specifically releasing greenhouse gases from waste disposal methods and improving public health and the environment.

Role of impact investing in the development of sustainable entrepreneurship

With the advent of societal and environmental solution-based businesses, traditional financing parlance is insufficient to bridge the financing gap. Moreover, financing sustainable businesses where the initial revenue stream remains uncertain is out of the scope of traditional financing sources. Traditional financing may increase a sustainable business's weighted average cost of capital (WACC) due to charging higher interest rates or financing at a very low valuation. Innovative financing modes such as impact investing can bridge the financing deficit. Impact investing is a broad term, and it can be categorized into several investment avenues that finance sustainable businesses (Gigante et al., 2023) However, its classification majorly lies in green bonds and crowdfunding. The issuance of green bonds is the same as regular bonds, but the money raised by green bonds is exclusively used for environmental projects (Ahmad & Mokhchy, 2023). Multinational corporations and financial institutions issue green bonds. Crowdfunding is another viable option for funding societal welfare projects. However, crowdfunding is best suited for the initial start of the business, and green bonds are mainly used for the business's working capital needs (Watson et al., 2023).

Role of digital technologies and innovation in promoting sustainable entrepreneurship

With the increasing penetration of artificial intelligence and blockchain technology, it is crucial for sustainable entrepreneurs to adopt the new technology to reduce operational costs. Most of these technologies have reduced the need for a workforce and integrated the whole system simultaneously. Digital technologies such as AI and blockchain can help maintain optimum service rates and robust supply chains (Aljabhan & Obaidat, 2023). Sustainable entrepreneurs often deal with uncertain queries related to societal and environmental phenomena, and artificial intelligence can aid in complex decision-making related to uncertain events as AI is highly capable of processing unstructured and vast amounts of data. Blockchain technology is termed as a decentralized system that can maintain transparency and accountability of the system by facilitating transparent transactions.

CHALLENGES OF SUSTAINABLE ENTREPRENEURSHIP IN EMERGING ECONOMIES

Sustainable business practices pose significant obstacles due to many concerns that necessitate resolution. Entrepreneurs often encounter challenges in reconciling the imperative of financial viability with ethical considerations as they endeavor to attain their twin objectives. Enterprises face complex obstacles related to financial resources, supply chain management, adherence to regulatory frameworks, and dynamic market demands. The main difficulty lies in obtaining adequate finance at a reasonable valuation, as angel investors and venture capitalists usually want scalability and exit options, which can be quite uncertain in sustainable companies. Sustainable businesses (SEs) in India mostly rely on grants, institutional loans, and non-institutional borrowing as their primary funding sources. The main equity sources in the social entrepreneurship sector consist of funds entrepreneurs contribute, encompassing both loans and equity, alongside early-stage investors. A limited number of traditional private equity firms, primarily concentrated on established industries like microfinance, healthcare, and agribusiness, have expanded their investment portfolio to include social enterprises (SEs). The main elements contributing to this phenomenon include emerging and untested marketplaces and corporate models, increased transaction costs for investors, and limited access to information required to understand the sector.

One additional challenge is the exorbitant expenses associated with inputs, as the manufacturing of sustainable goods heavily relies on using processed raw materials. The Indian market has a strong sensitivity to price, resulting in their products being occasionally overshadowed by conventional things due to their comparatively lower cost. Insufficient customer knowledge about the necessity of sustainable products is observed in India.

Economic Challenges

The consequence of limited capital access and a smaller budget is an increased probability of business failure. The less money an entrepreneur has to invest in the aforementioned activities to improve the probability of success, the less likely it becomes that the entrepreneur can prevent business failure. Failure is especially likely when the entrepreneur invests personal savings into the business as a source of capital. If the business fails, the entrepreneur incurs a loss of potential income, which can be critical for an entrepreneur in a developing economy. In developing economies where business and financial market infrastructure are poor, and there are limited social welfare and unemployment benefits, the entrepreneur bears a high opportunity cost and risks if business failure results in unemployment (Mahieu et al., 2021). Limited access to capital has several consequences for the entrepreneur. Firstly, it means the entrepreneur cannot develop their business idea. To follow a dream to succeed in business, an entrepreneur needs to invest in producing a good or service at a larger scale than the current one and/or invest in research and development and/or marketing and promotion. These investments requiring capital will improve the probability of success. Entrepreneurs who cannot access the capital required are forced to work with a smaller budget. SMEs are often considered to be more risky investments for lenders (Cumming & Hornuf, 2020). High failure rates of SMEs and the perceived higher costs of lending to SMEs mean many financial institutions choose to lend to consumers or larger enterprises (Harrison et al., 2022). This leaves SMEs with few options in lending sources and can often lead to them using informal forms of finance. While easier to access, these sources often leave entrepreneurs in vulnerable positions with high interest rates and the potential loss of key assets. The lack of access to capital is a major reason for the high rates of informality amongst SMEs in developing countries.

Lack of Infrastructure

Macroeconomic instability, accompanied by weak government institutions, corruption, social instability, high levels of debt, poor policy formulation, and an absence of policy-making capacity, often leads to an environment where infrastructure is underdeveloped. High and stable levels of economic growth are likely to elevate demand for infrastructure services, while demand will be depressed in low-income and unstable economic environments. Political and economic stability is particularly pertinent, as the nature and level of investment required for infrastructure often necessitate long-term commitments from both the public and private sectors. Infrastructure has been described as the bedrock that underpins economic activity. High-quality and wide-ranging infrastructure reduces the cost of doing business, increases the benefits from economic activity, and allows firms to compete in domestic and global markets. Infrastructure can be defined as the basic physical and organizational structures and facilities needed to operate a society or enterprise (Enholm et al., 2022). This definition highlights that infrastructure is more than roads, bridges, and transport; it includes a means for creating better opportunities for economic development. Brazil isn't such a highly populated city, but when people come, they come to a place like Rocinha where there are no roads, no land, and no housing to build a better future for themselves - Jamil, Rocinha resident.

High Levels of Poverty

Many researchers have noted that poverty is not just a lack of money or material possessions but is also a substantive constraint on the capability of people to live in a dignified way. This means poverty is more than just an economic issue; it produces a myriad of social and cultural implications that are rigorously addressed in the sustainable entrepreneurship discourse. These challenges are growing in both scale and complexity due to trends toward increased cognitive understanding of poverty and the underlying debates surrounding how to best address poverty in its many forms. One important issue in both practical and research terms is whether poverty should be explicitly addressed or can be dealt with as a part of broader entrepreneurial and economic development interventions (Cahayani, 2017). This is linked to a persistent tension between pro-poor and market-led development and poses a critical strategic issue for sustainable entrepreneurs. Another challenge that is sometimes overlooked is that poverty is a stigmatizing and disempowering condition experienced by people who are most marginalized in a given society. This means that when working with people living in poverty, there is a danger of essentializing them as a homogeneous grouping defined by their low economic status rather than acknowledging the vibrancy and diversity of their cultures, aspirations, and the many different sources of social and economic disadvantage that they face. Applying a 'poverty lens', on the one hand, may produce better targeting and emphasis on the specific needs of different groups living in poverty. On the other side, it may perpetuate stigmatization and exclusion of people living in poverty from involvement in initiatives that are framed as addressing something other than poverty. Both of these issues have far-reaching implications for the design and nature of initiatives to engage people living in poverty in sustainable entrepreneurship.

Environmental Challenges

To overcome these challenges, sustainable businesses should consider implementing cleaner production technologies that minimize or eliminate the production of pollutants and waste. They should also implement pollution prevention strategies that help reduce the amount of pollution created. An example of this could be reducing the use of hazardous materials in producing consumer goods. Finally, businesses can work on minimizing waste and pollution through waste reduction strategies (Moalem & Kerndrup, 2023; Tereshchenko et al., 2023). These strategies can be implemented to reuse and recycle products and materials to recover and reduce waste and pollution. Sustainable entrepreneurs in emerging economies are facing numerous challenges in developing their businesses. The increase in production and consumption has resulted in a rise in pollution and waste. It is estimated that businesses create 80% of pollution.

Social Challenges

Considering that value creation is at the core of entrepreneurship, the value-creating activities, mainly at the micro level, have strong potential for positive social and environmental change. This level of value creation moves beyond philanthropy and towards social entrepreneurship, where the primary focus is on creating social or environmental benefits. Social entrepreneurs often face similar issues to traditional entrepreneurs in balancing profitability with achieving desired social outcomes (Au et al., 2023; Smollan & Singh, 2024). While creating social benefits may be a strong motivator for traditional entrepreneurs, it may still be seen as a secondary agenda to wealth creation. This may still be true for entrepreneurs in emerging economies. Regardless of the type of entrepreneur, the perception remains that addressing social or environmental issues will detract from financial performance. This is a main issue for sustainable entrepreneurs, who aim to create social/environmental benefits and financial gain. In this climate, those entrepreneurs who seek to create benefits through traditional or social ventures are still at a disadvantage as they have to compete in the open market with those creating negative social/environmental externalities. This competitive environment does not Favor those who seek to create positive change. Social challenges generally include behavior or actions that may have positive or negative effects on the project and the people involved at any level in the project. Social challenges have long been overlooked in sustainable development literature. Literature in the entrepreneurship field is no exception. Scholars assumed that social issues would be addressed if economic issues were addressed. It is expected, though, given that the primary concern of entrepreneurs is business profitability.

Gender Inequality

Compared to established economies, the number of women entrepreneurs in an emerging economy is dramatically higher. This is mainly due to the fact that women will seek an alternate form of income when faced with poverty to survive and provide for their families. This may not necessarily be through choice, and women entrepreneurs in emerging economies generally do not start a business because of a great business opportunity spotted or that they wish to advance themselves, but in fact, it is to pull them out of unemployment or to improve their status in an existing job from a self-employment standpoint. Women entrepreneurs are driven by necessity rather than opportunity. This, in turn, diminishes the success level of these female entrepreneurs as their businesses will often be small-scale, slow-growing, and not sustainable (Fallah & Soori, 2023).

Inconsistent Policies and Regulations

Frequently, changes in regulations are made to fulfill special interests or favors. This became evident in India when the Supreme Court of India cancelled the allocation of 2014 coal block licenses that were issued between 1993 and 2010. The court ruled that these allocations were illegal and arbitrary as they were not auctioned and caused exchequer losses. This was because the coal was given away to power and steel companies at throwaway prices. This verdict had massive implications for many companies relying on that coal to fuel their power plants and steel mills, and the Government had to re-auction the coal blocks. The governments of many emerging economies often lack clear, stable, and consistent policies to regulate the business sector. Frequently, economic policies are reversed with a change in government, and rules and regulations are amended, making it difficult for small and medium enterprises to operate as it increases the cost of compliance.

Limited Access to Technology

The world is becoming increasingly reliant on technology. With this in mind, it is relatively new to the business scene in terms of implementation and has different penetration rates in different locations. It is difficult and much more expensive to start up and run an online business if there are limited resources for the internet and computers. Consider a sustainable entrepreneur in a developing area of China. There are many nights when the power goes out, and there are whole weeks when businesses are closed down because of a lack of resources to keep them operational (Shahid et al., 2023). Given that emerging economies are often faced with limited technology, sustainable entrepreneurs are usually forced into using older methods, such as setting up small shops, which are less efficient and less likely to have positive environmental impacts. This is a clear disadvantage for entrepreneurs willing to implement new high-tech solutions. Skill and knowledge of the latest technology are very important in producing goods and services since science and technology are the principal sources of invention and innovation in this modern era.

Considering the above-described opportunities and challenges, several sustainable entrepreneurship-based businesses have managed the obstacles and capitalized on the opportunities.

CASE STUDIES

Case 1: Binbag Recycling Services

Binbag Recycling Services, a Bengaluru-based startup established in 2014, demonstrated the perfect example of a sustainable entrepreneurship-based for-profit business. Binbag recycling services have emphasized the recycling of e-waste and IT assets. Recent statistics presented by the Central Pollution Control Board (CPCB); India is expected to generate 5.2 million metric tons of e-waste by 2025. With the advent of the circular economy concept, it is very essential to support the circular economy by converting e-waste and IT assets into reusable secondary resources. If e-waste is not recycled, it is expected that 120 million tons of e-waste will be generated globally, and Emerging economies will be the major contributors of global e-waste. Binbag is currently working with more than 100 companies to recycle e-waste. They invite quotations for e-waste collection, and after inspection, their teams collect the e-waste from the companies. Further, they segregate the e-waste based on the material and different purposes. Using recycled secondary raw materials further reduces the natural resource extraction and other manufacturing operations for raw materials. To carry out the operations sustainably, Binbag recycling services follow the 3A model: Awareness, Assets, and Axis. Awareness is meant to create and disseminate information about e-waste recycling to manufacturers. Assets depict the manufacturing and technological capability of the company to extract reusable material for operations. Axis represents the robustness of supply chain management of the Binbag recycling services. Furthermore, they believe in profit sharing with their stakeholders. Adequate financing is essential for the sustainable e-waste recycling business. Binbag services also follow "Go rupees for your E-waste" to finance their treatment operations and payments for collecting e-waste from manufacturers and retailers (Hazarika et al., 2021).

Case 2: Arken Enterprises (Desi Hangover)

Arken Enterprises, with the global brand name of Desi Hangover (Direct to Consumer), was established in 2014 by Hitesh Kenjale, Abha Agrawal, Omkar Pandharkame, and Lakshya Arora. The inception of Arken Enterprises stems from the establishment of the woven and handcrafted leather footwear brand Kolhapuris with a blend of traditional design. However, operating the business sustainably in the price-sensitive industry of footwear amidst low-cost machine-made footwear was a tedious task. Local artisans were also facing difficulties in producing leather-based footwear due to the unavailability of cheap raw materials and the absence of a robust supply chain mechanism. Further, the availability of cheap machine-built footwear hampers the demand for leather footwear. Arken Enterprises has capitalized on the opportunity by partnering with local artisans of leather footwear. However, convincing the cobbler community to partner with Arken enterprise was not easy as the potential benefits of partnering with the company were not evident. So, they conducted several workshops for cobbler engagement and eventually successfully persuaded them to partner with Arken Enterprises. Furthermore, the company has taken care of artisan families and their children's education by inserting an RFID (Radio frequency identification) chip in the footwear with artisan information. So that the customer may know the impact they have created by footwear purchase. Now, the founders have started working on creating demand for leather footwear. A major obstacle was to manufacture footwear at a low cost. Mass production of footwear was essential to achieve economies of scale, so they have fetched global demand. Strategically, the Desi Hangover bränd name was established to redefine the craft ecosystem of rural India. With increasing order size and demand, founders felt the need to raise funds. In 2022, they have raised $180,000 in pre-seed rounds from social alpha and CIIE.co. Therefore, Arken Enterprises is a perfect representation of sustainable entrepreneurship.

PROPOSED CONCEPTUAL FRAMEWORK

The proposed conceptual framework depicts the antecedent-consequence measures of sustainable entrepreneurship. Antecedent measures comprised of enablers of sustainable entrepreneurship, which are individual, organizational, and environmental enablers. On the other hand, consequence measures depict the triple bottom line outcome, which are people, profit, and planet. The proposed conceptual framework provides the future scope of the study by employing a structural equation modeling technique.

Figure 1. Conceptual Framework

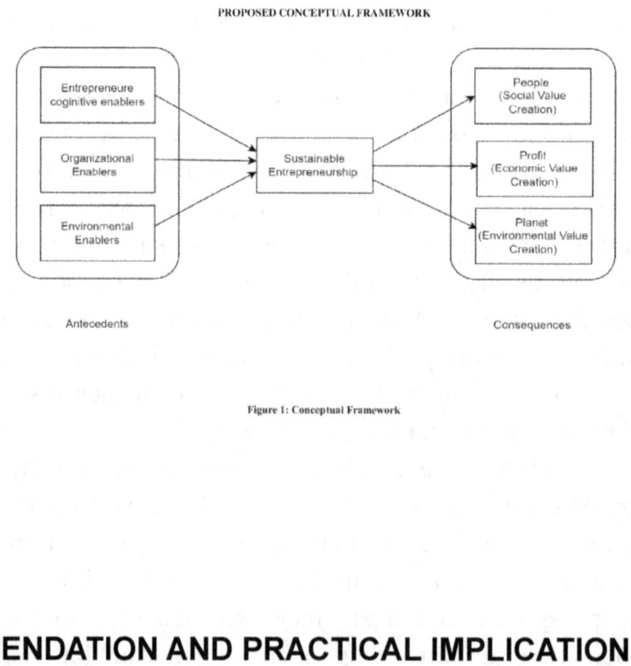

RECOMMENDATION AND PRACTICAL IMPLICATION

Sustainable entrepreneurship is an activity that generates and initiates change in a sustainable manner, and innovation is a vital component of any competitive economy. Identification of sustainable business opportunities is the first step, and the role of education institutions and state-sponsored training institutes is very crucial in imparting solution-based education to students. Developed nations have already reached saturation points in terms of infrastructure development. However, developing nations are being transformed in terms of infrastructure and other capacity-building programs, and implementing sustainable practices in infrastructural development in developing countries is the need of the hour to mitigate environmental issues. Previous literature has suggested that emerging economies have many entrepreneurial opportunities, but the conversion rate of transforming ideas into sustainable businesses is not encouraging. So, it is the collective responsibility of various stakeholders such as financial institutions, state schemes, and entrepreneurial incubation cells. Financial parlance for sustainable entrepreneurs in emerging economies needs special attention as founders face difficulties in raising finance in the early stage of business. Innovative financing methods such as crowdfunding, green bonds, and state-sponsored financing schemes are the immediate solution to the financing crunch for sustainable entrepreneurs. Economies of scale due to operational deficiency and poor order size can be solved by leveraging technological solutions and following cutting-edge marketing channels. The asset-light business model could be the most feasible business model for sustainable entrepreneurs as it reduces the asset cost to a large extent. These are the major recommendations and actionable implications for sustainable entrepreneurs who face financing and operational issues while running their businesses sustainably.

CONCLUSION

Sustainable entrepreneurship has successfully created a sphere focusing on social and environmental issues by providing innovative solutions. In general, there are three main potential positive implications of entrepreneurship in any given society, including the creation of new jobs, the introduction of new products and services, and the process of innovation investment. Sustainable entrepreneurship creates further implications by addressing the root causes of social and environmental problems and working toward creating sustainability. Therefore, the implications of sustainable entrepreneurship expand beyond mitigation into creating a sustainable economy and society. Globalization and technological advancements have led to adopting sustainable business practices in emerging economies. Innovation is creating new or improved products and services that can greatly benefit society and/or harm the environment. While new products and technologies have created many environmental problems, they are also essential to long-term environmental and social sustainability. Sustainable entrepreneurship is innovative in that it seeks to solve social and environmental problems and seeks new and different solutions than traditional for-profit business activity. New products and services can help solve pressing social and environmental problems and create opportunities for sustainable entrepreneurship by providing solutions to carry out those products and services in an environmentally friendly or socially beneficial manner. This phenomenon has attracted a lot of attention from various stakeholders. Entrepreneurship, whether it involves self-employment in small-scale agriculture or an off-farm diversification strategy, holds the potential as a sustainable livelihood pathway for many types of households in marginal areas. Given that entrepreneurship represents a viable pathway out of poverty for some types of households, the identification of the poor as a heterogeneous group implies that consideration should be given to targeting entrepreneurial support services at specific groups of potential and existing entrepreneurs. The implications for theory and practice are now revisited to concisely identify the potential managerial and policy impacts of this analysis in the area of rural development and the alleviation of poverty in developing countries. Through this analysis, it has been demonstrated that the heterogeneity of the poor in marginal areas of developing countries presents a challenge to both managerial practice and the design of supportive public policy. Failure to understand the motivations, aspirations, and constraints of different types of households from various resource, socioeconomic, and demographic circumstances runs the risk of simplistic targeting strategies, which seek to identify the poor solely in terms of an income threshold.

REFERENCES

Aayog, N. (2024, July). *Circular Economy Cell*.

Ahmad, S., & Mokhchy, J. (2023). Corporate social responsibilities, sustainable investment, and the future of green bond market: Evidence from renewable energy projects in Morocco. *Environmental Science and Pollution Research International*, 30(6), 15186–15197. DOI: 10.1007/s11356-022-23080-y PMID: 36166123

Aljabhan, B., & Obaidat, M. A. (2023). Privacy-preserving blockchain framework for supply chain management: Perceptive Craving Game Search Optimization (PCGSO). *Sustainability (Basel)*, 15(8), 6905. DOI: 10.3390/su15086905

Au, W. C., Drencheva, A., & Yew, J. L. (2023). Narrating career in social entrepreneurship: Experiences of social entrepreneurs. *Journal of Social Entrepreneurship*, 14(3), 343–369. DOI: 10.1080/19420676.2021.1890188

Avelar, S., Borges-Tiago, T., Almeida, A., & Tiago, F. (2024). Confluence of sustainable entrepreneurship, innovation, and digitalization in SMEs. *Journal of Business Research*, 170, 114346. DOI: 10.1016/j.jbusres.2023.114346

Baporikar, N. (2021). *Handbook of Research on Strategies and Interventions to Mitigate COVID-19 Impact on SMEs*. IGI Global. DOI: 10.4018/978-1-7998-7436-2

Bonfanti, A., De Crescenzo, V., Simeoni, F., & Adaui, C. R. L. (2024). Convergences and divergences in sustainable entrepreneurship and social entrepreneurship research: A systematic review and research agenda. *Journal of Business Research*, 170, 114336. DOI: 10.1016/j.jbusres.2023.114336

Bothra, N. (2024, May 23). *How India became the world's third largest startup hub in 15 years*. Forbes India.

Buendía-Martínez, I., & Carrasco Monteagudo, I. (2020). The role of CSR on social entrepreneurship: An international analysis. *Sustainability (Basel)*, 12(17), 6976. DOI: 10.3390/su12176976

Cahayani, A. (2017). The role of entrepreneurial spirit in Indonesian youths and housewives to reduce unemployment and poverty rate. In *Handbook of research on unemployment and labor market sustainability in the era of globalization* (pp. 140–156). IGI Global. DOI: 10.4018/978-1-5225-2008-5.ch009

Chaparro-Banegas, N., Ibañez Escribano, A. M., Mas-Tur, A., & Roig-Tierno, N. (2024). Innovation facilitators and sustainable development: A country comparative approach. *Environment, Development and Sustainability*, 26(4), 8467–8495. DOI: 10.1007/s10668-023-03055-w PMID: 37363019

Cumming, D. J., & Hornuf, L. (2020). *Marketplace lending of SMEs.*

Diacono, S., & Baldacchino, L. (2024). Identifying entrepreneurial opportunities in the circular economy. *Journal of Management & Organization*, 30(1), 165–187. DOI: 10.1017/jmo.2023.47

Economics. (2024). *Russia's Ease of Doing Business*. World Bank.

Enholm, I. M., Papagiannidis, E., Mikalef, P., & Krogstie, J. (2022). Artificial intelligence and business value: A literature review. *Information Systems Frontiers*, 24(5), 1709–1734. DOI: 10.1007/s10796-021-10186-w

Fallah, M. R., & Soori, M. (2023). Presenting a framework for the successful entry of women entrepreneurs into green entrepreneurship. *Journal of Science and Technology Policy Management*, 14(3), 467–486. DOI: 10.1108/JSTPM-03-2021-0041

Figge, F., Hahn, T., Schaltegger, S., & Wagner, M. (2002). The sustainability balanced scorecard–linking sustainability management to business strategy. *Business Strategy and the Environment*, 11(5), 269–284. DOI: 10.1002/bse.339

García-Jurado, A., Pérez-Barea, J. J., & Nova, R. J. (2021). A new approach to social entrepreneurship: A systematic review and meta-analysis. *Sustainability (Basel)*, 13(5), 2754. DOI: 10.3390/su13052754

GEM. (2020). *igniting startups for economic growth and social change in south africa*. Global Entrepreneurship Monitor.

George, A. (2021). *Green Entrepreneurs: Start-ups Accelerating Sustainability*. Asia Society.

Gigante, G., Sironi, E., & Tridenti, C. (2023). At the Frontier of Sustainable Finance: Impact Investing and the Financial Tradeoff; Evidence from Private Portfolio Companies in the United Kingdom. *Sustainability (Basel)*, 15(5), 3956. DOI: 10.3390/su15053956

Gupta, P., Chauhan, S., Paul, J., & Jaiswal, M. P. (2020). Social entrepreneurship research: A review and future research agenda. *Journal of Business Research*, 113, 209–229. DOI: 10.1016/j.jbusres.2020.03.032

Halberstadt, J., Schwab, A.-K., & Kraus, S. (2024). Cleaning the window of opportunity: Towards a typology of sustainability entrepreneurs. *Journal of Business Research*, 171, 114386. DOI: 10.1016/j.jbusres.2023.114386

Harrison, R., Li, Y., Vigne, S. A., & Wu, Y. (2022). Why do small businesses have difficulty in accessing bank financing? *International Review of Financial Analysis*, 84, 102352. DOI: 10.1016/j.irfa.2022.102352

Hazarika, G., Salunke, P., Wadhwani, K., & Sen, K. (2021). Sustainable Entrepreneurship–A Dyad Case Study on Recycling. *SMS Journal of Entrepreneurship & Innovation, 8*(Issue-1), 102–111.

IBEF. (2024). *Circular Economy for Sustainable Development in India*. 2024.

Jamgade, S. R., Raj, H., & Arman, M. (2024). Economy Percolating Effect of Ecotourism: Application of Triple Bottom Line (TBL) Theory. In *Achieving Sustainable Transformation in Tourism and Hospitality Sectors* (pp. 317–333). IGI Global.

Kamaludin, M. F., Xavier, J. A., & Amin, M. (2024). Social entrepreneurship and sustainability: A conceptual framework. *Journal of Social Entrepreneurship*, 15(1), 26–49. DOI: 10.1080/19420676.2021.1900339

Kickul, J., & Lyons, T. S. (2020). *Understanding social entrepreneurship: The relentless pursuit of mission in an ever changing world*. Routledge. DOI: 10.4324/9780429270406

Klofsten, M., Kanda, W., Bienkowska, D., Bocken, N., Mian, S., & Lamine, W. (2024). Start-ups within entrepreneurial ecosystems: Transition towards circular economy. *International Small Business Journal*, 42(4), 02662426241227520. DOI: 10.1177/02662426241227520

Mahieu, J., Melillo, F., Reichstein, T., & Thompson, P. (2021). Shooting stars? Uncertainty in hiring entrepreneurs. *Strategic Entrepreneurship Journal*, 15(4), 526–567. DOI: 10.1002/sej.1339

Mair, J., & Marti, I. (2006). Social entrepreneurship research: A source of explanation, prediction, and delight. *Journal of World Business*, 41(1), 36–44. DOI: 10.1016/j.jwb.2005.09.002

Mikhailova, E. A., Post, C. J., & Nelson, D. G. (2024). Integrating United Nations Sustainable Development Goals in Soil Science Education. *Soil Systems*, 8(1), 29. DOI: 10.3390/soilsystems8010029

Moalem, R. M., & Kerndrup, S. (2023). The entrepreneurial role of waste companies in transforming waste streams to value streams: Lessons from a Danish Municipal waste company. *Waste Management & Research*, 41(3), 620–634. DOI: 10.1177/0734242X221124048 PMID: 36169120

Mordovets, V. A., Ugolnikova, O. D., Kruglov, D. V., Shchipanov, E. F., & Averyanova, O. V. (2022). State Policy for Sustainable Development of Entrepreneurship in Russia: Minimizing Risks and Removing Barriers. *International Scientific and Practical Conference" Sustainable Development of Environment after Covid-19"(SDEC 2021)*, 325–330. DOI: 10.2991/assehr.k.220106.058

Mulibana, L., & Tshikovhi, N. (2024). Rural Entrepreneurship and Innovation in BRICS Economies: Secondary Evidence from Rural Areas in South Africa. *Sustainability (Basel)*, 16(6), 2408. DOI: 10.3390/su16062408

Nayak, R., & Pillai, K. R. (2024). Sustainable entrepreneurship research in emerging economies: An evidence from systematic review. *Journal of Entrepreneurship in Emerging Economies*, 16(3), 495–517. DOI: 10.1108/JEEE-03-2022-0099

Parshutina, I. G., Plakhova, L. V, Zakharkina, N. V, Sokolova, N. N., & Isakova, M. N. (2019). Formation of entrepreneurial climate in Russia for sustainable development of small business. *European Proceedings of Social and Behavioural Sciences.*

Saebi, T., Foss, N. J., & Linder, S. (2019). Social entrepreneurship research: Past achievements and future promises. *Journal of Management*, 45(1), 70–95. DOI: 10.1177/0149206318793196

Sarma, S., Attaran, S., & Attaran, M. (2024). Sustainable entrepreneurship: Factors influencing opportunity recognition and exploitation. *International Journal of Entrepreneurship and Innovation*, 25(1), 56–69. DOI: 10.1177/14657503221093007

Satsangi, P., & Dhir, A. (2024). *Role of Communities in Achieving Sustainable Development.* Academic Foundation.

Shahid, M. S., Hossain, M., Shahid, S., & Anwar, T. (2023). Frugal innovation as a source of sustainable entrepreneurship to tackle social and environmental challenges. *Journal of Cleaner Production*, 406, 137050. DOI: 10.1016/j.jclepro.2023.137050

Singh, S., Chauhan, A., & Dhir, S. (2020). Analyzing the startup ecosystem of India: A Twitter analytics perspective. *Journal of Advances in Management Research*, 17(2), 262–281. DOI: 10.1108/JAMR-08-2019-0164

Smollan, R., & Singh, S. (2024). How social entrepreneurs respond to enterprise failure. *Journal of Social Entrepreneurship*, 15(1), 1–25. DOI: 10.1080/19420676.2021.1890189

Sörensson, A., & Ghannad, N. (2024). Entrepreneurial opportunities and difficulties under COVID-19 for women entrepreneurs in Asia and Europe. *Journal of Entrepreneurship in Emerging Economies*, 16(1), 119–133. DOI: 10.1108/JEEE-02-2023-0052

Sorooshian, S. (2024). The Sustainable Development Goals of the United Nations: A Comparative Midterm Research Review. *Journal of Cleaner Production*, 453, 142272. DOI: 10.1016/j.jclepro.2024.142272

Statista. (2014, July 5). *Brazil: number of startups 2013-2023*. Statista Research Department.

Terán-Yépez, E., Marín-Carrillo, G. M., del Pilar Casado-Belmonte, M., & de las Mercedes Capobianco-Uriarte, M. (2020). Sustainable entrepreneurship: Review of its evolution and new trends. *Journal of Cleaner Production*, 252, 119742. DOI: 10.1016/j.jclepro.2019.119742

Tereshchenko, E., Happonen, A., Porras, J., & Vaithilingam, C. A. (2023). Green growth, waste management, and environmental impact reduction success cases from small and medium enterprises context: A systematic mapping study. *IEEE Access : Practical Innovations, Open Solutions*, 11, 56900–56920. DOI: 10.1109/ACCESS.2023.3271972

UNCTAD. (2023). *National Entrepreneurship Strategy - South Africa.*

Watson, R., Nielsen, K. R., Wilson, H. N., Macdonald, E. K., Mera, C., & Reisch, L. (2023). Policy for sustainable entrepreneurship: A crowdsourced framework. *Journal of Cleaner Production*, 383, 135234. DOI: 10.1016/j.jclepro.2022.135234

Zakari, A., & Oluwaseyi Musibau, H. (2024). Sustainable economic development in OECD countries: Does energy security matter? *Sustainable Development (Bradford)*, 32(1), 1337–1353. DOI: 10.1002/sd.2668

Chapter 11
Sustainable Innovation and Product Development:
Creating Environmentally Friendly and Socially Responsible Products

Sunayana Bhat
Christ University, India

Sonika Bhardwaj
https://orcid.org/0000-0003-2510-436X
Christ University, India

ABSTRACT

This chapter examines sustainable innovation and product creation in entrepreneurship. It discusses sustainable innovation, the significance of integrating sustainability into product development, and successful projects from diverse industries. Lifecycle thinking, eco-design, social impact assessment, and difficulties with sustainable product creation are discussed. The chapter concludes that sustainable entrepreneurship may solve environmental and social issues while boosting innovation and company success.

INTRODUCTION

Recently, a global shift toward sustainability in entrepreneurship and industry has occurred. Traditional corporate practices become unsustainable as climate change, resource depletion, and social inequity worsen. A new wave of entrepreneurs and

DOI: 10.4018/979-8-3693-4338-8.ch011

businesses has emerged, inspired by a desire to profit and improve society and the earth. This paradigm change emerged from sustainable entrepreneurship, which balances economic growth with environmental protection and social justice. Sustainable innovation and product development drive sustainable entrepreneurship (Vig, 2022). This chapter explores this dynamic interaction and shows entrepreneurs how to produce economically viable, environmentally friendly, and socially responsible products. By doing so, entrepreneurs may fulfil changing consumer wants and help create a more sustainable future. It explores sustainable innovation and product development principles, practices, and obstacles. Sustainable innovation in entrepreneurship and business will be examined. From there, we will explore design methods, tools, and approaches that enable entrepreneurs to build goods with the lowest environmental effect and maximum social value.

The chapter underscores the escalating need for sustainable entrepreneurship in response to global challenges such as climate change and social inequity. Traditional business practices, often focused on short-term profits, are increasingly recognized as unsustainable. In contrast, sustainable entrepreneurship aims to balance economic growth with environmental stewardship and social equity, tapping into consumer preferences for ethical and sustainable products. The conceptual framework integrates key concepts like sustainable innovation, Life Cycle Assessment (LCA), Design Thinking, and the Triple Bottom Line framework. Sustainable innovation involves creating products and processes that minimize environmental impact while enhancing social well-being. LCA evaluates environmental impacts throughout a product's lifecycle, while Design Thinking fosters creativity and empathy in developing sustainable solutions. The Triple Bottom Line framework balances people, planet, and profit in decision-making.

The theoretical framework incorporates Diffusion of Innovations Theory, which explains how new sustainable practices spread; the Resource-Based View, which emphasizes leveraging resources for competitive advantage; Stakeholder Theory, which highlights the importance of engaging diverse stakeholders; and Institutional Theory, which explores how societal norms and regulations influence sustainability adoption.

The chapter discusses the benefits of sustainable innovation, including improved brand reputation, operational efficiency, and social impact. Challenges such as material procurement, financial constraints, and supply chain ethics are addressed, with recommendations for overcoming these obstacles. By integrating these principles, entrepreneurs can align with shifting consumer preferences and gain strategic advantages, ultimately contributing to a more sustainable and equitable future.

The primary objective of this study is to explore the principles, practices, and challenges of sustainable innovation and product development within entrepreneurship. The study aims to demonstrate how entrepreneurs can create products that are economically viable, environmentally friendly, and socially responsible. Additionally, the study seeks to highlight the economic, social, and environmental benefits of adopting sustainable practices through case studies and real-world examples.

The rationale behind this study stems from the growing urgency to address environmental and social challenges. As traditional business practices become increasingly unsustainable, there is a pressing need for a new entrepreneurial paradigm that balances profit with ecological and social responsibility. By examining sustainable innovation and product development, this study aims to provide a comprehensive understanding of how businesses can contribute to a more sustainable future. The study also seeks to equip entrepreneurs with practical tools and strategies to overcome obstacles and successfully integrate sustainability into their operations.

BACKGROUND

The growing urgency for sustainable entrepreneurship reflects the escalating global crises of climate change, resource depletion, and social inequity. Traditional business models, which prioritize short-term financial gains, are increasingly seen as inadequate in addressing these complex, long-term challenges. As a result, there is a shift towards sustainable entrepreneurship—a holistic approach that aligns economic development with environmental and social responsibility. This shift is driven by several factors: the mounting evidence of environmental degradation, the scarcity of natural resources, and rising social inequalities.

Consumer expectations have also evolved, with a growing demand for products and services that reflect ethical and sustainable practices. Consumers are more informed and conscientious about the environmental and social impacts of their purchasing decisions, pushing businesses to integrate sustainability into their core operations. Companies that embrace sustainable practices not only respond to these demands but also leverage them to differentiate themselves in the marketplace. They can achieve enhanced brand loyalty, improve operational efficiencies, and mitigate risks associated with environmental and social issues.

Sustainable entrepreneurship thus represents a strategic approach to business that seeks to balance profit with positive contributions to society and the environment. This paradigm shift encourages businesses to innovate and redesign their processes, products, and supply chains in ways that reduce their ecological footprint and enhance social well-being. By doing so, they not only contribute to global sustainability goals but also position themselves for long-term success in a rapidly changing business environment.

UNDERSTANDING SUSTAINABLE INNOVATION

Sustainable innovation significantly departs from traditional corporate practices, combining economic growth, environmental protection, and social equity (Rasheed & Liu, 2023). Sustainable innovation balances current demands with future needs by promoting environmental responsibility, social equality, and economic viability (Parag et al., 2023). Entrepreneurs must embrace sustainable innovation for strategic reasons, not just corporate responsibility. It helps organizations differentiate and service the growing sector of environmentally and socially conscientious consumers (Varadarajan, 2015). By integrating sustainability into their innovation processes, entrepreneurs may reduce resource scarcity, regulatory compliance, and reputational risk. As investors favour sustainable businesses, their access to finance increases. Sustainable innovation creates long-term value by giving entrepreneurs the resilience and adaptability to overcome global challenges like climate change and social inequity (Schulte & Hallstedt, 2018). Tesla, Patagonia, Beyond Meat, and Interface demonstrate sustainable innovation's profitability and transformative power, inspiring young entrepreneurs who want to change the world.

A forward-thinking firm that balances economic growth, environmental protection, and social equality relies on sustainable innovation. Sustainable innovation promotes responsible resource management, equitable social development, and long-term financial viability (Rasheed & Liu, 2023). Businesses reduce their environmental impact using renewable energy, resource efficiency, and eco-friendly production. Sustainable innovation promotes social equity by fostering diversity, upholding human rights, and addressing poverty and inequality (Riti & Yang, 2016). It seeks market opportunities that provide financial returns and social benefits because economic success and sustainability are intertwined. Following these concepts, businesses may fulfil today's consumer needs and prosper in changing conditions. Sustainable innovation drives companies toward resilience, collaboration, and positive social impact, creating a more sustainable and equitable world.

Sustainable innovation is crucial to entrepreneurship because it drives corporate success and affects industries and communities (Lipnik & Lipnik, 2020). Innovative businesses that include sustainability meet the growing demand for eco-friendly and socially responsible goods and services and gain a competitive edge in the market. Sustainable innovation allows entrepreneurs to stand out and attract an increasing market of ethical and sustainable consumers (Tarnovskaya, 2023). It also mitigates resource scarcity, regulatory compliance, and reputational damage threats, improving resilience and long-term survival. Sustainable innovation also encourages creativity, adaptability, and teamwork, enabling entrepreneurs to recognize and capitalize on market possibilities while working toward a more sustainable and fair future. Sustainable innovation is a moral imperative for entrepreneurs that promotes positive change, innovation, and growth.

Multiple successful sustainable innovation efforts across industries show how incorporating environmental and social factors into business practices may improve business. Tesla's electric automobiles have transformed transportation by offering an environmentally benign alternative to fossil fuel-powered cars and promoting renewable energy. Patagonia pioneered sustainable clothing by promoting fair labour, recyclable materials, and supply chain transparency to reduce environmental impact and promote social responsibility. Beyond Meat has revolutionized meat production with plant-based alternatives, solving animal welfare and environmental problems. Google's renewable energy and carbon neutrality leadership inspires other tech titans to reduce their environmental impact. These examples show how sustainable innovation transforms business models and promotes a greener future across industries.

INTEGRATING SUSTAINABILITY INTO PRODUCT DEVELOPMENT

Lifecycle thinking, eco-friendly design, and social effect assessment are essential to sustainable product development. Entrepreneurs can find ways to optimize and innovate products from raw material extraction to disposal by taking a lifecycle strategy (Tsalis et al., 2022). This integrative approach reduces waste, environmental footprints, and social well-being. Material selection, energy efficiency, trash minimization, and packaging optimization improve ecological sustainability. Considerations for social implications ensure that products fit market demands and encourage fair labour, community engagement, affordability, and consumer health and safety (Kasradze et al., 2023). Entrepreneurs may create a more sustainable and fair future where products benefit society and the environment by including these factors in product development.

Sustainable product design demands a holistic strategy that stresses sustainability throughout product development. Entrepreneurs can use design strategies to reduce environmental impact and improve sustainability. To decrease resource depletion and pollution, choose renewable, recyclable, or biodegradable materials (Laycock et al., 2023). Optimizing energy efficiency from manufacturing to usage and disposal reduces carbon emissions and energy consumption. Design features that allow product disassembly, repair, or recycling minimize waste and promote circularity (Cordella & Kaps, 2018). Entrepreneurs also optimize packaging for reusability, recyclability, and environmental sustainability by reducing materials and employing eco-friendly alternatives. Using these design methods, entrepreneurs can build products that suit consumer requirements and promote sustainability (Branca et al., 2023)

Product development must evaluate social effects to suit market needs and benefit society. It involves considering how the product may affect workers, communities, and consumers (Alomoto et al., 2021). Fair wages, safe working conditions, and worker rights are essential across the supply chain. Engaging local communities to identify and address social repercussions like displacement, cultural heritage preservation, and community well-being is crucial. Entrepreneurs must also make their products affordable and accessible to all, especially marginalized or vulnerable groups. Product design must also prioritize consumer health and safety, reduce hazards, and conform to regulations and standards (Fontes et al., 2016). By considering these factors during product development, entrepreneurs can design products that generate economic value and promote social fairness and well-being, creating a more inclusive and sustainable society.

TOOLS AND TECHNIQUES FOR SUSTAINABLE PRODUCT DEVELOPMENT

To develop sustainable products, businesses can use many tools and methods to examine and enhance their products' environmental and social impacts. Life cycle assessment (LCA) evaluates a product or service's ecological implications from raw material extraction to disposal. LCA reveals resource consumption, energy use, emissions, and trash generation at each product life cycle stage (Klöpffer, 2014). Entrepreneurs can identify environmental hotspots and make informed decisions to reduce environmental impacts by completing LCAs. They can create more resource-efficient, pollutant-free, and sustainable products.

Eco-design methods and tools help product designers include environmental factors. These methods help entrepreneurs set environmental priorities, use eco-friendly materials and manufacturing techniques, and optimize product performance while reducing environmental effects. Design for Environment (DfE), Design for Sustainability (DfS), and Environmental Product Declarations (EPDs) assist businesses in evaluating their goods' environmental impact and prioritizing sustainability. Entrepreneurs can use eco-design methods and technologies to create innovative, market-competitive, and ecologically sustainable products (Kabongo, 2013).

Cradle-to-cradle (C2C) design concepts promote goods that resemble natural systems, where all materials are recycled or biodegraded, creating a closed-loop, regenerative economy. C2C design principles urge businesses to utilize materials that can be safely returned to natural or industrial cycles without waste or pollution. Material selection, product durability, recyclability, and biodegradability must be considered early in the design process (Meyer & Schneider, 2019). Using C2C design concepts, entrepreneurs can build goods that reduce environmental impact, regenerate ecosystems, and preserve natural resources for future generations. These methods and techniques for sustainable product creation can help entrepreneurs innovate, decrease environmental impact, and create goods that provide long-term value to consumers and society while building a more sustainable and resilient future.

CASE STUDIES AND BEST PRACTICES

A leading telecommunications company in India, Bharti Airtel, introduced the GreenTowers initiative to reduce carbon emissions from its network infrastructure and address environmental concerns. By adopting energy-efficient equipment, optimizing tower operations, and integrating renewable energy sources like solar power, Bharti Airtel effectively mitigated the ecological consequences of its telecommunications towers nationwide. In addition to showcasing the organization's dedication to sustainability, this endeavour establishes a benchmark for other telecommunications providers. GreenTowers, an initiative by Bharti Airtel that reduces operational expenses and carbon emissions, exemplifies the business advantages of integrating sustainability into core operations. As an industry disruptor in the Indian telecommunications sector, Reliance Jio has prioritized sustainability by implementing eco-friendly packaging methods. Reliance Jio has expanded consumer satisfaction and bolstered its brand reputation by implementing eco-friendly printing methods, using biodegradable and recyclable materials, and reducing plastic usage. The significance of sustainable package design and logistics in reducing waste and promoting environmental stewardship is highlighted in this case study. The environmentally friendly packaging utilized by Reliance Jio functions as an exemplary model for telecommunications companies aiming to reduce their ecological impact and appeal to consumers' inclination towards sustainable goods.

Nevertheless, the case of Bharati Airtel Limited vs. Reliance Jio Limited illuminates the intricate legal intricacies and competitive forces within the telecommunications sector. Reliance Jio Infocomm Limited lodged a formal grievance with the Competition Commission, invoking Section 19(1) of the Competition Act, 2002, to accuse Bharti Airtel, Idea Cellular Limited, and Vodafone India Limited of engaging in anticompetitive conduct. The telecom titans were charged in the complaint of exploiting their dominant market positions and participating in cartel-like activities with the Cellular Operators Association of India (COAI). The COAI allegedly prevented Reliance Jio from accessing Points of Interconnection (POIs). Telecommunications operators rely heavily on points of interconnection to connect their networks and enable subscribers to communicate without interruption. The allegation put forth by Reliance Jio indicated that its rivals, in collaboration with COAI, were intentionally impeding the deployment of its network, thus hindering its capacity to compete in the market effectively. This case underscores the jurisdictional complexities inherent in India's regulatory framework, specifically concerning the relationship between the Telecom Regulatory Authority of India (TRAI) and the Competition Commission. Despite the cartelization allegations against the incumbent operators and COAI by the Competition Commission, legal objections were brought before the Supreme Court due to jurisdictional disputes.

The legal disputes highlight the fierce rivalry and calculated manoeuvring that characterize the telecommunications sector, where participants may employ legal methods to safeguard their positions and interests. The consequences of these cases may have substantial effects on regulatory supervision, consumer choice, and market competition. The Bharati Airtel Limited v. Reliance Jio Limited case exemplifies the intricate relationship within the telecommunications industry between competition law, regulatory frameworks, and market dynamics. It highlights the significance of implementing solid regulatory supervision and enforcement mechanisms in the telecommunications industry to promote consumer welfare and ensure equitable competition. Indian competition law has witnessed substantial expansion, specifically in the telecommunications industry, which is the second-largest global market. Notwithstanding the legal complexities, the development of competition law in India is a testament to the country's dedication to cultivating equitable and competitive business conduct. Implementing the Competition Act 2002, which superseded the antiquated Monopolies and Restrictive Trade Practices Act 1969, represented a turning point in the regulatory framework of India. The legislative amendment demonstrated India's commitment to creating a structure that encourages market competition, protects consumers' interests, and facilitates unrestricted trade. The Competition Act regulates monopolistic practices and anticompetitive conduct to level the playing field for companies and safeguard the interests of consumers.

Notwithstanding the advancements, enduring jurisdictional conflicts have emerged between regulatory entities, including the Competition Commission of India (CCI) and the Telecom Regulatory Authority of India (TRAI), which explicitly concern predatory pricing. These disputes underscore the importance of establishing unambiguous regulatory limits to prevent redundancy and guarantee the efficient implementation of competition legislation. However, it is essential to note that TRAI and CCI are vital in promoting market efficiency and protecting competition. In contrast to TRAI, which is primarily concerned with overseeing the telecom industry and promoting ethical conduct, CCI is responsible for enforcing competition law in all sectors. Through their efforts to preserve competition and thwart market distortions, these regulatory bodies foster an environment that is advantageous for the growth of businesses while safeguarding the interests of consumers.

The expansion of competition law in India, particularly in the telecommunications industry, demonstrates the nation's dedication to promoting equitable and competitive business conduct. Notwithstanding the obstacles posed by jurisdiction, regulatory entities such as TRAI and CCI assume critical functions in fostering market competition, protecting consumer welfare, and augmenting market efficacy as a whole. Employing efficient enforcement and cooperative efforts, these regulatory frameworks help equalize opportunities for consumers and businesses. The telecom sector in India serves as a prime illustration of the intricate dynamics among regulatory frameworks, legal obstacles, and sustainability initiatives. Prominent corporations such as Bharti Airtel and Reliance Jio have exhibited their dedication to sustainability by undertakings like GreenTowers and eco-friendly packaging, thereby illustrating the sector's capacity for environmental stewardship. Nevertheless, legal disputes such as the Bharati Airtel Limited v. Reliance Jio Limited case emphasized the fierce rivalry and calculated manoeuvring that characterizes the sector. It underscores the criticality of solid regulatory supervision and enforcement systems.

The progression of competition law in India, specifically in the telecommunications industry, indicates the country's commitment to promoting equitable and competitive business conduct. The Competition Act of 2002 sought to promote consumer protection and market competition by replacing antiquated legislation that has encountered ongoing jurisdictional disputes between regulatory bodies such as TRAI and CCI. Consequently, the establishment of unambiguous regulatory boundaries has become imperative. Notwithstanding these obstacles, the TRAI and CCI protect competition and augment market efficacy, fostering a favourable milieu for enterprises and consumers. In light of the ongoing transformations in the telecommunications industry, it will be imperative that stakeholders, regulatory entities, and policymakers work together in concert to tackle issues related to sustainability, legal intricacies, and equitable competition. By fostering collaboration, innovation, and efficient enforcement, the telecommunications sector in India can surmount these obstacles and contribute positively towards a more sustainable and competitive future.

CASE STUDY 1

Bharti Airtel's GreenTowers Initiative

Bharti Airtel, a leading telecommunications company in India, faced significant environmental and operational challenges related to its extensive network infrastructure. The high energy consumption and carbon emissions from its telecommunications towers were key concerns that needed to be addressed.

Bharti Airtel introduced the GreenTowers initiative to reduce carbon emissions and operational expenses by adopting energy-efficient equipment, optimizing tower operations, and integrating renewable energy sources like solar power. By investing in energy-efficient equipment, Bharti Airtel reduced energy consumption and lowered operational costs. This initial investment in advanced technology paid off through significant energy savings over time. Optimizing tower operations involved upgrading existing infrastructure and implementing better management practices. This optimization reduced energy waste and further cut down on operational expenses. Incorporating solar power and other renewable energy sources reduced reliance on diesel generators, cutting fuel costs and decreasing carbon emissions.

A cost-benefit analysis of integrating sustainable practices reveals several financial implications. Initial costs include investing in energy-efficient equipment and renewable energy infrastructure, alongside expenses for training and optimizing operations. However, the benefits are substantial, featuring significant reductions in energy costs due to decreased consumption and lower fuel expenses from reduced reliance on diesel generators. Additionally, organizations can enhance their brand reputation and customer loyalty by demonstrating a commitment to sustainability. Potential tax incentives and subsidies for using renewable energy sources further offset the initial investment, making the overall financial case for sustainable practices compelling. The GreenTowers initiative by Bharti Airtel exemplifies the financial benefits of integrating sustainability into core operations. By reducing operational expenses and carbon emissions, Bharti Airtel not only improved its environmental footprint but also achieved substantial cost savings.

CASE STUDY 2

Reliance Jio's Eco-Friendly Packaging

As a major player in the Indian telecommunications sector, Reliance Jio sought to address environmental concerns related to packaging waste and its impact on consumer perception. The challenge was to reduce waste while maintaining or enhancing consumer satisfaction. Reliance Jio implemented eco-friendly packaging methods, including using biodegradable and recyclable materials, eco-friendly printing methods, and reducing plastic usage. This initiative aimed to minimize environmental impact and appeal to environmentally conscious consumers. By switching to biodegradable and recyclable materials for packaging, Reliance Jio reduced the environmental impact and waste management costs. The use of these materials also attracted eco-conscious consumers. Implementing eco-friendly printing methods reduced the use of harmful chemicals and materials, aligning with sustainability goals and reducing production costs over time. Reducing plastic usage in packaging not only decreased environmental harm but also reduced the costs associated with plastic materials.

A cost-benefit analysis of adopting eco-friendly packaging materials highlights both financial outlays and advantages. Initial costs involve investing in the development and sourcing of sustainable packaging, as well as potential increases in packaging expenses during the transition period. Nevertheless, the long-term benefits are significant. Reduced waste management and disposal costs contribute to savings over time, while enhanced brand reputation and increased consumer loyalty result from demonstrated eco-friendly practices. Additionally, businesses can capture a larger market share by appealing to environmentally conscious consumers. Financial incentives for sustainable packaging practices can further mitigate initial costs, making the overall investment in eco-friendly packaging economically advantageous. Reliance Jio's eco-friendly packaging initiative highlights the financial viability of sustainable practices. By reducing waste and production costs, and enhancing brand reputation, Reliance Jio achieved both environmental and economic benefits.

The Case of Bharati Airtel Limited vs. Reliance Jio Limited

The competitive dynamics between Bharti Airtel and Reliance Jio have been marked by legal disputes and regulatory challenges. Reliance Jio lodged a formal complaint with the Competition Commission of India (CCI), accusing Bharti Airtel, Idea Cellular Limited, and Vodafone India Limited of engaging in anti-competitive conduct. Reliance Jio alleged that its rivals, in collaboration with the Cellular Operators Association of India (COAI), were deliberately impeding the deployment of its network by restricting access to POIs. This hindered Reliance Jio's ability to compete effectively.

The case underscored the jurisdictional complexities between the Telecom Regulatory Authority of India (TRAI) and the Competition Commission of India (CCI). The legal disputes highlighted the need for clear regulatory boundaries to ensure efficient implementation of competition laws. The legal disputes between Bharti Airtel and Reliance Jio had significant financial implications for both companies and the market. Legal battles entail substantial costs, and the outcome of such cases can influence market dynamics, regulatory oversight, and consumer choice. The legal disputes between Bharti Airtel and Reliance Jio illustrate the fierce competition and strategic maneuvering within the telecommunications sector. The need for robust regulatory oversight and enforcement mechanisms is critical to promote fair competition and protect consumer welfare.

These case studies of Bharti Airtel and Reliance Jio demonstrate the significant financial and environmental benefits of adopting sustainable practices. By integrating energy-efficient equipment, renewable energy sources, and eco-friendly packaging, these companies have successfully reduced costs, enhanced brand reputation, and contributed to a more sustainable future. The cost-benefit analyses reveal that sustainable practices not only help protect the environment but also provide substantial economic advantages. Additionally, the legal dynamics between these companies underscore the importance of clear regulatory boundaries and effective enforcement to ensure fair competition in the market. By fostering collaboration, innovation, and efficient enforcement, the Indian telecommunications sector can surmount challenges related to sustainability, legal intricacies, and equitable competition. This collective effort will contribute positively towards a more sustainable and competitive future.

CASE STUDY 3

Apple Inc. is a global leader in technology, known for its innovative products and commitment to sustainability. In recent years, Apple has increasingly focused on minimizing its environmental footprint through various initiatives. One such approach is the implementation of Life Cycle Assessment (LCA) to evaluate and enhance the environmental performance of its products. As a major manufacturer of electronic devices, Apple faces significant environmental challenges, including resource depletion, greenhouse gas emissions, and electronic waste. The company recognized the need to adopt a more sustainable approach to product design and manufacturing to address these issues and align with its corporate responsibility goals. Apple employs Life Cycle Assessment (LCA) to comprehensively assess the environmental impacts of its products throughout their entire life cycles. LCA involves evaluating each stage of a product's life, from raw material extraction and manufacturing to distribution, use, and end-of-life disposal. This holistic approach allows Apple to identify key areas where environmental improvements can be made.

In a notable application of LCA, Apple redesigned its MacBook Air and Mac mini with a focus on sustainability. One of the most significant changes was the introduction of recycled aluminum enclosures for these products. Traditionally, aluminum production is energy-intensive and contributes to high carbon emissions.

By using recycled aluminum, Apple significantly reduced the carbon footprint associated with these devices. Through LCA, Apple identified that the use of recycled aluminum not only decreased greenhouse gas emissions but also reduced energy consumption during the manufacturing process. This was a crucial step in Apple's broader strategy to lower its overall environmental impact. Apple sourced aluminum from recycled post-consumer scrap, ensuring that the material used in the new enclosures met high standards of quality and performance while reducing reliance on virgin aluminum extraction.

The manufacturing process was optimized to integrate recycled aluminum without compromising the structural integrity or aesthetic appeal of the products. This required innovations in material processing and assembly techniques. The use of recycled aluminum in the MacBook Air and Mac mini resulted in a substantial reduction in carbon emissions. Apple reported that the carbon footprint of the new MacBook Air was nearly 47% lower than the previous generation. Similarly, the redesigned Mac mini saw a significant decrease in its environmental impact. Consumers responded positively to Apple's sustainability efforts, appreciating the company's commitment to environmental stewardship. The redesigned products maintained their competitive edge in the market, demonstrating that sustainability and high performance can go hand-in-hand. Apple introduced recycled aluminum enclosures for the MacBook Air and Mac mini, significantly reducing their carbon footprint. This change not only decreased greenhouse gas emissions but also reduced production costs associated with virgin aluminum extraction.

A cost-benefit analysis of integrating recycled materials into manufacturing processes reveals a range of financial impacts. The primary cost involves the initial investment in new manufacturing processes and the procurement of recycled materials. However, this investment is offset by significant long-term benefits. The use of recycled aluminum can reduce material costs over time, while decreased energy consumption leads to lower operational expenses. Additionally, adopting sustainable practices enhances brand reputation, which can boost sales and foster customer loyalty. Potential tax incentives and subsidies for utilizing recycled materials further contribute to the economic advantages, making the integration of recycled materials a financially beneficial strategy.

Apple's implementation of Life Cycle Assessment (LCA) in the redesign of the MacBook Air and Mac mini showcases the company's dedication to sustainable innovation. By leveraging LCA, Apple successfully identified and addressed key areas for environmental improvement, leading to significant reductions in carbon emissions and energy consumption. This case study highlights the importance of integrating LCA into product development processes to achieve meaningful sustainability goals. Through continued commitment to LCA and other sustainable practices, Apple sets a benchmark for the technology industry and inspires other companies to pursue environmental responsibility. Apple's use of LCA in redesigning the MacBook Air and Mac mini demonstrates how sustainable practices can lead to financial benefits. By reducing material and energy costs and enhancing brand reputation, Apple achieved both environmental and economic gains.

CASE STUDY 4

IKEA, a globally recognized leader in home furnishings, is committed to sustainability and reducing its environmental impact. As part of its broader sustainability strategy, IKEA employs Life Cycle Assessment (LCA) to evaluate and enhance the environmental performance of its products. This case study focuses on IKEA's innovative approach to sustainable product design, particularly through its KUNGSBACKA kitchen fronts, which are made from recycled materials. IKEA faces the challenge of balancing mass production with environmental sustainability. The company aims to minimize resource consumption, reduce waste, and lower its carbon footprint while maintaining affordability and quality for its customers. Adopting sustainable practices across its product lines is essential to meeting these goals.

To address these challenges, IKEA integrates Life Cycle Assessment (LCA) into its product development process. LCA provides a comprehensive evaluation of the environmental impacts associated with a product throughout its entire life cycle, from raw material extraction to production, use, and disposal. This approach enables IKEA to identify opportunities for reducing environmental impact and enhancing sustainability. One of the standout examples of IKEA's commitment to sustainable design is the KUNGSBACKA kitchen fronts. These fronts are made from recycled wood and PET bottles, showcasing IKEA's innovative use of recycled materials. The KUNGSBACKA kitchen fronts are manufactured using wood recovered from recycled industrial sources and PET plastic from post-consumer bottles. This approach reduces the need for virgin materials and helps divert waste from landfills. Reduction in Resource Use and Waste: By incorporating recycled wood and PET bottles, IKEA significantly reduces resource consumption and waste generation. The production of KUNGSBACKA fronts demonstrates how recycled materials can be effectively utilized to create high-quality, durable products.

IKEA sources recycled wood and PET bottles from reliable suppliers, ensuring that the materials meet stringent quality and environmental standards. This sustainable sourcing strategy helps conserve natural resources and supports the recycling industry. The production of KUNGSBACKA kitchen fronts involves innovative techniques to blend recycled wood and PET plastic seamlessly. The process ensures that the final product is both aesthetically pleasing and functionally robust. Through LCA, IKEA assesses the environmental benefits of using recycled materials. The analysis revealed that the KUNGSBACKA fronts have a significantly lower environmental impact compared to similar products made from virgin materials. The reduced need for new raw materials results in lower carbon emissions and decreased energy consumption. The KUNGSBACKA kitchen fronts have been well-received by consumers who value sustainability. IKEA's commitment to transparency and sustainability resonates with its customer base, reinforcing the brand's reputation as a leader in environmentally responsible home furnishings.

The KUNGSBACKA kitchen fronts are made from recycled wood and PET bottles, reducing the need for virgin materials and decreasing production costs.Integrating recycled materials into manufacturing involves several costs and benefits. Initial costs include investments in sourcing and processing recycled materials and redesigning manufacturing processes to accommodate these inputs. Despite these costs, the long-term benefits are substantial. Using recycled wood and PET bottles can significantly lower material costs and reduce waste disposal expenses. Additionally, adopting such sustainable practices enhances the brand image, appealing to environmentally conscious consumers. Potential financial incentives for using recycled materials further enhance the economic advantages, making the shift to recycled inputs a financially sound and strategically beneficial decision.

IKEA's use of Life Cycle Assessment (LCA) in the development of KUNGSBACKA kitchen fronts exemplifies the company's dedication to sustainable innovation. By leveraging recycled materials and optimizing the production process, IKEA successfully reduces the environmental impact of its products. This case study underscores the importance of integrating LCA into product design to achieve sustainability goals. IKEA's ongoing commitment to LCA and sustainable practices sets a powerful example for the industry and encourages other companies to adopt similar approaches. Through continuous innovation and sustainable development, IKEA aims to create a positive impact on the environment while providing affordable and high-quality products to its customers. IKEA's implementation of LCA in the development of KUNGSBACKA kitchen fronts highlights the financial viability of sustainable practices. By lowering material costs and waste disposal expenses, IKEA achieves significant economic and environmental benefits

CASE STUDY 5

Herman Miller is a renowned office furniture manufacturer known for its commitment to sustainable design and innovation. The company applies Cradle-to-Cradle (C2C) design principles to its product development, focusing on creating products that can be easily recycled or repurposed at the end of their life cycle. This case study highlights Herman Miller's application of C2C principles in the design of the

"Mirra" chair, emphasizing its sustainable features and the impact on the environment. As a leading manufacturer, Herman Miller faces the challenge of reducing the environmental impact of its products while maintaining high standards of quality and functionality. The company aims to design products that are not only durable and ergonomic but also sustainable throughout their life cycle. This includes ensuring that materials are safe for human and environmental health and that products can be disassembled and recycled efficiently.

Herman Miller adopts Cradle-to-Cradle (C2C) design principles to create products that support a circular economy. C2C principles focus on designing products with the intention of reusing materials in a closed-loop system, thereby minimizing waste and environmental impact. The design process considers the entire life cycle of the product, from material selection to end-of-life management.The "Mirra" chair is a prime example of Herman Miller's application of C2C principles. Designed with sustainability in mind, the Mirra chair incorporates several features that align with the goals of C2C design.Design for Disassembly: The Mirra chair is designed to be easily disassembled at the end of its useful life. This allows for efficient recycling of its components, ensuring that materials can be recovered and reused rather than ending up in landfills. Each part of the chair is labeled for recycling, facilitating the separation and processing of different materials.Safe Materials: Herman Miller carefully selects materials that are safe for both human and environmental health. The Mirra chair is made from non-toxic materials that do not release harmful substances during use or disposal. This commitment to using safe materials ensures that the chair meets high environmental and health standards.

Sustainable End-of-Life Management: At the end of its life cycle, the Mirra chair can be returned to Herman Miller for recycling. The company has established a take-back program that ensures the proper handling and recycling of the chair's components. This program supports the circular economy by keeping materials in use and reducing waste.The materials used in the Mirra chair are selected based on their environmental impact, safety, and recyclability. Herman Miller works closely with suppliers to ensure that all materials meet C2C standards and contribute to the overall sustainability of the product.The production process for the Mirra chair is designed to minimize waste and energy consumption. Herman Miller uses efficient manufacturing techniques that reduce the environmental footprint of the product. The application of C2C principles has significantly reduced the environmental impact of the Mirra chair. By designing for disassembly and using safe, recyclable materials, Herman Miller has created a product that supports a circular economy and reduces waste.

The Mirra chair has been well-received by customers who value sustainability and quality. Herman Miller's commitment to C2C design principles enhances its brand reputation and attracts environmentally conscious consumers. The Mirra chair's design facilitates easy disassembly, allowing for efficient recycling of components and reducing waste disposal costs.Adopting Cradle to Cradle (C2C) principles for designing and manufacturing chairs involves several costs, including initial expenses for implementing C2C design principles and setting up a take-back program for end-of-life products. However, these costs are outweighed by significant benefits. By reducing waste disposal and raw material extraction, businesses can lower operational costs. Revenue can be generated from recycling materials, while increased customer loyalty and sales stem from appealing to environmentally conscious consumers. Additionally, embracing C2C principles enhances brand reputation and provides a competitive advantage, making the investment in sustainable practices both economically and strategically advantageous.

Herman Miller's application of Cradle-to-Cradle (C2C) design principles in the development of the Mirra chair demonstrates the company's dedication to sustainable innovation. By focusing on design for disassembly, using safe materials, and ensuring sustainable end-of-life management, Herman Miller has created a product that supports a circular economy and reduces environmental impact. This case study highlights the importance of C2C principles in product design and showcases Herman Miller's leadership in sustainable manufacturing. Through continuous innovation and a commitment to sustainability, Herman Miller sets a benchmark for the industry and inspires other companies to adopt similar practices. Herman Miller's Mirra chair demonstrates the financial advantages of C2C design principles. By reducing waste disposal costs and generating revenue from recycled materials, Herman Miller achieves significant economic and environmental benefits.

CASE STUDY 6

Aveda, a pioneering company in the cosmetics industry, is dedicated to environmental sustainability and social responsibility. By incorporating Cradle-to-Cradle (C2C) design principles, Aveda emphasizes recyclable packaging and sustainable ingredient sourcing. This case study examines Aveda's innovative "Full Circle Recycling Program," highlighting its impact on reducing landfill waste and promoting a circular economy.The cosmetics industry faces significant environmental challenges, including packaging waste and the ethical sourcing of ingredients. Aveda recognized the need to address these issues by implementing sustainable practices that would minimize environmental impact while maintaining the high quality of their products.Aveda adopted Cradle-to-Cradle (C2C) design principles to create products that support a circular economy. C2C principles focus on designing products with the end of their life cycle in mind, ensuring that materials can be safely reused or recycled. This approach minimizes waste and reduces the environmental footprint of Aveda's products.Aveda's "Full Circle Recycling Program" is a key initiative demonstrating the company's commitment to C2C principles. This program encourages customers to return empty Aveda containers, which are then repurposed, recycled, or responsibly disposed of, thus reducing landfill waste.

Aveda uses recyclable materials for its product packaging, including post-consumer recycled (PCR) plastic and bioplastics. This choice of materials ensures that packaging can be efficiently recycled at the end of its use, contributing to a reduction in overall waste. Aveda sources ingredients sustainably, prioritizing organic, fair trade, and ethically harvested materials. This practice ensures that the production of Aveda products supports environmental conservation and fair labor practices, aligning with C2C principles.The Full Circle Recycling Program involves customers in the recycling process by encouraging them to return empty containers to Aveda stores. This engagement fosters a sense of environmental responsibility among consumers and increases awareness of sustainability issues.Returned containers are sorted and processed to recover recyclable materials. Aveda collaborates with specialized recycling partners to ensure that materials are repurposed effectively. Non-recyclable components are disposed of responsibly to minimize environmental impact. By using recyclable packaging and implementing the Full Circle Recycling Program, Aveda significantly reduces the amount of waste sent to landfills. The program has diverted millions of containers from landfills, demonstrating a tangible impact on waste reduction.

Consumers have responded positively to Aveda's sustainability initiatives. The Full Circle Recycling Program has strengthened customer loyalty and enhanced Aveda's brand reputation as an environmentally conscious company. Customers appreciate the opportunity to contribute to environmental conservation through their participation in the program.Aveda adopts C2C design principles, focusing on recyclable packaging and sustainable ingredient sourcing. The Full Circle Recycling Program exemplifies this approach by encouraging customers to return empty containers for repurposing. Aveda uses recyclable materials, including post-consumer recycled (PCR) plastic and bioplastics, reducing waste and production costs.

Investing in sustainable packaging materials and managing a recycling program involves certain costs, including the initial investment in eco-friendly materials and the ongoing expenses related to running the recycling initiative. However, these costs are balanced by several substantial benefits. Over time, using recycled packaging can lead to lower material costs and reduced waste disposal expenses. Additionally, adopting sustainable packaging enhances brand reputation and fosters customer loyalty, as consumers increasingly favor environmentally responsible practices. Furthermore, businesses may benefit from potential financial incentives for implementing sustainable practices, making the overall investment in sustainable packaging both financially and reputationally rewarding.

Aveda's application of Cradle-to-Cradle (C2C) design principles through the Full Circle Recycling Program highlights the company's dedication to sustainability. By using recyclable packaging and sourcing ingredients sustainably, Aveda addresses critical environmental challenges and promotes a circular economy. This case study illustrates the effectiveness of C2C principles in reducing waste and engaging consumers in sustainability efforts. Aveda's leadership in sustainable practices sets a benchmark for the cosmetics industry, inspiring other companies to adopt similar approaches. Through continued innovation and commitment to sustainability, Aveda contributes to a healthier planet and a more responsible industry.Aveda's Full Circle Recycling Program highlights the financial benefits of sustainable practices in the cosmetics industry. By reducing material and waste disposal costs and enhancing brand reputation, Aveda achieves both environmental and economic gains.

These case studies of Apple Inc., IKEA, Herman Miller, and Aveda demonstrate the significant financial and environmental benefits of adopting sustainable practices. By integrating Life Cycle Assessment (LCA) and Cradle-to-Cradle (C2C) design principles into their product development and operations, these companies have successfully reduced costs, enhanced brand reputation, and contributed to a more sustainable future. The cost-benefit analyses reveal that sustainable practices not only help protect the environment but also provide substantial economic advantages, reinforcing the importance of sustainability in today's business world.

LESSONS AND BEST PRACTICES FOR ENTREPRENEURS DEVELOPING SUSTAINABLE PRODUCTS

Successful telecom sustainable product development projects focus on connecting sustainability goals with business goals. Sustainability may boost innovation, lower costs, improve brand reputation, and open new markets, helping entrepreneurs succeed. Sustainable product development requires stakeholder engagement, including customers, suppliers, industry partners, and regulatory bodies. Entrepreneurs can obtain insights, establish shared goals, address issues, and develop support for sustainability efforts by cooperating with stakeholders, fostering a value chain culture of sustainability. Sustainable product creation demands continual innovation and R&D to find new technologies, materials, and design solutions that match client expectations and reduce environmental effects. Entrepreneurs must invest in sustainable technologies, product design, and production practices to survive in a fast-changing market.

Entrepreneurs must build rigorous measurements and monitoring systems to track their goods' environmental and social impact throughout their lifecycle. Entrepreneurs can evaluate their sustainable product development efforts, identify areas for improvement, and show progress toward sustainability goals by measuring KPIs like carbon emissions, energy consumption, waste generation, and social outcomes. Successful case studies and best practices can help telecom and other entrepreneurs produce sustainable products, driving innovation, producing revenue, and contributing to a more sustainable future. Top of Form

OVERCOMING CHALLENGES AND BARRIERS

Stakeholder ignorance of sustainability principles makes integrating sustainability into product development more accessible. Organizations may resist change, especially if sustainable practices demand significant investments or process changes (Fisher et al., 2021). If sustainable resources or eco-friendly technology are scarce or expensive, they can be challenging to source. Finally, quantifying product environmental and social impacts throughout their lifecycle is complex and resource-intensive.

Building a sustainable culture from the top down with leadership commitment and clear sustainability goals can help firms overcome opposition to sustainable innovation. Training employees on sustainability ideas and practices can help them comprehend the benefits of incorporating them into their jobs. Organizations can also reward sustainable behaviour through recognition programs or sustainability-related performance indicators. Sharing value and aligning interests with suppliers and consumers can also help embrace sustainable practices.

Sustainable product creation is often hindered by the belief that sustainable methods are expensive or that the ROI needs to be clarified. Cost-benefit assessments can show the long-term economic benefits of sustainability, such as energy savings, resource efficiency, and brand reputation. Accessing government subsidies, green financing channels, or corporate sustainability funds for sustainable initiatives can also reduce financial limitations. Conflicting or confusing rules or compliance expenses can limit sustainable product development. Organizations can work with regulators to promote sustainable policies and practices while adhering to legal constraints (Vilochani et al., 2023). By embracing voluntary sustainability standards or certifications, organizations can concretely showcase their dedication to upholding ethical and environmental standards. These standards facilitate market entry and consumer confidence by providing a framework for measuring and verifying a company's sustainability performance. By implementing established benchmarks, such as Fair-Trade certification for ethical sourcing and ISO 14001 for environmental management, organizations demonstrate their commitment to sustainable operations while distinguishing themselves within the market.

Sustainable marketing and business practices are essential for e-commerce companies to reduce their environmental impact and contribute to a sustainable future. These practices involve adopting eco-friendly packaging, minimizing energy consumption, and partnering with sustainable suppliers. Companies can enhance consumer trust and credibility by implementing such measures while actively promoting environmental conservation. Challenges associated with sustainable marketing can be addressed by transparently communicating sustainability efforts to consumers, obtaining certifications, and showcasing sustainability initiatives. By aligning with sustainability principles, e-commerce companies can reduce their environmental footprint, foster consumer loyalty, and contribute to a more environmentally conscious business landscape (Singha et al., 2023). Interdisciplinary collaboration and partnerships are essential for shaping future generations' perceptions of the earth and fostering sustainable practices (Singha & Singh, 2024).

Furthermore, organizations may find voluntary sustainability standards highly beneficial in surmounting the financial and regulatory obstacles inherent in sustainable product development and innovation. Proactive engagement, strategic planning, and collaboration with value-chain stakeholders are essential for overcoming these obstacles. Pursuing opportunities to incorporate sustainability principles into business operations and product development processes constitutes proactive engagement. It may entail performing thorough sustainability assessments, identifying areas that require enhancement, and establishing ambitious sustainability objectives that align with industry standards and stakeholder demands.

Strategic planning is vital to achieve certification objectives and successfully implement sustainable practices. Organizations must formulate comprehensive sustainability strategies that specify precise aims, benchmarks, and schedules for execution. It entails synchronizing sustainability initiatives with fundamental business objectives, the efficient allocation of resources, and the oversight of advancements made towards sustainability targets.

Participation of value-chain stakeholders is also essential for overcoming financial and regulatory obstacles and fostering substantial change. It is recommended that businesses actively participate in partnerships and cooperative initiatives with non-governmental organizations (NGOs), suppliers, consumers, and regulatory agencies to promote sustainability goals and facilitate collective action. Through the active engagement of stakeholders at every stage of the value chain, organizations can discern mutually agreed-upon objectives, tackle shared obstacles, and harness combined knowledge and assets to propel sustainable innovation and product development.

To summarize, businesses can proactively showcase their commitment to environmental and social responsibility, improve market entry, and cultivate consumer confidence by embracing voluntary sustainability standards or certifications. Organizations must adopt proactive stakeholder engagement, strategic planning, and value-chain partner collaboration to surmount the financial and regulatory obstacles linked to sustainable innovation. Businesses can achieve long-term economic success and contribute positively to the environment and society by incorporating sustainability into their operations and embracing it as a fundamental value.

RECOMMENDATIONS AND SOLUTIONS

To integrate sustainable innovation and product development effectively, entrepreneurs should:

Use eco-friendly materials, prioritize energy efficiency, and design for recyclability or biodegradability from the start. This approach minimizes environmental impact and enhances product sustainability.

Evaluate the environmental impact throughout a product's lifecycle to identify areas for improvement, reduce resource use, and lower emissions.

Encourage creativity and support new, sustainable technologies and processes. An environment that values innovation can lead to breakthroughs in addressing environmental and social challenges.

Involve customers, suppliers, and communities in the development process to ensure products meet diverse needs and enhance acceptance.

Leverage government grants, tax credits, and funding from responsible investors to offset the costs of green technologies and materials.

Collaborate with suppliers to source sustainable materials and implement fair labor practices, maintaining high standards of environmental and social responsibility.

Regularly assess and enhance sustainability practices, monitor performance, and demonstrate commitment.

Provide training on sustainable practices and technologies to foster a culture of sustainability.

Collaborate with businesses, research institutions, and NGOs to amplify sustainability efforts.

Balance people, planet, and profit to guide responsible decision-making and resilient business practices.

By following these strategies, entrepreneurs can drive sustainable innovation, contribute to a more equitable future, and achieve long-term success.

DISCUSSION

Contemporary businesses are increasingly focusing on sustainable product development as they navigate environmental concerns, shifting consumer preferences, and the pursuit of long-term success with social impact. Sustainable innovation involves more than just eco-friendly products; it requires rethinking organizational practices and supply chains to minimize environmental harm and maximize social benefits. Entrepreneurs play a crucial role in this transformation, using sustainable practices to carve out a competitive edge and access new markets driven by eco-conscious consumers and investors.

However, integrating sustainability poses challenges, including internal resistance, financial constraints, and regulatory hurdles. Overcoming these requires fostering a culture of environmental stewardship and investing in green technologies to reduce costs. Supportive policies and incentives from governments can also drive adoption by creating a conducive environment for sustainable practices.

Successful case studies highlight the practical benefits of sustainable innovation, offering valuable lessons for businesses. Collaboration with stakeholders such as suppliers, consumers, and NGOs is essential for developing effective sustainable solutions. Innovation and strategic partnerships can help businesses address complex environmental and social issues, enhance their brand, and contribute to a more sustainable future. Embracing sustainability as a core principle can yield significant advantages, including cost savings, market differentiation, and positive societal impact.

FUTURE RESEARCH DIRECTIONS

Future research should focus on adapting sustainable business models to evolving market dynamics, technological advancements, and regulatory frameworks. Longitudinal studies are needed to assess the success factors and challenges of sustainable ventures over time. Key areas for exploration include the integration of automation, blockchain, and artificial intelligence (AI) in sustainable product development. AI's potential in optimizing energy efficiency and supply chain management, blockchain's role in enhancing supply chain transparency, and additive manufacturing's impact on resource-efficient production warrant further investigation.

Understanding consumer behavior towards sustainable products is crucial; research should explore how sustainable practices influence purchasing decisions and attitudes. Additionally, the role of stakeholder collaboration in driving innovation and achieving sustainability goals needs examination. Policy and regulation also play a significant role; future studies should investigate their impact on corporate sustainability practices and identify opportunities for leveraging regulatory frameworks.

Cross-cultural and institutional analyses could reveal how different environments influence sustainable entrepreneurship. A multidisciplinary approach, incorporating stakeholder engagement, consumer behavior, policy analysis, and cultural contexts, will provide comprehensive insights and support the advancement of sustainable innovation and product development.

CONCLUSION

Sustainable innovation and product development represent a crucial evolution in modern entrepreneurship, balancing economic growth with environmental and social responsibility. This chapter has explored the principles and practices of sustainable innovation, highlighting the importance of creating products that are economically viable while being environmentally friendly and socially beneficial. The conceptual framework, including sustainable design, life cycle assessment, and stakeholder involvement, provides a comprehensive approach for aligning product development with sustainability goals. Theoretical insights from the Diffusion of Innovations, Resource-Based View, Stakeholder Theory, and Institutional Theory further contextualize the adoption and impact of these practices.

Recommendations emphasize practical strategies for integrating sustainability, such as adopting eco-friendly design principles, engaging stakeholders, and leveraging financial incentives. Integrating sustainability is not just about compliance but offers a strategic advantage that drives long-term success, enhances brand reputation, and meets growing consumer demand. As global awareness of environmental and social issues rises, entrepreneurs who prioritize sustainability will not only achieve competitive differentiation but also contribute to a more equitable and sustainable future. This chapter underscores that sustainable innovation is key to fostering a resilient and responsible business landscape, benefiting both enterprises and society.

REFERENCES

Alomoto, W., Niñerola, À., & Pié, L. (2021). Social impact assessment: A systematic review of literature. *Social Indicators Research*, 161(1), 225–250. DOI: 10.1007/s11205-021-02809-1

Branca, G., Resciniti, R., & Babin, B. J. (2023). Sustainable packaging design and the consumer perspective: A systematic literature review. *Italian Journal of Marketing*. DOI: 10.1007/s43039-023-00084-1

Cordella, M., & Kaps, R. (2018). Sustainability of bio-based products: Linking life cycle thinking with standards, certification and labelling schemes. In *Springer eBooks* (pp. 469–474). DOI: 10.1007/978-3-319-66981-6_52

Fisher, J., Arora, P., Chen, S., Rhee, S., Blaine, T., & Simangan, D. (2021). Four propositions on integrated sustainability: Toward a theoretical framework to understand the environment, peace, and sustainability nexus. *Sustainability Science*, 16(4), 1125–1145. DOI: 10.1007/s11625-021-00925-y PMID: 33717363

Fontes, J. L. I., Tarne, P., Traverso, M., & Bernstein, P. (2016). Product social impact assessment. *The International Journal of Life Cycle Assessment*, 23(3), 547–555. DOI: 10.1007/s11367-016-1125-6

Kabongo, J. D. (2013). Design for environment. In *Springer eBooks* (pp. 780–786). DOI: 10.1007/978-3-642-28036-8_40

Kasradze, M., Štreimikienė, D., & Lauzadyte-Tutliene, A. (2023). Measuring the impact of corporate social responsibility in the energy sector. *Environmental Science and Pollution Research International*, 30(51), 109973–110009. DOI: 10.1007/s11356-023-30131-5 PMID: 37798520

Klöpffer, W. (2014). Introducing Life Cycle Assessment and its presentation in 'LCA compendium.' In *LCA compendium* (pp. 1–37). DOI: 10.1007/978-94-017-8697-3_1

Laycock, B., Pratt, S., & Halley, P. J. (2023). A perspective on biodegradable polymer biocomposites - from processing to degradation. *Functional Composite Materials*, 4(1), 10. Advance online publication. DOI: 10.1186/s42252-023-00048-w

Lipnik, A., & Lipnik, M. C. (2020). Sustainable innovation: Definitions, priorities and emerging issues. In *Sustainability and innovation* (pp. 41–56). DOI: 10.1007/978-3-030-46750-0_2

Meyer, A., & Schneider, P. (2019). Cradle-to-cradle for sustainable development: From eco-design to a circular economy. In *Springer eBooks* (pp. 321–330). DOI: 10.1007/978-3-030-11352-0_273

Parag, Y., Elimelech, E., & Opher, T. (2023). Bottled water: An evidence-based overview of economic viability, environmental impact, and social equity. *Sustainability (Basel)*, 15(12), 9760. DOI: 10.3390/su15129760

Rasheed, M., & Liu, J. (2023). Unleashing the power of innovation promoters for sustainable economic growth: A global perspective. *Environmental Science and Pollution Research International*, 30(45), 100979–100993. DOI: 10.1007/s11356-023-29313-y PMID: 37642909

Riti, J. S., & Yang, S. (2016). Renewable energy, energy efficiency, and eco-friendly environment (R-E5) in Nigeria. *Energy, Sustainability and Society*, 6(1), 13. Advance online publication. DOI: 10.1186/s13705-016-0072-1

Schulte, J., & Hallstedt, S. I. (2018). Company risk management in light of the sustainability transition. *Sustainability (Basel)*, 10(11), 4137. DOI: 10.3390/su10114137

Singha, S., & Singh, R. (2024). Cross-Disciplinary Collaborations and Partnerships for Sustainability Education: Including Community-Based Learning, Industry Partnerships, and International Collaborations. In Goi, C. L. (Ed.), *Teaching and Learning for a Sustainable Future: Innovative Strategies and Best Practices* (Vol. 1, pp. 17–37). IGI., DOI: 10.4018/978-1-6684-9859-0.ch002

Singha, S., Singha, R., Rebeka, S. P., & Ruben, V. M. (2023). Sustainable marketing in e-commerce: Strategies for environmental impact reduction. In Masengu, R., Bigirimana, S., Chiwaridzo, O. T., Benson, R., & Blossom, C. (Eds.), *Sustainable Marketing, Branding, and Reputation Management: Strategies for a Greener Future* (pp. 444–464). IGI Global., DOI: 10.4018/979-8-3693-0019-0.ch023

Tarnovskaya, V. (2023). Sustainability as the source of competitive advantage. How sustainable is it? In *International Business and Management Series* (pp. 75–89). DOI: 10.1108/S1876-066X20230000037005

Tsalis, T. A., Stefanakis, A., & Nikolaou, I. E. (2022). A framework to evaluate the social life cycle impact of products under the circular economy thinking. *Sustainability (Basel)*, 14(4), 2196. DOI: 10.3390/su14042196

Varadarajan, R. (2015). Innovating for sustainability: A framework for sustainable innovations and a model of sustainable innovations orientation. *Journal of the Academy of Marketing Science*, 45(1), 14–36. DOI: 10.1007/s11747-015-0461-6

Vig, S. (2022). Sustainable development through sustainable entrepreneurship and innovation: A single-case approach. *Social Responsibility Journal*, 19(7), 1196–1217. DOI: 10.1108/SRJ-02-2022-0093

Vilochani, S., McAloone, T. C., & Pigosso, D. C. A. (2023). Management practices for sustainable product development: Insights from a systematic literature review. *Proceedings of the Design Society*, 3, 2505–2514. DOI: 10.1017/pds.2023.251

ADDITIONAL READING

Jiang, Y., Cai, W., & Wang, Y. (2024). Change starts within: Does managerial ability matter to green innovation? *Humanities & Social Sciences Communications*, 11(1), 827. Advance online publication. DOI: 10.1057/s41599-024-03331-8

Neu, W. T., Qian, X., & Yu, P. (Eds.). (2024). *The Synergy of Sustainable Entrepreneurship*. IGI Global., https://www.igi-global.com/publish/call-for-papers/call-details/7276

Popescu, C. R., Yu, P., & Wei, Y. (Eds.). (2023). *Achieving the Sustainable Development Goals Through Infrastructure Development* (pp. 1–303). IGI Global., DOI: 10.4018/979-8-3693-0794-6

Singha, R., & Singha, S. (2024). Application of Experiential, Inquiry-Based, Problem-Based, and Project-Based Learning in Sustainable Education. In Goi, C. (Ed.), *Teaching and Learning for a Sustainable Future: Innovative Strategies and Best Practices* (pp. 109–128). IGI Global., DOI: 10.4018/978-1-6684-9859-0.ch006

Singha, R., Singha, S., & Jasmine, E. (2024). Encouraging Sustainable Living Through HR Initiatives. In Popescu, C., Martínez-Falcó, J., Marco-Lajara, B., Sánchez-García, E., & Millán-Tudela, L. (Eds.), *Building Sustainable Human Resources Management Practices for Businesses* (pp. 52–73). IGI Global., DOI: 10.4018/979-8-3693-1994-9.ch004

Singha, R., Singha, S., Natal, M. S., Ruben, V. M., Mize, E., & Haokip, A. D. (2024). Developing Anticipatory and Cognitive Skills for Sustainable Management. In Cepni, E. (Ed.), *Chaos, Complexity, and Sustainability in Management* (pp. 46–59). IGI Global., DOI: 10.4018/979-8-3693-2125-6.ch003

Singha, S. (2024). Fostering a Culture of Sustainability Through Human Resources Practices. In Popescu, C., Martínez-Falcó, J., Marco-Lajara, B., Sánchez-García, E., & Millán-Tudela, L. (Eds.), *Building Sustainable Human Resources Management Practices for Businesses* (pp. 107–124). IGI Global., DOI: 10.4018/979-8-3693-1994-9.ch007

Singha, S. (2024). Engaging Stakeholders for a Sustainable Future: Catalysts of Green Economy and Renewable Energy Transitions. In Castanho, R. (Ed.), *Green Economy and Renewable Energy Transitions for Sustainable Development* (pp. 208–223). IGI Global., DOI: 10.4018/979-8-3693-1297-1.ch012

Yu, L., & Wu, W. (2024). The impact of perceived environmental corporate social responsibility on idea generation and idea implementation. *Humanities & Social Sciences Communications*, 11(1), 486. Advance online publication. DOI: 10.1057/s41599-024-02971-0

KEY TERMS AND DEFINITIONS

Business Growth: Expanding a business's operations, market share, and profitability over time.

Eco-Design: The integration of environmental considerations into the design of products, aiming to minimize environmental impact throughout the lifecycle.

Entrepreneurship: Entrepreneurship is setting up and running a business, typically with innovative ideas and approaches.

Environmental Responsibility: The obligation of individuals and organizations to minimize ecological harm and promote sustainability.

Product Development: The design, creation, and delivery of new products or services to the market.

Social Impact: The effect that an organization's actions have on the well-being of society and communities.

Sustainability: The practice of meeting present needs without compromising the ability of future generations to meet their own needs.

Sustainable Innovation: The process of creating novel solutions that meet present needs without compromising the ability of future generations to meet their own.

Chapter 12
Venture Philanthropy and Its Applications in Impact Entrepreneurship and Systems Change and Private–Public Collaboration

Farrell Tan
Soristic Impact Collective, Singapore

Pauline Tan
Soristic Impact Collective, Singapore

ABSTRACT

Venture philanthropy utilises principles of venture capital and philanthropy. It presents a new form of high-engagement funding, progressing from traditional models of chequebook or armchair philanthropy. The capacity building, longer-term funding, and emphasis on financial sustainability reflects the management intensiveness of venture philanthropy, but with the potential for catalysing new forms of innovation and multi-sectoral partnerships.Venture philanthropy has been demonstrated to be important catalysts for impact entrepreneurship and providing new sources of unconventional financing to impact entrepreneurs. Aside from financing impact-oriented ventures, venture philanthropy has also been involved in other roles, such as policy advocacy, convening networks between the public and private sector, and initiating social innovation for new service delivery models. Finally, the chapter closes with some examples of venture philanthropy in the Asian context.

DOI: 10.4018/979-8-3693-4338-8.ch012

1. INTRODUCTION TO VENTURE PHILANTHROPY

The concept of venture philanthropy can be traced as far back as the 1960s in the US, though it only gained prominence in the 1990s (EVPA, 2018). In a Harvard Business Review paper, Letts, Ryan and Grossman (1997) challenged philanthropic foundations to apply venture capital approaches in their grantmaking to support grantees in to support grantees in developing longer-term organisation capacity to better serve the evolving needs of society to better serve various needs in society. A 2011 study on 755 grantmaking organisations found that there could be a mismatch between the needs of some non-profit organisations and the prevalent funding practices of philanthropic organisations, as non-profit organisations needed flexible and longer-term funding, and capacity building to be able to respond to their changing environments (McCray, 2014). For these organisations, the lack of such financial resources and organisational capabilities restricts their ability to scale their impact, or even develop the basic infrastructure necessary to sustain its own operations (Roundy et al., 2017). It is imperative that new approaches to philanthropic funding was required. Concurrently, philanthropists themselves were also less content to engage in the typical chequebook giving, and gradually sought new ways for greater performance and accountability (Chia, 2015; Shaw et al., 2013). Chia (2015) also attributes the shift in philanthropic landscape to the shifting profiles of philanthropists themselves, where the new generation of philanthropists are more educated, and have better international exposure than their predecessors. These shifting trends also occurred against a backdrop of government austerity and shifting fiscal spaces, thereby providing opportunities for new philanthropic approaches to emerge (Sciortino, 2017a). Venture philanthropy thus appeared to fill these gaps. As a matter of definition, practitioner circles have used "venture philanthropy" interchangeably with other terms such as "social venture capital" or "high engagement philanthropy" (Scarlata & Alemany, 2008). It is not the objective of this book chapter to debate the nuances between the terms, given that all of them have conceptual similarities.

In venture philanthropy, approaches such as providing long-term funding, tailored financing, organisational capacity building, developing long-term relationships, and instituting organisational performance measures were meant to support non-profit organisations to build long-term strategic and operational capacity, with financial sustainability in mind (Pepin, 2005; Buckland et al, 2013). These approaches incorporated were typically used by venture capitalists, and were more management intensive, performance-seeking, and more willing to make high-risk but also high-impact bets (Scaife, 2008). Essentially, venture philanthropists are looking not to be just passive funders, but value-adding and high engagement funders beyond the provision of grants (Scarlata & Alemany, 2010). Some of the more common capacity building activities offered by venture philanthropists include providing networking opportunities, mentoring, refining financial and operational processes, enhancing fundraising strategies and consulting for strategic development (AVPN & Ernst & Young, 2019). In addition, the deal origination, screening, and post-funding management processes of venture philanthropists were also found to bear similar resemblance to that utilised by venture capitalists (Gordon, 2014). For example, venture philanthropists could proactively outreach to high potential ideas, co-create social innovation ideas prior to and after the deployment of funding. Not all venture philanthropists would however have similar modus operandi, and venture philanthropists can lie on a spectrum of how much of these venture capitalist values they espouse they espouse (Scarlata & Alemany, 2008):

Table 1. Categories of Venture Philanthropists (Scarlata & Alemany, 2008)

Venture-Generated Philanthropic Funds	• Philanthropic funds contributed from successful venture capital investments • Such philanthropic funds can exist independently from its parent venture capital fund, and may or may not incorporate venture capital principles in its disbursement of funds
Venture-Influenced Philanthropic Funds	• Reflects some of the principles of venture capitalists, such as risk-taking, emphasis on performance outcomes and more stringent due diligence processes • However, these funds may not have the in-house management expertise to engage in more intensive capacity building of its grantees or investees
Venture-Parallel Philanthropic Funds	• Philanthropic funds whose approaches most closely mirrors those of venture capitalists • Key distinguishing factor is the high engagement levels with grantees or investees

The development of this new concept though, was not without resistance. Some thought that this represented the blurring of boundaries between business and philanthropy, with non-profit organisations having to adopt business-like practices, or a clash of cultures between traditional non-profit organisations and that of venture capitalists (Moody, 2008). Other concerns also involve how the traditional role of government in providing public goods could be subverted by the increasing presence of the private sector and philanthropy (Rowe, 2023b). Nevertheless, employing venture capital approaches to philanthropy have been found to contribute to higher levels of innovation and technological development, formation of strategic partnerships, multi-stakeholder initiatives, and policy advocacy (Kortum & Lerner, 1998; Shaw et al., 2021).

Venture philanthropists can look to fund organisations that have innovative and untested solutions with a high growth potential or a track record of growth. To further maintain growth trajectories, besides financial capital, they are willing to provide strategic and operational expertise and social capital (Hafenmayer, 2013). In this model shift, researchers have also highlighted how semantics have changed, as venture philanthropists redefine existing terms such as referring to 'grantees' as 'investees, such as referring to "grantees" as "investees" or "non-profit leader" as "social entrepreneurs" (Martin & Rob, 2006). Further details of typical practices in venture philanthropy are provided in the table below (John, 2006; EVPA, 2018).

Table 2. Core Features of Venture Philanthropy

Core Feature	Description
High Engagement	Venture philanthropy entails high levels of mutual engagement between the philanthropist, and the receiving organisation, whether non-profit organisations or social enterprises. This contrasts against this contrasts against more passive philanthropic approaches which have been coined "armchair philanthropy" or "chequebook giving" (Scaife, 2008). Examples of engagement could be board-level appointments by the venture philanthropist to guide in strategic decision making, or participating in the day-to-day operations. In essence, venture philanthropists are more inclined to engage with their funded organisations as compared to more passive philanthropic models.. In some instances, venture philanthropists can also engage with organisations to co-create solutions (Gordon, 2014).
Multi-Year Support	Funding is provided over longer periods of time, often with increasingly challenging performance targets or outcomes to unlock subsequent tranches of funding. The design of this funding is intended to incentivise organisations for growth and to scale their impact. Venture philanthropists could financially-back their funded organisations across multiple phases of growth, such as such as during the initial pilot phase, scale proven interventions, scale proven interventions, to the eventual organisation maturity and achievement of financial and impact sustainability (Grossman et al., 2013)
Tailored Financing	Where non-returnable grants have been the financial instrument of choice for traditional philanthropists, venture philanthropists are more inclined to use a variety of financial instruments, such as loans, mezzanine, or quasi-equity instruments (Scarlata & Alemany, 2010). Instruments that also provide a financial return alongside social returns could be more often used in financing for social enterprises, whereby the venture philanthropists are looking to achieve some nominal financial returns. This allows the venture philanthropist to recycle capital back into new funding opportunities.
Organisational Capacity Building and Non-Financial Support	Venture philanthropists look to build organisational capacity of their funded organisations, with the understanding that organisation capacity and management teams are important precursors for scaling impact (Grossman et al., 2013). This model of capacity building is similar to that employed by venture capitalists, where capacity gaps within the organisation are identified, and the venture philanthropist participates in closing those gaps, such as through strategic hiring or bringing in external consultants. Other areas of support could be in providing access to new networks of funders, executive coaching, marketing and communications and strategic planning. For early-stage companies, capacity building could also involve basic levels of professionalisation, such as development of a business concept, vision, mission and value statements (Ingstad et al., 2014).
Performance Measurement	Measuring performance and outcomes is a key feature in venture philanthropy, as organisations could be set programme and organisation-level targets to achieve. The targets could also be linked to funding disbursements, where funds are disbursed upon achievement of pre-agreed targets.The setting of targets could also enhance accountability, and nudge the organisation's management to acquire new capabilities that would help with achieving the performance targets.

With the above principles in mind, new venture philanthropy funds were started and embedded these principles in their operations, capital deployment strategies and engagements with funded organisations. A point to note is that venture philanthropists do not only actively engage with their funded companies, and can also be involved in building networks, and breaking down existing operating silos between organisations (Pepin, 2005). It is with the development of these strategic networks that venture philanthropists can help illuminate pathways to new opportunities. The supposed benefits of venture philanthropy are not only aspirational or hypothetical on the part of venture philanthropists, and recipients of such funding and capacity building approaches have clearly espoused the complementary skills of venture philanthropists (Ingstad et al., 2014). For example, Ingstand et al's (2014) research on social entrepreneurs receiving philanthropic venture capital found that some social entrepreneurs valued the advice and guidance at least as important as funding, while also being able to tap on the business experience of funders.

The table below illustrates some of these venture philanthropy funds that were incorporated following the initial years of the conceptualisation of venture philanthropy (Community Wealth Ventures, Inc., 2002). The examples selected are intended to portray the diversity of venture philanthropy approaches, such as the type of organisations being funded, and the various financial instruments that can be utilised to deploy the funding. However, certain key features in the venture capitalist approach are highly evident.

Table 3. Examples of Venture Philanthropy Funds (Community Wealth Ventures, Inc., 2002)

Fund Name	New Profit Inc	New Schools Venture Fund	The Roberts Enterprise Development Fund
Date of Fund Incorporation	1998	1997	1997
Fund Description	Venture capital fund for the nonprofit sector, with the objective of investing in and partnering with innovative, high-performing nonprofit organisations. The fund supports social entrepreneurs to scale their organisations by providing performance-based growth capital, along with management support, network access, strategy consulting and growth planning.	Nonprofit fund harnessing the power of entrepreneurs to improve public education in America. The fund aims to combine the intellectual strength of a think tank with the action-oriented nature of a venture capital fund. At the core of the fund's beliefs are that social entrepreneurs can have a direct and catalytic effect on improving the public education system.	The fund is intended to raise standards of excellence in nonprofit and philanthropic communities. Utilises a social venture capital approach, such as building capacity of nonprofit organisations, and bringing social-purpose organisations to market for financial sustainability.
Funding Approach	Mainly deploys financial capital as grants that have slightly differentiated purposes. Provides an initial nonperformance-based grant with incentive capacity building support with the objective of developing organisation strategic plans. This follows with subsequent multi-year, larger quantum performance-based grant funding to support organisational growth.	Through a rigorous due diligence process, aims to uncover the potential of entrepreneurial teams or ventures that: ● Can be scaled to impact thousands of students ● Have sound revenue models or alternative funding plans ● Have expertise in education and business management Utilises a variety of financing instruments such as grants, loans and equity investments.	Evaluates funding opportunities based on the following: ● The integration of the organisation's social purpose and mission into its organisational strategy ● Quality of its operating systems, business and social impact plans ● Ability of the organisation to benefit from the fund's capacity building and other non-financial support Primarily disburses funding via grants.

continued on following page

Table 3. Continued

Fund Name	New Profit Inc	New Schools Venture Fund	The Roberts Enterprise Development Fund
Length of Funding Relationships	Estimated at 4 to 5 years.	Does not have a specified tenure, but expects multi-year relationships with funded organisations.	Funding is designed to be long-term, with some relationships stretching to over 10 years. The fund is acceptable to continuing funding relationships, as long as enterprises require funding and that financial and social outcomes in business plans are met.
Exit Strategy	The fund's exit will be dependent on the funded organisation building capacities in the following areas: ● Developing networks to access new sources of growth capital ● Developing effective board-level leadership ● Building organisational capacity in performance measurement, fundraising strategies and infrastructure ● Developing new sources of revenue ● Building of organisational brands	No explicit conditions that trigger an exit, but plans for exits via capacity building, developing revenue and fundraising plans, and setting organisations on growth trajectories.	Conditional on enterprises being able to generate significant amounts of net income over time, and demonstrating that they are able to financially sustain their continued growth.

As highlighted in the table above, the financing instruments used can range from grants, to loan or quasi-equity instruments that provide funders with some level of financial and impact returns (Martin, 2007). In academic or practitioner fields, impact investing and strategic philanthropy could also have similar definitions and forms as venture philanthropy given that these approaches focus on engaging with funded companies, increasing the scale of impact, establishing accountability and measures of performance (Agrawal & Hockerts, 2021; Shaw et al., 2021). In other instances, venture philanthropists could also express their identities differently, whether with a priority on social welfare issues, or to adopt a more commercially-driven approach (Onishi, 2019). For the purpose of this book chapter, we do not attempt to differentiate these approaches; however, use venture philanthropy as the reference point while acknowledging that it could be synonymous with impact investing and strategic philanthropy.

Also, venture philanthropy can also be a flexible financing approach applied to a wide range of organisations. Across the spectrum of socially-motivated organisations are non-profit organisations, to social enterprises and socially-driven businesses, all of which could be recipients of venture philanthropy or impact-oriented financing (Roundy et al., 2017).

Figure 1. Spectrum of Financing Approaches

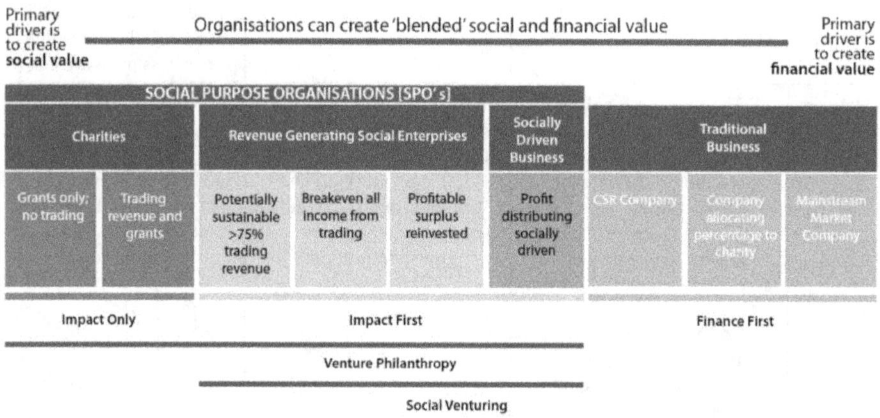

Source: EVPA, 2010

Some studies have suggested that venture philanthropists were more likely to use commercial financing instruments, when the funded organisations demonstrated greater income-generation potential, thus providing the venture philanthropist with exit opportunities or potential to participate in financial upside (Spiess-Knafl & Aschari-Lincoln, 2015). The objective of financial returns or exit opportunities can stem from the desire to recycle capital or in the case of having some financial returns, to also look to grow the philanthropists' ability to make increasing venture philanthropic contributions over time.

In reality, the landscape for financing instruments and financing targets can be complex, with funders utilising a variety of instruments according to their motivation and priorities for financial and impact returns, while funding a range of social-purpose organisations, all at different positions of the continuum between business and impact (Roundy et al., 2017). We attempt to illustrate a simplified landscape of financing instruments and funding targets in the table (EVPA, 2010; World Economic Forum, 2015).

Table 4. Organisation Type and Funding Approaches

	Funding Targets		
	Non-Profit Organisation	**Hybrid (Social Enterprises)**	**Corporation / Inclusive Business**
Organisation Profile	Usually non-profit organisations that prioritise impact	Hybrid type organisations that attempt to maximise across the business and impact domains	Primarily for-profit businesses, but are also explicit in creating value for all stakeholders, and contributing to sustainable development (Schaltegger et al., 2019)
Type of Instruments	● Non-recoverable grants	● Convertible grants ● Convertible loans ● Loans with concessionary interest rates ● Equity	● Convertible loan ● Loans with concessionary interest rates (contingent on impact outcomes) ● Equity
Description	No repayment expected, and used for funding targets that are in the early-stage, with little cash flow, business or impact visibility	Typically lower-cost financing, but with also mechanisms to allow for funders to participate in financial upside via conversion to equity	While some of the instruments can be in similar form to that deployed for hybrid-type organisations, the mechanisms could provide for more financial returns to the investors

(Source: EVPA, 2010; World Economic Forum, 2015)

Other models have also attempted to illustrate how venture philanthropists can participate in various stages of an impact-oriented organisation depending on its funding objectives and risk appetite (Grossman et al., 2013). The model demonstrates how different types of funding, provided at various stages of the organisation, can have objectives that guide the organisation on a growth trajectory towards long-term sustainability.

Figure 2. Funding Approaches with Organisational Growth

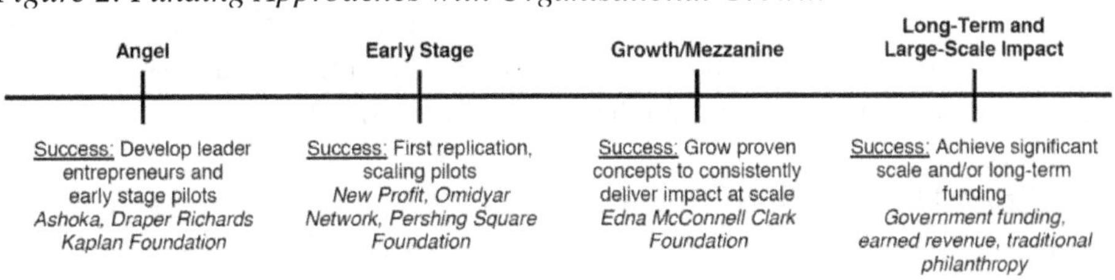

Conceptually, the concept of venture philanthropy is highly appealing, given the emphasis on building long-term organisational capacity, infrastructure, skills and networks and it is with these capacities that non-profit organisations are better to create longer-term and more sustainable impact (Katz, 2005). Though it is not to say that venture philanthropy would eventually displace traditional forms of philanthropy, given that philanthropy is a culmination of individual preference, culture, legal and economic conditions and it is likely that diverse approaches to philanthropy would remain (Martin, 2007; Sciortino, 2017a).

Having provided an introduction to venture philanthropy, in the next section, we will cover the importance of venture philanthropy in catalysing the growth of impact enterprises.

2. The Role and Importance of Venture Philanthropy

The concept of philanthropy, as demonstrated above, is not limited to just reconfiguring traditional philanthropy and non-profit organisations but can be applied to a wide range of contexts as will be explored further in this section.

2.1 Venture Philanthropy and Entrepreneurship

The intersection between sustainable development, and entrepreneurship, collectively defined as sustainability entrepreneurship, has been recognised for its ability to contribute to sustainable development, given its potential for creative destruction and addressing market failures around social and environmental issues (Hall et al., 2010). Entrepreneurship, new venture development, and social entrepreneurship provides for the simultaneous contribution to economic and social progress, where any intervention for poverty alleviation needs to be sustained beyond just the provision of basic human needs which is in the traditional realm of non-profit organisations (Dees, 2008). Building new enterprises that solve sustainability issues can also be an attractive proposition, as attempting to re-orient existing businesses towards sustainability can be challenging due to the trade-offs it faces in doing so (Schaltegger et al., 2019). Often, building impact-oriented enterprises would require new and unconventional entrepreneurial approaches across the entire value chain, such as product design, manufacturing, and distribution (Larsson, 2000).

Case Brief: How Venture Philanthropy and Social Enterprises Alleviate Social Issues (Di Lorenzo & Scarlata, 2019)

Using a difference-in-difference research method, researchers examined if social enterprises that receive venture philanthropy funding contributed to alleviating income inequality in their location of operations in India between the periods of 1987 and 2004. The researchers used data from Ashoka Foundation, which is an active investor of early-stage impact enterprises across various geographical regions. Ashoka Foundation is known to utilise principles of venture philanthro-

py, such as capacity building of funded ventures, employing unique financing instruments, and connecting funded organisations with its network of investors, specialists and consultants.

In this study, the difference-in-difference method utilised by the researchers attempted to isolate the contributions of Ashoka-funded social enterprises, by comparing Indian municipalities which had at least one Ashoka-funded social enterprise against municipalities whereby the group of social enterprises did not operate in.

With income inequality as the dependent variable, the research found that municipalities with venture philanthropy-funded social enterprises experienced a decrease in income inequality levels. In addition, these municipalities experienced higher rates of decline in income inequality, compared to municipalities without venture philanthropy-funded social enterprises. While there are limitations addressed by the researchers, such as reliance only on data of social enterprises funded by Ashoka, or country-specific contexts, there is some indication on how the intersection between venture philanthropy and social entrepreneurship can contribute to economic and social progress.

Unconventional entrepreneurs require unconventional financing; therefore, within the context of building early-stage impact enterprises, venture philanthropy plays a critical role. Resource-constrained entrepreneurs can only stand to benefit from the in-house business and management expertise accumulated by venture philanthropic organisations (Ingstad et al., 2014). Venture philanthropy essentially bridges the traditionally separate realms of business and philanthropy with funders seeking a combination of financial and impact returns (Dees, 2008). This funding approach is highly synergistic with the concept of impact enterprises due to their dual financial and impact objectives. Yet, there could still exist funding gaps within the context of youth entrepreneurship for sustainable development.

A 2018 survey of 207 youth entrepreneurs found that youth entrepreneurs face a lack of access to financing, and given their relatively lesser professional experience, also requires expert advice, capacity building and incubation to develop and scale their ideas (Amesheva et al., 2019). Financiers could also perceive younger entrepreneurs to be of higher risk, given their inexperience and lack of collateral and assets. Also, the pursuit of dual objectives could also be more resource-demanding, thus it can be expected that impact enterprises have a longer runway to profitability (Bull & Crompton, 2006). This means that early-stage impact enterprises face greater challenges in attempting to cross the "valley of death" compared to other startups (OECD, 2022). This longer runway to profitability and pursuit of other objectives could exclude them from the interests of commercial funders, thereby requiring financial support from other kinds of funders with more unique or dual interests (Agrawal & Hockerts, 2021). While these ventures are still in the early-stage, grants can be an important resource for them to firstly make the necessary investments to build organisational capacity, while also serving as a signal to future investors or stakeholders on their credibility (Lall & Park, 2022).

In a study of 7,358 social impact startups and 2,671 environmental impact startups participating in the Global Accelerator Learning Initiative during the periods between 2013 to 2019, Beyhan & Fındık (2022) found that startups with prior equity or philanthropic support were more likely to be selected by startup accelerators. In addition to the signalling and legitimacy effect of receiving early-stage funding, these enterprises were able to dedicate resources to test their business model, improve their products and validate product-market fit. These criteria around market validation, product value proposition, and growth potential have been found to be common evaluation criteria used by accelerators, regardless of whether these accelerators were commercially or impact focused (Butz & Mrożewski, 2021). Their selection into startup accelerators further strengthens their access to capital and other capacity building resources, setting them on pathways for growth. Importantly, these early-stage grants also provide them with the runway to execute on their business and impact plans, and eventually settle on the appropriate revenue and funding models that are aligned with their organisational needs (Searing et al., 2022). Following participation in impact-oriented accelerator programmes, these early-stage ventures were also more likely to secure external investments to resource their growth trajectory (Lall et al., 2020).

Overall, there is research to suggest the importance of early-stage venture philanthropic grant financing, that helps with plugging financing gaps while providing impact-oriented ventures with the resources they need for growth. As these enterprises grow, they then require new forms of funding. Impact-oriented venture capital is a common source of financing, whereas it bears similarities to venture capital in funding high-growth early-stage ventures, it is also inclined to back organisations that fulfil social and environmental needs. In addition to employing similar principles of venture philanthropy or venture capital, such as building capacity in investee companies, backing growth potential, and using innovative financing instruments, some impact-oriented venture capital could also be inclined to accept financial returns below the market rate of traditional venture capital (Scarlata & Alemany, 2010). These new sources of impact-oriented venture capital have also increased the availability of new sources of capital to impact enterprises, which were traditionally heavily reliant on traditional philanthropic sources or government financing (Thillai Rajan et al., 2014).

Case Brief: The Impact of Impact-Oriented Venture Capital (Croce et al., 2021)

A study was conducted on 92, impact-oriented venture capital funds (IOVCs), which were actively investing as of December 2018. The objective of the study was to identify trends and patterns that were evident in this new emerging field of venture philanthropy and impact finance at the international level, however of which no such study existed then.

At a descriptive level, these IOVCs were found to be interested in impact themes such as basic services (e.g. education, food and water), creating employment opportunities, contributing to climate change challenges, and improving people's access to microcredit and financing. While most of the IOVCs targeted market financial returns, a small minority appeared willing to accept lower financial returns as a trade-off for impact creation.

Researchers also examined the type of investee companies that these IOVCs were likely to invest in. The findings demonstrated that the IOVCs appeared to be less concerned with investee profitability during periods prior to the investment, if growth potential is apparent. Also, in time periods following investments by IOVCs, investee companies were also likely to show an increase in assets and revenue. On this note, it lends support to the notion that the capacity building efforts provided and utilised in venture philanthropy and venture capital approaches could produce tangible financial outcomes for their investee companies.

However, although there appears to be alignment between impact enterprises and venture philanthropy, this is not necessarily a seamless match, with some of the following challenges still being identified in these funding relationships (Magomedova & Bastida-Vialcanet, 2022; Arena et al., 2018).

Table 5. Common Challenges in Venture Philanthropy (Magomedova & Bastida-Vialcanet, 2022; Arena et al., 2018).

Funders' overreliance on commercial evaluation techniques for decision making	To reduce their financial risk exposure, financiers could rely too heavily on evaluation techniques and financial metrics that are more applicable for commercially-focused enterprises. Impact enterprises without a commercially competitive business model could be excluded from such financing markets.
Funders' exertion of control over the company	Venture philanthropists have a tendency to be involved in capacity building of funded companies, and in some instances could also have board-level representation. While this could overcome the lack of business competencies in funded companies, there is also the risk that funders' control becomes overbearing and resulting in organisational conflict.
Over-emphasis on commercial results	As some venture philanthropists or impact-oriented financiers could still expect some level of financial returns, the expression of these expectations on funded companies could result in decision-making tensions, and funded companies may be required to compromise on their social mission.
Lack of resources to measure performance	The low resource nature of early-stage companies could mean that initiatives to measure performance and outcomes are de-prioritised, instead prioritising activities that could have more immediate commercial pay-offs for the organisation's sustainability.
Impact enterprises face challenging economic and impact trade-offs	In a similar vein to the previous point, this recognises the challenges facing impact enterprises to make the right decisions, where there are economic or impact trade-offs. This challenge can be compounded further if the enterprise has multiple groups of stakeholders, all with differing objectives.

The above points attempt to summarise challenges faced by venture philanthropists and impact enterprises, despite the conceptual dovetailing. It is imperative that the providers and recipients of impact-oriented capital are aware of the various challenges in the funding relationship after capital has been deployed, or initiate conversations around some of these potential challenges even prior to any funding.

2.2 Venture Philanthropy and Systems Change

In addition to contributing to funding gaps, strategic venture philanthropy has the potential to catalyse systems change to solve complex issues (Kania et al., 2014). In this instance, venture philanthropy shares similar definitions with that of catalytic philanthropy, whereby philanthropy contributes to systems change beyond just contributing to solutions targeting specific social issues (Kramer, 2009). Such changes could influence how government policies and systems are shaped. Venture philanthropists with this modus operandi, can generally be categorised in the following table (Shaw et al., 2021).

Table 6. Types of Strategic Venture Philanthropists

Role	Policy Advocate	Convenor of Networks	Innovator
Objective	Philanthropists in this category have policy goals, and engage with policy makers with the objective of public policy reform	Creating shared objectives and priorities between ecosystem players, mitigating tensions between ecosystem players, identifying ecosystem gaps	Initiate innovation in service provision, whether as part of existing systems or new systems
Activities	● Identify gaps in existing policies, or identify potential for transformational shifts in policy ● Provide policy makers with information and data to enable policy change ● Develop partnerships with government or government service programmes	● Intermediary role between public and private sector actors ● Facilitating transmission of knowledge between ecosystem players ● Developing and strengthening relationships and the collective ecosystem ● Developing multi-stakeholder partnerships to utilise the various strengths of different types of ecosystem players	● Investing in new and innovative service delivery models ● Provision of early-stage risk capital to fund the development of new solutions ● Measuring impact of new solutions and demonstrating effectiveness with existing models ● Capacity building and scaling of new solutions whether through public or private revenue models
Expertise	Thorough understanding of policy, policy impacts, and policy cycles	Experts in convening and developing relationships, mediating tensions, building consensus	Understanding of social innovation, service design, impact evaluation, and public and private revenue models for sustainability

While the table attempts to profile or segment the different types of roles between venture philanthropic players, the reality is that venture philanthropists can play multiple roles, with varying levels of intensity. The various roles also reflect how venture philanthropists sit at the crucial intersection within public and private sector systems.

Philanthropic players that are involved in public advocacy can play various complementary or adversarial roles against existing government services (Sandfort, 2008). Complementary roles could see philanthropists contribute to either emerging or existing unmet needs, while adversarial roles involve philanthropists nudging government bodies to make changes to public policy. What is a common denominator in these different roles is in how philanthropic funding complements public funding. In some instances, philanthropic funding is also recognised to be more nimble in identifying and responding to emerging issues, and without the bureaucratic structures of government, can address these issues at a lower cost (Maclean et al., 2013).

As an illustration, the image below demonstrates how the different funding types have different objectives as responses to social issues are developed and mainstreamed.

Figure 3. Complementing Roles of Philanthropy and Public Financing (Sandfort, 2008)

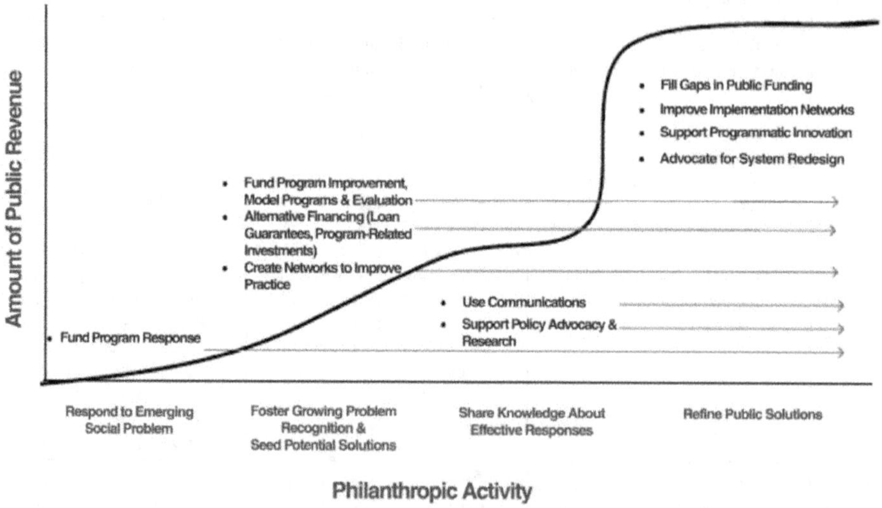

In the beginning, philanthropic capital is used to seed newly identified social issues, and to trial new solutions to improve practice. Also, philanthropic capital can supplement public financing deficits (Sandfort, 2008). A variety of financial instruments can be used, sometimes in complement with small amounts of public financing as a reflection of the government's interest. Gradually as new practices become mainstreamed, with effectiveness demonstrated, larger amounts of public financing can be deployed to scale the solution, while allowing the initial philanthropic organisation to exit. An example of how venture philanthropists can participate in identifying existing social issues, and elevating these issues for change at the policy level is illustrated in the case brief below.

Case Brief: Policy and Program Support for Public Education (Zeichner & Peña-Sandoval, 2015)

The New Schools Venture Fund (NSVF) was founded in 1998 by venture capitalists and social entrepreneurs with the objective of developing capacity for teachers. Its approach involves disrupting traditional models of teacher training, and focuses more on making teacher education more evidence-based, and equipping teachers to handle the practical challenges in the teaching process itself. In addition, accountability is also important as teachers are expected to be able to demonstrate that they can improve educational outcomes in students. These approaches were intended

Not content with making changes to the public education at the level of practice, staff from the NSVF, were also instrumental in contributing to legislation reform, to deregulate teacher training, thereby allowing for more innovative teacher capacity building methods to emerge. Consequently, in May 2023, the GREAT Act was introduced in both the Senate and House of Representatives in the 113th Congress. The objectives of the GREAT Act was intended to increase the rigour of teacher selection, implement hands-on training that would equip teachers to be highly effective, and require teachers to demonstrate their ability to improve students' educational outcomes.

Philanthropists also play the role of convener, given their neutral positioning within the private and public sector, thus being able to create the platform for debate and strategic partnerships (Shaw et al., 2021). Such cross-sector or multi-stakeholder strategic partnerships are also important, considering that social issues can be highly complex problems that linear cause-and-effect relationships and single stakeholder actions are unable to solve (Kania et al., 2014). Given its complexity, it can be expected that no single party would have the requisite capabilities and resources to solve social issues independently. Different parties, such as non-profit organisations, government bodies and the private sector, all with different capabilities therefore need to be brought together and aligned towards a common objective, highlighting the importance of a convening platform facilitated by venture philanthropists (Rowe, 2023b); Shaw et al 2021).

Case Brief: Convener of Networks (Rowe, 2023a)

Social Ventures Australia (SVA) is a venture philanthropy started in 2002, initiated by a prominent network of business consultancies and philanthropists. With a mandate to engage with governments and networks to influence change in policy and practice in the education sector, SVA has been able to advocate for systems-wide change and provide funding to network organisations all with the objective of influencing how systems operate.

As a matter of positioning with networks, SVA has been also noted to position at the intersection of government policy, philanthropy, private corporations, education research organisations and education institutions. Its hub-and-spoke positioning in this complex network of different entities has been identified as one of the reasons SVA has been able to create systems change, via the transferring of knowledge, shared values and economic benefits.

Venture philanthropists can also play the role of catalysing innovation, or more specifically social innovation. Some discourses see differences in definition within social entrepreneurship and social innovation, with social innovation being more agnostic to the forms of organisations that creates innovative services to meet a social need (Phillips et al., 2015). Social entrepreneurship has an inclination to achieve this social innovation through the use of a business vehicle or market-driven models, whereas social innovation could be more neutral to how the means are achieved, as long as it is achieved (Maclean et al., 2013). Nevertheless, both social innovation and social entrepreneurship share the same eventual objective of meeting social needs through innovation.

Despite its potential to contribute to social issues, there have been instances where social innovators have highlighted the insufficiency, or inability to readily access government financing for these solutions (Audretsch et al., 2022). Even where financing is available, the type of financing can be short-term or on a project-basis, rather than longer-term financing that allows the innovation to be scaled. As such, herein lies the opportunity for longer-term venture philanthropy to step in.

Case Brief: Social Innovation Supported by Venture Philanthropy (Onie et al., 2018)

Health Leads is a social enterprise with the objective of addressing the basic needs of patients, and mainstreaming this into the existing healthcare system. Over the course of the piloting and scaling of its social innovation, Health Leads received funding from venture philanthropic organisations such as New Profit and the Robert Wood Johnson Foundation.

Approximately at its time of inception in 1996, the US healthcare system was not designed to address the social needs of its patients, nor were frontline healthcare staff equipped to assess the social needs of patients. With venture philanthropy funding, Health Leads was able to develop and standardise its Health Leads model, whereby patients are screened for unmet social needs, gain professional support in resource information and how to access resources, with eventual follow-up to patients securing of resources.

As Health Leads scaled, it continued to receive financial backing from the Robert Wood Johnson Foundation, which provided multiple rounds of funding standardise and scale its solution and test new models for financial sustainability.

3. VENTURE PHILANTHROPY IN ASIA

In this next section, we provide some examples of the application of venture philanthropy in Asia across different contexts, such as social entrepreneurship, private-public partnerships, public-led and public-complement. These examples generally demonstrate the flexibility of the approach of venture philanthropy, however amidst this flexibility, at its core attempts to use capital to catalyse change. The focus on case studies is simultaneously a reflection of some of the challenges in philanthropy research. Firstly, the sensitive and personal nature of giving limits available data for large-scale empirical studies, and the diversity and lack of publicly available data across different Asian regions means that an aggregated comprehensive picture of venture philanthropy as a concept in Asia is challenging to obtain (Chia, 2015).

Countries in the Asia region are highly diverse, due to varying levels of development, roles of public authorities, religion and culture to name a few (Aggad, 2023). However, some perspectives see some commonalities in the traditional values in Asia countries, in espousing the "survival values" which prioritises economic security (Bidet & Defourny, 2019). This view sees that the state generally engages in policies that promote economic growth, with social policies subordinate to economic objectives (Holliday, 2000). In addition, Asian philanthropists are also more likely to take the cue from the government and support these government initiatives (Shapiro et al., 2018). Some of these state values or culture could eventually translate to the nature of social enterprises, in that social enterprises undertake activities that mirror these economic and social values, while simultaneoously functioning to serve gaps that emerge from government policies (Bidet & Defourny, 2019). For example, in a recent study by the British Council on the state of social enterprises in the ASEAN region, creating employment opportunities was a common dominant impact theme amongst social enterprises in a number of countries (British Council, 2021). This might suggest that the objectives of social enterprises reflect the "survival values" and seek to provide economic security to marginalised groups who are otherwise unable to do so. In some instances, employment opportunities provided by social enterprises have also been found to be more resilient compared to traditional enterprises, possibly due to more worker-focused approaches in management practices (OECD, 2022). Other forms of social social enterprises could operate within rural and urban settings, either fulfilling specific product or service gaps in underserved markets or bridging the rural-urban product markets. Examples of typologies of some of these social enterprises are in the table below:

Table 7. Typology of Impact Enterprises in Rural-Urban Contexts (Thillai Rajan et al., 2014)

Typology	Description
Rural-to-Rural	• Enterprises who source for inputs from non-urban and rural areas and whose primary customers are also within these non-urban and rural areas • Such enterprises could be set up to fulfil product or service supply-demand opportunity in these non-urban and rural contexts • Income opportunity limited to the purchasing power of non-urban and rural populations
Urban-to-Rural	• Companies who source inputs from urban areas, but serves customers in non-urban areas • Examples of such businesses would be microfinance
Rural-to-Urban	• Companies that source inputs from rural areas, and selling these products and services to customers in urban areas • One of the more well-perceived business models, due to the income opportunities it provides to the rural population
Urban-to-Urban	• Models that could still fulfil underserved needs in urban populations, such as healthcare and education • While it does not have the sort of income transfer to urban populations, still possible to create social impact, given that urban populations could still be underserved in some areas

Although the benefits of youth and social entrepreneurship are apparent, early-stage impact enterprises in the Asia Pacific still face clear funding gaps, as a majority of these impact enterprises either rely on initial family and friends funding, or government grants and programme-related funding (Guelich & Bosma, 2018). Consequently, these funding gaps could limit either the employment or entrepreneurship opportunities for some segments of the population in the Asia region, such as youths, in attempting to extricate themselves from structural issues such as lack of access to education, political instability and conflict, and government failure to adequately provide basic services. Against this backdrop, there are some signs that impact-oriented capital has identified and started entering the region as demonstrated by the table below (Prasad et al., 2020). The total amount of capital deployed by development finance institutions and private impact financiers into impact enterprises totalled USD6.7 billion between 2017 and 2019, almost 60% of the total funding deployed compared to the preceding 10-year period from 2017 to 2016. Also, the number of deals for the 2017 to 2019 period amounted to almost 70% of the total deals in the preceding 10-year period. However, the financing was still largely driven by development finance institutions, suggesting the opportunity for more private impact financiers to plug this funding gap (Prasad et al., 2020).

Table 8. Impact-Oriented Capital Deployments (2007 to 2019)

	Capital Deployed (USD Billion)				Number of Deals			
	2007 to 2016	**2017**	**2018**	**2019**	**2007 to 2016**	**2017**	**2018**	**2019**
Total	11.3	1.7	2.6	2.4	449	115	91	92

Source: Prasad et al., 2020

To catalyse the entry of new capital to finance impact opportunities, many governments in Asia are attempting to fill this financing gap, with governments from Singapore, Hong Kong, South Korea, India, Malaysia, Taiwan and Indonesia having established impact-oriented financing to enable the creation of social enterprises (Shapiro et al., 2018). In addition to financing, these funds also utilise principles of venture capital, and are involved in the capacity building such as building networks, mentoring and incubation activities.

The following case brief below demonstrates an example of private-public collaboration in impact-oriented financing. While the Indonesian Impact Alliance collaboration is still in its nascent years, having only started in 2023, and thus its efficacy is unknown, it does demonstrate opportunities in how different stakeholders can collaborate to tackle funding gaps for early-stage impact enterprises.

Case Brief: Public-Private Collaboration for Catalysing Innovative Impact Financing (Jasonson & Sklair, 2024)

The Indonesian Impact Alliance is a collaboration formed in May 2023, with support from the Indonesian Government, United Nations Development Programme, Ford Foundation, and several other social enterprises and impact financiers. The objective of this multi-stakeholder collaboration was to help with the development of impact financing in Indonesia to support the impact entrepreneurship ecosystem.

The Alliance will use innovative financing mechanisms such as blended finance, that would simultaneously address funding gaps for early-stage impact enterprises, and catalyse new private capital into the sector via de-risking mechanisms. The Alliance also intends to contribute to the development of a supportive regulatory landscape for impact capital.

In other instances, the government could also take a more prominent role in leading venture philanthropic efforts to catalyse new grassroots social innovation, or in plugging financing gaps. In the following case brief below, government-initiated venture philanthropy could catalyse new social finance markets for socially valuable initiatives, and depending on the context, could be government-led or government-initiated with follow-on support from the private sector. Also, both case briefs demonstrate the importance of understanding where existing funding gaps are, and how various players can participate in closing these funding gaps, through the use of innovative financing instruments (Spiess-Knafl & Aschari-Lincoln, 2015).

While this model of venture philanthropy differs from the initial conceptualisations from Western economies that venture philanthropy is a private sector-led endeavour (Rowe, 2023a), it still provides an example of how venture philanthropic capital, whether provided for by private or public entities, can be catalysts for social innovation (Jing & Gong, 2012; Yoon & Lee, 2020). However, where venture philanthropy is government-led or initiated, care needs to be taken to avoid the crowding out effect, where excessive government involvement limits the ability of social innovation to serve actual needs on the ground, and instead organisations seek funding according to the government's pre-determined funding criteria (Li, 2018).

Case Brief: Government-Initiated Social Financing (Korea Social Value and Solidarity Foundation Annual Report, 2022; Yoon & Lee, 2020)

The Korea Social Value and Solidarity Foundation ("SVS") was a measure introduced by the Korean government in 2019, to catalyse the development of a social finance market, which would in turn contribute to the financing of socially innovative projects and enterprises. The SVS incorporates venture philanthropy principles, such as using innovative financing instruments, and providing capacity for funded companies. The funded companies collectively have a broad range of impact areas, such as social housing, education, elderly care, social innovation and financial inclusion.

While the SVS was initiated by the government, over time, it has garnered the support of other players in the private sector, with the SVS playing the role of wholesale funding allocation to other social finance intermediaries, which have the primary responsibility of originating and executing funding for social economy organisations. The SVS also has diverse financial and social return objectives, depending on the nature of the companies being funded, and can target market rate financial returns, capital recovery, or at risk of loss.

Other venture philanthropy concepts emerged with the objective of solving longer-term structural societal issues which could have longer-term drag on economic and societal potential.

Case Brief: Medium to Long-Term Financing for Social Impact (Aggad, 2023; Chia, 2015)

The Japan Venture Philanthropy Fund ("JVPF") was the first venture philanthropy fund in Japan, and was jointly formed by the Nippon Foundation and Social Investment Partners. Incorporating the principles of venture capital, the JVPF would provide tailored financing using a variety of financing instruments such as grants, loans and equity, help investee companies build long-term business and financing plans, and continuously engage with investee companies to provide long-term management support.

Prior to funding, Social Investment Partners would conduct rigorous due diligence on potential funding targets, co-create business plans, define KPIs and impact targets. This process is also expected to require significant investment of resources by potential investees. However, if potential investees are successful in this process, they can expect to receive an optimal funding plan that suits the need of the business, and the availability of unrestricted funding to achieve multi-year objectives.

In addition, the impact mandate of the JVPF is clear, with the objective of contributing to structural social issues such as inequality in educational opportunity, declining birth rates and consequently a declining participating workforce, and enhancing the resilience of communities.

In other instances, the private sector can also proactively pursue impact-financing or impact-oriented opportunities, without any prompts or leadership by the government. The positive outcome of private sector participation is that high potential impact enterprises are limited to, or heavily reliant on government funding and political cycles (Bull & Crompton, 2006; Wong & Yap, 2019).

Case Brief: Private Sector-Driven Impact Enterprises (Radclyffe-Thomas, 2015; Wong & Yap, 2019)

SOW Asia was founded by a former investment banker in 2009, with the objective of being a trusted partner and investor for social-impact organisations to scale in Hong Kong and throughout Asia. SOW Asia's accelerator, Hong Kong's first accelerator program exclusively for social enterprises, would accelerate the business model of social enterprises to progress beyond prototypes and market trials, such that these social enterprises would be ready to receive investment and scale.

An example of an investee company is Bonham Strand Tailors ("BST"), a bespoke commercial tailor entity founded in 2012. The mission of BST was to preserve the culture of western suit tailoring in Hong Kong, while providing a dignified livelihood for displaced old tailors who are facing increasing business costs. To mitigate risk, BSR operated on an asset-pooling model, whereby experienced tailors are aggregated within the same location, and had access to a common pool of resources such as machinery, equipment and profit pool.

While BST had a social mission, it was also a for-profit entity, where products were charged at market rate, to maximise financial sustainability, earnings for its tailors and financial returns for its investors. Brand and identity development, such as partnering with European fabric houses, helped to built loyalty and profile amongst its customers, rather than relying on a 'guilt' or 'empathy' premium. SOW Asia was involved in the early scale-up phase of the business, having deployed its investment in 2013 and exiting in 2016.

Venture philanthropy can also directly fill gaps in existing public services, especially where there could be limitations on public financing. This model sees venture philanthropy as a partner to the government, in funding demonstration projects, using funding leverage to change existing behaviours and attitudes, and prompting experimentation and innovation (Knott & McCarthy, 2007).

Case Brief: Venture Philanthropy and Education in India (Sahasranamam & Mitra, 2019)

The Faizal and Shabana Foundation was set up in 2007, with the objective of uplifting the lives of the underprivileged in society. The Government of India's efforts to formalise education for all has seen some successes, with over 200 million children provided with access to education; however, there were still challenges facing the education system. While enrollment in primary education was high, there were considerable drop-out rates as children progressed to secondary school, while other structural issues such as teacher absenteeism, and physical infrastructure in schools were less than desirable.

Given the foundation's objectives, the founder Faizal Kottikollom considered how the foundation can play in contributing to these gaps in the education system. Considering between the traditional philanthropic model and the venture philanthropy model, a choice was made to utilise the more professional approach offered by the venture philanthropy model. This choice culminated in the project named "Promoting Regional Schools to International Standards through Multiple Interventions" (PRISM).

The first phase of the project involved infrastructure development, with donations of physical IT equipment, and development of other physical infrastructure such as physical exercise facilities, canteens and science laboratories. Following this first phase, education curriculum issues were addressed, and capacity building for teachers were conducted.

Similar to performance measurement features in the venture philanthropy model, tangible impact measurement outcomes were also instituted. Short-term goals included academic achievement of students, while longer-term goals included having students progress to professional courses.

To contribute to financial sustainability, the school's kitchen, which was equipped by the foundation with state-of-the-art facilities, would engage in commercial food catering and sales in its spare capacity to generate revenues. Finally, the foundation planned an exit strategy whereby it would maintain the school's infrastructure for a 5-year period, following which key responsibilities would be maintained by the PRISM committee and schools' management.

Venture philanthropy may not be limited to foundations, as private corporations can also perform venture philanthropic roles, as an extension of its broader corporate bottom-of-pyramid strategies to achieve both financial and social outcomes. This approach recognises that corporate venture philanthropy can serve as a competitive advantage (Simon, 1995). As demonstrated in the brief below, corporate venture philanthropy can be undertaken to propagate solutions that are aligned with the corporates' business strategy, thus being able to utilise existing corporate capabilities. This form of corporate philanthropy also represents a gradual shift in traditional forms of corporate social responsibility, towards more strategic approaches, which could be more focused and connected to its core businesses (John et al., 2017). In addition, benefits do not solely accrue to the investee companies, as the corporation is able to benefit in numerous non-financial ways, such as the development of new business opportunities.

Case Brief: Corporate Venture Philanthropy (Leborgne□Bonassié et al., 2019)

Danone Group SA (Danone) is a prominent global food processing company with a multitude of products in dairy, nutrition, and medical nutrition products. In 2005, Danone collaborated with Nobel Peace Prize winner, Muhammad Yunus to establish Grameen Danone Foods in Bangladesh. While the initial intention was to develop nutrient-rich food products that were affordable and nutritious, as a way to reduce malnutrition amongst communities in Bangladesh. Following the initial success of this endeavour, Danone created an impact-focused investment fund, Danone.communities, with the objective of providing early stage venture philanthropic capital to social enterprises that are aligned with Danone's core business.

In line with the approaches of venture philanthropy, Danone.communities' objective was to provide support to inclusive business solutions with clear business and impact value propositions, enable impact-motivated entrepreneurs, while also using its corporate expertise and network to build capacity in these early-stage ventures. For some of its investee companies, Danone provided capacity building in the form of product development, operations and marketing.

In all, examples of Danone.communities' funded social enterprises include businesses that provided safe drinking water to communities in Cambodia, increasing supply of locally-produced milk in Senegal, improving nutrition for low-income families in France, providing access to drinking water for communities in Mexico, and tackling child malnutrition in China.

The benefits did not solely accrue to the investee companies, as Danone also generated non-financial returns for itself, such as new market knowledge, innovation ideas, higher levels of employee engagement and a better market reputation.

As a matter of definition, corporate philanthropy can have complex relationships with the business itself (Sciortino, 2017b). As Sciortino (2017b) demonstrates, philanthropic and corporate business units can exist on a continuum of either complete integration or separation. Along this continuum, philanthropic units could share or distinguish its branding, funding, management and contributions from the business units. The next example demonstrates how different choices of philanthropic activities can exist within the same corporate context.

Case Brief: Different Forms of Corporate Philanthropy (John et al., 2017)

The Singtel group is one of Singapore's largest telecommunications conglomerate, and through its regional expansion strategy, also owns stakes in regional operators in markets such as Australia and India.

As part of its corporate philanthropy efforts, the Singtel Touching Lives Fund ("STLF") raises funds for charities helping the less privileged children and youths in Singapore since its inception in 2002. In addition to paying for the fundraising costs for these charities, Singtel also matches employee contributions to the STLF dollar for dollar.

As a demonstration of the progression of its corporate philanthropy efforts, Singtel launched the Singtel Future Makers program in 2016, with the objective of building capacity and scaling social impact start-ups. The program is a 6-month long accelerator program for social enterprises, startups or non-profit organisations that leverage innovative or technological solutions to solve social problems. The accelerator program culminates in a demo day pitch, and start-ups can expect to receive some grant funding. Beyond this grant funding, program participants can also receive mentorship, access to customer base or continued business relationships with the Singtel group.

Overall, this section provides examples of how venture philanthropy can be provided for in multiple contexts, such as public-private collaborations, public-led or public-complement, and privately-led. The selection of examples is intended to demonstrate the flexibility of the application of venture philanthropy, and how it can be deployed depending on each individual country's social and economic contexts.

4. CONCLUSION

This chapter started with a brief narrative on the origins of and key features of venture philanthropy, and how the concept of venture philanthropy attempts to break away from traditional models of philanthropy. Venture philanthropy can be a diverse concept, comprising different funders' objectives, target organisations to fund, and financial instruments used. It can also overlap with other concepts such as impact finance. The objective of this book chapter is not to differentiate the concepts, considering that both approaches actively engage with funded companies to build capacities with the ultimate goal of scaling up socially and environmentally beneficial solutions.

Venture philanthropy also plays important roles in plugging funding gaps for entrepreneurship for sustainable development, and catalysing systems change. Venture philanthropists, through their funding and offering of capacity building, can contribute to policy change, convene networks and mediate tensions between multiple stakeholder groups, or prompt new social innovation. Within the Asia context, the concept of venture philanthropy has been utilised in many settings in the public, private, and cross sector collaboration.

Overall, the potential for venture philanthropy is undeniable. For aspiring venture philanthropists, this chapter aims to provide insights on developing your funding strategy and variation of approaches you can undertake. For academic researchers, this chapter may prompt new research ideas in areas such as the role and importance of venture philanthropy in sustainable development.

5. REFERENCES

Aggad, F. (2023). Comparative multilateral philanthropy: The cases of the European Union Commission and the Asian Development Bank on crisis and non-crisis philanthropic engagements. In Moyo, B., Qobo, M., & Ngwenya, N. (Eds.), *African Philanthropy* (pp. 104–122). Edward Elgar Publishing., DOI: 10.4337/9781803927879.00013

Agrawal, A., & Hockerts, K. (2021). Impact investing: Review and research agenda. *Journal of Small Business and Entrepreneurship*, 33(2), 153–181. DOI: 10.1080/08276331.2018.1551457

Arena, M., Bengo, I., Calderini, M., & Chiodo, V. (2018). Unlocking finance for social tech start-ups: Is there a new opportunity space? *Technological Forecasting and Social Change*, 127, 154–165. DOI: 10.1016/j.techfore.2017.05.035

Audretsch, D. B., Eichler, G. M., & Schwarz, E. J. (2022). Emerging needs of social innovators and social innovation ecosystems. *The International Entrepreneurship and Management Journal*, 18(1), 217–254. DOI: 10.1007/s11365-021-00789-9

AVPN & Ernst & Young (2019). Exploring the Venture Philanthropy Ecosystem in India. An Asian Venture Philanthropy Network and Ernst & Young Joint Publication.

Beyhan, B., & Fındık, D. (2022). Selection of Sustainability Startups for Acceleration: How Prior Access to Financing and Team Features Influence Accelerators' Selection Decisions. *Sustainability (Basel)*, 14(4), 2125. DOI: 10.3390/su14042125

Bidet, E., & Defourny, J. (2019). *Social Enterprise in Asia: Theory, Models and Practice* (1st ed.). Routledge., DOI: 10.4324/9780429265761

British Council (2021). The State of Social Enterprise in South East Asia.

Buckland, L., Hehenberger, L., & Hay, M. (2013). The Growth of European Venture Philanthropy. Stanford Social Innovation Review Summer 2013.

Bull, M., & Crompton, H. (2006). Business practices in social enterprises. *Social Enterprise Journal*, 2(1), 42–60. DOI: 10.1108/17508610680000712

Butz, H., & Mrożewski, M. J. (2021). The Selection Process and Criteria of Impact Accelerators. An Exploratory Study. *Sustainability (Basel)*, 13(12), 6617. DOI: 10.3390/su13126617

Chia, A. (2015). *Potential and Prospects for Philanthropy in Implementing Post-2015 Development Goals*. ADB Sustainable Development Working Paper Series. No. 38 April 2015.

Community Wealth Ventures, Inc. (2002). *Venture Philanthropy 2002*. Advancing Nonprofit Performance Through High-Engagement Grantmaking. Copyright by Venture Philanthropy Partners, Inc.

Croce, A., Ughetto, E., Scellato, G., & Fontana, F. (2021). Social impact venture capital investing: An explorative study. *Venture Capital*, 23(4), 345–369. DOI: 10.1080/13691066.2021.1982069

Dees, J. G. (2008). Philanthropy and Enterprise: Harnessing the Power of Business and Social Entrepreneurship for Development. *Innovations: Technology, Governance, Globalization*, 3(3), 119–132. DOI: 10.1162/itgg.2008.3.3.119

Di Lorenzo, F., & Scarlata, M. (2019). Social Enterprises, Venture Philanthropy and the Alleviation of Income Inequality. *Journal of Business Ethics*, 159(2), 307–323. DOI: 10.1007/s10551-018-4049-1

EVPA (2010). Establishing a Venture Philanthropy Organisation in Europe. A Practical Guide.

EVPA (2018). The Investing for Impact Toolkit.

Gordon, J. (2014). A stage model of venture philanthropy. *Venture Capital*, 16(2), 85–107. DOI: 10.1080/13691066.2014.897014

Grossman, A., Appleby, S., & Reimers, C. (2013). *Venture Philanthropy: Its Evolution and Its Future*. Harvard Business School 2013.

Guelich, U. & Bosma, N. (2018). Youth Entrepreneurship in Asia and the Pacific 2019. Youth Co:Lab, Global Entrepreneurship Research Association, UNDP and Global Entrepreneurship Monitor.

Hafenmayer, W. (2013). Venture philanthropy: Approach, features, and challenges. *Trusts & Trustees*, 19(6), 535–541. DOI: 10.1093/tandt/ttt084

Hall, J. K., Daneke, G. A., & Lenox, M. J. (2010). Sustainable development and entrepreneurship: Past contributions and future directions. *Journal of Business Venturing*, 25(5), 439–448. DOI: 10.1016/j.jbusvent.2010.01.002

Holliday, I. (2000). Productivist Welfare Capitalism: Social Policy in East Asia. *Political Studies*, 48(4), 706–723. DOI: 10.1111/1467-9248.00279

Ingstad, E. L., Knockaert, M., & Fassin, Y. (2014). Smart money for social ventures: An analysis of the value-adding activities of philanthropic venture capitalists. *Venture Capital*, 16(4), 349–378. DOI: 10.1080/13691066.2014.988379

Jasonson, E., & Sklair, J. (2024). *Philanthropy and Innovative Financing in Asia and the Middle East. Cambridge Judge Business School*. Centre for Strategic Philanthropy.

Jing, Y., & Gong, T. (2012). Managed Social Innovation: The Case of Government-Sponsored Venture Philanthropy in Shanghai. *Australian Journal of Public Administration*, 71(2), 233–245. DOI: 10.1111/j.1467-8500.2012.00767.x

John, R. (2006). *Venture Philanthropy: The Evolution of High Engagement Philanthropy in Europe*. Skoll Centre for Social Entrepreneurship.

John, R., Chia, A., & Ito, K. (2017). *Corporate Philanthropy in Asia: Innovations that unlock the resources of business for the common good*. Entrepreneurial Social Finance in Asia: Working Paper No. 5 DOI: 10.13140/RG.2.2.20242.25289

Kania, J., Kramer, M. & Russell, P. (2014). Strategic Philanthropy for a Complex World. Stanford Social Innovation Review Summer 2014.

Katz, S. N. (2005). What Does It Mean to Say That Philanthropy Is "Effective"? The Philanthropists' New Clothes.

Knott, J. H., & McCarthy, D. (2007). Policy Venture Capital: Foundations, Government Partnerships, and Child Care Programs. *Administration & Society*, 39(3), 319–353. DOI: 10.1177/0095399706298052

Kortum, S., & Lerner, J. (1998). Does Venture Capital Spur Innovation? National Bureau of Economic Research Working Paper 6846.

Kramer, R. (2009). Catalytic Philanthropy. *Stanford Social Innovation Review*.

Lall, S. A., Chen, L.-W., & Roberts, P. W. (2020). Are we accelerating equity investment into impact-oriented ventures? *World Development*, 131, 104952. DOI: 10.1016/j.worlddev.2020.104952

Lall, S. A., & Park, J. (2022). How Social Ventures Grow: Understanding the Role of Philanthropic Grants in Scaling Social Entrepreneurship. *Business & Society*, 61(1), 3–44. DOI: 10.1177/0007650320973434

Larson, A. L. (2000). Sustainable innovation through an entrepreneurship lens. *Business Strategy and the Environment*, 9(5), 304–317. DOI: 10.1002/1099-0836(200009/10)9:5<304::AID-BSE255>3.0.CO;2-O

Letts, C. W., Ryan, W. P., & Grossman, A. S. (1997). Virtuous Capital: What Foundations Can Learn from Venture Capitalists. [Issue.]. *Harvard Business Review*, (March-April), 1997. PMID: 10165448

Li, S. (2018). Crowding-Out Effects of Government Guided Venture Philanthropy. *American Journal of Industrial and Business Management*, 08(03), 433–445. DOI: 10.4236/ajibm.2018.83028

Maclean, M., Harvey, C., & Gordon, J. (2013). Social innovation, social entrepreneurship and the practice of contemporary entrepreneurial philanthropy. *International Small Business Journal*, 31(7), 747–763. DOI: 10.1177/0266242612443376

Magomedova, N., & Bastida-Vialcanet, R. (2022). Unmasking the Barriers to Financing Social Enterprises. *Voluntas*, 33(3), 550–560. DOI: 10.1007/s11266-022-00498-z

Martin, M. (2007). *The Value Proposition of Venture Philanthropy*. Viewpoints.

Martin, M., & Rob, J. (2006). *Venture Philanthropy in Europe: Landscape and Driving Principles*. Book Chapter.

McCray, J. (2011). *Is Grantmaking Getting Smarter? A national study of philanthropic practice.*

Moody, M. (2008). "Building a Culture": The Construction and Evolution of Venture Philanthropy as a New Organizational Field. *Nonprofit and Voluntary Sector Quarterly*, 37(2), 324–352. DOI: 10.1177/0899764007310419

OECD. (2022). *Unlocking the Potential of Youth-Led Social Enterprises.* OECD Global Action Promoting Social & Solidarity Economy Ecosystems.

Onie, R. D., Lavizzo-Mourey, R., Lee, T. H., Marks, J. S., & Perla, R. J. (2018). Integrating Social Needs Into Health Care: A Twenty-Year Case Study Of Adaptation And Diffusion. *Health Affairs*, 37(2), 240–247. DOI: 10.1377/hlthaff.2017.1113 PMID: 29401027

Onishi, T. (2019). Venture Philanthropy and Practice Variations: The Interplay of Institutional Logics and Organizational Identities. *Nonprofit and Voluntary Sector Quarterly*, 48(2), 241–265. DOI: 10.1177/0899764018819875

Pepin, J. (2005). Venture capitalists and entrepreneurs become venture philanthropists. *International Journal of Nonprofit and Voluntary Sector Marketing*, 10(3), 165–173. DOI: 10.1002/nvsm.10

Phillips, W., Lee, H., Ghobadian, A., O'Regan, N., & James, P. (2015). Social Innovation and Social Entrepreneurship: A Systematic Review. *Group & Organization Management*, 40(3), 428–461. DOI: 10.1177/1059601114560063

Prasad, M., Gokhale, A., & Agarwal, N. (2020). *The Advance of Impact Investing in South East Asia. 2020 Update*. Australian Aid, Investing in Women & Intellecap.

Radclyffe-Thomas, N. (2015). Stitching across time: Heritage and history in contemporary Hong Kong fashion. *Clothing Cultures*, 2(3), 241–255. DOI: 10.1386/cc.2.3.241_1

Roundy, P., Holzhauer, H., & Dai, Y. (2017). Finance or philanthropy? Exploring the motivations and criteria of impact investors. *Social Responsibility Journal*, 13(3), 491–512. DOI: 10.1108/SRJ-08-2016-0135

Rowe, E. E. (2023a). Philanthrocapitalism and the State: Mapping the Rise of Venture Philanthropy in Public Education in Australia. *ECNU Review of Education*, 6(4), 518–540. DOI: 10.1177/20965311221128840

Rowe, E. E. (2023b). Venture philanthropy in public schools in Australia: Tracing policy mobility and policy networks. *Journal of Education Policy*, 38(1), 1–22. DOI: 10.1080/02680939.2021.1973569

Sahasranamam, S., & Mitra, S. (2019). Faizal & Shabana Foundation: A venture philanthropic approach to education. *Emerald Emerging Markets Case Studies*, 9(1), 1–21. DOI: 10.1108/EEMCS-04-2018-0052

Sandfort, J. (2008). Using Lessons From Public Affairs to Inform Strategic Philanthropy. *Nonprofit and Voluntary Sector Quarterly*, 37(3), 537–552. DOI: 10.1177/0899764008320270

Scaife, W. (2008). Venturing into Venture Philanthropy: Is More Sustainable Health and Medical Research Funding Possible Through Venture Philanthropy and Social Entrepreneurship? *Journal of Nonprofit & Public Sector Marketing*, 20(2), 245–260. DOI: 10.1080/10495140802224902

Scarlata, M., & Alemany, L. (2008). Philanthropic Venture Capital: Can the Key Elements of Venture Capital Be Applied Successfully to Social Enterprises? SSRN *Electronic Journal*. DOI: 10.2139/ssrn.1099277

Scarlata, M., & Alemany, L. (2010). Deal Structuring in Philanthropic Venture Capital Investments: Financing Instrument, Valuation and Covenants. *Journal of Business Ethics*, 95(S2), 121–145. DOI: 10.1007/s10551-011-0851-8

Schaltegger, S., Hörisch, J., & Freeman, R. E. (2019). Business Cases for Sustainability: A Stakeholder Theory Perspective. *Organization & Environment*, 32(3), 191–212. DOI: 10.1177/1086026617722882

Sciortino, R. (2017a). Philanthropy, Giving, and Development in Southeast Asia. *Austrian Journal of South-East Asian Studies, Vol 10 No 2*, 129-138 Pages. https://doi.org/DOI: 10.14764/10.ASEAS-2017.2-1

Sciortino, R. (2017b). Philanthropy in Southeast Asia: Between Charitable Values, Corporate Interests, and Development Aspirations. *Austrian Journal of South-East Asian Studies, Vol 10 No 2*, 139-163 Pages. DOI: 10.14764/10.ASEAS-2017.2-2

Searing, E. A. M., Poledrini, S., Young, D. R., & Nyssens, M. (2022). The hybrid nature of social enterprises how does it affect their revenue sources? *Social Enterprise Journal*, 18(2), 321–343. DOI: 10.1108/SEJ-02-2021-0010

Shapiro, R. A., Mirchandani, M., & Jang, H. (2018). *Pragmatic Philanthropy*. Springer Singapore., DOI: 10.1007/978-981-10-7119-5

Shaw, A., Canavan, J., & Dolan, P. (2021). Strategic philanthropy's investment in public systems: A framework for intervention. *International Journal of Management Reviews*, 23(3), 411–425. DOI: 10.1111/ijmr.12269

Shaw, E., Gordon, J., Harvey, C., & Maclean, M. (2013). Exploring contemporary entrepreneurial philanthropy. *International Small Business Journal*, 31(5), 580–599. DOI: 10.1177/0266242611429164

Simon, F. L. (1995). Global corporate philanthropy: A strategic framework. *International Marketing Review*, 12(4), 20–37. DOI: 10.1108/02651339510097711

Spiess-Knafl, W., & Aschari-Lincoln, J. (2015). Understanding mechanisms in the social investment market: What are venture philanthropy funds financing and how? *Journal of Sustainable Finance & Investment*, 5(3), 103–120. DOI: 10.1080/20430795.2015.1060187

Thillai Rajan, A., Koserwal, P., & Keerthana, S. (2014). The Global Epicenter of Impact Investing: *An Analysis of Social Venture Investments in India.Journal of Private Equity*, 17(2), 37–50. DOI: 10.3905/jpe.2014.17.2.037

Wong, M. C. S., & Yap, R. C. Y. (2019). Social Impact Investing for Marginalized Communities in Hong Kong: Cases and Issues. *Sustainability (Basel)*, 11(10), 2831. DOI: 10.3390/su11102831

World Economic Forum. (2015). Blended Finance Vol. 1: A Primer for Development Finance and Philanthropic Funds. ReDesigning Development Finance Initiative. A Joint Initiative of the World Economic Forum and the OECD.

Yoon, K.-S., & Lee, S.-Y. (2020): Policy Systems and Measures for the Social Economy in Seoul, UNRISD Working Paper, No. 2020-6, United Nations Research Institute for Social Development (UNRISD), Geneva

Zeichner, K., & Peña-Sandoval, C. (2015). Venture Philanthropy and Teacher Education Policy in the U.S.: The Role of the New Schools Venture Fund. *Teachers College Record*, 117(5), 1–44. DOI: 10.1177/016146811511700508

Chapter 13

Triz Methodology for Design of Water Saving System in a Household Toliet

Omar Eduardo Sánchez Estrada
https://orcid.org/0000-0002-0108-0642
Universidad Autónoma del Estado de México, Mexico

Raymundo Ocaña Delgado
https://orcid.org/0000-0002-3851-5777
Universidad Autónoma del Estado de México, Mexico

Mario Gerson Urbina Perez
Universidad Autónoma del Estado de México, Mexico

ABSTRACT

Renowned scientists have developed creativity theories, have related different discoveries, and have manipulated creative inventions to apply them; however, results are always questionable. Genrich Altshuler, an expert scholar on patents, created the TRIZ Methodology or Theory of Inventive Problem Solving, (Altshuller & Altov, 1996), which has scientifically proved its scopes, based on the study of more than two million patents in different countries (Shirwaiker & Okudan, 2011). According to Carvalho and Back (2001), the TRIZ methodology is developed from interconnecting different methods and algorithms in order to identify, decompose and solve problems from different areas and applications in an innovative manner. Unmeasurable water usage and waste in cities, due to different companies, the state and population, is increasing day after day. Therefore, this research work has

DOI: 10.4018/979-8-3693-4338-8.ch013

the objective to define design technical-conceptual criteria and usage of technical contradictions established in the TRIZ method in order to promote and facilitate prefiguration of water saving systems.

INTRODUCTION

Throughout the years, science and technology have revolutionized the problem-solving approach in different fields and levels, and invention comes from these concepts as a challenging activity for scientists, considered as a turning point to discover hidden answers to determined uncertainties. In the 1940s, it was believed that inventors carried out their creative process fortuitously, it was simply the state of mind at the time in order to materialize the invention and to promote advances in science and technology (Rodriguez et al., 2015). Teti and D'Addona (2011) state that the application of the TRIZ method allows innovation through analysis and resolution of contradictions. This methodology is integrated by different methods, tools and algorithms, which take into account the evolution of socio-technical systems and levels of invention (li et al., 2012). In addition, it facilitates the categorization and modeling of problems, by means of concepts and tools aligned to systematic approaches and generic criteria, and it is also feasible to understand possible future product or service trends (Sivan and Kanthavel, 2004).

TRIZ can be considered as the integration of conceptual and technical tools for understanding and solving problems assertively (Gadd, 2011). It is worth highlighting the concept of contradictions, which arise when two needs that integrate simple and complex technical problems that occur in a product or process are in conflict; however, both of them are the key to problem solving (Lopez, 1999). According to the method, another relevant concept is that of ideality, and this is recognized as the natural tendency of all technical systems based on a developing evolution process, and it is represented as the sum of the total useful functions of a system divided by the sum of the total harmful effects (Altshuller et al., 1996). Currently, business, management and technology systems organizations are making a study to find solutions through functional analysis, which can be described as a tool that allows to identify functions and characteristics within the management and technological system, as well as to protect the business system. This work shows the errors, damages, unnecessary functions, excessive cost of components and the definition of the proposed system (Sklyarova et al., 2020).

Meanwhile, the global water shortage has created a concern for inhabitants of all regions in the world; collection and storage systems are an alternative to subsequently treat water already used in toilets and in different areas in a household. According to the World Health Organization (WHO) (2017), by the year 2100, millions of people will not have access to water service. It is noteworthy that poor management of the resource, technical capacities and economic factors in developing countries are components that aggravate the problem (Thiam et al., 2021). On the other hand, researchers work for the saving and reuse of this valuable resource, in countries such as China, waterfalls, ecological wetland waterscapes and artificial lakes among others have been developed, the projects promote a good circulation and utilization of rainwater (Xie et al., 2021). Although planning the ecological landscape is a valuable starting point, such action proposes to set the places where the different multilayer plants will be located, those with lower layer that grow under the shade of light and do not consume as much water, as well as the way in which plants and foliage are placed reduces the force of rain when precipitating, managing to reduce surface runoff (he, 2021).

Consequently, TRIZ has motivated companies such as Toyota to develop the methodology in the Research and Development department; Samsumg and its work together with Russian companies have achieved 50 patents in just 12 months and have obtained savings over 100 million dollars (Purchasecontrol, 2020). Based on the theory, it is possible to combine solutions for contradictions and procedures for creativity, imagination, creativity and associative thinking, that is, different areas of the psyche (Mi Dahlgaard-Park, S, 2006). Furthermore, it was found that the theory can be applied in most decision-making processes, as well as in organizational management, which allows project leaders to leave behind the intuition and improvisation of technical-practical solutions, this has driven the search for thought-leading executives in order to make the right decisions in a timely manner (Wang, Zhang & Zhang, 2015). All of the above have the potential to be reinterpreted for their application in water saving systems in a household toilet.

The use of TRIZ with a focus on system development expands the possibility of managing, using and reusing the vital liquid efficiently in different living spaces. Everything starts with a specific problem, which is disarticulated to obtain more relevant aspects of it, which turns it into an abstract problem that can be solved through a pre-established solution for such abstract approach; finally, the solution must be defined as a specific solution to address the specific original problem. Thus, a water saving system developed through the resolution of technical contradictions in a complex system favors a better prognosis regarding depletion of the valuable resource (Butt, 1997). TRIZ as a set of tools for the creative process not only opens the possibility of approaching problems logically and systematically towards the conceptualization of any system, it also accelerates initiatives to commercialize it in any region of the world.

Therefore, shortage and good management of water resources represents one of the most important challenges for scientists in the world. The inability to manage water resources technically and financially, especially in developing countries, represents a major problem in terms of health, employment and environmental care. It is worth noting that the World Health Organization estimates that 2.1 billion people around the world do not have a drinking water service (UN, 2017). In addition, 97 percent of this resource found on the planet is contained in the oceans, which makes it difficult to use for domestic, industrial or agricultural consumption and use. Only 3 percent is fresh water, while no agreements have emerged among countries that are considered economic and technological world powers to plan, develop and implement projects (viable, feasible and desirable) to save the water consumed in household toilets, mainly in countries with higher poverty rates (Fuenfschilling & Truffer, 2016).

Hence, the main objective of this research focuses on defining the design criteria through the TRIZ method based on the understanding of abiotic, biotic and socioeconomic systems, the organization in a harmonious balance of materials, the integration of technological requirements and the configuration of responses to biological needs or psychological effects related to form, color, volume or space.

PREVIOUS ANALYSIS

For the TRIZ method development, the concept defined as contradictions is a key to identify a conflict among needs of a product, which are in contradiction in the origin of every technical problem, in their conception they must be analyzed and associated to solve specific requirements, such contradictions are classified as technical, physical and human: (a) technical contradiction, it occurs when solution proposals are made concerning the improvement of some attributes or functions of a useful object, artifact, instrument or system, which are affected automatically; (b) physical contradiction, it arises when the same physical element or component presents two contradictory conditions; and (c) human contradiction, it occurs when users resist or simply block a possible change (Rantanen & Domb, 2010). From their simplest structure, problems generally integrate different contradictions, resulting from technical, physical or human problems. The contradiction matrix use simplifies the analysis to work with any of the three, it shapes different types of problem with a simple division between two parameters of the same category. It should be emphasized that Altshuller assumed that there are universal principles for innovation, which accelerates creativity and technological progress. Thus, the principles of invention can be a practical guide to resolve contradictions in any water-saving system in a household toilet. Table 1 describes the 39 technological systems parameters, and Table 2 the 40 invention principles developed by Altshuller.

Table 1. Altshuller parameters of technological systems

1 Weight of a moving object	11 Tension, pressure	21 Power	31 Effects of damages collateral
2 Weight of an object stationary	12 Form	22 Loss of energy	32 Manufactureability or ease of manufacturing
3 Length of an object mobile	13 Stability of the object.	23 Loss of material	33 Convenience of use.
4 Length of an object stationary	14 Resistance	24 Loss of information	34 Ease of repair
5 Area of a moving object	15 Durability of an object mobile	25 Waste of time	35 Adaptability
6 Area of an object stationary	16 Durability of an object stationary	26 Amount of Substance or matter	36 Complexity of device or object
7 Volume of an object mobile	17 Temperature	27 Reliability	37 Complexity of control
8 Volume of an object stationary	18 Brilliance	28 Accuracy in measurement	38 Level of automation
9. Velocity	19 Energy expended by the object mobile	29 Accuracy in manufacture	39 Productivity
10. Strength	20 Energy expended by the object stationary	30 External damage that affects an object	

Source: (Altshuller and Altov 1996)

Table 2. 40 principles of Altshuller's invention

1 Segmentation	2 Extraction	3 Local quality	4 Asymmetry
5 Combination	6 Universality	7 Nesting	8 Anti-weight
9 Preliminary anti-action	10 Preliminary action	11 Beforehand cushioning	12 Equipotentiality
13 Investment	14 Sphericity	15 Dynamics	16. Partial actions, on clutches or excessive
17 Move to a new dimension	18 Vibrations mechanical	19 Periodic Action	20. Continuity of useful action

continued on following page

Table 2. Continued

21 Pass quickly	22 Convert damage into benefit.	23 Feedback	24 Intermediaries
25 Self-service	26 Copying	27 Cheap short-lived objects	28 Mechanics substitution
29 Use of systems hydraulic or pneumatic	30 Flexible membranes or thin films	31 Use of Porous Materials	32 Color changes
33 Homogeneity	34 Rejection and regeneration of parts	35 Transformation of states chemical or physical	36 Transitions of Phase
37 Thermal Expansion	38 Accelerated oxidation	39 Inert environment	40 Materials compounds

Source: (Altshuller and Altov 1996)

Therefore, designing systems for water saving in dwelling house and other areas has been addressed for several centuries, the processes and systems proposed at the time have also been arranged with different contradictions, for example, increasing water flow in an "X" water stream, naturally enhances the amount of material to be used to contain water, the TRIZ method as an analysis and systematization tool streamlines the solution of the problem (Sivan & Kanthavel 2013). Figure 1 exemplifies Altshuller's contradiction matrix in water-saving systems for a household.

Figure 1. Matrix of Contradictions

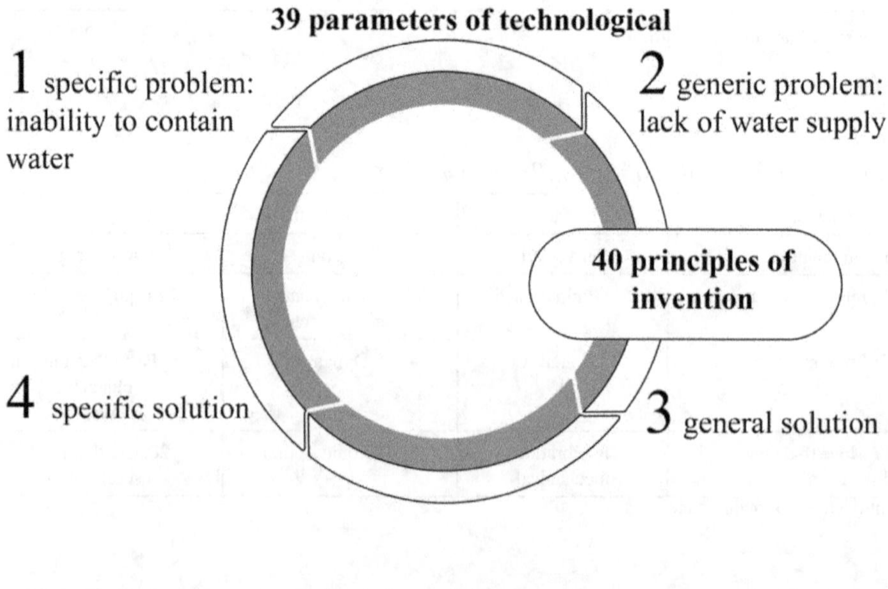

Functional analysis (creativity)

Water saving is not a priority in the supply systems of household toilets, the operation that occurs in every toilet equipment is identified from interaction characteristics in each one of them, that is to say, generally there is no interconnection in all the furniture, which breaks the idea of saving and managing water. So, there is a need in the supply systems design and it is precisely that an interconnected system could work to address contradictions from the TRIZ method.

Within water saving systems in toilets there are different errors related to contradictions (technical, physical and human), which are described below:

Table 3. Identified contradictions

Techniques	Physics	Human
Irregular supply	Water leaks in different components	Irresponsabilidad
Lack of water recovery	Low quality materials	Different activities
Interconnected systems	Component incompatibility	Lack of communication between users
Water contamination	Deficient valves	Lack of knowledge
Lag in function	Poor configuration of the conventional system	Resistance to change

Table 4. Damage, unnecessary functions and excessive cost

Damage	Unnecessary functions	Excessive cost
Pipeline	Waste of water	W.C, sink and shower
Toilet furniture	Low quality materials	Recovery systems
Containers	Component incompatibility	Heating and lighting systems
Watering can	Deficient valves	Ecological education
Sewer system	Poor system	Construction

Creative thinking for system design

Solving problems creatively starts from identifying the need, going through the categorization of factors such as creativity, sustainability, user, context, investment, etc. This shows how complex it can be to consolidate creative thinking. Planners, designers, engineers or scientists do not share a common definition for creativity, which leads to some uncertainty in the face of problems with permanent evolution; however, it does not mean that it is not addressed on a daily basis, regardless of its conceptual multidimensionality, which refers to a high level of analysis, synthesis, interpretation and techniques, but it is still far from consensus (Williams, Ostwald & Askland, 2010). Therefore, finding a concept is required to accelerate the cognitive process and to reconfigure ways to solve specific problems (Kim et al. 2007).

Creativity for design related to problem definition, conceptualization, functionality, ergonomics, aesthetics, sustainability and originality are factors that modify the manufacturing, use, disuse, disassembly and life cycle of projects. Creativity has been defined as the ability to create an appropriate and innovative product (Lubart, 1994; Sternberg & Lubart, 1996; Amabile, 1997; Sternberg, 2001). Teachers and researchers specializing in the field seek to transfer knowledge and agree upon them to generate ideas and determine their effectiveness, based on the functional analysis of systems and multidimensionality of problems to be solved, without omitting the quality and level of originality (Shroyer, Lovins, Turns, Cardella, & Atman, 2018), such a process accelerates identifying creativity evaluation indicators (Demirkan & Afacan 2012). For Altshueller, creative thinking: a) eliminates contradictions through creative solutions; b) creative solutions are defined by a limited number of methods to eliminate contradictions; and c) it is feasible to develop effective tactics to find meaning among different types of contradictions. Randomness for creative problem solving is not acceptable, but is governed by systematization.

Altshuller defines two types of problems: those of known solution and those of unknown solution, the former referring to those shown in books, magazines, internet, scientific articles, and the latter, defined as creative problems. Figure 2 presents the creativity cycle for the solution of creative problems in water saving systems in household toilets.

Figure 2. Cycle creativity

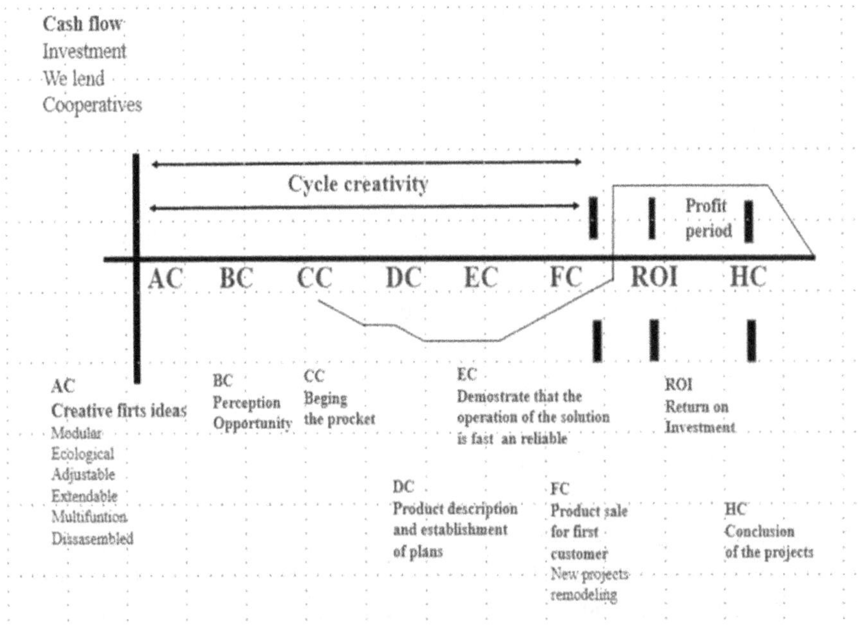

Source: (Adapted from Ekmekci & Koksal, 2015)

Design Theory

Technical, physical or human problems must be approached from codification and categorization of their components. From the design practice it is important to build a user profile to identify the different use sequences that occur in the interactions between objects or systems of objects and people, as well as to work with the trinomial (object-person-environment). This enables decomposition of systems into their different parts and facilitates the identification of different contradictions. If we consider that design is based on the construction of shape, ergonomics, aesthetics and sustainability, among other factors, it may be more practical to systematize problems. It should be noted that each of these concepts integrates an important number of factors, which are logically intertwined and make design to be efficient in its multiple sections.

Shape Construction

Every idea developed starts from a conceptual beginning, which means that everything created, developed or manufactured must consider the basic principle of construction that will be given according to the purpose, conditions, method or technique to carry it out. For designers it is easy to identify that a structural shape starts from mental configuration given to something, that is, it seeks to prefigure ideas from different approaches and strategies, for example, geometry seeks linearity, symmetry, axiality, modularity or just organic structure. This supports the analysis of objects or systems of objects, since it will be simpler to identify characteristics or functions determined for each useful object.

Ergonomics

Every object that goes through the design process in some way has been manufactured with the idea of facilitating interactions, whether manual, semi-automatic or automatic, working from preventive, corrective, dynamic or static ergonomics, in order to determine the best performance in different intervals of use and to improve quality of life. Each use sequence that occurs among primary users (those who will be in permanent contact with the object) and secondary users (those who have incidental contact with the product), salespeople, transporters, packers, etc., is considered to address factors related to the surroundings: environmental, lighting, thermal and acoustic, among others. This science supports defragmentation of components according to their use, safety, comfort and dimensions. Therefore, ergonomics not only facilitates identification of interactions, but it also reveals possible technical, physical and human contradictions that may arise in different systems.

Aesthetics

Object condition well-valued by consumers, if an object or system is beautiful, pleasant, identifiable, balanced and congruent in its shapes, it will surely facilitate identification of human contradictions, which is basic to apply the TRIZ method, because perception and adaptability of people with objects or systems, show different conditions of use, function, maintenance and reuse.

Sustainability

The main objective of this article is to define conceptual parameters for the project beginning, going through the theoretical-practical characteristics of use, function, structure, interaction, identification and communication of the object, based on the useful object that will be ecologically bearable, economically viable and socially equitable, together with transversality of cultural, political and state requirements. Therefore, development of innovative packaging with low environmental impact will promote the construction of a new, more sustainable material culture. At present, this factor is of paramount importance, since ideation, as the first phase of design, must consider objects that are ecologically bearable, economically viable and socially, politically and culturally equitable. Manufacturing with energy savings, reduction of operations and optimization of production phases, not only reveals the most common contradictions in different systems, but also the waste and excessive use of resources to produce objects. Thus, disassembly as a primary action in sustainable design should also be worked on in the first phase of ideation, and with it to determine whether it will be a destructive disassembly or not, to carry out recycling, remanufacturing or reuse through implementation of the four evaluation characteristics:

> *Identification easiness:* speed to identify the parts and disassemble them, easiness to recognize location and joining systems.
> *Accessibility:* determining the ease with which disassembly tools can access the attachment point and item to be disassembled.
> *Ease of detachment:* properties of a component joining element to separate from another or from the rest of the product.
> *Ease of handling:* easiness of handling that components have throughout the disassembly process.

Figure 3. Overall programme structure

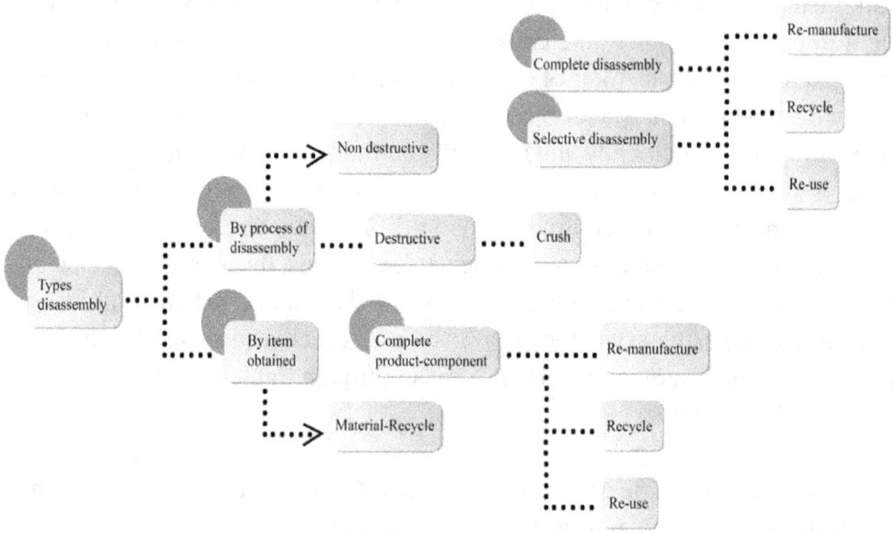

Source: (Srinivasan et al., 1997; Greedel & Allenby, 1995)

The main objective of the Design for Disassembly (DFD) is to choose phases and sequences as chains of actions that will occur one after the other (Srinivasan et al., 1997), the graph called "nodes and meshes" is simple disassembly, where the physical parts are represented as nodes and the existing connections between the parts as meshes. It should be noted that disassembly allows the designer to locate technical contradictions that are not so visible.

Figure 4. Connection diagram "nodes and mashes"

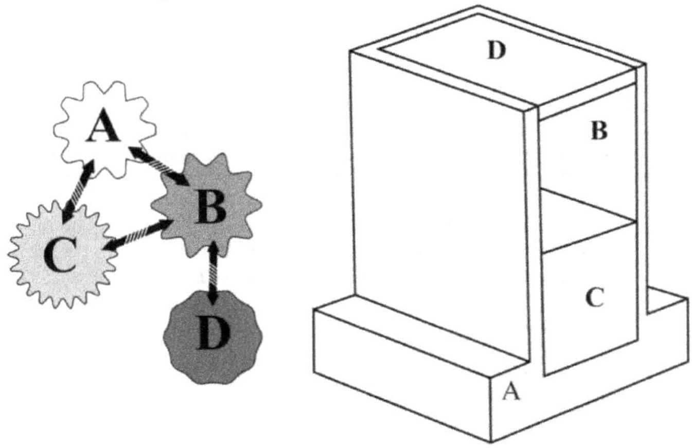

Source: (Cappelli et al., 2007)

For developing sustainable projects, the aim is to select materials with low environmental impact, based on a rigorous analysis of the product's life cycle, disassembly by phases, elimination of any possible use of toxic materials, gas emissions from the adhesives, chemical compounds and coatings used for finishing, (Calkins, 2008). In addition, it is also necessary to consider psychosocial factors associated with: a) ecological thinking; b) defense of sustainability theories; and c) fostering values and habits for the construction of a new sustainable integral culture. It is worth mentioning that selection of materials is based on: a) initial conceptualization of the project; b) design by phases; c) manufacture and assembly; d) availability and replacement; e) preservation of shape at different temperatures; and f) resistance to corrosion and wear. Thus, design interconnects possible solutions through physical, chemical, mechanical, thermal, electrical and manufacturing parameters (Gonzalez & Meza, 2004). The following is suggested for selecting materials with low environmental impact.

Table 5. Simple TRIZ application of inventive problem-solving theory

Technical Contradiction	Physical contradiction	Altshuller parameters	Inventive principles
Variable to be improved (Adaptability) Benefit (Multifunction) Variable That is affected (Durability)	Physical variable that is improved (Function) Physical variable that is affected (Durability of an object stationary)	Identified parameter (35) Adaptability Identified parameter (14) Resistance	Principle of inventiveness identified (35, 3, 32, 6)

Source: (own elaboration)

Figure 5. The matrix of contradictions proposesthe inventive principles that according to Altshuller should be used in the solution of the contradiction (35,3,32,6)

	Variable that is affected / Variable to be improved	Tension or pressure	Shape	Stability of the composition of the object	Resistance	Durability o fan object
		11	12	13	14	15
35	Adaptability				35, 3, 32, 6	
36	Complexity of a mechanism				2, 13, 28	

CONCLUSION

Creativity development in any area of application has lagged significantly when it comes to reconfiguring and addressing specific problems. The Theory of Inventive Problem Solving (TRIZ) not only fragments and systematizes problems, but offers a wide scope for addressing problems of high impact and benefit, related to the development of material culture. Understanding technical, physical and human contradictions opens the possibility of interconnecting different solutions to different problems, in addition to accelerating technology in its multiple dimensions; however, this also accelerates the critical and productive thinking of developers and professionals in any area. Under these terms, design must be technically and theoretically aligned to the methodology concepts and parameters in order to fully exploit creating multidimensional objects that meet the requirements for which they were manufactured, in addition to questioning the paradigms related to product development, weakening the value system that integrates economy, production and quality of life. In addition to the above, there is a need to address problems related to natural resources, their exploitation and the impact it leaves on the planet.

REFERENCES

Al'tshuller, G. S. (1996). And suddenly the inventor appeared: TRIZ, the theor

Amabile, T. M. (1997). Entrepreneurial creativity through motivational synergy. *The Journal of Creative Behavior*, 31(1), 18–26. DOI: 10.1002/j.2162-6057.1997.tb00778.x

Butts, K. H. (1997). The strategic importance of water. *The US Army War College Quarterly: Parameters*, 27(1), 1.

Calkins, M. (2008). *Materials for sustainable sites: a complete guide to the evaluation, selection, and use of sustainable construction materials*. John Wiley & Sons.

Cappelli, F., Delogu, M., Pierini, M., & Schiavone, F. (2007). *Design for disassembly: a methodology for identifying the optimal disassembly sequence*. Journal of Engineering Design, 18(6), 563-575. Retrevied from DOI: 10.1080/09544820601013019

CARVALHO., MD, & Back, N. (2001, September). Use of the fundamental concepts of TRIZ and the method of inventive principles in product development. In *Brazilian Congress of Product Development management* (Vol. 3).

Demirkan, H., & Afacan, Y. (2012). Assessing creativity in design education: Analysis of creativity factors in the first-year design studio. *Design Studies*, 33(3), 262–278. DOI: 10.1016/j.destud.2011.11.005

Ekmekci, I., & Koksal, M. (2015). *Triz methodology and an application example for product development.* Procedia-Social and Behavioral Sciences, 195(Suppl. C), 2689-2698. Retrevied from DOI: 10.1016/j.sbspro.2015.06.481

Fuenfschilling, L., & Truffer, B. (2016). The interplay of institutions, actors and technologies in socio-technical systems—An analysis of transformations in the Australian urban water sector. *Technological Forecasting and Social Change*, 103, 298–312. DOI: 10.1016/j.techfore.2015.11.023

Gadd, K. (2011). *TRIZ for engineers: enabling inventive problem solving*. John wiley & sons. DOI: 10.1002/9780470684320

González, H. Á., & Mesa, D. H. (2004). The importance of the method in the selection of materials. *Scientia et technica*, 10(24), 175–180.

Graedel, T. E., Allenby, B. R., & Comriɛ, P. R. (1995). Matrix approaches to abridged life cycle assessment. *Environmental Science & Technology*, 29(3), 134A–139A. DOI: 10.1021/es00003a751

He, J. (2021). Planning and design of water-saving green plant landscape under human intervention after a great earthquake. *Arabian Journal of Geosciences*, 14(23), 1–10. DOI: 10.1007/s12517-021-08748-y

Kim, M. H., Kim, Y. S., Lee, H. S., & Park, J. A. (2007). An underlying cognitive aspect of design creativity: Limited Commitment Mode control strategy. *Design Studies*, 28(6), 585–604. DOI: 10.1016/j.destud.2007.04.006

Li, Z., Tate, D., Lane, C., & Adams, C. (2012). A framework for automatic TRIZ level of invention estimation of patents using natural language processing, knowledge-transfer and patent citation metrics. *Computer Aided Design*, 44(10), 987–1010. DOI: 10.1016/j.cad.2011.12.006

López, E. (1999) *La metodología TRIZ y su impacto en la innovación industrial en México.*

Lubart, T. I. (1994). *Creativity*. In R. J. Sternberg (Ed), Handbook of Perception and Cognition: Thinking and problem solving. (1st. ed., pp. 289-332). Academic Press.

Mendes, G., Arroyo-Rodríguez, V., Almeida, W. R., Pinto, S. R. R., Pillar, V. D., & Tabarelli, M. (2016). Plant trait distribution and the spatial reorganization of tree assemblages in a fragmented tropical forest landscape. *Plant Ecology*, 217(1), 31–42. DOI: 10.1007/s11258-015-0557-6

Mi Dahlgaard-Park, S. (2006). Inventive thinking through TRIZ: A practical guide. *The TQM Magazine*, 18(3), 312–314. DOI: 10.1108/09544780610660040

Purchasecontrol (2020). *¿Can The TRIZ Method Help Improve Your Company?*https://www.purchasecontrol.com/blog/triz-method/

Rantanen, K., & Domb, E. (2010). *TRIZ simplificado: Nuevas aplicaciones de resolución de problemas para ingenieros y profesionales de la fabricación*. Prensa CRC.

Rodríguez, J. L. M., Machado, A. S., & Robaina, R. (2015). Design of cylindrical spur gears using TRIZ. *ITEGAM-JETIA, 1*(3).

Shirwaiker, R. A., & Okudan, G. E. (2011). Contributions of TRIZ and axiomatic design to leanness in design: An investigation. *Procedia Engineering*, 9, 730–735. DOI: 10.1016/j.proeng.2011.03.162

Shroyer, K., Lovins, T., Turns, J., Cardella, M. E., & Atman, C. J. (2018). *Timescales and ideaspace: An examination of idea generation in design practice.* Design Studies, 57, 9-36. Retrevied from DOI: 10.1016/j.destud.2018.03.004

Sivan, H., & Kanthavel, K. (2013). TRIZ: A Perfect Tool for Process Innovation by Tackling Engineering contradictions. *IOSR Journal of Mechanical and Civil Engineering*, •••, 21–26.

Sklyarova, O. A., Musaelyan, A. K., Bukhov, N. V., Medvedeva, L. S., & Bidzhieva, A. S. (2020). Application of TRIZ Technique in the Organizations' Activity. [IJEBA]. *International Journal of Economics & Business Administration*, 8(4), 563–571.

Sklyarova, O. A., Musaelyan, A. K., Bukhov, N. V., Medvedeva, L. S., & Bidzhieva, A. S. (2020). Application of TRIZ Technique in the Organizations' Activity. [IJEBA]. *International Journal of Economics & Business Administration*, 8(4), 563–571.

Srinivasan, H., Shyamsundar, N., & Gadh, R. (1997). A framework for virtual disassembly analysis. *Journal of Intelligent Manufacturing*, 8(4), 277–295. DOI: 10.1023/A:1018537611535

Sternberg, R. J., & Lubart, T. I. (1996). *Investing in creativity*. American psychologist, 51(7), 677-688. Retrevied from DOI: 10.1037/0003-066X.51.7.677

Teti, R., & D'Addona, D. (2011). TRIZ based tool management in supply networks. *Procedia Engineering*, 9, 680–687. DOI: 10.1016/j.proeng.2011.03.155

Thiam, D. R., Dinar, A., & Ntuli, H. (2021). Promotion of residential water conservation measures in South Africa: The role of water-saving equipment. *Environmental Economics and Policy Studies*, 23(1), 173–210. DOI: 10.1007/s10018-020-00286-3

Wang, M., Zhang, D., & Zhang, L. (2015). Introduction of TRIZ theory for the conflict-solving in the building energy and environment management system innovation. *Procedia Engineering*, 121, 2232–2239. DOI: 10.1016/j.proeng.2015.09.201

Williams, A., Ostwald, M. J., & Askland, H. H. (2010). *Creativity, design and education: Theories, positions and challenges*. Australian Learning & Teaching Council.

World Health Organization (WHO). (2017). United Nations Children's Fund (UNICEF). *Progress on drinking water, sanitation and hygiene*, 140

Xie, Q., Lee, C., Lu, Z., & Yuan, X. (2021). Interactions with artificial water features: A scoping review of health-related outcomes. *Landscape and Urban Planning*, 215, 104191. DOI: 10.1016/j.landurbplan.2021.104191

KEY TERMS AND DEFINITIONS

Design: Creative projet activity that is developed from various methodologies to address ergonomics, aesthetics, semiotics, sustainability to improve the quality of life of living beings.

Creativity: Activity that must be exercised and applied assertively using methods such as solving inventive problems.

Disassembly: Action that must be planned from the first stage of design to strengthen the life cycle of the product as well as its recovery for production of new objects

Sustainability: Promote that it is economically sustainable, ecologically bearable, and socially, politically, and culturally equitable.

Accessibility: Determining the ease with which disassembly tools can access the attachment point and item to be disassembled to dismantele the product into its different components

Ergonomics: Define the highest performance of interactions between people and systems to avoid any type of injuries, through the study of human factors

Semiotics: The identification of systems favors interactions, as well as the perception of those who use them.

Compilation of References

Aayog, N. (2024, July). *Circular Economy Cell* .

Abdullahi, M., & Sallau, A. S. (2023). Social Entrepreneurship as Panacea for Sustainable Community Development. [CIJDS]. *Caleb International Journal of Development Studies*, 06(01), 55–61. DOI: 10.26772/cijds-2023-06-01-03

Abeydeera, S., Kearins, K., & Tregidga, H. (2016). Does Buddhism Enable a Different Sustainability Ethic at Work? *Journal of Corporate Citizenship*, 62(62), 109–130. https://www.jstor.org/stable/90003767. DOI: 10.9774/GLEAF.4700.2016.ju.00013

Abolafia, M. (1996). *Making Markets: Opportunism and Restraint on Wall Street.* Harvard University Press.

Acs, Z. J., Autio, E., & Szerb, L. (2014). National systems of entrepreneurship: Measurement issues and policy implications. *Research Policy*, 43(3), 476–494. DOI: 10.1016/j.respol.2013.08.016

Acs, Z. J., Stam, E., Audretsch, D. B., & O'Connor, A. (2017). The lineages of the entrepreneurial ecosystem approach. *Small Business Economics*, 49(1), 1–10. DOI: 10.1007/s11187-017-9864-8

ADB. (2016). *Renewable Energy in Asia: The Role of the Private Sector.* Asian Development Bank.

ADB. (2018). *Asian Development Outlook 2018: How Technology Affects Jobs.* Asian Development Bank.

Aggad, F. (2023). Comparative multilateral philanthropy: The cases of the European Union Commission and the Asian Development Bank on crisis and non-crisis philanthropic engagements. In Moyo, B., Qobo, M., & Ngwenya, N. (Eds.), *African Philanthropy* (pp. 104–122). Edward Elgar Publishing., DOI: 10.4337/9781803927879.00013

Agrawal, A., & Hockerts, K. (2021). Impact investing: Review and research agenda. *Journal of Small Business and Entrepreneurship*, 33(2), 153–181. DOI: 10.1080/08276331.2018.1551457

Ahmad, M. N. (2020). Electric vehicle charging stations in India (the challenges and barriers being faced by charge point operators and a look at possible solutions)

Ahmad, S. Z., & Xavier, S. R. (2012). Entrepreneurial environments and growth: Evidence from Malaysia GEM data. *Journal of Chinese Entrepreneurship*, 4(1), 50–69. DOI: 10.1108/17561391211200939

Ahmad, S., & Mokhchy, J. (2023). Corporate social responsibilities, sustainable investment, and the future of green bond market: Evidence from renewable energy projects in Morocco. *Environmental Science and Pollution Research International*, 30(6), 15186–15197. DOI: 10.1007/s11356-022-23080-y PMID: 36166123

Ahuja, M. (2020). Promoting inclusive access and empowerment through AI in social entrepreneurship. *The Journal of Development Studies*, 56(4), 789–806.

Ajzen, I. (1991). The theory of planned behavior. *Organizational Behavior and Human Decision Processes*, 50(2), 179–211. DOI: 10.1016/0749-5978(91)90020-T

Al Saiqal, N. Y., Ryan, J. C., & Parcero, O. J. (2019). Entrepreneurial intention and UAE youth: Unique influencers of entrepreneurial intentions in an emerging country context. *Journal of East-West Business*, 25(2), 144–165. DOI: 10.1080/10669868.2018.1536012

Alammari, A., Khalif, A. A., & DarougI, A. A. (2019). Restructuring the Libyan economy with available and unexploited resources of the tourism sector. *Volume II*, 398.

Alchian, A., & Demsetz, H. (1972). Production, information costs and economic organization. *The American Economic Review*, 62, 777–795.

Aldrich, H., & Zimmer, C. (1986). Entrepreneurship through social networks. In Sexton, D. L., & Smilor, R. W. (Eds.), *The art and science of entrepreneurship* (pp. 3–23). Ballinger.

Aljabhan, B., & Obaidat, M. A. (2023). Privacy-preserving blockchain framework for supply chain management: Perceptive Craving Game Search Optimization (PCGSO). *Sustainability (Basel)*, 15(8), 6905. DOI: 10.3390/su15086905

Alomoto, W., Niñerola, À., & Pié, L. (2021). Social impact assessment: A systematic review of literature. *Social Indicators Research*, 161(1), 225–250. DOI: 10.1007/s11205-021-02809-1

Al'tshuller, G. S. (1996). And suddenly the inventor appeared: TRIZ, the theor

Alvedalen, J., & Boschma, R. (2017). A critical review of entrepreneurial ecosystems research: Towards a future research agenda. *European Planning Studies*, 25(6), 887–903. DOI: 10.1080/09654313.2017.1299694

Amabile, T. M. (1997). Entrepreneurial creativity through motivational synergy. *The Journal of Creative Behavior*, 31(1), 18–26. DOI: 10.1002/j.2162-6057.1997.tb00778.x

Amaleshwari, U. A., & Jeevitha, R. (2023). Entrepreneurial orientation and circular business practices: A conceptual framework. *Journal of Management and Public Policy*, 14(2), 16–26.

Anagnostopoulos, I. (2018). Fintech and regtech: Impact on regulators and banks. *Journal of Economics and Business*, 100, 7–25. https://doi.org/. 07. 003DOI: 10.1016/j.jeconbus.2018

Andrade, J. A. (2012). Universidades empreendedoras e o contexto do nordeste brasileiro. *Revista Gestão & Tecnologia*, 12(2), 4–32. DOI: 10.20397/2177-6652/2012.v12i2.368

Anuj Ramatri. (2020, January 20). *The man who Recycled our Cigarette Waste | Anuj Ramatri* [Video]. YouTube. https://www.youtube.com/watch?v=qVuRu1c6PIs

Arena, M., Bengo, I., Calderini, M., & Chiodo, V. (2018). Unlocking finance for social tech start-ups: Is there a new opportunity space? *Technological Forecasting and Social Change*, 127, 154–165. DOI: 10.1016/j.techfore.2017.05.035

Arigela, S. (2022, December). Veerendra., Manam, Ravindra., Adireddy, Ramesh., K., Manoz, Kumar, Reddy., Chandra, Sekhar. (2022). Electric vehicles charging in India: Infrastructure planning and policy aspects. *Energy Storage*, 4(6), e335. Advance online publication. DOI: 10.1002/est2.335

Armanios, D. E., Eesley, C. E., Li, J., & Eisenhardt, K. M. (2017). How entrepreneurs leverage institutional intermediaries in emerging economies to acquire public resources. *transformations and transitions*, 173-197. *Strategic Management Journal*, 38(7), 1373–1390. DOI: 10.1002/smj.2575

Arner, D. W., Barberis, J., & Buckley, R. P. (2015). The evolution of Fintech: A new post-crisis paradigm. *SSRN*, 47, 1271–1315. https://heinonline.org/HOL/LandingPage?handle=hein.journals/geojintl47&div=41&id=&page=. DOI: 10.2139/ssrn.2676553

Arrow, K. (1963). Uncertainty and the welfare economics of medical care. In *Essays in the Theory of Risk Bearing*: 117–219. Chicago: Markham, 1971.

Ashari, H., Abbas, I. K. A., Abdul-Talib, A. N., & Mohd Zamani, S. N. (2021). Entrepreneurship and Sustainable Development Goals: A Multigroup Analysis of the Moderating Effects of Entrepreneurship Education on Entrepreneurial Intention. *Sustainability (Basel)*, 14(1), 431. DOI: 10.3390/su14010431

Audretsch, D. B., Eichler, G. M., & Schwarz, E. J. (2022). Emerging needs of social innovators and social innovation ecosystems. *The International Entrepreneurship and Management Journal*, 18(1), 217–254. DOI: 10.1007/s11365-021-00789-9

Auerswald, P., & Dani, L. (2017). Economic ecosystems. In Clarke, G., Feldman, M., Gertler, M., & Wojcik, D. (Eds.), *New Oxford Handbook of Economic Geography*. Oxford University Press.

Aus, R. (2011). Trash to trend: Using upcycling in fashion design [Unpublished doctoral dissertation]. Estonian Academy of Arts.

Autio, E., George, G., & Alexy, O. (2011). International Entrepreneurship and Capability Development—Qualitative Evidence and Future Research Directions. *Entrepreneurship Theory and Practice*, 35(1), 11–37. DOI: 10.1111/j.1540-6520.2010.00421.x

Autio, E., Nambisan, S., Thomas, L. D. W., & Wright, M. (2018). Digital affordances, spatial affordances, and the genesis of entrepreneurial ecosystems. *Strategic Entrepreneurship Journal*, 12(1), 72–95. DOI: 10.1002/sej.1266

Au, W. C., Drencheva, A., & Yew, J. L. (2023). Narrating career in social entrepreneurship: Experiences of social entrepreneurs. *Journal of Social Entrepreneurship*, 14(3), 343–369. DOI: 10.1080/19420676.2021.1890188

Avelar, S., Borges-Tiago, T., Almeida, A., & Tiago, F. (2024). Confluence of sustainable entrepreneurship, innovation, and digitalization in SMEs. *Journal of Business Research*, 170, 114346. DOI: 10.1016/j.jbusres.2023.114346

AVPN & Ernst & Young (2019). Exploring the Venture Philanthropy Ecosystem in India. An Asian Venture Philanthropy Network and Ernst & Young Joint Publication.

Baik, S. H., Jin, Y. G., & Yoon, Y. T. (2018). Determining equipment capacity of electric vehicle charging station operator for profit maximization. *Energies*, 11(9), 2301.

Banerjee, A. V., & Duflo, E. (2019). *Good Economics for Hard Times*. PublicAffairs.

Baporikar, N. (2021). *Handbook of Research on Strategies and Interventions to Mitigate COVID-19 Impact on SMEs*. IGI Global. DOI: 10.4018/978-1-7998-7436-2

Barral, M. R. M., Ribeiro, F. G., & Canever, M. D. (2018). Influence of the university environment in the entrepreneurial intention in public and private universities. *RAUSP Management Journal*, 53(1), 122–133. DOI: 10.1016/j.rauspm.2017.12.009

Bartley, T., & Schneiberg, M. (2002). Rationality and institutional contingency: The varying politics of economic regulation in the fire insurance industry. *Sociological Perspectives*, 45(1), 47–79. DOI: 10.1525/sop.2002.45.1.47

Bataineh, M. J., Marcuello, C., Sánchez-Sellero, P., & Universidad de Zaragoza. (2023). Toward sustainability: the role of social entrepreneurship in creating social-economic value in renewable energy social enterprises. *REVESCO. Revista de Estudios Cooperativos*. DOI: 10.5209/reve.85561

Baum, J. R., Frese, M., Baron, R. A., & Katz, J. A. (2007). Entrepreneurship as an area of psychology study: An introduction. *The Psychology of Entrepreneurship*, 1, 18.

Bellah, R. N., Madsen, R., Sullivan, W. M., Swidler, A., & Tipton, S. M. (1991). *The good society*. Knopf.

Belz, F. M., & Binder, J. K. (2017). Sustainable Entrepreneurship: A Convergent Process Model. *Business Strategy and the Environment*, 26(1), 1–17. DOI: 10.1002/bse.1887

Beyhan, B., & Fındık, D. (2022). Selection of Sustainability Startups for Acceleration: How Prior Access to Financing and Team Features Influence Accelerators' Selection Decisions. *Sustainability (Basel)*, 14(4), 2125. DOI: 10.3390/su14042125

Bidet, E., & Defourny, J. (2019). *Social Enterprise in Asia: Theory, Models and Practice* (1st ed.). Routledge., DOI: 10.4324/9780429265761

Bird, B. (1988). Implementing entrepreneurial ideas: The case for intention. *Academy of Management Review*, 13(3), 442–453. DOI: 10.2307/258091

Blyth, M. (2001). The Transformation of the Swedish Model: Economic Ideas, Distributional Conflict, and Institutional Change. *World Politics*, 54(1), 1–26. DOI: 10.1353/wp.2001.0020

Bombonatti Filho, O. (n.d.). CIRCULAR ECONOMY – A NEW MANAGEMENT MODEL FOR THE PLANET ECONOMIA CIRCULAR – UM NOVO MODELO DE GESTAO PARA O PLANETA. *19th CONTECSI International Conference on Information Systems and Technology Management*. DOI: 10.5748/19CONTECSI/PSE/SOC/6961

Bonfanti, A., De Crescenzo, V., Simeoni, F., & Loza Adaui, C. R. (2024). Convergences and divergences in sustainable entrepreneurship and social entrepreneurship research: A systematic review and research agenda. *Journal of Business Research*, 170, 114336. DOI: 10.1016/j.jbusres.2023.114336

Bosma, N., Content, J., Sanders, M., & Stam, E. (2018). Institutions, entrepreneurship, and economic growth in Europe. *Small Business Economics*, 51(2), 483–499. DOI: 10.1007/s11187-018-0012-x

Bothra, N. (2024, May 23). *How India became the world's third largest startup hub in 15 years*. Forbes India.

Branca, G., Resciniti, R., & Babin, B. J. (2023). Sustainable packaging design and the consumer perspective: A systematic literature review. *Italian Journal of Marketing*. DOI: 10.1007/s43039-023-00084-1

Brishty, S. P., Islam, Q. T., Alam, S. R. & Akif, A. (2025). Cyclo Fibers: Pioneering Sustainable Textile Production in Bangladesh. SAGE Publications: SAGE Business Cases Originals.

British Council (2021). The State of Social Enterprise in South East Asia.

Brouwer, M., & Thoden van Velzen, U. (2023). *Multi-dimensional sustainability assessment of product-packaging combinations : MuDiSa: a calculation tool to assess the sustainability of product-packaging combinations in multiple dimensions of sustainability*. DOI: 10.18174/633072

Brown, R., & Mason, C. (2014). Inside the high-tech black box: A critique of technology entrepreneurship policy. *Technovation*, 34(12), 773–784. DOI: 10.1016/j.technovation.2014.07.013

Brundtland, G. (1987). *Report of the World Commission on Environment and Development: Our Common Future*. United Nations General Assembly document A/42/427.

Brundtland, G. H. (1987). *Our common future: The World Commission on Environment and Development*. Oxford University Press.

Brush, C. G., De Bruin, A., & Welter, F. (2009). A gender-aware framework for women's entrepreneurship. *International Journal of Gender and Entrepreneurship*, 1(1), 8–24. DOI: 10.1108/17566260910942318

Bruton, G., Khavul, S., Siegel, D., & Wright, M. (2015). New financial alternatives in seeding entrepreneurship: Microfinance, crowdfunding, and peer–to–peer innovations. *Entrepreneurship Theory and Practice*, 39(1), 9–26. DOI: 10.1111/etap.12143

Buckland, L., Hehenberger, L., & Hay, M. (2013). The Growth of European Venture Philanthropy. Stanford Social Innovation Review Summer 2013.

Buendía-Martínez, I., & Carrasco Monteagudo, I. (2020). The role of CSR on social entrepreneurship: An international analysis. *Sustainability (Basel)*, 12(17), 6976. DOI: 10.3390/su12176976

Bull, M., & Crompton, H. (2006). Business practices in social enterprises. *Social Enterprise Journal*, 2(1), 42–60. DOI: 10.1108/17508610680000712

Busenitz, L. W., Gomez, C., & Spencer, J. W. (2000). Country institutional profiles: Unlocking entrepreneurial phenomena. *Academy of Management Journal*, 43(5), 994–1003. DOI: 10.2307/1556423

Butts, K. H. (1997). The strategic importance of water. *The US Army War College Quarterly: Parameters*, 27(1), 1.

Butz, H., & Mrożewski, M. J. (2021). The Selection Process and Criteria of Impact Accelerators. An Exploratory Study. *Sustainability (Basel)*, 13(12), 6617. DOI: 10.3390/su13126617

Cahayani, A. (2017). The role of entrepreneurial spirit in Indonesian youths and housewives to reduce unemployment and poverty rate. In *Handbook of research on unemployment and labor market sustainability in the era of globalization* (pp. 140–156). IGI Global. DOI: 10.4018/978-1-5225-2008-5.ch009

Calkins, M. (2008). *Materials for sustainable sites: a complete guide to the evaluation, selection, and use of sustainable construction materials*. John Wiley & Sons.

Candeias, J. C., & Sarkar, S. (2024). Entrepreneurial Ecosystems Policy Formulation: A Conceptual Framework. *The Academy of Management Perspectives*, 38(1), 77–105. DOI: 10.5465/amp.2022.0047

Candeias, J., & Sarkar, S. (2022). Entrepreneurial Ecosystems and distinguishing features of effective policies–an evidence-based approach. *Entrepreneurship and Regional Development*, 34(5-6), 343–375. DOI: 10.1080/08985626.2022.2045634

Cappelli, F., Delogu, M., Pierini, M., & Schiavone, F. (2007). *Design for disassembly: a methodology for identifying the optimal disassembly sequence*. Journal of Engineering Design, 18(6), 563-575. Retrevied from DOI: 10.1080/09544820601013019

Carbonara, E., Tran, H. T., & Santarelli, E. (2020). Determinants of novice, portfolio, and serial entrepreneurship: An occupational choice approach. *Small Business Economics*, 55(1), 123–151. DOI: 10.1007/s11187-019-00138-9

CARVALHO., MD, & Back, N. (2001, September). Use of the fundamental concepts of TRIZ and the method of inventive principles in product development. In *Brazilian Congress of Product Development management* (Vol. 3).

Cavallo, A., Ghezzi, A., & Balocco, R. (2019). Entrepreneurial ecosystem research: Present debates and future directions. *The International Entrepreneurship and Management Journal*, 15(4), 1291–1321. DOI: 10.1007/s11365-018-0526-3

Central Bank of Sri Lanka. (2019). *Annual Report 2019*. Central Bank of Sri Lanka.

Cetindamar, D., Gupta, V., Karadeniz, E., & Egrican, N. (2012). What the numbers tell: The impact of human, family and financial capital on women and men's entry into entrepreneurship in Turkey. *Entrepreneurship and Regional Development*, 24(1–2), 29–51. DOI: 10.1080/08985626.2012.637348

Chaney, L. H., & Martin, J. (2007). *Intercultural Business Communication* (4th ed.). Pearson Prentice Hall.

Chaparro-Banegas, N., Ibañez Escribano, A. M., Mas-Tur, A., & Roig-Tierno, N. (2024). Innovation facilitators and sustainable development: A country comparative approach. *Environment, Development and Sustainability*, 26(4), 8467–8495. DOI: 10.1007/s10668-023-03055-w PMID: 37363019

Chaudhary, S., Kaur, P., Alofaysan, H., Halberstadt, J., & Dhir, A. (2023). Connecting the dots? Entrepreneurial ecosystems and sustainable entrepreneurship as pathways to sustainability. *Business Strategy and the Environment*, 32(8), 5935–5951. DOI: 10.1002/bse.3466

Chia, A. (2015). *Potential and Prospects for Philanthropy in Implementing Post-2015 Development Goals*. ADB Sustainable Development Working Paper Series. No. 38 April 2015.

Chohra, M. (2019). A critical review of the academic entrepreneurial ecosystem in developing countries: The case of Algeria. *International Journal of Technology Management & Sustainable Development*, 18(3), 243–259. DOI: 10.1386/tmsd_00008_1

Chokkalingam, B., Padmanaban, S., Siano, P., Krishnamoorthy, R., & Selvaraj, R. (2017). Real-time forecasting of EV charging station scheduling for smart energy systems. *Energies*, 10(3), 377. DOI: 10.3390/en10030377

Code Effort Private Limited. (2023). *Code Effort*. Retrieved March 22, 2024, from https://www.codeefforts.com/about

Cohen, B., & Winn, M. I. (2007). Market imperfections, opportunity and sustainable entrepreneurship. *Journal of Business Venturing*, 22(1), 29–49. DOI: 10.1016/j.jbusvent.2004.12.001

Community Wealth Ventures, Inc. (2002). *Venture Philanthropy 2002*. Advancing Nonprofit Performance Through High-Engagement Grantmaking. Copyright by Venture Philanthropy Partners, Inc.

Connell, K. Y. H., & Kozar, J. (2017). Introduction to special issue on sustainability and the triple bottom line within the global clothing and textiles industry. *Fashion and Textiles*, 4(1), 1–3.

Corbett, A. C. (2007). Learning asymmetries and the discovery of entrepreneurial opportunities. *Journal of Business Venturing*, 22(1), 97–118. DOI: 10.1016/j.jbusvent.2005.10.001

Cordella, M., & Kaps, R. (2018). Sustainability of bio-based products: Linking life cycle thinking with standards, certification and labelling schemes. In *Springer eBooks* (pp. 469–474). DOI: 10.1007/978-3-319-66981-6_52

Cortes, A. (2017). A Triple Bottom Line Approach for Measuring Supply Chains Sustainability Using Data Envelopment Analysis. *European Journal of Sustainable Development*, 6(3), 119–128. DOI: 10.14207/ejsd.2017.v6n3p119

Coviello, N. E., & Jones, M. V. (2004). Methodological issues in international entrepreneurship research. *Journal of Business Venturing*, 19(4), 485–508. DOI: 10.1016/j.jbusvent.2003.06.001

Covin, J. G., & Slevin, D. P. (1989). Strategic management of small firms in hostile and benign environments. *Strategic Management Journal*, 10(1), 75–87. DOI: 10.1002/smj.4250100107

Croce, A., Ughetto, E., Scellato, G., & Fontana, F. (2021). Social impact venture capital investing: An explorative study. *Venture Capital*, 23(4), 345–369. DOI: 10.1080/13691066.2021.1982069

Cumming, D. J., & Hornuf, L. (2020). *Marketplace lending of SMEs*.

Dacin, P. A., Dacin, M. T., & Matear, M. (2010). Social entrepreneurship: Why we don't need a new theory and how we move forward from here. *The Academy of Management Perspectives*, 24(3), 37–57.

Dancin, M. T., Dancin, D. A., & Tracey, P. (2011). Social Entrepreneurship: A Critique and Future Directions. *Organization Science*, 22(5), 1203–1213. DOI: 10.1287/orsc.1100.0620

Davidson, E., & Vaast, E. (2010). *Digital entrepreneurship and its sociomaterial enactment* 2010 43rd Hawaii International Conference on System Sciences, IEEE (2010), pp. 1-10

Dean, T. J., & McMullen, J. S. (2007). Toward a theory of sustainable entrepreneurship: Reducing environmental degradation through entrepreneurial action. *Journal of Business Venturing*, 22(1), 50–76. DOI: 10.1016/j.jbusvent.2005.09.003

Deb, S., Tammi, K., Kalita, K., & Mahanta, P. (2018). Review of recent trends in charging infrastructure planning for electric vehicles. *Wiley Interdisciplinary Reviews. Energy and Environment*, 7(6), e306. DOI: 10.1002/wene.306

Deb, S., Tammi, K., Kalita, K., & Mahanta, P. (2019). Charging station placement for electric vehicles: A case study of Guwahati city, India. *IEEE Access : Practical Innovations, Open Solutions*, 7, 100270–100282. DOI: 10.1109/ACCESS.2019.2931055

Dees, J. G. (2008). Philanthropy and Enterprise: Harnessing the Power of Business and Social Entrepreneurship for Development. *Innovations: Technology, Governance, Globalization*, 3(3), 119–132. DOI: 10.1162/itgg.2008.3.3.119

Demirkan, H., & Afacan, Y. (2012). Assessing creativity in design education: Analysis of creativity factors in the first-year design studio. *Design Studies*, 33(3), 262–278. DOI: 10.1016/j.destud.2011.11.005

Deshpande, A. M., & Deshpande, K. U. (2015, August). Creating a platform to foster the growth of electric vehicles in Indian market by increasing the electric vehicle public charging stations. In *2015 IEEE International Transportation Electrification Conference (ITEC)* (pp. 1-4). IEEE.

Di Lorenzo, F., & Scarlata, M. (2019). Social Enterprises, Venture Philanthropy and the Alleviation of Income Inequality. *Journal of Business Ethics*, 159(2), 307–323. DOI: 10.1007/s10551-018-4049-1

Di Zhang, D., & Bruning, E. (2011). Personal characteristics and strategic orientation: Entrepreneurs in Canadian manufacturing companies. *International Journal of Entrepreneurial Behaviour & Research*, 17(1), 82–103. DOI: 10.1108/13552551111107525

Dia, R. R., Akif, A., Islam, Q. T., Hossain, M. A. (2025). Interactive Cares Bangladesh: Empowering Bangladesh's Future Through Education and the SDGs. SAGE Publications: SAGE Business Cases Originals.

Diacono, S., & Baldacchino, L. (2024). Identifying entrepreneurial opportunities in the circular economy. *Journal of Management & Organization*, 30(1), 165–187. DOI: 10.1017/jmo.2023.47

Dobbin, F. (1994). *Forging Industrial Policy*. Cambridge University Press. DOI: 10.1017/CBO9781139174183

Doran, J., McCarthy, N., & O'Connor, M. (2018). The role of entrepreneurship in stimulating economic growth in developed and developing countries. *Cogent Economics & Finance*, 6(1), 1442093. DOI: 10.1080/23322039.2018.1442093

Doron, A. (1998) The Introduction of Supplementary Means Tested Benefits: A Breach in the Universality of the National Insurance Old Age Pension System' (in Hebrew). In Ginosar, P. (ed) *Iyunim Betkumat Yisrael [Studies in Zionism, the Yishuv and the State of Israel: A Research Annual]* Vol. 8, Sede Boqer, The Ben Gurion Research Center, pp. 398 –423.

Dutta, S., Lanvin, B., & Wunsch-Vincent, S. (2016). *Global innovation index 2016: Winning with global innovation*. Cornell University, INSEAD, and the World Intellectual Property Organization (WIPO).

E3S Web of Conferences. (2024). Sustainable fashion and textile recycling.

Economics. (2024). *Russia's Ease of Doing Business*. World Bank.

Eisenhardt, K. M., & Schoonhoven, C. B. (1990). Organizational growth: Linking founding team, strategy, environment, and growth among US semiconductor ventures, 1978-1988. *Administrative Science Quarterly*, 35(3), 504–529. DOI: 10.2307/2393315

Ekmekci, I., & Koksal, M. (2015). *Triz methodology and an application example for product development.* Procedia-Social and Behavioral Sciences, 195(Suppl. C), 2689-2698. Retrevied from DOI: 10.1016/j.sbspro.2015.06.481

Elia, G., Margherita, A. & Passiante, G. (2020). Digital entrepreneurship ecosystem: how digital technologies and collective intelligence are reshaping the entrepreneurial process. *Technol. Forecast. Soc. Chang.,* 150 (2020), Article 119791

Elkington, J. (2018). 25 Years ago I coined the phrase "Triple Bottom Line." Here's why it's time to rethink it. Harvard Business Review. Retrieved from https://hbr.org/2018/06/25-years-ago-i-coined-the-phrase-triple-bottom-line-heres-why-im-giving-up-on-it

Elkington, J. (1994). Towards the Sustainable Corporation: Win-Win-Win Business Strategies for Sustainable Development. *California Management Review*, 36(2), 90–100. DOI: 10.2307/41165746

Ellen MacArthur Foundation. (2017). A new textiles economy: Redesigning fashion's future.

Eller, F. J., Gielnik, M. M., Wimmer, H., Tholke, C., Holzapfel, S., Tegtmeier, S., & Halberstadt, J. (2020). Identifying business opportunities for sustainable development: Longitudinal and experimental evidence contributing to the field of sustainable entrepreneurship. *Business Strategy and the Environment*, 29(3), 1387–1403. DOI: 10.1002/bse.2439

Emmanuel Inalegwu Akoh. (2023). *Social entrepreneurship as a tool for sustainable development in the townships in KwaZulu-Natal province*. https://doi.org/DOI: 10.51415/10321/4826

Enholm, I. M., Papagiannidis, E., Mikalef, P., & Krogstie, J. (2022). Artificial intelligence and business value: A literature review. *Information Systems Frontiers*, 24(5), 1709–1734. DOI: 10.1007/s10796-021-10186-w

European Commission. (2017). *Circular economy in practice—reducing textile waste*. EASME.

EV infrastructure, (2022, June) Part 1: Assessment of India's Current Electric Vehicle (EV) Charging Infrastructure.

EV infrastructure, (2022, June) Part 2: Developing Electric Vehicle Charging Infrastructure in India–Business Opportunities and Risks.

EV infrastructure, (2022, June) Part 3: EV Charging Infrastructure in India – Strategic Recommendations

EVPA (2010). Establishing a Venture Philanthropy Organisation in Europe. A Practical Guide.

EVPA (2018). The Investing for Impact Toolkit.

Fallah, M. R., & Soori, M. (2023). Presenting a framework for the successful entry of women entrepreneurs into green entrepreneurship. *Journal of Science and Technology Policy Management*, 14(3), 467–486. DOI: 10.1108/JSTPM-03-2021-0041

Farrukh, M., Lee, J. W. C., & Shahzad, I. A. (2019). Intrapreneurial behavior in higher education institutes of Pakistan: The role of leadership styles and psychological empowerment. *Journal of Applied Research in Higher Education*, 11(2), 273–294. DOI: 10.1108/JARHE-05-2018-0084

Feldman, M. P. (2001). The entrepreneurial event revisited: Firm formation in a regional context. *Industrial and Corporate Change*, 10(4), 861–891. DOI: 10.1093/icc/10.4.861

Fifka, M., & Idowu, S. (2013). Sustainability and Social Innovation. In Idowu, S., & Capaldi, N. (Eds.), *Encyclopedia of Corporate Social Responsibility* (pp. 309–315).

Figge, F., Hahn, T., Schaltegger, S., & Wagner, M. (2002). The sustainability balanced scorecard–linking sustainability management to business strategy. *Business Strategy and the Environment*, 11(5), 269–284. DOI: 10.1002/bse.339

Finnish Standard Association. (1983). *Hospital textiles. Sheet polyester-cotton; SFS 2945*. Finnish Standard Association.

Finnish Standard Association. (2010). *Quantitative chemical analysis. Part 1: General principles of testing; SFS 1833-11*. Finnish Standard Association.

Fischer, A., & Pascucci, S. (2017). Institutional incentives in circular economy transition: The case of material use in the Dutch textile industry. *Journal of Cleaner Production*, 155, 17–32. DOI: 10.1016/j.jclepro.2016.12.038

Fisher, J., Arora, P., Chen, S., Rhee, S., Blaine, T., & Simangan, D. (2021). Four propositions on integrated sustainability: Toward a theoretical framework to understand the environment, peace, and sustainability nexus. *Sustainability Science*, 16(4), 1125–1145. DOI: 10.1007/s11625-021-00925-y PMID: 33717363

Fletcher, K. (2008). *Sustainable fashion and textiles: Design journeys*. Earthscan/James & James.

Fontes, J. L. I., Tarne, P., Traverso, M., & Bernstein, P. (2016). Product social impact assessment. *The International Journal of Life Cycle Assessment*, 23(3), 547–555. DOI: 10.1007/s11367-016-1125-6

Formentini, G., & Ramanujan, D. (2023). EXAMINING THE ROLE AND FUTURE POTENTIAL OF DESIGN FOR DISASSEMBLY METHODS TO SUPPORT CIRCULAR PRODUCT DESIGN. *Proceedings of the Design Society*, 3, 1735–1744. DOI: 10.1017/pds.2023.174

Fritsch, M. (2013). New business formation and regional development: A survey and assessment of the evidence. *Foundations and Trends in Entrepreneurship*, 9(13), 249–364. DOI: 10.1561/0300000043

Fritsch, M., & Wyrwich, M. (2014). The long persistence of regional levels of entrepreneurship: Germany, 1925–2005. *Regional Studies*, 48(6), 955–973. DOI: 10.1080/00343404.2013.816414

Fuenfschilling, L., & Truffer, B. (2016). The interplay of institutions, actors and technologies in socio-technical systems—An analysis of transformations in the Australian urban water sector. *Technological Forecasting and Social Change*, 103, 298–312. DOI: 10.1016/j.techfore.2015.11.023

Fukuda-Parr, S., & Muchhala, B. (2020). The Southern origins of sustainable development goals: Ideas, actors, aspirations. *World Development*, 126, 104706. DOI: 10.1016/j.worlddev.2019.104706

Gadd, K. (2011). *TRIZ for engineers: enabling inventive problem solving*. John wiley & sons. DOI: 10.1002/9780470684320

Gal, J. (2004). *Social Security in Israel*. Magnes Press. (in Hebrew)

Gam, H. J., & Banning, J. (2011). Addressing sustainable apparel design challenges with problem-based learning. *Clothing & Textiles Research Journal*, 29(3), 202–215. DOI: 10.1177/0887302X11414874

Ganesh, U., Sinha, S., Gokhale, A., Kaushal, A., Gupta, A., & Thukral, C. (2019). Innovations for Scaling Green Sectors.

García-Jurado, A., Pérez-Barea, J. J., & Nova, R. J. (2021). A new approach to social entrepreneurship: A systematic review and meta-analysis. *Sustainability (Basel)*, 13(5), 2754. DOI: 10.3390/su13052754

Garg, M., & Kumar, P. (2023). Social Entrepreneurship and Sustainable Development: A Bibliometric Analysis. *Colombo Business Journal*, 14(2), 99–131. DOI: 10.4038/cbj.v14i2.159

Gazzola, P., Pavione, E., Pezzetti, R., & Grechi, D. (2020). Trends in the fashion industry. The perception of sustainability and circular economy: A gender/generation quantitative approach. *Sustainability (Basel)*, 12(7), 2809. DOI: 10.3390/su12072809

Geissdoerfer, M., Morioka, S. N., de Carvalho, M. M., & Evans, S. (2018). Business models and supply chains for the circular economy. *Journal of Cleaner Production*, 190, 712–721. DOI: 10.1016/j.jclepro.2018.04.159

GEM. (2018). *Global Entrepreneurship Monitor 2018/19 Global Report*. GEM Consortium.

GEM. (2020). *igniting startups for economic growth and social change in south africa*. Global Entrepreneurship Monitor.

Genus, A. (2021). Sustainable entrepreneurship research in the 2020s: An introduction. *Business Strategy and the Environment*, 30(3), 1419–1422. DOI: 10.1002/bse.2705

George, A. (2021). *Green Entrepreneurs: Start-ups Accelerating Sustainability*. Asia Society.

GFA & BCG. (2017). *Pulse of the fashion industry*. Global Fashion Agenda and the Boston Consulting Group.

Gigante, G., Sironi, E., & Tridenti, C. (2023). At the Frontier of Sustainable Finance: Impact Investing and the Financial Tradeoff; Evidence from Private Portfolio Companies in the United Kingdom. *Sustainability (Basel)*, 15(5), 3956. DOI: 10.3390/su15053956

Giovannoni, E., & Fabietti, G. (2013). What is sustainability? A review of the concept and its applications. *Integrated reporting: Concepts and cases that redefine corporate accountability, 21-40.*

Giudici, A., Reinmoeller, P., & Ravasi, D. (2018). Open-system orchestration as a relational source of sensing capabilities: Evidence from a venture association. *Academy of Management Journal*, 61(4), 1369–1402. DOI: 10.5465/amj.2015.0573

GIZ. (2018). *Comparative Analysis of SME Policies in South Asia*. Deutsche Gesellschaft für Internationale Zusammenarbeit (GIZ).

Global Entrepreneurship Development Institute (GEDI). (2019). *Global Entrepreneurship Index 2019*. Global Entrepreneurship Development Institute.

Global Wellness Institute. (2018). *Global Wellness Economy Monitor*. Global Wellness Institute.

González, H. Á., & Mesa, D. H. (2004). The importance of the method in the selection of materials. *Scientia et technica*, 10(24), 175–180.

Gordon, J. (2014). A stage model of venture philanthropy. *Venture Capital*, 16(2), 85–107. DOI: 10.1080/13691066.2014.897014

Graedel, T. E., Allenby, B. R., & Comrie, P. R. (1995). Matrix approaches to abridged life cycle assessment. *Environmental Science & Technology*, 29(3), 134A–139A. DOI: 10.1021/es00003a751

Green Hermitage. (n.d.). The circular economy in fashion

Greif, A. (1998). Self-enforcing political systems and economic growth: Late medieval Genoa. In Bates, R., Greif, A., Levi, M., Rosenthal, J. L., & Weingast, B. (Eds.), *Analytical Narratives: 23–63*. Princeton University Press. DOI: 10.2139/ssrn.49207

Greve, H. (1995). Jumping ship: The diffusion of strategy abandonment. *Administrative Science Quarterly*, 40(3), 444–473. DOI: 10.2307/2393793

GRI. (2016). *Sustainability Reporting Guidelines*. Global Reporting Initiative.

Grossman, A., Appleby, S., & Reimers, C. (2013). *Venture Philanthropy: Its Evolution and Its Future*. Harvard Business School 2013.

Grzymala, Z. (2023). *Circular Economy as a Sustainable Development Marketing Tool.*, DOI: 10.4018/978-1-6684-8681-8.ch015

Guba, E. G., & Lincoln, Y. S. (1994). Competing paradigms in qualitative research. In Denzin, N. K., & Lincoln, Y. S. (Eds.), *Handbook of qualitative research* (pp. 105–117). Sage Publications, Inc.

Guelich, U. & Bosma, N. (2018). Youth Entrepreneurship in Asia and the Pacific 2019. Youth Co:Lab, Global Entrepreneurship Research Association, UNDP and Global Entrepreneurship Monitor.

Guerrero, M., Liñán, F., & Cáceres-Carrasco, F. R. (2021). The influence of ecosystems on the entrepreneurship process: A comparison across developed and developing economies. *Small Business Economics*, 57(4), 1733–1759. DOI: 10.1007/s11187-020-00392-2

Günzel-Jensen, F., Siebold, N., Kroeger, A., & Korsgaard, S. (2020). Do the United Nations' Sustainable Development Goals matter for social entrepreneurial ventures? A bottom-up perspective. Journal of Business Venturing Insights.

Gupta, N., & Matharu, M. (2022). Examining the enablers of sustainable entrepreneurship – an interpretive structural modelling technique. *Journal of Entrepreneurship in Emerging Economies*, 14(5), 701–726. DOI: 10.1108/JEEE-10-2021-0416

Gupta, P., Chauhan, S., Paul, J., & Jaiswal, M. P. (2020). Social entrepreneurship research: A review and future research agenda. *Journal of Business Research*, 113, 209–229. DOI: 10.1016/j.jbusres.2020.03.032

Gupta, R. S., Tyagi, A., & Anand, S. (2021). Optimal allocation of electric vehicles charging infrastructure, policies and future trends. *Journal of Energy Storage*, 43, 103291. DOI: 10.1016/j.est.2021.103291

Hafenmayer, W. (2013). Venture philanthropy: Approach, features, and challenges. *Trusts & Trustees*, 19(6), 535–541. DOI: 10.1093/tandt/ttt084

Halberstadt, J., Schwab, A.-K., & Kraus, S. (2024). Cleaning the window of opportunity: Towards a typology of sustainability entrepreneurs. *Journal of Business Research*, 171, 114386. DOI: 10.1016/j.jbusres.2023.114386

Haldar, S. (2019). Towards a conceptual understanding of sustainability-driven entrepreneurship. *Corporate Social Responsibility and Environmental Management*, 26(6), 1157–1170. DOI: 10.1002/csr.1763

Hall, J. K., Daneke, G. A., & Lenox, M. J. (2010). Sustainable Development and Entrepreneurship: Past Contributions and Future Directions. *Journal of Business Venturing*, 25(5), 439–448. DOI: 10.1016/j.jbusvent.2010.01.002

Hamilton, J. A. (2024). *Textile recycling—A review*. ResearchGate.

Hanum, L., Noor, I., & Wahyudi, L. E. (2023). Individual and Social Influence on the Sustainable Social Entrepreneurs Development. *Jurnal Ilmu Sosial Dan Humaniora*, 12(2), 288–295. DOI: 10.23887/jish.v12i2.62081

Harrison, R. T., & Leitch, C. (2010). Voodoo institution or entrepreneurial university? Spin-off companies, the entrepreneurial system and regional development in the UK. *Regional Studies*, 44(9), 1241–1262. DOI: 10.1080/00343400903167912

Harrison, R., Li, Y., Vigne, S. A., & Wu, Y. (2022). Why do small businesses have difficulty in accessing bank financing? *International Review of Financial Analysis*, 84, 102352. DOI: 10.1016/j.irfa.2022.102352

Hart, S. L., & Dowell, G. (2011). A natural-resource-based view of the firm: Fifteen years after. *Journal of Management*, 37(5), 1464–1479. DOI: 10.1177/0149206310390219

Hazarika, G., Salunke, P., Wadhwani, K., & Sen, K. (2021). Sustainable Entrepreneurship–A Dyad Case Study on Recycling. *SMS Journal of Entrepreneurship & Innovation, 8*(Issue-1), 102–111.

Hechavarría, D. M., & Ingram, A. E. (2019). Entrepreneurial ecosystem conditions and gendered national-level entrepreneurial activity: A 14-year panel study of GEM. *Small Business Economics*, 53(2), 431–458. DOI: 10.1007/s11187-018-9994-7

Heimer, C. (1985). *Reactive Risk and Rational Action: Managing Moral Hazard in Insurance Contracts*. University of California Press. DOI: 10.1525/9780520318465

He, J. (2021). Planning and design of water-saving green plant landscape under human intervention after a great earthquake. *Arabian Journal of Geosciences*, 14(23), 1–10. DOI: 10.1007/s12517-021-08748-y

Hemavathi, S., & Shinisha, A. (2022). A study on trends and developments in electric vehicle charging technologies. *Journal of Energy Storage*, 52, 105013. DOI: 10.1016/j.est.2022.105013

Hockerts, K. (2017). Determinants of social entrepreneurial intentions. *Entrepreneurship Theory and Practice*, 41(1), 105–130. DOI: 10.1111/etap.12171

Hockerts, K., & Wustenhagen, R. (2010). Greening Goliaths versus emerging Davids — Theorizing about the role of incumbents and new entrants in sustainable entrepreneurship. *Journal of Business Venturing*, 25(5), 481–492. DOI: 10.1016/j.jbusvent.2009.07.005

Hofstad, H., & Torfing, J. (2016). Collaborative innovation as a tool for environmental, economic and social sustainability in regional governance. *Scandinavian Journal of Public Administration*, 19(4), 49–70. DOI: 10.58235/sjpa.v19i4.14992

Hofstede, G. (2001). *Cultures and Organizations.* Software of the Mind. McGraw-Hill.

Holliday, I. (2000). Productivist Welfare Capitalism: Social Policy in East Asia. *Political Studies*, 48(4), 706–723. DOI: 10.1111/1467-9248.00279

Hollingsworth, J. R. & Wolfgang Streeck (1994). Countries and sectors: Concluding remarks on performance, convergence, and competitiveness. In J. R. Hollingsworth, P. Schmitter, and W. Streeck (eds.), *Governing Capitalist Economies*: 270–300. Oxford: Oxford University Press.

Hooi, H. C., Ahmad, N. H., Amran, A., & Rahman, S. A. (2016). The functional role of entrepreneurial orientation and entrepreneurial bricolage in ensuring sustainable entrepreneurship. *Management Research Review*, 39(12), 1616–1638. DOI: 10.1108/MRR-06-2015-0144

Horne, J., Recker, M., Michelfelder, I., Jay, J., & Kratzer, J. (2020). Exploring entrepreneurship related to the sustainable development goals - mapping new venture activities with semi-automated content analysis. *Journal of Cleaner Production*, 242, 118052. DOI: 10.1016/j.jclepro.2019.118052

Howaldt, J. (2018). Harnessing AI for innovation in social entrepreneurship. *Technology Innovation Management Review*, 8(1), 12–20.

Hussien, D. A., Omran, W. A., & Sharkawy, R. M. (2023, March). Smart charging of electric vehicles in charging stations. In 2023 5th International Youth Conference on Radio Electronics, Electrical and Power Engineering (REEPE) (Vol. 5, pp. 1-5). IEEE.

IBEF. (2024). *Circular Economy for Sustainable Development in India*. 2024.

IEEE Future Directions. (2022). Wrapping up the year: Sustainability in fashion.

IEEE Xplore. (2023). Sustainable fashion: The future directions.

IEEE Xplore. (n.d.). Recycling in the fashion industry.

IEEE Xplore. (n.d.). Sustainable fashion practices for the future.

IEEE Xplore. (n.d.). Sustainable textile innovations.

IFOAM. (2017). *The World of Organic Agriculture: Statistics and Emerging Trends 2017*. International Federation of Organic Agriculture Movements.

Immergut, E. (1992). The rules of the game: The logic of health policymaking in France, Switzerland, and Sweden. In S. Steinmo, Kathleen Thelen, and Frank Longstreth (eds.), *Structuring Politics*: 57–89. Cambridge, UK: Cambridge University Press.

Inalegwu Akoh, E., & Mpele Lekhanya, L. (2022). Social entrepreneurship and networking challenges: Impact on sustainable development in South Africa. *Problems and Perspectives in Management*, 20(4), 195–209. DOI: 10.21511/ppm.20(4).2022.15

Information and Communication Technology Agency (ICTA). (2020). *Digital Economy Strategy of Sri Lanka*. Information and Communication Technology Agency.

Ingstad, E. L., Knockaert, M., & Fassin, Y. (2014). Smart money for social ventures: An analysis of the value-adding activities of philanthropic venture capitalists. *Venture Capital*, 16(4), 349–378. DOI: 10.1080/13691066.2014.988379

International Labour Organization (ILO). (2023). *Impact of multiple crises on Sri Lanka's micro, small and medium-sized enterprises*. International Labour Organization.

IPCC. (2014). [*Impacts, Adaptation, and Vulnerability. Part A: Global and Sectoral Aspects*. Contribution of Working Group II to the Fifth Assessment Report of the Intergovernmental Panel on Climate Change.]. *Climatic Change*, •••, 2014.

Ipiranga, A. S. R., Freitas, A. A. F., & Paiva, D. (2010). O empreendedorismo acadêmico no contexto da interação universidade-empresa-governo. *Cadernos EBAPE*, 8(4), 676-693. https://doi.org/DOI: 10.1590/s1679-39512010000400000

Islam, Q. T., & Akif, A. (2024). Paperman Foundation India: Driving Sustainability through Circular Economy and Creating Impact. SAGE Publications: SAGE Business Cases Originals.

Islam, Q. T., Talukder, M. S., & Haque, K. L. (2022). Sustainable Development Through the Circular Economy: Experience From Emerging Economies. In Redefining Global Economic Thinking for the Welfare of Society (pp. 75-93). IGI Global.

Islam, Q. T., Zabir, F., Singh, T. (2025). Code Effort's Model: A Case Study in SDG-Driven Environmental Entrepreneurship. SAGE Publications: SAGE Business Cases Originals.

Jaén, I., Fernandez-Serrano, J., & Francisco, L. (2013). Valores culturales, nivel de ingresos y actividad emprendedora. *Revista de Economía Mundial*, 35, 35–52.

Jamgade, S. R., Raj, H., & Arman, M. (2024). Economy Percolating Effect of Eco-tourism: Application of Triple Bottom Line (TBL) Theory. In *Achieving Sustainable Transformation in Tourism and Hospitality Sectors* (pp. 317–333). IGI Global.

Jasonson, E., & Sklair, J. (2024). *Philanthropy and Innovative Financing in Asia and the Middle East. Cambridge Judge Business School*. Centre for Strategic Philanthropy.

Jayasena, H. A. H., & Selker, J. S. (2004). Thousand Years of Hydraulic Civilization Some Sociotechnical Aspects of Water Management. *Proceedings of the Workshop on Water and Politics: Understanding the Role of Politics in Water Management*. World Water Council.

Jing, Y., & Gong, T. (2012). Managed Social Innovation: The Case of Government-Sponsored Venture Philanthropy in Shanghai. *Australian Journal of Public Administration*, 71(2), 233–245. DOI: 10.1111/j.1467-8500.2012.00767.x

John, R., Chia, A., & Ito, K. (2017). *Corporate Philanthropy in Asia: Innovations that unlock the resources of business for the common good*. Entrepreneurial Social Finance in Asia: Working Paper No. 5 DOI: 10.13140/RG.2.2.20242.25289

John, R. (2006). *Venture Philanthropy: The Evolution of High Engagement Philanthropy in Europe*. Skoll Centre for Social Entrepreneurship.

Johnson, D., Gianiodis, P., Harrison, R., & Bock, A. (2022). From laboratory to clinic: Science commercialization within university-centered entrepreneurial ecosystems. *R&D Management*. online first. DOI: 10.1111/radm.12535

Johnson, D., Bock, A. J., & George, G. (2019). Entrepreneurial dynamism and the built environment in the evolution of university entrepreneurial ecosystems. *Industrial and Corporate Change*, 28(4), 941–959. DOI: 10.1093/icc/dtz034

Johnson, M. P., & Schaltegger, S. (2020). Entrepreneurship for Sustainable Development: A Review and Multilevel Causal Mechanism Framework. *Entrepreneurship Theory and Practice*, 44(6), 1141–1173. DOI: 10.1177/1042258719885368

Juma, N., Olabisi, J., & Griffin-EL, E. (2023). External enablers and entrepreneurial ecosystems: The brokering role of the anchor tenant in capacitating grassroots ecopreneurs. *Strategic Entrepreneurship Journal*, 17(2), 372–407. DOI: 10.1002/sej.1462

Jung, K., Eun, J.-H., & Lee, S.-H. (2017). Exploring competing perspectives on government-driven entrepreneurial ecosystems: Lessons from centres for creative economy and innovation (CCEI) of South Korea. *European Planning Studies*, 25(5), 827–847. . 2017.1282083DOI: <ALIGNMENT.qj></ALIGNMENT>10. 1080/ 09654313

Kabongo, J. D. (2013). Design for environment. In *Springer eBooks* (pp. 780–786). DOI: 10.1007/978-3-642-28036-8_40

Kaestner, L., Scope, C., Neumann, N., & Woelfel, C. (2023). SUSTAINABLE CIRCULAR PACKAGING DESIGN: A SYSTEMATIC LITERATURE REVIEW ON STRATEGIES AND APPLICATIONS IN THE COSMETICS INDUSTRY. *Proceedings of the Design Society*, 3, 3265–3274. DOI: 10.1017/pds.2023.327

Kahle, J. H., Marcon, É., Ghezzi, A., & Frank, A. G. (2020). Smart Products value creation in SMEs innovation ecosystems. *Technological Forecasting and Social Change*, 156, 120024. DOI: 10.1016/j.techfore.2020.120024

Kalakanti, A. K., & Rao, S. (2022). Charging Station Planning for Electric Vehicles. *Systems*, 10(1), 6. DOI: 10.3390/systems10010006

Kalendzhjan, S. O., & Kadol, N. F. (2022). *Social entrepreneurship as a catalyst for sustainable socio-economic development*. https://doi.org/DOI: 10.56199/dpcsebm.kvzv9880

Kamaludin, M. F., Xavier, J. A., & Amin, M. (2024). Social entrepreneurship and sustainability: A conceptual framework. *Journal of Social Entrepreneurship*, 15(1), 26–49. DOI: 10.1080/19420676.2021.1900339

Kania, J., Kramer, M. & Russell, P. (2014). Strategic Philanthropy for a Complex World. Stanford Social Innovation Review Summer 2014.

Kasradze, M., Štreimikienė, D., & Lauzadyte-Tutliene, A. (2023). Measuring the impact of corporate social responsibility in the energy sector. *Environmental Science and Pollution Research International*, 30(51), 109973–110009. DOI: 10.1007/s11356-023-30131-5 PMID: 37798520

Katz, S. N. (2005). What Does It Mean to Say That Philanthropy Is "Effective"? The Philanthropists' New Clothes.

Kavianipour, M., Fakhrmoosavi, F., Singh, H., Ghamami, M., Zockaie, A., Ouyang, Y., & Jackson, R. (2021). Electric vehicle fast charging infrastructure planning in urban networks considering daily travel and charging behaviour. *Transportation Research Part D, Transport and Environment*, 93, 102769. DOI: 10.1016/j.trd.2021.102769

Khan, M. A. I., Syed, A. J., & Azharuddin, S. (2023). Social Entrepreneurship: Driving Change and Creating Positive Societal Impact. Social Entrepreneurship: Driving Change and Creating Positive Societal Impact.

Khan, S. (2024). Innovation and Sustainable Development in Entrepreneurship. *SMS Journal of Entrepreneurship & Innovation*, 10(1), 69–81. DOI: 10.21844/smsjei.v10i01.30006

Khan, W., Ahmad, F., Ahmad, A., Alam, M. S., & Ahuja, A. (2018). Electric vehicle charging infrastructure in India: viability analysis. In *ISGW 2017: Compendium of Technical Cases* (pp. 193–206). Springer. DOI: 10.1007/978-981-10-8249-8_17

Kickul, J., & Lyons, T. S. (2020). *Understanding social entrepreneurship: The relentless pursuit of mission in an ever changing world.* Routledge. DOI: 10.4324/9780429270406

Kim, W. C., & Mauborgne, R. A. (2014). *Blue ocean strategy, expanded edition: How to create uncontested market space and make the competition irrelevant.* Harvard business review Press.

Kim, H., & Damhorst, M. L. (1998). Environmental concern and apparel consumption. *Clothing & Textiles Research Journal*, 16(3), 126–133. DOI: 10.1177/0887302X9801600303

Kim, M. H., Kim, Y. S., Lee, H. S., & Park, J. A. (2007). An underlying cognitive aspect of design creativity: Limited Commitment Mode control strategy. *Design Studies*, 28(6), 585–604. DOI: 10.1016/j.destud.2007.04.006

Kiran, P. R., Chaubey, A., & Shastri, R. K. (2024). Incorporating the ESG framework to analyse entrepreneurial opportunities among tribal people. *Management of Environmental Quality*, 35(2), 249–269. DOI: 10.1108/MEQ-08-2023-0247

Kirby, D. (2006). Creating entrepreneurial universities in the UK: Applying entrepreneurship theory to practice. *The Journal of Technology Transfer*, 31(5), 599–603. DOI: 10.1007/s10961-006-9061-4

Kirchherr, J., Reike, D., & Hekkert, M. (2017). Conceptualizing the circular economy: An analysis of 114 definitions. *Resources, Conservation and Recycling*, 127, 221–232. DOI: 10.1016/j.resconrec.2017.09.005

Kizhakkan, A. R., Rathore, A. K., & Awasthi, A. (2019, December). Review of electric vehicle charging station location planning. In 2019 IEEE Transportation Electrification Conference (ITEC-India) (pp. 1-5). IEEE. DOI: 10.1109/ITEC-India48457.2019.ITECINDIA2019-226

Klofsten, M., Kanda, W., Bienkowska, D., Bocken, N., Mian, S., & Lamine, W. (2024). Start-ups within entrepreneurial ecosystems: Transition towards circular economy. *International Small Business Journal*, 42(4), 02662426241227520. DOI: 10.1177/02662426241227520

Klöpffer, W. (2014). Introducing Life Cycle Assessment and its presentation in 'LCA compendium.' In *LCA compendium* (pp. 1–37). DOI: 10.1007/978-94-017-8697-3_1

Knight, J. (2001). Explaining the rise of neoliberalism: The mechanisms of institu-tional change. In Campbell, J., & Perderson, O. (Eds.), *The Rise of Neo-liberalism and the Institutional Analysis: 27-50*. Princeton University Press. DOI: 10.1515/9780691188225-006

Knott, J. H., & McCarthy, D. (2007). Policy Venture Capital: Foundations, Government Partnerships, and Child Care Programs. *Administration & Society*, 39(3), 319–353. DOI: 10.1177/0095399706298052

Kore, H. H., & Koul, S. (2022). Electric vehicle charging infrastructure: Positioning in India. *Management of Environmental Quality*, 33(3), 776–799. DOI: 10.1108/MEQ-10-2021-0234

Koreh, M., & Shalev, M. (2009, October). Dialectics of institutional change: The transformation of social insurance financing in Israel. *Socio-economic Review*, 7(4), 553–584. DOI: 10.1093/ser/mwp018

Korhonen, J., Nuur, C., Feldmann, A., & Birkie, S. E. (2018). Circular Economy as an Essentially Contested Concept. *Journal of Cleaner Production*, 175, 544–552. DOI: 10.1016/j.jclepro.2017.12.111

Kortum, S., & Lerner, J. (1998). Does Venture Capital Spur Innovation? National Bureau of Economic Research Working Paper 6846.

Koval, V., Arsawan, I. W. E., Suryantini, N. P. S., Kovbasenko, S., Fisunenko, N., & Aloshyna, T. (2022). Circular Economy and Sustainability-Oriented Innovation: Conceptual Framework and Energy Future Avenue. *Energies*, 16(1), 243. DOI: 10.3390/en16010243 PMID: 35910686

Kramer, R. (2009). Catalytic Philanthropy. *Stanford Social Innovation Review*.

Kraus, S., Palmer, C., Kailer, N., Kallinger, F. L., & Spitzer, J. (2018). Digital entrepreneurship: A research agenda on new business models for the twenty-first century. *International Journal of Entrepreneurial Behaviour & Research*, 25(2), 353–375. DOI: 10.1108/IJEBR-06-2018-0425

Kreutzer, K. (2022). Social Enterprises. *Edward Elgar Publishing Limited EBooks*, 121–123, 121–123. Advance online publication. DOI: 10.4337/9781800375499.social.enterprises

Krill Design. (n.d.). Krill Design. https://en.krilldesign.net/

Kshetri, N. (2009). Entrepreneurship in post-socialist economies: A typology and institutional contexts for market entrepreneurship. *Journal of International Entrepreneurship*, 7(3), 236–259. DOI: 10.1007/s10843-009-0039-9

Kshetri, N. (2010). Business perceptions of regulative institutions in Central and Eastern Europe. *Baltic Journal of Management*, 5(3), 356–377. DOI: 10.1108/17465261011079758

Kuckertz, A. (2019). Let's take the entrepreneurial ecosystem metaphor seriously! *Journal of Business Venturing Insights*, 11, e00124. DOI: 10.1016/j.jbvi.2019.e00124

Kumar, K, J., Kumar, S., & VS, N. (. (2022). Standards for electric vehicle charging stations in India: A review. *Energy Storage*, 4(1), e261. DOI: 10.1002/est2.261

Kumar, P., & Dash, K. (2013). Potential need for electric vehicles, charging station infrastructure and its challenges for the Indian market. *Advance in Electronic and Electric Engineering*, 3(4), 471–476.

Lall, S. A., Chen, L.-W., & Roberts, P. W. (2020). Are we accelerating equity investment into impact-oriented ventures? *World Development*, 131, 104952. DOI: 10.1016/j.worlddev.2020.104952

Lall, S. A., & Park, J. (2022). How Social Ventures Grow: Understanding the Role of Philanthropic Grants in Scaling Social Entrepreneurship. *Business & Society*, 61(1), 3–44. DOI: 10.1177/0007650320973434

Lam, A. Y., Leung, Y. W., & Chu, X. (2013, October). Electric vehicle charging station placement. In *2013 IEEE International Conference on Smart Grid Communications (SmartGridComm)* (pp. 510-515). IEEE. DOI: 10.1109/SmartGridComm.2013.6688009

Lam, A. Y., Leung, Y. W., & Chu, X. (2014). Electric vehicle charging station placement: Formulation, complexity, and solutions. *IEEE Transactions on Smart Grid*, 5(6), 2846–2856. DOI: 10.1109/TSG.2014.2344684

Larson, A. L. (2000). Sustainable innovation through an entrepreneurship lens. *Business Strategy and the Environment*, 9(5), 304–317. DOI: 10.1002/1099-0836(200009/10)9:5<304::AID-BSE255>3.0.CO;2-O

Laycock, B., Pratt, S., & Halley, P. J. (2023). A perspective on biodegradable polymer biocomposites - from processing to degradation. *Functional Composite Materials*, 4(1), 10. Advance online publication. DOI: 10.1186/s42252-023-00048-w

Leblebici, H., Salancik, G., Copay, A., & King, T. (1991). Institutional change and the transformation of interorganizational fields: An organizational history of the U.S. broadcasting industry. *Administrative Science Quarterly*, 36(3), 333–363. DOI: 10.2307/2393200

Lemaster, K., & Jackson, V. F. (2009). Sustainable Airport Projects: Going Beyond LEED. *Airport Magazine*, 20.

Leong, B., Wee, A. K. S., & Yuen-Ping, H. (2008). Is an enterprise framework necessary for an entrepreneurial university? A comparison of technology start-ups in Singapore and Sweden. *Science & Public Policy*, 35(9), 647–656. DOI: 10.3152/030234208X287038

Letts, C. W., Ryan, W. P., & Grossman, A. S. (1997). Virtuous Capital: What Foundations Can Learn from Venture Capitalists. [Issue.]. *Harvard Business Review*, (March-April), 1997. PMID: 10165448

Lewis, D., Bowers, R., Heslop, L., & Tawfic, S. (2024). From Ecosystems to Advicescapes: Business, Development and Advice in Sri Lanka and Bangladesh. *Journal of South Asian Development*, 0(0), 345–363. Advance online publication. DOI: 10.1177/09731741241239120

Li, J., Li, J., Zhu, X., Yao, Y., & Casu, B. (2020). Risk spillo-vers between FinTech and traditional financial institutions: Evidence from the US. *International Review of Financial Analysis*, 71, 101544. https://doi.org/. 101544DOI: 10. 1016/j.irfa.2020

Lipnik, A., & Lipnik, M. C. (2020). Sustainable innovation: Definitions, priorities and emerging issues. In *Sustainability and innovation* (pp. 41–56). DOI: 10.1007/978-3-030-46750-0_2

Li, S. (2018). Crowding-Out Effects of Government Guided Venture Philanthropy. *American Journal of Industrial and Business Management*, 08(03), 433–445. DOI: 10.4236/ajibm.2018.83028

Lisitsa, M., Khutieva, E., Doroshenko, O., Konareva, A., & Trifonova, L. (2022). *Circular Economy as an Alternative to Green Economy*. DOI: 10.2991/aer.k.220308.029

Li, Y., & Zahra, S. A. (2012). Formal institutions, culture, and venture capital activity: A cross-country analysis. *Journal of Business Venturing*, 27(1), 95–111. DOI: 10.1016/j.jbusvent.2010.06.003

Li, Z., Tate, D., Lane, C., & Adams, C. (2012). A framework for automatic TRIZ level of invention estimation of patents using natural language processing, knowledge-transfer and patent citation metrics. *Computer Aided Design*, 44(10), 987–1010. DOI: 10.1016/j.cad.2011.12.006

Loop Biotech. (2023, May 22). *The inventors of the World's First Living Coffin | Loop Biotech* [Video]. YouTube. https://www.youtube.com/watch?v=uQXOls5Mefs

Loop Biotech. (2024, March 4). About us - *Bob Hendrikx & Lonneke Westhoff.* https://loop-biotech.com/about-us/

López, E. (1999) *La metodología TRIZ y su impacto en la innovación industrial en México.*

Lorenz, M. P., Ramsey, J. R., & Richey, R. G.Jr. (2018). Expatriates' international opportunity recognition and innovativeness: The role of metacognitive and cognitive cultural intelligence. *Journal of World Business*, 53(2), 222–236. DOI: 10.1016/j.jwb.2017.11.004

Loviscek, V. (2021). Triple Bottom Line toward a Holistic Framework for Sustainability: A Systematic Review. *Revista de Administração Contemporânea.*

Lubart, T. I. (1994). *Creativity.* In R. J. Sternberg (Ed), Handbook of Perception and Cognition: Thinking and problem solving. (1st. ed., pp. 289-332). Academic Press.

Lubberink, R. (2019). Social Entrepreneurship and Sustainable Development. *Methods in Molecular Biology (Clifton, N.J.)*, 1965, 1–11. DOI: 10.1007/978-3-319-71058-7_47-1

Maaßen, C., Rovira, R., & Urbano, D. (2023). A Process Model for Sustainable Entrepreneurship: Evidence from a Highly Entrepreneurial European Region. *Journal of Social Entrepreneurship*, in press, 1–32. DOI: 10.1080/19420676.2023.2221262

Maclean, M., Harvey, C., & Gordon, J. (2013). Social innovation, social entrepreneurship and the practice of contemporary entrepreneurial philanthropy. *International Small Business Journal*, 31(7), 747–763. DOI: 10.1177/0266242612443376

Magnuson, W. (2018). Regulating Fintech. *Vanderbilt Law Review*, 71(4), 1167-1226. https://heinonline. org/HOL/ Landi ngPage? handle= hein. journ als/ vanlr 71& div= 33&id=&page=

Magomedova, N., & Bastida-Vialcanet, R. (2022). Unmasking the Barriers to Financing Social Enterprises. *Voluntas*, 33(3), 550–560. DOI: 10.1007/s11266-022-00498-z

Mahieu, J., Melillo, F., Reichstein, T., & Thompson, P. (2021). Shooting stars? Uncertainty in hiring entrepreneurs. *Strategic Entrepreneurship Journal*, 15(4), 526–567. DOI: 10.1002/sej.1339

Mair, J., & Marti, I. (2006). Social entrepreneurship research: A source of explanation, prediction, and delight. *Journal of World Business*, 41(1), 36–44. DOI: 10.1016/j.jwb.2005.09.002

Maldonado Castro, A., Maldonado Castro, J., Yela Burgos, R., & Moreno Suqilanda, E. (2022). Circular economy and its impact on environmental sustainability. *Centro Sur*, 6(4). Advance online publication. DOI: 10.37955/cs.v6i4.286

Malecki, E. J. (2018). Entrepreneurship and entrepreneurial ecosystems. *Geography Compass*, 12(3), e12359. DOI: 10.1111/gec3.12359

Manolova, T. S., Eunni, R. V., & Gyoshev, B. S. (2008). Institutional environments for entrepreneurship: Evidence from emerging economies in Eastern Europe. *Entrepreneurship Theory and Practice*, 32(1), 203–218. DOI: 10.1111/j.1540-6520.2007.00222.x

Mansouri, S., & Momtaz, P. P. (2022). Financing sustainable entrepreneurship: ESG measurement, valuation, and performance. *Journal of Business Venturing*, 37(6), 106258. Advance online publication. DOI: 10.1016/j.jbusvent.2022.106258

Martin, M., & Parsapour, A. (2012). Upcycling wastes with biogas production: An energy and economic analysis. In Proceedings of the Venice 2012: International Symposium on Energy from Biomass and Waste, Venice, Italy, 12–15 November 2012.

Martin, M. (2007). *The Value Proposition of Venture Philanthropy*. Viewpoints.

Martin, M., & Rob, J. (2006). *Venture Philanthropy in Europe: Landscape and Driving Principles*. Book Chapter.

Martino, B. (2023). Biomimicry in Building Architecture. *University of Colorado Honors Journal*, 118, 118. Advance online publication. DOI: 10.33011/cuhj20231867

Marvel, M. R. (2013). Human capital and search–based discovery: A study of high–tech entrepreneurship. *Entrepreneurship Theory and Practice*, 37(2), 403–419. DOI: 10.1111/j.1540-6520.2011.00465.x

Mason, C., Cooper, S., & Harrison, R. (2002). Venture capital and high technology clusters: the case of Ottawa. In Oakey, R., During, W., & Kauser, S. (Eds.), *New Technology-Based Firms in the New Millennium* (Vol. II, pp. 261–278). Pergammon.

McCray, J. (2011). *Is Grantmaking Getting Smarter? A national study of philanthropic practice*.

McWilliams, A., Siegel, D. S., & Wright, P. M. (2006). Corporate Social Responsibility: Strategic Implications. *Journal of Management Studies*, 43(1), 1–18. DOI: 10.1111/j.1467-6486.2006.00580.x

Mendes, G., Arroyo-Rodríguez, V., Almeida, W. R., Pinto, S. R. R., Pillar, V. D., & Tabarelli, M. (2016). Plant trait distribution and the spatial reorganization of tree assemblages in a fragmented tropical forest landscape. *Plant Ecology*, 217(1), 31–42. DOI: 10.1007/s11258-015-0557-6

Metawea, M. (2020). The role of financial institutions in supporting entrepreneurial success: Case of Egypt. American Journal of Business and Operations Research.

Meyer, A., & Schneider, P. (2019). Cradle-to-cradle for sustainable development: From eco-design to a circular economy. In *Springer eBooks* (pp. 321–330). DOI: 10.1007/978-3-030-11352-0_273

Mi Dahlgaard-Park, S. (2006). Inventive thinking through TRIZ: A practical guide. *The TQM Magazine*, 18(3), 312–314. DOI: 10.1108/09544780610660040

Mikhailova, E. A., Post, C. J., & Nelson, D. G. (2024). Integrating United Nations Sustainable Development Goals in Soil Science Education. *Soil Systems*, 8(1), 29. DOI: 10.3390/soilsystems8010029

Ministry of Industry and Commerce. (2017). *National Policy Framework for Small and Medium Enterprise (SME) Development.* Government of Sri Lanka.

Mishra, S., Verma, S., Chowdhury, S., Gaur, A., Mohapatra, S., Dwivedi, G., & Verma, P. (2021). A comprehensive review on developments in electric vehicle charging station infrastructure and present scenario of India. *Sustainability (Basel)*, 13(4), 2396. DOI: 10.3390/su13042396

Mittelstadt, B. D. (2016). Ethical considerations in AI deployment for social entrepreneurship. *Ethics and Information Technology*, 18(4), 249–267.

Moalem, R. M., & Kerndrup, S. (2023). The entrepreneurial role of waste companies in transforming waste streams to value streams: Lessons from a Danish Municipal waste company. *Waste Management & Research*, 41(3), 620–634. DOI: 10.1177/0734242X221124048 PMID: 36169120

Molchanova, R. V. (2023). CIRCULAR ECONOMY IN THE CONSTRUCTION INDUSTRY. *EKONOMIKA I UPRAVLENIE: PROBLEMY, RESHENIYA, 4/3*(136), 110–116. DOI: 10.36871/ek.up.p.r.2023.04.03.013

Molla, A., & Biru, A. (2023). The evolution of the Fintech entrepreneurial ecosystem in Africa: An exploratory study and model for future development, *Technological Forecasting and Social Change*,186. *Technological Forecasting and Social Change*, 122123, 122123. Advance online publication. DOI: 10.1016/j.techfore.2022.122123

Moody, M. (2008). "Building a Culture": The Construction and Evolution of Venture Philanthropy as a New Organizational Field. *Nonprofit and Voluntary Sector Quarterly*, 37(2), 324–352. DOI: 10.1177/0899764007310419

Mora, M., Akinci, B., & Alarcón, L. (2019). Integrating Social Sustainability in Value Stream Mapping: Panelized Post-Disaster Temporary Housing Case Study. *Proceedings of the 36th International Symposium on Automation and Robotics in Construction (ISARC)*. DOI: 10.22260/ISARC2019/0076

Mordovets, V. A., Ugolnikova, O. D., Kruglov, D. V., Shchipanov, E. F., & Averyanova, O. V. (2022). State Policy for Sustainable Development of Entrepreneurship in Russia: Minimizing Risks and Removing Barriers. *International Scientific and Practical Conference" Sustainable Development of Environment after Covid-19"(SDEC 2021)*, 325–330. DOI: 10.2991/assehr.k.220106.058

Motoyama, Y., & Knowlton, K. (2016). From Resource Munificence to Ecosystem Integration: The Case of GovernmentSponsorship in St. Louis. *Entrepreneurship and Regional Development*, 28(5–6), 448–470. DOI: 10.1080/08985626.2016.1186749

Mulibana, L., & Tshikovhi, N. (2024). Rural Entrepreneurship and Innovation in BRICS Economies: Secondary Evidence from Rural Areas in South Africa. *Sustainability (Basel)*, 16(6), 2408. DOI: 10.3390/su16062408

Mura, R., Vicentini, F., Botti, L. M., & Chiriacò, M. V. (2024). Achieving the circular economy through environmental policies: Packaging strategies for more sustainable business models in the wine industry. *Business Strategy and the Environment*, 33(2), 1497–1514. DOI: 10.1002/bse.3556

Nair, S., Rao, N., Mishra, S., & Patil, A. (2017, December). India's charging infrastructure— biggest single point impediment in EV adaptation in India. In 2017 IEEE transportation electrification conference (ITEC-India) IEEE.

National Center for Biotechnology Information. (2020). Environmental impacts of fashion.

Nayak, R., & Pillai, K. R. (2024). Sustainable entrepreneurship research in emerging economies: An evidence from systematic review. *Journal of Entrepreneurship in Emerging Economies*, 16(3), 495–517. DOI: 10.1108/JEEE-03-2022-0099

Ncube, A., Mtetwa, S., Bukhari, M., Fiorentino, G., & Passaro, R. (2023). Circular Economy and Green Chemistry: The Need for Radical Innovative Approaches in the Design for New Products. *Energies*, 16(4), 1752. DOI: 10.3390/en16041752

Neessen, P. C. M., Voinea, C. L., & Dobber, E. (2021). Business Models of Social Enterprises: Insight into Key Components and Value Creation. *Sustainability (Basel)*, 13(22), 12750. DOI: 10.3390/su132212750

Nelder, C., & Rogers, E. (2019). *Reducing EV charging infrastructure costs*. Rocky Mountain Institute.

Njue, N. G., & Kariuki, S. N. (2024). Contextual and Structural Factors, Project Modelling and Sustainability of Entrepreneurial Development Projects: A Conceptual Framework. *European Journal of Business Management and Research*, 9(2), 35–42. DOI: 10.24018/ejbmr.2024.9.2.1713

Noll, R., & Owen, B. (1983). *The Political Economy of Deregulation*. American Enterprise Institute.

North, D. (1981). *Structure and Change in Economic History*. W. W. Norton.

North, D. (1990). *Institutions, Institutional Change and Economic Performance*. Cambridge University. DOI: 10.1017/CBO9780511808678

Nowshin, S. (2024, May 6). *Magical mushrooms: How mycelium is changing industries beyond food*. Sifted. https://sifted.eu/articles/mushroom-tech-mycelium-loop-biotech

NSF. (2019). *National Science Foundation of Sri Lanka*. National Science Foundation.

Nuralam, I. P. SE, M., & Putri, N. V. W. (2023). Fostering Sustainable Entrepreneurship in Emerging Market: an Interdisciplinary Perspective.

OECD. (2014). *Entrepreneurial ecosystems and growth oriented entrepreneurship*. https://www.oecd.org/cfe/leed/Entrepreneurial-ecosystems.pdf

OECD. (2017). *Enhancing the Contributions of SMEs in a Global and Digitalised Economy*. Organisation for Economic Co-operation and Development.

OECD. (2022). *Unlocking the Potential of Youth-Led Social Enterprises*. OECD Global Action Promoting Social & Solidarity Economy Ecosystems.

Oham, C. A. (2022). *Okeoma John-Paul Okeke*. Advances in Business Strategy and Competitive Advantage Book Series. Strategic Formulation and Implementation of Social Entrepreneurs., DOI: 10.4018/978-1-7998-7724-0.ch001

Olson, M. (1971). *The Logic of Collective Action*. Harvard University Press.

Öner, M. A., & Kunday, Ö. (2016). A study on Schumpeterian and Kirznerian entrepreneurship in Turkey: 2006–2013. *Technological forecasting and social change*, 102(2), 62–71. https://doi.org/. techfore.2015. 09. 005DOI: 10. 1016/ j

Onie, R. D., Lavizzo-Mourey, R., Lee, T. H., Marks, J. S., & Perla, R. J. (2018). Integrating Social Needs Into Health Care: A Twenty-Year Case Study Of Adaptation And Diffusion. *Health Affairs*, 37(2), 240–247. DOI: 10.1377/hlthaff.2017.1113 PMID: 29401027

Onishi, T. (2019). Venture Philanthropy and Practice Variations: The Interplay of Institutional Logics and Organizational Identities. *Nonprofit and Voluntary Sector Quarterly*, 48(2), 241–265. DOI: 10.1177/0899764018819875

Ostgaard, T. A., & Birley, S. (1994). Personal networks and firm competitive strategy: A strategic or coincidental match? *Journal of Business Venturing*, 9(4), 281–305. DOI: 10.1016/0883-9026(94)90009-4

Ostrom, E. (1990). *Governing the Commons*. Cambridge, UK: Cambridge University Press. Perugini, F. (2023). Space–time analysis of entrepreneurial ecosystems. *The Journal of Technology Transfer*, 48(1), 240–291.

Özpolat, A., & Nakıpoğlu Özsoy, F. (Eds.). (2022). *Circular Economy in the Framework of Sustainable Development Policy*. Özgür Yayınları., DOI: 10.58830/ozgur.pub11

Pailman, W., Kruger, W., & Prasad, G. (2015). Mobile payment innovation for sustainable energy access. *2015 International Conference on the Domestic Use of Energy (DUE)*, 39-44.

Parag, Y., Elimelech, E., & Opher, T. (2023). Bottled water: An evidence-based overview of economic viability, environmental impact, and social equity. *Sustainability (Basel)*, 15(12), 9760. DOI: 10.3390/su15129760

Pareek, S., Sujil, A., Ratra, S., & Kumar, R. (2020, February). Electric vehicle charging station challenges and opportunities: A future perspective. In 2020 International Conference on Emerging Trends in Communication, Control and Computing (ICONC3) (pp. 1-6). IEEE.

Pareek, S., Sujil, A., Ratra, S., & Kumar, R. (2020, February). Electric vehicle charging station Challenges and opportunities: a future perspective. In 2020 International Conference on Emerging Trends in Communication, Control and Computing (ICONC3) IEEE. DOI: 10.1109/ICONC345789.2020.9117473

Parrish, B. D. (2010). Sustainability-driven entrepreneurship: Principles of organization design. *Journal of Business Venturing*, 25(5), 510–523. DOI: 10.1016/j.jbusvent.2009.05.005

Parshutina, I. G., Plakhova, L. V, Zakharkina, N. V, Sokolova, N. N., & Isakova, M. N. (2019). Formation of entrepreneurial climate in Russia for sustainable development of small business. *European Proceedings of Social and Behavioural Sciences*.

Pastran, A., Colli, E., & Poclaba, C. (2021). Sustainable entrepreneurship: A new way of doing business. *Journal of the International Council for Small Business*, 2(2), 147–158. DOI: 10.1080/26437015.2021.1882915

Patricia, P. (2024). The Role Of Entrepreneurship Education In Universities To Pursue Sustainable Development Goals. *Feedforward*, 4(1), 23–23. DOI: 10.19166/ff.v4i1.8129

Patzelt, H., & Shepherd, D. A. (2011). Recognizing Opportunities for Sustainable Development. *Entrepreneurship Theory and Practice*, 35(4), 631–652. DOI: 10.1111/j.1540-6520.2010.00386.x

Pepin, J. (2005). Venture capitalists and entrepreneurs become venture philanthropists. *International Journal of Nonprofit and Voluntary Sector Marketing*, 10(3), 165–173. DOI: 10.1002/nvsm.10

Phillips, W., Lee, H., Ghobadian, A., O'Regan, N., & James, P. (2015). Social Innovation and Social Entrepreneurship: A Systematic Review. *Group & Organization Management*, 40(3), 428–461. DOI: 10.1177/1059601114560063

Pinkse, J., & Groot, K. (2015). Sustainable Entrepreneurship and Corporate Political Activity: Overcoming Market Barriers in the Clean Energy Sector. *Entrepreneurship Theory and Practice*, 39(3), 633–654. DOI: 10.1111/etap.12055

Pol, V. G. (2010). Upcycling: Converting waste plastics into paramagnetic, conducting, solid, pure carbon microspheres. *Environmental Science & Technology*, 44(12), 4753–4759. DOI: 10.1021/es100243u PMID: 20481621

Pomare, C. (2018). *A Multiple Framework Approach to Sustainable Development Goals (SDGs) and Entrepreneurship*. Entrepreneurship and the Sustainable Development Goals. DOI: 10.1108/S2040-724620180000008006

Popa, A. (2023). Circular economy as a strategy of regional and local development. *Strategii Si Politici de Management in Economia Contemporana*, 178–187. DOI: 10.53486/icspm2022.29

Popescu, C. R., & Yu, P. (Eds.). (2024). *Intersecting Environmental Social Governance and AI for Business Sustainability*. IGI Global., DOI: 10.4018/979-8-3693-1151-6

Popescu, C. R., Yu, P., & Wei, Y. (Eds.). (2023). *Achieving the Sustainable Development Goals Through Infrastructure Development*. IGI Global., DOI: 10.4018/979-8-3693-0794-6

Porras-Paez, A., & Schmutzler, J. (2019). Orchestrating an entrepreneurial ecosystem in an emerging country: The lead actor's role from a social capital perspective. *Local Economy*, 34(8), 767–786. DOI: 10.1177/0269094219896269

Powell, W., Koput, k. & Smith-Doerr, L. (. (1996). Technological change and the locus of innovation: Networks of learning in biotechnology. *Administrative Science Quarterly*, 41, 116–145. DOI: 10.2307/2393988

Prasad, M., Gokhale, A., & Agarwal, N. (2020). *The Advance of Impact Investing in South East Asia. 2020 Update*. Australian Aid, Investing in Women & Intellecap.

Presidential Expert Committee. (2019). *The report on Sustainable Sri Lanka 2030 Vision and Strategic Path*. Presidential Secretariat, Government of Sri Lanka.

Pretty, J., Benton, T. G., Bharucha, Z. P., Dicks, L. V., Flora, C. B., Godfray, H. C. J., Goulson, D., Hartley, S., Lampkin, N., Morris, C., Pierzynski, G., Prasad, P. V. V., Reganold, J., Rockström, J., Smith, P., Thorne, P., & Wratten, S. (2018). Global assessment of agricultural system redesign for sustainable intensification. *Nature Sustainability*, 1(8), 441–446. DOI: 10.1038/s41893-018-0114-0

Prokopenko, O., Chechel, A., Koldovskiy, A., & Kldiashvili, M. (2024). Innovative Models of Green Entrepreneurship: Social Impact on Sustainable Development of Local Economies. Ekonomìka, Ekologìâ. *Socìum*, 8(1), 89–111. DOI: 10.61954/2616-7107/2024.8.1-8

Purchasecontrol (2020). *¿Can The TRIZ Method Help Improve Your Company?*https://www.purchasecontrol.com/blog/triz-method/

Qian, H., Acs, Z. J., & Stough, R. R. (2013). Regional systems of entrepreneurship: The nexus of human capital, knowledge and new firm formation. *Journal of Economic Geography*, 13(4), 559–587. DOI: 10.1093/jeg/lbs009

Rabiee, A., Ghiasian, A., & Chermahini, M. A. (2018). Long term profit maximization strategy for charging scheduling of electric vehicle charging station. *IET Generation, Transmission & Distribution*, 12(18), 4134–4141. DOI: 10.1049/iet-gtd.2018.5592

Radclyffe-Thomas, N. (2015). Stitching across time: Heritage and history in contemporary Hong Kong fashion. *Clothing Cultures*, 2(3), 241–255. DOI: 10.1386/cc.2.3.241_1

Rafi, S., Dia, R. R., Gazi, M. A., & Islam, Q. T. (2024). Fairphone: The Phone That Protects the Planet. SAGE Publications: SAGE Business Cases Originals. Ali, K. S., Islam, Q. T., Zabir, F., & Hossain, M. A. (2024). SWAP: A Sustainable Solution to Our E-Waste Problem. SAGE Publications: SAGE Business Cases Originals.

Rantanen, K., & Domb, E. (2010). *TRIZ simplificado: Nuevas aplicaciones de resolución de problemas para ingenieros y profesionales de la fabricación*. Prensa CRC.

Rasheed, M., & Liu, J. (2023). Unleashing the power of innovation promoters for sustainable economic growth: A global perspective. *Environmental Science and Pollution Research International*, 30(45), 100979–100993. DOI: 10.1007/s11356-023-29313-y PMID: 37642909

Rastogi, C. (2018). M-Kopa Solar: Lighting up the Dark Continent. *South Asian Journal of Business and Management Cases*, 7(1), 93–103. DOI: 10.1177/2277977918774648

Recycled Fibers, C. Y. C. L. O. (2022, May 18). *About - CYCLO® Recycled Fibers*. CYCLO® Recycled Fibers. https://www.cyclofibers.com/about/

ResearchGate. (n.d.). A terminology for downcycling. • Grounded. (n.d.). Sustainable fashion: 4 ways fashion brands can be more sustainable.

ResearchGate. (n.d.). Achieving sustainability through zero waste fashion—a review.

Reynolds, P., Bosma, N., Autio, E., Hunt, S., De Bono, N., Servais, I., Lopez-Garcia, P., & Chin, N. (2005). Global entrepreneurship monitor: Data collection design and implementation 1998–2003. *Small Business Economics*, 24(3), 205–231. DOI: 10.1007/s11187-005-1980-1

Riti, J. S., & Yang, S. (2016). Renewable energy, energy efficiency, and eco-friendly environment (R-E5) in Nigeria. *Energy, Sustainability and Society*, 6(1), 13. Advance online publication. DOI: 10.1186/s13705-016-0072-1

Rodríguez, J. L. M., Machado, A. S., & Robaina, R. (2015). Design of cylindrical spur gears using TRIZ. *ITEGAM-JETIA, 1*(3).

Roleders, V. V. (2023). CIRCULAR ECONOMY MODEL IN INDUSTRIAL ECOSYSTEMS. *The Actual Problems of Regional Economy Development*, 1(19), 243–254. DOI: 10.15330/apred.1.19.243-254

Rotefoss, B., & Kolvereid, L. (2005). Aspiring, nascent and fledgling entrepreneurs: An investigation of the business start-up process. *Entrepreneurship and Regional Development*, 17(2), 109–127. DOI: 10.1080/0898562050074049

Roundy, P., Holzhauer, H., & Dai, Y. (2017). Finance or philanthropy? Exploring the motivations and criteria of impact investors. *Social Responsibility Journal*, 13(3), 491–512. DOI: 10.1108/SRJ-08-2016-0135

Rowe, E. E. (2023a). Philanthrocapitalism and the State: Mapping the Rise of Venture Philanthropy in Public Education in Australia. *ECNU Review of Education*, 6(4), 518–540. DOI: 10.1177/20965311221128840

Rowe, E. E. (2023b). Venture philanthropy in public schools in Australia: Tracing policy mobility and policy networks. *Journal of Education Policy*, 38(1), 1–22. DOI: 10.1080/02680939.2021.1973569

Saebi, T., Foss, N. J., & Linder, S. (2019). Social entrepreneurship research: Past achievements and future promises. *Journal of Management*, 45(1), 70–95. DOI: 10.1177/0149206318793196

SAGE Journals. (2022). Sustainable fashion practices.

Sahasranamam, S., & Mitra, S. (2019). Faizal & Shabana Foundation: A venture philanthropic approach to education. *Emerald Emerging Markets Case Studies*, 9(1), 1–21. DOI: 10.1108/EEMCS-04-2018-0052

Sahoo, P. (2006). *Foreign Direct Investment in South Asia: Policy, Trends, Impact and Determinants*. ADB Institute Discussion Paper No 56. Asian Development Bank Institute.

Sajan, Jerome. (2022). An Economic Feasibility Study of Electric Vehicle Charging Stations in India. DOI: 10.1007/978-981-19-2091-2_17

Sandfort, J. (2008). Using Lessons From Public Affairs to Inform Strategic Philanthropy. *Nonprofit and Voluntary Sector Quarterly*, 37(3), 537–552. DOI: 10.1177/0899764008320270

Santos -Corrada, M. D. L. M., Méndez-Tejeda, R., Flecha-Ortiz, J. A., & Lopez, E. (2024). An analysis of sustainable consumption practices through the role of the consumer behavior in the circular economy. *Journal of Consumer Behaviour*, 23(1), 229–242. DOI: 10.1002/cb.2183

Saranya, K. G., Hema, A., & Joanish Muthu, J. (2023). A review on sustainable biodiversity challenges and opportunities. *World Journal of Advanced Research and Reviews*, 17(1), 679–685. DOI: 10.30574/wjarr.2023.17.1.0069

Sarkis, J., Gonzalez-Torre, P., & Adenso-Diaz, B. (2010). Stakeholder pressure and the adoption of environmental practices: The mediating effect of training. *Journal of Operations Management*, 28(2), 163–176. DOI: 10.1016/j.jom.2009.10.001

Sarma, S., Attaran, S., & Attaran, M. (2024). Sustainable entrepreneurship: Factors influencing opportunity recognition and exploitation. *International Journal of Entrepreneurship and Innovation*, 25(1), 56–69. DOI: 10.1177/14657503221093007

Satsangi, P., & Dhir, A. (2024). *Role of Communities in Achieving Sustainable Development.* Academic Foundation.

Save, B., Sheikh, A., & Goswami, P. (2019, December). Recent developments, challenges, and possible action plans for electric vehicle charging infrastructure in India. In 2019 9th International Conference on Power and Energy Systems (ICPES) DOI: 10.1109/ICPES47639.2019.9105530

Saxenian, A. (1994). *Regional Competitive Advantage: culture and competition in Silicon Valley and Route* (Vol. 128). Harvard University Press.

Scaife, W. (2008). Venturing into Venture Philanthropy: Is More Sustainable Health and Medical Research Funding Possible Through Venture Philanthropy and Social Entrepreneurship? *Journal of Nonprofit & Public Sector Marketing*, 20(2), 245–260. DOI: 10.1080/10495140802224902

Scarlata, M., & Alemany, L. (2008). Philanthropic Venture Capital: Can the Key Elements of Venture Capital Be Applied Successfully to Social Enterprises? SSRN *Electronic Journal*. DOI: 10.2139/ssrn.1099277

Scarlata, M., & Alemany, L. (2010). Deal Structuring in Philanthropic Venture Capital Investments: Financing Instrument, Valuation and Covenants. *Journal of Business Ethics*, 95(S2), 121–145. DOI: 10.1007/s10551-011-0851-8

Schaltegger, S., & Burritt, R. (2018). *Contemporary environmental accounting: Issues, concepts and practice*. Routledge.

Schaltegger, S., Hörisch, J., & Freeman, R. E. (2019). Business Cases for Sustainability: A Stakeholder Theory Perspective. *Organization & Environment*, 32(3), 191–212. DOI: 10.1177/1086026617722882

Schaltegger, S., & Wagner, M. (2011). Sustainable entrepreneurship and sustainability innovation: Categories and interactions. *Business Strategy and the Environment*, 20(4), 222–237. DOI: 10.1002/bse.682

Schmiedeknecht, M. (2019). Social Innovation and Entrepreneurship Supporting the Sustainable Development Goals (SDGs)–Fostering Social Value Creation. The Future of the UN Sustainable Development Goals.

Schmutzler, J., Andonova, V., & Diaz-Serrano, L. (2019). How context shapes entrepreneurial self-efficacy as a driver of entrepreneurial intentions: A multi-level approach. *Entrepreneurship Theory and Practice*, 43(5), 880–920. DOI: 10.1177/1042258717753142

Schulte, J., & Hallstedt, S. I. (2018). Company risk management in light of the sustainability transition. *Sustainability (Basel)*, 10(11), 4137. DOI: 10.3390/su10114137

Schulte, M. (2017). AI-driven analytics for impact assessment in social entrepreneurship. *Journal of Social Entrepreneurship*, 8(1), 89–106.

ScienceDirect. (n.d.). A review on textile recycling processes.

ScienceDirect. (n.d.). Environmental impacts of textile recycling.

ScienceDirect. (n.d.). Recycling processes in the textile industry.

Sciortino, R. (2017a). Philanthropy, Giving, and Development in Southeast Asia. *Austrian Journal of South-East Asian Studies, Vol 10 No 2*, 129-138 Pages. https://doi.org/DOI: 10.14764/10.ASEAS-2017.2-1

Sciortino, R. (2017b). Philanthropy in Southeast Asia: Between Charitable Values, Corporate Interests, and Development Aspirations. *Austrian Journal of South-East Asian Studies, Vol 10 No 2*, 139-163 Pages. DOI: 10.14764/10.ASEAS-2017.2-2

Searing, E. A. M., Poledrini, S., Young, D. R., & Nyssens, M. (2022). The hybrid nature of social enterprises how does it affect their revenue sources? *Social Enterprise Journal*, 18(2), 321–343. DOI: 10.1108/SEJ-02-2021-0010

Seelos, C., & Mair, J. (2017). *Innovation and scaling for impact: How effective social enterprises do it*. Stanford University Press.

Sehnem, S., Lara, A. C., Benetti, K., Schneider, K., Marcon, M. L., & da Silva, T. H. H. (2023). Improving startups through excellence initiatives: Addressing circular economy and innovation. *Environment, Development and Sustainability*, 26(6), 15237–15283. Advance online publication. DOI: 10.1007/s10668-023-03247-4 PMID: 37362985

Seier, M., Archodoulaki, V.-M., Koch, T., Duscher, B., & Gahleitner, M. (2023). Prospects for Recyclable Multilayer Packaging: A Case Study. *Polymers*, 15(13), 2966. DOI: 10.3390/polym15132966 PMID: 37447609

Seikkula-Leino, J., Jónsdóttir, S., Håkansson-Lindqvist, M., Westerberg, M., & Eriksson-Bergström, S. (2021). Responding to Global Challenges through Education: Entrepreneurial, Sustainable, and Pro-Environmental Education in Nordic Teacher Education Curricula. Sustainability.

Semenza, J. (2012). Creating Sustainable Communities: The Quadruple Bottom Line. *EcoHealth*, 9(4), 499–501. DOI: 10.1007/s10393-012-0795-1

Sennett, R. (1998). *The corrosion of character*. Norton.

Shabbir, M. S. (2023). Exploring the relationship between sustainable entrepreneurship and the United Nations sustainable development goals: A comprehensive literature review. *Sustainable Development (Bradford)*, 31(4), 3070–3085. DOI: 10.1002/sd.2570

Shahid, M. S., Hossain, M., Shahid, S., & Anwar, T. (2023). Frugal innovation as a source of sustainable entrepreneurship to tackle social and environmental challenges. *Journal of Cleaner Production*, 406, 137050. DOI: 10.1016/j.jclepro.2023.137050

Shaikh, M. J., & Hyder, M. (2023). Green Packaging as a Positive Catalyst for Green Environment: Implementation in Emerging Markets around the Globe. *Pakistan Journal of Humanities and Social Sciences*, 11(1). Advance online publication. DOI: 10.52131/pjhss.2023.1101.0382

Shane, S., Locke, E. A., & Collins, C. J. (2003). Entrepreneurial motivation. *Human Resource Management Review*, 13(2), 257–279. DOI: 10.1016/S1053-4822(03)00017-2

Shane, S., & Venkataraman, S. (2000). The promise of entrepreneurship as a field of research. *Academy of Management Review*, 25(1), 217–226. https://www.jstor.org/stable/259271. DOI: 10.5465/amr.2000.2791611

Shapiro, R. A., Mirchandani, M., & Jang, H. (2018). *Pragmatic Philanthropy*. Springer Singapore., DOI: 10.1007/978-981-10-7119-5

Shaw, A., Canavan, J., & Dolan, P. (2021). Strategic philanthropy's investment in public systems: A framework for intervention. *International Journal of Management Reviews*, 23(3), 411–425. DOI: 10.1111/ijmr.12269

Shaw, E., Gordon, J., Harvey, C., & Maclean, M. (2013). Exploring contemporary entrepreneurial philanthropy. *International Small Business Journal*, 31(5), 580–599. DOI: 10.1177/0266242611429164

Shepherd, D. A., & Patzelt, H. (2011). The New Field of Sustainable Entrepreneurship: Studying Entrepreneurial Action Linking "What is to be Sustained" with "What is to be Developed". *Entrepreneurship Theory and Practice*, 35(1), 137–163. DOI: 10.1111/j.1540-6520.2010.00426.x

Sheppard, C. J., Gopal, A. R., Harris, A., & Jacobson, A. (2016). Cost-effective electric vehicle charging infrastructure siting for Delhi. *Environmental Research Letters*, 11(6), 064010.

Shirwaiker, R. A., & Okudan, G. E. (2011). Contributions of TRIZ and axiomatic design to leanness in design: An investigation. *Procedia Engineering*, 9, 730–735. DOI: 10.1016/j.proeng.2011.03.162

Shriberg, M. (2002). Institutional assessment tools for sustainability in higher education: Strengths, weaknesses, and implications for practice and theory. *International Journal of Sustainability in Higher Education*, 3(3), 254–270. DOI: 10.1108/14676370210434714

Shrivastav, A. V., Khan, S. S., Gupta, R. K., Ekshinge, P. R., & Parmeshwar, N. (2020). Electric Vehicle Charging Station (Case study on infrastructure of EV charging station). *Journal of Emerging Technologies and Innovative Research*, 7, 2017–2033.

Shroyer, K., Lovins, T., Turns, J., Cardella, M. E., & Atman, C. J. (2018). *Timescales and ideaspace: An examination of idea generation in design practice.* Design Studies, 57, 9-36. Retrevied from DOI: 10.1016/j.destud.2018.03.004

Simon, F. L. (1995). Global corporate philanthropy: A strategic framework. *International Marketing Review*, 12(4), 20–37. DOI: 10.1108/02651339510097711

Singha, S., Singha, R., Rebeka, S. P., & Ruben, V. M. (2023). Sustainable marketing in e-commerce: Strategies for environmental impact reduction. In Masengu, R., Bigirimana, S., Chiwaridzo, O. T., Benson, R., & Blossom, C. (Eds.), *Sustainable Marketing, Branding, and Reputation Management: Strategies for a Greener Future* (pp. 444–464). IGI Global., DOI: 10.4018/979-8-3693-0019-0.ch023

Singha, S., & Singh, R. (2024). Cross-Disciplinary Collaborations and Partnerships for Sustainability Education: Including Community-Based Learning, Industry Partnerships, and International Collaborations. In Goi, C. L. (Ed.), *Teaching and Learning for a Sustainable Future: Innovative Strategies and Best Practices* (Vol. 1, pp. 17–37). IGI., DOI: 10.4018/978-1-6684-9859-0.ch002

Singh, S., Chauhan, A., & Dhir, S. (2020). Analyzing the startup ecosystem of India: A Twitter analytics perspective. *Journal of Advances in Management Research*, 17(2), 262–281. DOI: 10.1108/JAMR-08-2019-0164

Sirine, H., & Yustina, E. P. D. (2022). Business Model Canvas: The Implementation Method of Corporate Social Entrepreneurship. *Jagaditha: Jurnal Ekonomi & Bisnis*, 9(2), 176–184. DOI: 10.22225/jj.9.2.2022.176-184

Sivan, H., & Kanthavel, K. (2013). TRIZ: A Perfect Tool for Process Innovation by Tackling Engineering contradictions. *IOSR Journal of Mechanical and Civil Engineering*, •••, 21–26.

Sklyarova, O. A., Musaelyan, A. K., Bukhov, N. V., Medvedeva, L. S., & Bidzhieva, A. S. (2020). Application of TRIZ Technique in the Organizations' Activity. [IJEBA]. *International Journal of Economics & Business Administration*, 8(4), 563–571.

Slevin, D. P., & Covin, J. G. (1990). New venture strategic posture, structure, and performance: An industry life cycle analysis. *Journal of Business Venturing*, 5(2), 123–135. DOI: 10.1016/0883-9026(90)90004-D

Smollan, R., & Singh, S. (2024). How social entrepreneurs respond to enterprise failure. *Journal of Social Entrepreneurship*, 15(1), 1–25. DOI: 10.1080/19420676.2021.1890189

Sobel, R. S. (2008). Testing Baumol: Institutional quality and the productivity of entrepreneurship. *Journal of Business Venturing*, 23(6), 641–655. DOI: 10.1016/j.jbusvent.2008.01.004

Sörensson, A., & Ghannad, N. (2024). Entrepreneurial opportunities and difficulties under COVID-19 for women entrepreneurs in Asia and Europe. *Journal of Entrepreneurship in Emerging Economies*, 16(1), 119–133. DOI: 10.1108/JEEE-02-2023-0052

Soroka, A., Robinson, M., Gosling, J., Hoggins, L., Hall, J., & Naim, M. M. (2023). *Circular Economy Models in the Construction Sector: A Plastics Recycling Use Case.*, DOI: 10.1007/978-981-19-9205-6_14

Sorooshian, S. (2024). The Sustainable Development Goals of the United Nations: A Comparative Midterm Research Review. *Journal of Cleaner Production*, 453, 142272. DOI: 10.1016/j.jclepro.2024.142272

Sperber, S., & Linder, C. (2019). Gender-specifics in start-up strategies and the role of the entrepreneurial ecosystem. *Small Business Economics*, 53(2), 533–546. DOI: 10.1007/s11187-018-9999-2

Spiess-Knafl, W., & Aschari-Lincoln, J. (2015). Understanding mechanisms in the social investment market: What are venture philanthropy funds financing and how? *Journal of Sustainable Finance & Investment*, 5(3), 103–120. DOI: 10.1080/20430795.2015.1060187

Spigel, B. (2017). The Relational Organization of Entrepreneurial Ecosystems. *Entrepreneurship Theory and Practice*, 41(1), 49–72. DOI: 10.1111/etap.12167

Spigel, B., & Harrison, R. (2018). Toward a process theory of entrepreneurial ecosystems. *Strategic Entrepreneurship Journal*, 12(1), 151–168. DOI: 10.1002/sej.1268

SpringerLink. (2020). Sustainable fashion: Concepts and practices of.

Sreenivasan, A. & Suresh, M. (2023). Exploring the contribution of sustainable entrepreneurship toward sustainable development goals: A bibliometric analysis. *Green Technologies and Sustainability*, 3(1).

Sri Lanka Association of Software and Service Companies (SLASSCOM). (2019). *Sri Lanka Startup Report 2019*. Sri Lanka Association of Software and Service Companies.

Sri Lanka Tourism Development Authority (SLTDA). (2023). *Annual Statistical Report 2023*. Sri Lanka Tourism Development Authority. https://www.sltda.gov.lk/en/annual-statistical-report

Srinivasan, H., Shyamsundar, N., & Gadh, R. (1997). A framework for virtual disassembly analysis. *Journal of Intelligent Manufacturing*, 8(4), 277–295. DOI: 10.1023/A:1018537611535

SSRG International Journals. (2023). Achieving sustainability through zero waste fashion—A review. *International Journal of Humanities and Social Science*, 10(1), 105.

Stahl, G. K., & Maznevski, M. L. (2021). Unraveling the effects of cultural diversity in teams: A retrospective of research on multicultural work groups and an agenda for future research. *Journal of International Business Studies*, 52(1), 4–22. DOI: 10.1057/s41267-020-00389-9 PMID: 33487775

Stam, E. (2015). Entrepreneurial ecosystems and regional policy: A sympathetic critique. *European Planning Studies*, 23(9), 1759–1769. DOI: 10.1080/09654313.2015.1061484

Stam, E., & Van de Ven, A. (2021). Entrepreneurial Ecosystem Elements. *Small Business Economics*, 56(2), 809–832. DOI: 10.1007/s11187-019-00270-6

Statista. (2014, July 5). *Brazil: number of startups 2013-2023*. Statista Research Department.

Steigertahl, L., & Mauer, R. (2023). Investigating the success factors of the Nordic entrepreneurial ecosystem – talent transformation as a key process. *International Journal of Entrepreneurship and Innovation*, 24(1), 7–18. DOI: 10.1177/14657503211051217

Sternberg, R. J., & Lubart, T. I. (1996). *Investing in creativity*. American psychologist, 51(7), 677-688. Retrevied from DOI: 10.1037/0003-066X.51.7.677

Stoyanova-Koval, S., Slutskyi, Y., & Varhatiuk, M. (2023). CIRCULAR ECONOMY DEVELOPMENT TRENDS IN THE WORLD. *Economic Scope*. DOI: 10.32782/2224-6282/183-18

Stuart, R., & Abetti, P. A. (1987). Start-up ventures: Towards the prediction of initial success. *Journal of Business Venturing*, 2(3), 215–230. DOI: 10.1016/0883-9026(87)90010-3

Sullivan, W. M. (1995). *Work and integrity: The crisis and promise of professionalism in America.* HarperGoUins.

Syed Mohammed, A., Anuj, Lodhi, A. S., & Murtaza, Q. (2022). Techno-economic feasibility of hydrogen based electric vehicle charging station: A case study. *International Journal of Energy Research*, 46(10), 14145–14160.

Taieb, A. H., & Ben Amor, M. (2023). Eco-design Design Strategy: Case Study Biomimicry Approach in Design Product Materials. *Asian Journal of Environment & Ecology*, 21(3), 1–20. DOI: 10.9734/ajee/2023/v21i3460

Tarei, P. K., Chand, P., & Gupta, H. (2021). Barriers to the adoption of electric vehicles: Evidence from India. *Journal of Cleaner Production*, 291, 125847. DOI: 10.1016/j.jclepro.2021.125847

Tarnovskaya, V. (2023). Sustainability as the source of competitive advantage. How sustainable is it? In *International Business and Management Series* (pp. 75–89). DOI: 10.1108/S1876-066X20230000037005

Terán-Yépez, E., Marín-Carrillo, G. M., del Pilar Casado-Belmonte, M., & de las Mercedes Capobianco-Uriarte, M. (2020). Sustainable entrepreneurship: Review of its evolution and new trends. *Journal of Cleaner Production*, 252, 119742. DOI: 10.1016/j.jclepro.2019.119742

Tereshchenko, E., Happonen, A., Porras, J., & Vaithilingam, C. A. (2023). Green growth, waste management, and environmental impact reduction success cases from small and medium enterprises context: A systematic mapping study. *IEEE Access : Practical Innovations, Open Solutions*, 11, 56900–56920. DOI: 10.1109/ACCESS.2023.3271972

Teti, R., & D'Addona, D. (2011). TRIZ based tool management in supply networks. *Procedia Engineering*, 9, 680–687. DOI: 10.1016/j.proeng.2011.03.155

Textile Exchange. (n.d.). Downcycling.

Textiles & Clothing Sustainability. (2015). Sustainable fashion. *RE:view*.

Thelen, K. (2003). How Institutions Evolve: Insights from Comparative-Historical Analy-sis. In Mahoney, J., & Rueschemeyer, D. (Eds.), *Comparative Historical Analysis in the Social Sciences* (pp. 208–239). Cambridge University Press. DOI: 10.1017/CBO9780511803963.007

Theobald, H., & Hampel, S. (2013). Radical Institutional Change and Incremental Transformation: Long-Term Care Insurance in Germany. In Ranci, C., & Pavolini, E. (Eds.), *Reforms in Long-Term Care Policies in Europe*. Springer., DOI: 10.1007/978-1-4614-4502-9_6

Theodoraki, C., & Catanzaro, A. (2021). Widening the borders of entrepreneurial ecosystem through the international lens. *The Journal of Technology Transfer*. Advance online publication. DOI: 10.1007/s10961-021-09852-7

Thiam, D. R., Dinar, A., & Ntuli, H. (2021). Promotion of residential water conservation measures in South Africa: The role of water-saving equipment. *Environmental Economics and Policy Studies*, 23(1), 173–210. DOI: 10.1007/s10018-020-00286-3

Thillai Rajan, A., Koserwal, P., & Keerthana, S. (2014). The Global Epicenter of Impact Investing: *An Analysis of Social Venture Investments in India.Journal of Private Equity*, 17(2), 37–50. DOI: 10.3905/jpe.2014.17.2.037

Thomas, A. S., & Mueller, S. L. (2000). A case for comparative entrepreneurship: Assessing the relevance of culture. *Journal of International Business Studies*, 31(2), 287–301. DOI: 10.1057/palgrave.jibs.8490906

Thornton, P. (2002). The rise of the corporation in a craft industry: Conflict and conformity in institutional logics. *Academy of Management Journal*, 45(1), 81–101. DOI: 10.2307/3069286

Timofei, O. (2023). Circular business models for increasing product usage. *Competitiveness and Innovation in the Knowledge Economy*, 74–78, 74–78. Advance online publication. DOI: 10.53486/cike2022.08

Torfing, J., & Ansell, C. (2017). Strengthening political leadership and policy innovation through the expansion of collaborative forms of governance. *Public Management Review*, 19(1), 37–54. DOI: 10.1080/14719037.2016.1200662

Torres, P., & Godinho, P. (2022). Levels of necessity of entrepreneurial ecosystems elements. *Small Business Economics*, 59(1), 29–45. DOI: 10.1007/s11187-021-00515-3

Townley, B. (2002). The role of competing rationalities in institutional change. *Academy of Management Journal*, 45(1), 163–179. DOI: 10.2307/3069290

Trivedi, N., Gujar, N. S., Sarkar, S., & Pundir, S. P. S. (2018, March). Different fast charging methods and topologies for EV charging. In 2018 IEEMA Engineer Infinite Conference (eTechNxT) (pp. 1-5). IEEE. DOI: 10.1109/ETECHNXT.2018.8385313

Tsalis, T. A., Stefanakis, A., & Nikolaou, I. E. (2022). A framework to evaluate the social life cycle impact of products under the circular economy thinking. *Sustainability (Basel)*, 14(4), 2196. DOI: 10.3390/su14042196

Tula, S. T., Ofodile, O. C., Okoye, C. C., Nifise, A. O. A., & Odeyemi, O. (2024). Entrepreneurial ecosystems in the USA: A comparative review with European models. *International Journal of Management & Entrepreneurship Research*, 6(2), 451–466. DOI: 10.51594/ijmer.v6i2.799

Tyagi, B., Sasidharan, C., & Das, S. (2019). A case study on potential impact of electric vehicle charging for an electricity distribution utility in India. In *Second large scale integration of renewable energy conference*, Delhi.

UNCTAD. (2018). *World Investment Report 2018: Investment and New Industrial Policies. United Nations Conference on Trade and Development.*

UNCTAD. (2023). *National Entrepreneurship Strategy - South Africa.*

UNDP. (2018). *Promoting Inclusive and Sustainable Economic Growth.* United Nations Development Programme.

UNDP. (2020). *Human Development Report 2020: The Next Frontier.* Retrieved from https://hdr.undp.org/sites/default/files/hdr2020.pdf

United Nations. (2015). *Transforming our world: The 2030 Agenda for Sustainable Development.* Retrieved from https://sustainabledevelopment.un.org/post2015/transformingourworld

Varadarajan, R. (2015). Innovating for sustainability: A framework for sustainable innovations and a model of sustainable innovations orientation. *Journal of the Academy of Marketing Science*, 45(1), 14–36. DOI: 10.1007/s11747-015-0461-6

Venkatraman, N. (1989). The concept of fit in strategy research: Toward verbal and statistical correspondence. *Academy of Management Review*, 14(3), 423–444. DOI: 10.2307/258177

Vietor, R. (1994). *Contrived Competition: Regulation and Deregulation in America.* Belknap. DOI: 10.4159/harvard.9780674436794

Vig, S. (2022). Sustainable development through sustainable entrepreneurship and innovation: A single-case approach. *Social Responsibility Journal*, 19(7), 1196–1217. DOI: 10.1108/SRJ-02-2022-0093

Viktoriia Ilchenko. (2023). Social Entrepreneurship as a Tool to Achieve the Goals of Sustainable Development. *Ринкова економіка: сучасна теорія і практика управління, 21*(3(52)), 114–126. DOI: 10.18524/2413-9998.2022.3(52).275788

Vilochani, S., McAloone, T. C., & Pigosso, D. C. A. (2023). Management practices for sustainable product development: Insights from a systematic literature review. *Proceedings of the Design Society*, 3, 2505–2514. DOI: 10.1017/pds.2023.251

Vuorio, A. M., Puumalainen, K., & Fellnhofer, K. (2018). Drivers of entrepreneurial intentions in sustainable entrepreneurship. *International Journal of Entrepreneurial Behaviour & Research*, 24(2), 359–381. DOI: 10.1108/IJEBR-03-2016-0097

Wagner, R., & Kabalska, A. (2023). Between Involvement and Profit: Value (Un-) Captured by a Born-Social Start-Up. *Journal of Social Entrepreneurship*, •••, 1–26. DOI: 10.1080/19420676.2023.2199765

Walid, A. (2023). *Omran., R.M., Sharkawy*. Smart Charging of Electric Vehicles in Charging Stations., DOI: 10.1109/REEPE57272.2023.10086885

Wang, M., Zhang, D., & Zhang, L. (2015). Introduction of TRIZ theory for the conflict-solving in the building energy and environment management system innovation. *Procedia Engineering*, 121, 2232–2239. DOI: 10.1016/j.proeng.2015.09.201

Watson, R., Nielsen, K. R., Wilson, H. N., Macdonald, E. K., Mera, C., & Reisch, L. (2023). Policy for sustainable entrepreneurship: A crowdsourced framework. *Journal of Cleaner Production*, 383, 135234. DOI: 10.1016/j.jclepro.2022.135234

Weeraratne, B. (2016). Sustainable Consumption and Production in Sri Lanka. *Sri Lanka Journal of Social Sciences*, 39(1), 1–8.

Wei, Y. (2022). Regional governments and opportunity entrepreneurship in underdeveloped institutional environments: An entrepreneurial ecosystem perspective. *Research Policy*, 51(1), 104380. DOI: 10.1016/j.respol.2021.104380

Wesseh, P. K.Jr, Lin, B., Zhang, Y., & Wesseh, P. S. (2024). Sustainable entrepreneurship: When does environmental compliance improve corporate performance? *Business Strategy and the Environment*, 33(4), 3203–3221. DOI: 10.1002/bse.3657

Westley, F. (2017). Collaboration and ecosystem building in AI-driven social entrepreneurship. *Stanford Social Innovation Review*, 15(3), 76–88.

Wielemaker, M., & Gedajlovic, E. (2011). Governance and capabilities: Asia's entrepreneurial performance and stock of venture forms. *Asia Pacific Journal of Management*, 28(1), 75–185. DOI: 10.1007/s10490-010-9221-9

Williams, A., Ostwald, M. J., & Askland, H. H. (2010). *Creativity, design and education: Theories, positions and challenges*. Australian Learning & Teaching Council.

Williamson, O. (1975). *Markets and Hierarchies*. Free.

Wilson, J. Q. (1980). The politics of regulation. In Wilson, J. Q. (Ed.), *The Politics of Regulation: 357-394*. Basic Books.

Wong, M. C. S., & Yap, R. C. Y. (2019). Social Impact Investing for Marginalized Communities in Hong Kong: Cases and Issues. *Sustainability (Basel)*, 11(10), 2831. DOI: 10.3390/su11102831

Woodfield, P., Woods, C., & Shepherd, D. (2017). Sustainable entrepreneurship: Another avenue for family business scholarship? *Journal of Family Business Management*, 7(1), 122–132. DOI: 10.1108/JFBM-12-2015-0040

Woollard, D. (2010). Towards a theory of university entrepreneurship. *Industry and Higher Education*, 24(6), 413–427. DOI: 10.5367/ihe.2010.0017

World Bank. (2019). *Doing Business 2020: Comparing Business Regulation in 190 Economies*. World Bank Group.

World Bank. (2022). *Strategic Plan for Sri Lanka Tourism 2022 – 2025*. The World Bank. https://www.sltda.gov.lk/en/download-2

World Economic Forum. (2015). Blended Finance Vol. 1: A Primer for Development Finance and Philanthropic Funds. ReDesigning Development Finance Initiative. A Joint Initiative of the World Economic Forum and the OECD.

World Health Organization (WHO). (2017). United Nations Children's Fund (UNICEF). *Progress on drinking water, sanitation and hygiene*, 140

World Intellectual Property Organization (WIPO). (2024). *Global Innovation Index 2024: Unlocking the Promise of Social Entrepreneurship*. Geneva: WIPO. DOI: 10.34667/tind.50062

WTTC. (2018). *Travel and Tourism Economic Impact 2018*. World Travel and Tourism Council.

Wyche, S., Chidziwisano, G. H., Uwimbabazi, F., & Simiyu, N. (2018). Defamiliarizing the Domestic: Exploring "M-Kopa Solar" and Sustainable Practices in Rural Kenyan Households. *Proceedings of the 1st ACM SIGCAS Conference on Computing and Sustainable Societies*, 21. DOI: 10.1145/3209811.3211888

Xie, Q., Lee, C., Lu, Z., & Yuan, X. (2021). Interactions with artificial water features: A scoping review of health-related outcomes. *Landscape and Urban Planning*, 215, 104191. DOI: 10.1016/j.landurbplan.2021.104191

Yadav, C., & Garg, Ar. Y. (2023). DESIGN FOR DISASSEMBLY IN ARCHITECTURE. *INTERANTIONAL JOURNAL OF SCIENTIFIC RESEARCH IN ENGINEERING AND MANAGEMENT, 07*(04). DOI: 10.55041/IJSREM18950

Yang, D. (2023). Financial and Marketing Performance of P&G and Unilever. *BCP Business & Management*, 46, 49–57. DOI: 10.54691/bcpbm.v46i.5076

Yang, F., & Yang, M. M. (2023). Examining motivation of IT vendors to share knowledge with clients. *International Journal of Information Management*, 71, 102646. DOI: 10.1016/j.ijinfomgt.2023.102646

Yoon, K.-S., & Lee, S.-Y. (2020): Policy Systems and Measures for the Social Economy in Seoul, UNRISD Working Paper, No. 2020-6, United Nations Research Institute for Social Development (UNRISD), Geneva

Yu, P., Lang, H., Galang, J. I., & Xu, Y. (2023). The Role of Digital Twin in Accelerating the Digital

Yun, J. J., Lee, M., Park, K., & Zhao, X. (2019). Open innovation and serial entrepreneurs. *Sustainability (Basel)*, 11(18), 5055. DOI: 10.3390/su11185055

Yu, P., Chen, D., & Ahuja, A. (2022). Smart and Sustainable Economy: How COVID-19 Has Acted as a Catalyst for China's Digital Transformation. In Kautish, S., & Kaur, G. (Eds.), *AI-Enabled Agile Internet of Things for Sustainable FinTech Ecosystems* (pp. 106–146). IGI Global., DOI: 10.4018/978-1-6684-4176-3.ch006

Yu, P., Chen, J., Sampat, M., & Misuko, N. (2022). The Digital Transformation of Rural Agricultural Business Management: A Case Study of China. In Bilgaiyan, S., Singh, J., & Das, H. (Eds.), *Empirical Research for Futuristic E-Commerce Systems: Foundations and Applications* (pp. 23–52). IGI Global., DOI: 10.4018/978-1-6684-4969-1.ch002

Yu, P., Ge, Y., Mandizvidza, K., & Mulli, J. (2023). How Can Small and Medium Enterprises in the Chinese Market Achieve Sustainable Development Goals Through Blockchain? In Taleb, D., Abdelli, M., Khalil, A., & Sghaier, A. (Eds.), *Examining the Vital Financial Role of SMEs in Achieving the Sustainable Development Goals* (pp. 52–85). IGI Global., DOI: 10.4018/978-1-6684-4834-2.ch004

Yu, P., Gong, R., & Sampat, M. (2022). Blockchain Technology in China's Digital Economy: Balancing Regulation and Innovation. In Tehrani, P. (Ed.), *Regulatory Aspects of Artificial Intelligence on Blockchain* (pp. 132–157). IGI Global., DOI: 10.4018/978-1-7998-7927-5.ch007

Yu, P., Gu, H., Zhao, Y., & Ahuja, A. (2022). Digital Transformation Driven by Internet Data Center: Case Studies on China. In Piaggesi, D., Landazuri, H., & Jia, B. (Eds.), *Cases on Applying Knowledge Economy Principles for Economic Growth in Developing Nations* (pp. 203–230). IGI Global., DOI: 10.4018/978-1-7998-8417-0.ch011

Yu, P., Hu, X., Prakash, A., Misuko, N. W., & Haiyue, G. (Eds.). (2023). *Opportunities and Challenges of Industrial IoT in 5G and 6G Networks*. IGI Global., DOI: 10.4018/978-1-7998-9266-3

Yu, P., Jiao, A., & Sampat, M. (2022). The Effect of Chinese Green Transformation on Competitiveness and the Environment. In Ordóñez de Pablos, P., Zhang, X., & Almunawar, M. (Eds.), *Handbook of Research on Green, Circular, and Digital Economies as Tools for Recovery and Sustainability* (pp. 257–279). IGI Global., DOI: 10.4018/978-1-7998-9664-7.ch014

Yu, P., Liu, X., Mahendran, R., & Lu, S. (2022). Analysis and Comparison of Business Models of Leading Enterprises in the Chinese Hydrogen Energy Industry. In Felseghi, R., Cobîrzan, N., & Raboaca, M. (Eds.), *Clean Technologies and Sustainable Development in Civil Engineering* (pp. 179–216). IGI Global., DOI: 10.4018/978-1-7998-9810-8.ch008

Yu, P., Liu, Z., & Hanes, E. (2022). Supply Chain Resiliency, Efficiency, and Visibility in the Post-Pandemic Era in China: Case Studies of MeiTuan Waimai, and Ele. me. In Ramakrishna, Y. (Ed.), *Handbook of Research on Supply Chain Resiliency, Efficiency, and Visibility in the Post-Pandemic Era* (pp. 195–225). IGI Global., DOI: 10.4018/978-1-7998-9506-0.ch011

Yu, P., Liu, Z., Hanes, E., & Mumtaz, J. (2022). Integration of IoT and Blockchain for Smart and Secured Supply Chain Management: Case Studies of China. In Goyal, S., Pradeep, N., Shukla, P., Ghonge, M., & Ravi, R. (Eds.), *Utilizing Blockchain Technologies in Manufacturing and Logistics Management* (pp. 179–207). IGI Global., DOI: 10.4018/978-1-7998-8697-6.ch010

Yu, P., Liu, Z., & Sampat, M. (2023). Enhancing the Resilience of Food Cold Chain Logistics Through Digital Transformation: A Case Study of China. In Masudin, I., Almunawar, M., Restuputri, D., & Sud-On, P. (Eds.), *Handbook of Research on Promoting Logistics and Supply Chain Resilience Through Digital Transformation* (pp. 200–224). IGI Global., DOI: 10.4018/978-1-6684-5882-2.ch014

Yu, P., Lu, S., Hanes, E., & Chen, Y. (2022). The Role of Blockchain Technology in Harnessing the Sustainability of Chinese Digital Finance. In Swarnalatha, P., & Prabu, S. (Eds.), *Blockchain Technologies for Sustainable Development in Smart Cities* (pp. 155–186). IGI Global., DOI: 10.4018/978-1-7998-9274-8.ch009

Yu, P., Song, J., Sampat, M., & Hanes, E. (2023). Digital Twins: Accelerating the Digital Transformation in the Chinese Transportation Sector. In Fields, Z. (Ed.), *Multidisciplinary Approaches in AI, Creativity, Innovation, and Green Collaboration* (pp. 121–154). IGI Global., DOI: 10.4018/978-1-6684-6366-6.ch007

Yu, P., Xue, W., & Mahendran, R. (2022). The Development and Impact of China's Digital Transformation in the Medical Industry. In Rodrigues, M., & Proença, J. (Eds.), *Impact of Digital Transformation on the Development of New Business Models and Consumer Experience* (pp. 97–128). IGI Global., DOI: 10.4018/978-1-7998-9179-6.ch006

Yu, P., Zhang, Y., Sampat, M., & Chen, Y. (2023). Research on Cross-Industry Digital Transformation Under the New Normal: A Case Study of China. In Marco-Lajara, B., Martínez-Falcó, J., & Millán-Tudela, L. (Eds.), *Corporate Sustainability as a Tool for Improving Economic, Social, and Environmental Performance* (pp. 246–277). IGI Global., DOI: 10.4018/978-1-6684-7422-8.ch013

Zaheer, H., Breyer, Y. & Dumay, J. (2019). Digital entrepreneurship: an interdisciplinary structured literature review and research agenda. *Technol. Forecast. Soc. Chang.*, 148 (2019), Article 119735.

Zaiţ, D. (2002). *Management intercultural. Valorizarea diferenţelor culturale.* Editura Economică.

Zakari, A., & Oluwaseyi Musibau, H. (2024). Sustainable economic development in OECD countries: Does energy security matter? *Sustainable Development (Bradford)*, 32(1), 1337–1353. DOI: 10.1002/sd.2668

Zăpucioiu, L.-F., Sterie, M.-C., & Dimitriu, T. A. (2023). The Relevance of the Circular Economy in the Context of Sustainable Development. *Proceedings of the International Conference on Business Excellence, 17*(1), 1534–1543. DOI: 10.2478/picbe-2023-0138

Zeichner, K., & Peña-Sandoval, C. (2015). Venture Philanthropy and Teacher Education Policy in the U.S.: The Role of the New Schools Venture Fund. *Teachers College Record*, 117(5), 1–44. DOI: 10.1177/016146811511700508

Zhao, H., & Seibert, S. (2006). The big five personality dimensions and entrepreneurial status: A meta- analytical review. *The Journal of Applied Psychology*, 91(2), 259–271. DOI: 10.1037/0021-9010.91.2.259 PMID: 16551182

Zilber, T. (2002). Institutionalization as an interplay between actions meanings, and actors: The case of a rape crisis center in Israel. *Academy of Management Journal*, 45(1), 234–254. DOI: 10.2307/3069294

About the Contributors

Russ Neu, an influential leader driven by social impact and innovation, is the Founder and CEO of Social Collider, an esteemed aggregator of resources for social enterprises and impact organizations in Singapore. In 2020, he was appointed Visiting Professor under the prestigious Innovation for Impact Partnership initiative of the United Nations Development Programme (UNDP). Russ's literary contributions are equally noteworthy. In 2018, he authored the compelling book "It Made A Difference To This One," a poignant narrative about an NGO that has transformed the lives of more than 20,000 children affected by AIDS in China, capturing the essence of social responsibility. Russ's expertise extends to venture capitalism as well. He holds the position of Venture Partner, Impact Initiatives, at Quest Ventures, a leading venture fund that supports technology companies with the potential for scalability and replicability in vast internet communities. Prior to his current ventures, Russ held the significant role of global lead for diversity and inclusion at Flex, a renowned solution provider that designs and manufactures products for intelligent living. During his tenure, he played a pivotal role in conceptualizing and implementing programs that benefited both the company and society at large. His unwavering dedication to social good led to a remarkable increase in the hiring of persons with disabilities from a mere 5 to an impressive 350 in Zhuhai, China. Russ's leadership extended beyond corporate initiatives, as he spearheaded pioneering service learning projects that were integral to staff development at Flex. Under his guidance, Flex staff embarked on impactful endeavors, including the construction of schools in Nepal and Laos, positively impacting the lives of 4,000 villagers and school children directly and an additional 2,000 indirectly through book donations and teacher training programs. Before joining Flex, Russ held a position at the Ministry of Education in Singapore. His dedication to educational equity prompted his secondment to Laos as part of the Singapore International Foundation program, where he focused on improving access to education for senior public officials. Furthermore, he initiated the Laos-Singapore Charity Run in Vientiane, fostering a spirit of community and philanthropy. Russ holds a Bachelor's degree from the prestigious National University of Singapore and an MBA from Tsinghua University, pursued in collaboration with MIT, funded by a scholarship from the Korea Development Bank. His writings have graced the pages of The Straits Times and other esteemed publications, while his chronicles of Laos were compiled into a well-received book.

Qian Xiaojun is a distinguished academic and administrator in the field of Leadership and Organization Management. With a profound educational background, she obtained her Ph.D. in Mathematics in 1992 from Purdue University, Indiana, USA, preceded by an M.S. in Mathematics in 1988 from the same esteemed institution. Professor Qian's academic journey began with a B.S. in Applied Mathematics from Tsinghua University in 1982, laying the foundation for her future scholarly pursuits. Professor Qian has dedicated her career to Tsinghua University, serving as a full professor at the Department of Leadership and Organization Management and holding the esteemed position of vice chairperson of the Degree Review Committee in the School of Economics and Management. Her contributions to the university's academic and administrative landscape have been invaluable. Furthermore, Professor Qian's engagement in civic responsibilities is evident through her contribution in the 12th CPPCC Beijing Municipal Committee, demonstrating her dedication to serving the community beyond the university walls. Professor Qian's leadership roles within Tsinghua SEM have been instrumental in shaping the school's academic trajectory. She served as the Director of Planning and Quality Assurance Office from 2006 to 2013, ensuring the maintenance of academic standards and quality. Prior to that, she held the position of Director of MBA Programs from 2001 to 2006, guiding the development and implementation of MBA curricula. Additionally, Professor Qian's tenure as Assistant Dean responsible for Academic Degrees from 2006 to 2009 underscores her commitment to academic rigor and excellence. Professor Qian Xiaojun's dedication to academia, her contributions to Tsinghua University, and her engagement in public service have solidified her reputation as an exceptional scholar, administrator, and leader in the field of Leadership and Organization Management.

Poshan (Sam) Yu a Chinese Australian, is a versatile individual who excels in a range of roles and industries. With a dynamic skill set, he serves as a consultant, adjunct professor, keynote speaker, research award winner, SSCI journal editor, author, ad-hoc reviewer, entrepreneur, venture capitalist, and OzAsia festival ambassador. Additionally, he brings his financial expertise to over 30 media platforms in China as a guest financial news commentator. Sam's academic contributions extend to various prestigious institutions. He teaches at the University of Victoria Program at Soochow University in China and holds the position of an external professor of financial technology and finance at SKEMA Business School,

China. Furthermore, he is a visiting professor at Krirk University in Thailand, EU-Asia research coordinator at the European Business Institute of Luxembourg, and a visiting researcher at the Australian Studies Centre of Shanghai University. Notably, he is also a guest professor at Emlyon Business School China and an adjunct faculty member at George Washington University's master program at Renmin University of China. Previously, he taught as a casual academic at the University of South Australia Business School and was a visiting scholar at the Chinese University of Hong Kong. Furthermore, Sam is actively engaged with several organizations and holds significant positions. As a regional partner in China for FasterCapital, based in Dubai, United Arab Emirates, he plays a vital role in fostering entrepreneurship. He also serves as a vice president at Tinbowah Investment in Beijing and holds an honorary vice president position at the Belt and Road Blockchain Association. Additionally, he contributes as a business mentor for AIC RAISE in Coimbatore, India, the Griffith Industry Mentoring Program in Australia, and University College London. Beyond his professional endeavors, Sam acts as the marketing manager at CAMathories™, an organization founded by a group of Cambridge University alumni and faculty members dedicated to early childhood education, mathematics, science, and advanced technologies. Sam's research interests are extensive and encompass a wide range of topics. They include public-private partnerships, financial technology, regulatory technology, educational technology, mergers and acquisitions, private equity, venture capital, start-ups, intellectual property, art finance, wine, and China's "One Belt One Road" policy.

Himanshu is an Assistant Professor based at the NSUT, New Delhi, India. He was also a doctoral fellow at the Indian Institute of Technology, Roorkee, India. He holds the degree of M.Com. and B.Com. (Hons.) from the University of Delhi. He has qualifed UGC NET-JRF in both disciplines, Commerce and Management. He is currently a member of the British Accounting & Finance Association, American Accounting Association, and Indian Commerce Association. He has been a member of the Academy for Global Business Advancement. He has published research papers in reputed journals indexed in Scopus, Web of Science, and Australian Business Deans Council list. He is the reviewer of various ABDC listed journals. He has received the Best Paper Award in the International Conference organized by IBS Hyderabad. He has presented papers at national and international conferences at institutions of national repute (for instance, the British Accounting Association and the American Accounting Association, associated conferences). His research areas include fair value reporting, fnancial management, earnings management, and accounting for managers.

Ayyoob A is a distinguished Senior Research Scholar in Commerce, currently pursuing his Ph.D. at the Department of Commerce and Management Studies (DCMS), School of Business Studies, University of Calicut, Kerala. His research delves into the intricate realms of Corporate Governance, Corporate Sustainability, Strategic CSR, ESG, DEIB, and SDGs, marking him as a pivotal figure in his field. Among his impressive scholarly contributions is a notable paper on Diversity, Equity, and Inclusion (DE&I) published by Routledge, alongside several other papers focused on sustainability, which are under review in prestigious journals indexed in Scopus and ABDC. Mr. Ayyoob A's dedication to advancing sustainability is evident through his consistent delivery of valuable insights, profoundly influencing both theoretical frameworks and practical applications within his domain. His commitment is further demonstrated by his active participation in the academic community, having attended and presented papers at various international and national conferences organized by esteemed institutions. Beyond his research endeavors, Mr. Ayyoob A extends his expertise through consultancy services to researchers and students, both domestically and internationally. His consultancy work is complemented by his role as an educator, where he handles lectures and workshops focusing on research methodology and data analysis. His ability to demystify complex concepts and impart practical knowledge has made him a sought-after mentor and speaker. In his academic journey, Mr. Ayyoob A has not only contributed significantly to the body of knowledge in his field but also demonstrated a profound commitment to fostering a deeper understanding of sustainability and corporate responsibility. His multifaceted contributions, from groundbreaking research to impactful teaching and consultancy, underscore his role as a key influencer in the realms of commerce and management studies. Through his unwavering dedication and scholarly excellence, Mr. Ayyoob A continues to inspire and shape the future of corporate sustainability and governance.

Sonika Bhardwaj is an esteemed Associate Professor within the School of Law at Christ (Deemed to be University). With a passion for legal scholarship and education, Dr. Bhardwaj has dedicated herself to shaping the next generation of legal minds.

Sunayana Bhat is a dedicated PhD Research Scholar at Christ University in Bangalore, India. Her academic journey is marked by a passion for exploring new frontiers in her field and a commitment to advancing knowledge.

Muhammad Chowdhury Faisol is an internationally certified and trained pracademic with 18 years of experience in academia and corporate. Before ULAB, he was a faculty member at the University of Glasgow, UK, and North South

University, Bangladesh, and a visiting scholar at a few other universities in Dhaka. Alongside teaching, he served C-Suit positions in some of Bangladesh's largest business conglomerates and worked closely with several large enterprises as an HRM consultant. He was also a certified Interpreter for the Scottish Courts and Tribunal Services, Police Scotland, Scottish Prison Service, law firms, public schools, and housing societies in Scotland, UK. Besides his educational degrees, he was also trained in qualitative research methodology at the University of Oxford and business & management leadership at the University of Glasgow. He frequently delivers speeches and presents his research in international knowledge outlets and think tanks. He has received numerous research grants from various international institutions and professional bodies. He has authored a book, published peer-reviewed journal articles, and attended over 200 business conferences, seminars, and workshops. He is also associated with many professional institutions and associations across the globe

Raymundo Delgado Affiliation: Autonomous Mexico State University, UAEM Zumpango University Center, Industrial Design Raymundo Ocaña Education: 1987-1992 Graduate in Industrial Design, Autonomous University of the State of México. 1998-1999 Specialist in Strategic Design of Industrial Products, UAEM. 2001-2004 Master in Education, Franco Mexicana University. 2009-2011 Doctor in Education, Open University of Tlaxcala. Business Address: Plazuela San Juan 12, Zumpango, State of México, México. Research and Professional Experience: Full-Time Research Professor, UAEM Zumpango since 2001. Professional Appointments: Member of the Institutional Quality Committee, Member of the Curricular Committee of the Faculty of Architecture and Design, and member of the Institutional Curricular Innovation Network of the UAEM; advisor of 35 degree projects, 45 published articles, 60 presentations and collaborator in 4 research projects. And, Academic Coordinator of the degree in Industrial Design (1996-2005), Academic Deputy Director (2005-2013) and Director (2016-2020), the latter in the UAEM Zumpango campus. Honors: Recognition in the Program for Teacher Professional Development (PRODEP) Profile since 2005. Publications from the Last 3 Years: Ocaña, Delgado R. & Rodríguez, Leonel A.M. (2023) The sketch, a basic design tool. México: UAEMex. Ocaña, D., Rodríguez, L., Leonel R., Estevez, V. (2023) Assertiveness as a Factor in School Dropout During the COVID-19 Pandemic. In Costa, E., Pedrini, J. (Ed.), A comunicação e os contextos comunicativos 3. (Atenea Editora., DOI: https://doi.org/10.22533/at.ed.933231707). Ocaña, D. R., Rodríguez, L., González, B. (2022) Interaction of Graphic Design and Public Administration. In Zarur, Cortez (Ed.) Diseño Gráfico: enfoques de formación y campo laboral en Administración Pública. (1ra. ed., pp. 47- 59) UAEMex. Soto, R., Ocaña, D., Rodríguez, L., Sánchez, E. (2022) Creativity and the industrial designer… an essential skill. In Corrent, N. (Ed.) Ciências sociais aplicadas: Estado, organizações e desenvolvimento regional

2 (Atenea Editora., https://doi.org/10.22533/at.ed.45722041014). Ocaña, D., Rodríguez, L., Urbina, P., Sánchez, E. (2021) Enrollment in industrial design at CU UAEM Zumpango, analysis of its behavior 1987- 2020 at first admission. In Puppim, R. (Ed.) Design: contribuições significativas para o desenvolvimento sustentável. (Atenea Editora., https://doi.org/10.22533/at.ed.9282114102).

Harshit Gouri graduate from St. Stephen's College, University of Delhi, India. His research interests include Micro and Macro Economics Principles, Human Resource, Consumer Behavior, Neuromarketing and AI.-

Kelin Guo, MBA from EM Lyon Business School, with more than 10 years of experience in supply chain services and integrated marketing communications.

Quazi Islam is an internationally certified and trained academic, researcher, and trainer with 9 years of experience in industry and academia. His research concentration includes Sustainable Development, Circular Economy, Organizational Behavior, Human Resources, CSR. He is also involved in the course and syllabus designing and developing various Strategy and HR topics, including diversity and inclusion. He started his career in the Banking industry with Standard Chartered Bank in their international banking division as an Officer in foreign trade services. Later he joined Eastern Bank as a Management Trainee and was promoted to Associate Manager in the SME and consumer relationship banking division. He has obtained his Masters in Human Resources & Management from the University of Dundee, Scotland, United Kingdom, with a Distinction and was awarded the 'MSc Management Award' as a class valedictorian for 2017. Prior to that, he graduated from North South University with a distinction, double-majoring in Finance & Accounting and Human Resource Management.

Quazi Islam is an internationally certified and trained academic, researcher, and trainer with 9 years of experience in industry and academia. His research concentration includes Sustainable Development, Circular Economy, Organizational Behavior, Human Resources, CSR. He is also involved in the course and syllabus designing and developing various Strategy and HR topics, including diversity and inclusion. He started his career in the Banking industry with Standard Chartered Bank in their international banking division as an Officer in foreign trade services. Later he joined Eastern Bank as a Management Trainee and was promoted to Associate Manager in the SME and consumer relationship banking division. He has obtained his Masters in Human Resources & Management from the University of Dundee, Scotland, United Kingdom, with a Distinction and was awarded the 'MSc Management Award' as a class valedictorian for 2017. Prior to that, he graduated from North South University with a distinction, double-majoring in Finance & Accounting and Human Resource Management.

Shengyuan Lu is an independent researcher. His research interests include RegTech, FinTech and Cryptocurrencies.

Vedashree Mali serves as an Assistant Professor at the WPU School of Business, MIT World Peace University in Pune. She obtained her Ph.D. in Microfinance from North Maharashtra University, where her research focused on Microfinance for Small and Micro enterprises. Her research interests encompass Microfinance, Financial Inclusion, and Fintech. Dr. Mali has made significant contributions to the field, with numerous publications in reputable journals and presentations at both national and international conferences. She actively participates in Management Development Programs, providing finance training to non-finance professionals and imparting financial literacy to micro entrepreneurs. Currently, Dr. Vedashree is dedicated to researching the role of technology in financial inclusion, rural development, and green finance.

Suprya Paigude is an assistant professor at MIT World Peace University in Pune. Dr. Supriya has been the assistant director of the Centre of Industry Academic Partnership (CIAP) at MIT WPU. She has over 15 years of academic experience at MIT World Peace University. She has published numerous research papers in peer-reviewed international and national journals that are indexed in Scopus. Additionally, she has delivered research papers at national and international conferences, seminars, and conventions.

Palak Patel, Associate Professor and Vice Principal in Parul Institute of Design, Parul University, Vadodara, Gujarat.

Akhilesh Chandra Prabhakar earned his M.Phil. and Ph.D. degrees in Economics from the prestigious Jawaharlal Nehru University, New Delhi. With over a decade of academic experience in Ethiopia and Malaysia, he has established himself as a distinguished scholar and educator. Dr. Prabhakar's extensive body of research encompasses economic development, poverty, inequality, employment, SME development, regional trade, technological cooperation, and infrastructure initiatives, including contributions to the Silk Road Economic Zone. From 2005 to 2011, Dr. Prabhakar held various academic positions at Addis Ababa University, the University of Gondar, Debre Berhan University, and Debre Tabor University, serving under Ethiopia's Ministry of Education in collaboration with the United Nations Development Programme (UNDP). In 2011, he joined Universiti Utara Malaysia as a Senior Lecturer in Economics and Finance, significantly enhancing the institution's reputation as a leading academic hub in Asia. During his tenure from 2011 to 2015, Dr. Prabhakar published four SCOPUS-indexed research papers in ABDC-category journals, authored two books including The Current Global Economic Recession, published by Emerald Publishing Group (London)—supervised two Ph.D. candidates, and played a pivotal role in developing master's program curricula. Subsequently, Dr. Prabhakar served as an Associate Professor of Economics at the Mittal School of Business, Lovely Professional University, where he authored the book Regional Trade and Development Strategy in the Era of Globalization, published by IGI Global. Since 2022, Dr. Prabhakar has been a senior faculty member at the School of Business, Papua New Guinea University of Technology. Here, he has published over 15 research papers, including Colonial Echoes: Unraveling Economic Legacies and Geopolitical Shifts in the South Pacific Islands, featured in a Scopus-indexed Q2 journal. Additionally, he has authored two forthcoming books—Sustainable and Inclusive Economic Development and BRICS: A New Global Order—approved for publication by Taylor & Francis (Canada). He has also edited two upcoming works—AI and Social Entrepreneurship and Rural Social Entrepreneurship Development: Network-Based Manufacturing System Mode—to be published by IGI Global (USA). Moreover, Dr. Prabhakar has developed two modules for the Directorate of Distance and Flexible Learning (DODL) and supervised 28 EMBA and MBA students, two of whom have published research papers under his guidance. Dr. Prabhakar's research interests lie at the intersection of Social Entrepreneurship, BRICS-SCO and Global South Integration, and the De-dollarization Initiative as an alternative payment mechanism among Global South nations.

Sabyasachi Pramanik is a professional IEEE member. He obtained a PhD in Computer Science and Engineering from Sri Satya Sai University of Technology and Medical Sciences, Bhopal, India. Presently, he is an Associate Professor, Department of Computer Science and Engineering, Haldia Institute of Technology, India. He has many publications in various reputed international conferences, journals, and book chapters (Indexed by SCIE, Scopus, ESCI, etc). He is doing research in the fields of Artificial Intelligence, Data Privacy, Cybersecurity, Network Security, and Machine Learning. He also serves on the editorial boards of several international journals. He is a reviewer of journal articles from IEEE, Springer, Elsevier, Inderscience, IET and IGI Global. He has reviewed many conference papers, has been a keynote speaker, session chair, and technical program committee member at many international conferences. He has authored a book on Wireless Sensor Network. He has edited 8 books from IGI Global, CRC Press, Springer and Wiley Publications.

Rayed Rahman is a Research Assistant at North South University, he is an economics graduate with interest in sustainability and research.

Atanu Roy is a marine engineer from Kolkata, India. He completed his Marine Engineering four-year training under the West Bengal State Council of Technical Education (WBSCTE). Started a sailing career a foreign company, in 2003 and became Chief Engineer in 2011. During his period of sailing, he also started to associate with the maritime shore industry. He worked with Indian Maritime University (IMU) Kolkata campus, MERI as an assistant professor in 2015, and The Neotia University (TNU) in 2016 as a visiting faculty. During this period, he achieved an Extra First-Class Marine Engineer Certificate of Competency level in 2017, which is considered the highest grade of certificate of competency as a marine engineer officer. Becomes a faculty member at Ethiopian Maritime Training Institute (EMTI) in Ethiopia, Africa in 2017. Presently he is working at The Neotia University as an Assistant Professor in the Marine Department. Atanu Roy has a professional affiliation as a Fellow of the Institute of Marine Engineers (FIMarE), India and the Institute of Engineers, India (IEI).

Aparna Sajeev is an Assistant Professor at the Department of Commerce and Management Studies, School of Business Studies, University of Calicut. She pursued her doctoral degree in macro-policy management at the Faculty of Management Studies, University of Delhi. Her key research areas include sustainable Development and Climate Change, Sustainable Finance, Psychometric Analysis, and Impact Assessment. She has three years of Education industry experience as a Senior Research Manager - Impact Assessment and continues her work in education sector engagements as a consultant. She collaborated with the Berkeley Evaluation and Assessment Research Center. With over a decade of research experience, she is presently a research supervisor at the Department of Commerce, University of Calicut. She received a 2 million Won -Selected Research Paper award from Kyunghee University, Seoul (2020).

Omar Sánchez Doctor in education from the Autonomous University of the State of Mexico, with a postdoctoral stay at the Center for Studies and Research for Teaching Development, member of the national level 1 researcher system, full-time professor of the degree in Industrial Design, responsible for mobility international and degree committee, author of the book, disaster response, victims and sustainable industrial design.

Sachin Prakash Srivastava is currently working as an assistant professor at MIT World Peace University, Pune, India. He obtained his B.Tech in Mechanical Engineering and Ph.D. in Finance from Dayalbagh Educational Institute, Agra,

India. Prior to joining MIT World Peace University, he was a research associate at the Indian Institute of Management, Ahmedabad, India. His area of research is Entrepreneurship and Sustainability. He has worked for a brief period on Tribal empowerment programs based on SDGs in Rajaborari Estate in Harda, Madhya Pradesh, India.

Sonali Srivastava is presently working as an Assistant Professor at Symbiosis Centre for Management Studies, (SCMS) Nagpur, Maharashtra, India. She is a doctorate in Finance from Dayalbagh Educational Institute, Agra. She has an academic experience of more than 8 years with several reputed institutions i.e. VIT Bhopal University, MNNIT Allahabad, IIM Ahmedabad, Ministry of Finance and Amity University. She has published a number of research papers in peer reviewed international and national journals indexed in Scopus and WOS. She has also presented research papers in international and national conferences, seminars and conventions. Dr Sonali has organized a number of Conferences and Short-term courses. She is appointed as an external paper setter in many universities. She has authored books titled "Advanced Auditing and Recent Advances in Accounting, Taxation & Auditing". She is a member of various professional bodies and Member of the Reviewer Board of Various Journals.

H.A.K.N.S. Surangi is a professor in entrepreneurship at the University of Kelaniya, Sri Lanka. She completed her PhD at the University of Lincoln, United Kingdom. She has a longstanding interest in female entrepreneurship, gender, ethnic minority entrepreneurship, entrepreneurial networking and small business development in Asian countries. H.A.K.N.S. Surangi can be contacted at:surangins@kln.ac.lk

Md. Shamim Talukder is currently an Assistant Professor in the Department of Management at North South University, Bangladesh. He received Ph.D. degree major in Management Science and Engineering from the School of Management, Huazhong University of Science and Technology, Wuhan, China and MBA in Management Information Systems from the University of Dhaka, Bangladesh. His research interests converge at the intersection of End User Computing and Human-Computer Interaction, encompassing a spectrum of subjects such as consumer behavior, ethical AI Use, gerontechnology, technology adoption and diffusion, sustainability, and misinformation. He focuses on unraveling the intricate relationship between individuals, society, and technology, emphasizing optimizing accessibility, usability, and overall user experience. He employed predominantly quantitative research methods while also demonstrating competence in mixed methods. Through these methodological lenses, his investigations aim to offer valuable insights into the dynamic realm of human-computer interaction, contributing to its continued evolution and its profound implications for society. His research has been published in journals such as Technological Forecasting and Social Change, Internet Research, Industrial Management and Data Systems, Technology in Society, Journal of Systems and Information Technology, and The British Food Journal. He is a reviewer for many peer-reviewed journals, including Technological Forecasting and Social Change, Internet Research, Computer in Human Behavior, Information Technology and People, Enterprise Information Systems, and the Journal of Systems and Information Technology.

Shruti Tiwari, Sr. Development officer of Centre for Multidisciplinary and Interdisciplinary Education/ NEP Cell, Professor in Design, Parul Institute of Design, Parul University, Vadodara, Gujarat, India.

Mario Urbina Perez Master in industrial design, full-time professor of the degree in industrial design, specialist in development of electronic interfaces for design research. Recognized teacher before the Secretary of Public Education in Mexico.

Omar Vargas-González Professor, research assistant and former Head of Computer Systems Department at Tecnológico Nacional de México Campus Ciudad Guzmán, professor at Telematic Engineering at Centro Universitario del Sur Universidad de Guadalajara with a master degree in Computer Systems. Has been trained in Innovation and Multidisciplinary Entrepreneurship at Arizona State University (2018) and a Generation of Ecosystems of Innovation, Entrepreneurship and Sustainability for Jalisco course by Harvard University T.H. Chan School of Health. At present conduct research on diverse fields such as Entrepreneurship, Economy, Statistics, Mathematics and Information and Computer Sciences. Has collaborated in the publication of many scientific articles and conducted diverse Innovation and Technological Development projects.

Index

G

H

I

P

R

S

T

W

www.ingramcontent.com/pod-product-compliance
Lightning Source LLC
LaVergne TN
LVHW080345011026
849161LV00009B/2195